FISCAL ASPECTS OF AVIATION MANAGEMENT

Southern Illinois University Press Series in Aviation Management

FISCAL ASPECTS OF AVIATION MANAGEMENT

Robert W. Kaps

Southern Illinois University Press

Carbondale and Edwardsville

Copyright © 2000 by the Board of Trustees,
Southern Illinois University
Printed in the United States of America
03 02 01 00   4 3 2 1

"A Fuelish Problem" by Perry Flint, reprinted with permission from
Air Transport World magazine, December 1990, pp. 56–57.

Library of Congress Cataloging-in-Publication Data

Kaps, Robert W., 1943-
    Fiscal aspects of aviation management / Robert W. Kaps.
        p.   cm. — (Southern Illinois University Press series in aviation management)
    Includes bibliographical references and index.
    1. Aeronautics, Commercial—Finance. 2. Airlines—Finance.
3. Airports—Finance. I. Title. II. Series.

HE9782.K36 2000
387.7'1—dc21   99-43190
ISBN 0-8093-2250-1 (pbk. : alk. paper)   CIP

The paper used in this publication meets the minimum requirements
of American National Standard for Information Sciences—Permanence
of Paper for Printed Library Materials, ANSI Z39.48-1992.♾

CONTENTS

PREFACE

During the last twenty years, American business has become perhaps the most complex institution in our rapidly changing society. Much of this evolution has resulted from the rapid growth and structural changes of corporate America. The continuous upsizing, downsizing, outsourcing, and a host of other "ings" so prevalent to the American, and even worldwide, business scene have caused considerable financial changes to be inaugurated.

Much of this changing scene of American business may also be a by-product of the wave of deregulation that swept the nation's business structures in the 1970s and 1980s. Deregulation of the trucking, banking, telephone, and airline industries has changed traditional business landscapes. Events after the Airline Deregulation Act of 1978 have significantly altered the air transportation industry. This legislation has likewise affected public airports and the way fixed base operators (FBOs) function.

The corporation, initially conceived simply as a convenient means of marshaling capital and transacting business, has become a vigorous influence among the social institutions of our day. Profit is, and will continue to be, the major reason for the existence of any business. Today, however, the survival of business as an independent institution depends not on profit alone but also on the values and understanding of the employees. Established corporations, such as United Airlines (UAL) and Avis, have become "employee owned." These paradigm shifts have created new approaches and changing views toward the traditional corporation, its products, services, employees, and stakeholders. Because the employee may also be the ultimate corporate authority (owner), it behooves the captains of these monolithic structures to have knowledgeable employees, somewhat grounded in the particulars of the financial world and the industry in which they exist. It was with this belief that this book was prepared.

In 1993, I began teaching a financial course for aviation students at Southern Illinois University Carbondale. The previous instructor had labored through the same course without benefit of a text suitable to the aviation concern.

So why write another introduction to a quasi-financial course, especially when there are numerous texts available that address fiscal aspects of management in a more concise and comprehensive manner than is contained in *Fiscal Aspects of Aviation Management*? The answer is simple. While no criticism is intended of any of the existing books, very few if any address the subject matter from an aviation viewpoint. The purpose of this text is to prepare students for careers in the aviation field. Having over twenty years in the airline industry and over thirty-two years in aviation, I wanted to bring an excitement about today's aviation business to aviation students.

The elements of fiscal management follow generally accepted accounting principles and, as such, resemble the fiscal aspects of any other industry or enterprise. Thus, although the content of this undertaking primarily follows the activity of a fictitious airline (Air Atlantis), the applications and procedures apply to all elements of finance and accounting of the aviation industry. Where exceptions to this general rule occur, citations are noted. For a portion of this area, a special chapter was undertaken to address the fiscal issues pertaining to airports.

In the development of Air Atlantis (AirA) for inclusion in this text, there are by necessity a number of nuances germane only to the airline industry. For the most part, these nuances exist only in the area of terminology. Despite such reference to airline terminology, this book is designed to provide the student with a basic set of terms, tools, and techniques to be utilized in the analysis of financial and economic conditions of all sectors within the aviation community and business in general. Each chapter focuses on a financial category and analyzes one primary and several secondary topics within that category.

I am grateful to the many people who have helped me in this undertaking by explaining some of the complex issues: James Hill from the accounting firm of Ernst & Young; David O'Reilly, vice president of Bank of America; Rick Macaluso from the investment company of A. G. Edwards; Sandy Singer from the St. Louis (Lambert) International Airport; Jacqueline (Guenniwig) Rosser, a former student now employed by the National Air Transportation Association; Purvi Shah, an undergraduate research assistant; and Jamie LeBlanc, who credits the text with inspiring him to start his own fixed base operator business.

Special acknowledgment is made of the contributions of David A. NewMyer, chairman of the Aviation Management and Flight Department at Southern Illinois University. His augmentation of the course and curriculum development and his major contribution to chapter 10, concerning airport financing, pushed this project along.

Rick Lanman, a former student and now a colleague, handled the editing and general ancillary material development. Without Rick this project would still rest in a box waiting for a guardian angel to pull the pieces together. Besides the work mentioned, Rick acted in the capacity of a drill instructor. His ubiquitous presence served as a reminder that the project must be completed. He would have made Jack Webb proud. One paragraph of recognition cannot do justice to the commitment and time he has given to this project.

In the initial development of this text, Jeff Hartung, a former director of GTE Airphone Company, laid out several abstracts concerning financial issues that were ultimately incorporated. The original idea to fictionalize an airline was his, and much of the Air Atlantis scenario was his contribution.

To the many students at Southern Illinois University Carbondale in the Department of Aviation Management and Flight who reacted to the material and sometimes suffered through first, second, and third drafts, a special thank-you, for it was your interest that made the endeavor worthwhile.

FISCAL ASPECTS OF AVIATION MANAGEMENT

1

FINANCIAL MANAGEMENT
AND ACCOUNTING PROCEDURES

The modern aviation enterprise must conduct business in a rapidly changing and highly competitive environment. A premium is therefore placed on the ability to react with speed and precision to constantly changing market conditions. Management and even the labor unions within the industry must be concerned with all aspects of the organization's operations. To handle these responsibilities, most organizations make extensive use of data and reports generated by the organization's financial personnel.

Within each business, a firm must establish functional strategies. These strategies generally correspond to such areas of management as marketing, production, human resources, research and development, and the study of fiscal and financial elements. Financial strategies include debt policies, dividend policies, asset management programs, and the capitalization structure of the firm. Figure 1-1 shows a normal pattern of business action effects.

A debt policy is a financial strategy that permits a company to determine whether it will borrow money or use cash on hand to fund its operation. In the management of debt funds, there is a responsibility for having sufficient funds for the firm to conduct its business and to pay its bills. Money must be located to finance receivables (money owed to the firm by others) and inventories, to purchase assets, and to identify sources of long-term financing. Cash must be available to pay dividends and other benefit actions by the board of directors. Some companies, like the former Texas Air conglomerate, were highly leveraged, that is, they borrowed large sums of money against their assets, thus providing the capital required to purchase other airlines. Leveraging allowed Texas Air to buy People Express and Eastern Air Lines (both now defunct), becoming at that time one of the largest airlines in the world. Conversely, Disney Enterprises built the Epcot Center almost entirely from cash flow and cash on hand.

The management of debt funds associates both liquidity and profitability aspects. If the firm's funds are inadequate, the firm may default on the payment of

1

Figure 1-1. Business Action Effects

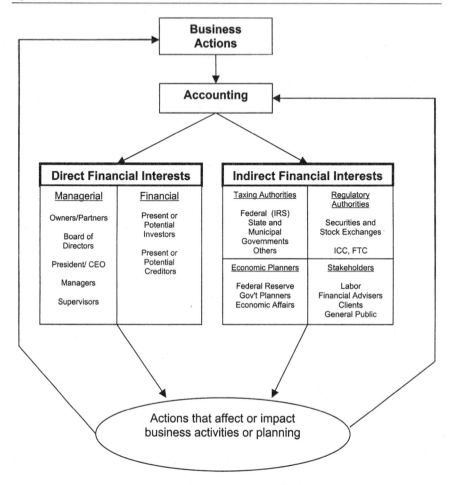

bills, interest on its debt, or repayment of the principal when a loan is due. If the firm does not carefully choose its financing methods, it may pay excessive interest with a subsequent decline in profits.

Companies approach financial strategies from different perspectives. Some pay out most of their profits as dividends to stockholders, while others retain much of their profit for future growth. Corporations can raise money by selling shares in their business to investors, who thus become owners of the business. Dividends are the investors' reward for the risk of investing. How a company approaches dividend policies can influence present and future stockholders, company growth, liquidity, and future profitability.

A firm's dividend policy has the effect of dividing the firm's after-tax profit into funds to finance long-term growth, funds to be distributed to shareholders, or both. Because dividend policies affect both long-term financing and the return distributed to shareholders, the firm may adopt two possible approaches to dividends: first, as a long-term financing decision and, second, as a maximization of wealth. The latter, although more philosophical than the former, recognizes that each payment of dividends has a strong influence on the market price of the company's stock.

Asset management is how the firm plans to earn income on its assets. Assets are the resources by which the firm is able to conduct business, including buildings, machinery, vehicles, inventory, money, and anything else owned or leased by the firm. A firm's assets must be carefully managed, and many decisions must be made concerning their use. For example, some companies use cash on hand to invest in the stock market, purchasing other companies' stock or debt instruments. Other companies may use cash on hand or other liquid assets to earn interest at commercial banks. Asset management and decision making cross liquidity and profitability lines. Converting idle equipment into cash improves liquidity. Reducing costs improves profitability.

Finally, *capitalization* refers to the precise mix of stock and debt issues, how stock is backed, and other relevant issues germane to how a business is financed. It is a financial strategy that determines what types of stock will be used to fund a firm's operations. Funds may be viewed as the firm's liquid assets. Funds include cash held by the firm, money borrowed by the firm, and money gained from the purchases of common and preferred stock. These financial strategies and procedures will be discussed more fully in chapters 3 and 4.

Indispensable to any discussion of fiscal aspects of transportation, or financial management in general, is the topic of accounting procedures. Accounting is essential to both business and government. Accountants are employed in nearly every business community in the world. In this introductory chapter, we will examine what accountants do, what concepts and rules they apply, and how these rules are derived. Later we will explore the most important part of accounting: the basic financial reports of economic activity.

Fiscal elements or aspects of a subject matter are, by definition, related to financial matters or, more particularly, to the elements of taxation, revenue, and public debt. Whether speaking of the public or the private domain, fiscal aspects are developed by financial managers or are borrowed from accounting, economics, and other fields related to the management of money. Finance, or financial management, is an applied field of business administration having its own theories and principles fundamentally concerned with application. Fiscal aspects of a subject matter then can borrow from financial principles, but they are broader in scope, leaving room for unique theories and problematic processes. They can be differentiated from accounting and economics as well as incorporated into each. Fiscal aspects are related to the totality of business finance.

As a business discipline, finance can be carefully differentiated from both economics and accounting. Accounting is concerned with recording, reporting, and measuring of business transactions. Using a widely accepted double-entry bookkeeping system, accounting provides data on an organization's activities. The data may be historical, as in the case of an aircraft repair business's previous year's balance sheet, or a forecast of required available seat miles, as in the case of next year's operating budget. Finance uses the information provided by the accounting system to make decisions that help organizations achieve their objectives. Stated briefly, accounting is a data-collection process dealing with accurate recording and reporting.

It is the accountant's responsibility to keep records of financial transactions such as taxes, income, expenses, and sales. More important, however, is the accountant's analysis of how such transactions affect business. By performing various arithmetic and statistical analyses, accountants can determine how well a business is being managed and how financially viable it is.

Modern business relies more on reports than on direct personal knowledge of its own or others' business activities. Potential investors use financial records to compare companies before investing in stocks. Banks use financial records to evaluate whether to make loans. Labor unions use them in their determination of how large a raise to demand at the negotiating table. Government agencies use such reports to determine the amount of taxes owed by an individual company. And, most important to the business itself, managers use this information to decide the company's future and to control operations.

The Need for Accounting Information in Business

The objective of accounting is to provide information on economic activity that is relevant to decision makers. But there are those who use this information for other than traditional managerial purposes. Just as there are two main users of accounting information—the internal user, primarily the manager, and the external user, the stakeholder—there are also two main systems of accounting to address these ends—managerial and financial accounting.

A firm's internal accounting information should provide data that will enable managers to plan, assess, control, and make operational decisions. Managerial accounting, sometimes called budgeting, involves planning for the future. Prepared on an expected, or pro forma, basis, budgeting information is forecasting business activity. Once a budget is developed, the firm attempts to follow the plan and achieve the projected results. The process of developing such plans and comparing actual results—differences called *variances*—is the primary function of managerial accounting.

While managerial accounting serves a firm's internal needs by providing recent information, financial accounting focuses primarily on historical reports. The information that financial accountants compile is intended primarily for external uses by investors, creditors, potential investors, employees and their unions, government agencies, and others. The information provided to these groups usually consists of the results of operation (the income statement), the financial position of the company (the balance sheet), and a statement of cash flows for a specific period.

Financial accounting is regulated in an attempt to ensure that the resulting reports are clear, reliable, and relatively consistent between comparable reporting periods. The principal regulatory body is the Securities and Exchange Commission. In addition, the American Institute of Certified Public Accountants (AICPA) sets ethical standards for the accounting profession, and the independent Financial Accounting Standards Board (FASB) sets procedural standards. Of course, the Internal Revenue Service has particular interest in the reports produced for all companies.

Because managerial accounting serves internal purposes, it is not constrained by government regulations and generally accepted accounting principles. Managerial accounting provides information for the exclusive use of the particular organization. Thus managerial accountants are free to generate any information that managers find useful. But information prepared for use by others outside the firm is subject to regulations previously discussed.

Because managerial accounting is point specific, many organizations develop particular methodologies to identify cost and price products. Boeing Corporation, for example, is extremely cost-conscious in terms of the per-unit cost of products. Cost accounting is the branch of managerial accounting that determines per-unit cost of products manufactured. In a merchandising business, the invoice can determine the per-unit cost of an article sold. But in a manufacturing plant, values are added as a result of productive efforts that cannot be found on a vendor's invoice; it must be determined from the accounting records.

Major differences exist between managerial and financial accounting. However, both provide a wealth of information to their specific users. Although the differences are many, similarities occur because a firm uses only one management information system. The accounting information generated is used for both financial accounting and managerial purposes, making the starting points for each the same. Additionally, both procedures are concerned with issuing financial reports about the firm's activities for a specific period. Financial accounting focuses on the firm as a whole, and managerial accounting focuses on smaller segments of the same company.

Whereas overlap may sometimes be differentiated by the particular outcomes desired, managerial and financial accounting use a similar method of classifying account information. As a primary focus of the balance sheet, it is necessary to understand their importance and relevance to the accounting procedure. Both forms of accounting distinguish five categories of accounts: asset, liability, equity, revenue, and expense.

Asset accounts. An asset is any resource that permits a company to conduct business. It is anything owned by the company that has value. Also included in this definition are the intangible assets, which occupy a different level of existence. An intangible asset has no physical existence. Instead, it has value as an abstract commodity. Indicative of these are names of businesses that have a special meaning. For example, Trans World Airlines' logo is so well known that another company tried to buy the rights to it. Other examples include patents, copyrights, and trademarks.

Assets are divided into three distinct areas.

- Current assets are those that will, or can, be converted into cash within the current accounting period.
- Fixed assets are resources of the firm that will be used to generate revenue. These assets will not be converted into cash, like current assets, unless they are sold, damaged, or otherwise replaced.
- Intangible assets are those that do not represent physical property.

Liability accounts. Liability accounts comprise the debts of the business, that is, what the company owes. As with assets, liabilities are divided into three subgroups.

- Current liabilities are debts that must be paid during the current accounting period, usually one year. Examples would be salaries paid to employees and taxes that will be paid to the government.
- Long-term liabilities are debts that will not be paid in the current accounting period but that are still owed. Loan payments for equipment are an example.
- Obligations under capital lease are also considered a liability account. These are rent agreements, for example, that cannot be canceled by either party. In economic terms, the company borrowed the money for the asset.

Equity accounts. Equity accounts are established for a variety of ownership types. *Equity* is a term used to represent the ownership rights in a company or piece of equipment. *Equity* is another word for "what the company owns." When we look at the accounting equations later, we'll see that assets minus liabilities equals owner's equity.

Often equity and capital are interchangeable. Capital is the investment made to secure equity. Equity revolves around three major types of accounts.

- Preferred stock is an equity security that gives the holder a preference over other forms of stock for dividend distribution and return of investment in cases of company liquidation.

• Common stock is the true ownership of a company. It represents the residual ownership of a company.
• Retained earnings are the ownership rights that have accrued because the firm has been profitable. The company retained some of the income earned and has reinvested it in the company.

Revenue accounts. Revenues are inflows of assets. Generally, revenues are in the form of cash. Revenue can also enter the company as the tangible form of accounts receivable. These are issued in exchange for a company's products and services. In many businesses the term *revenue* is used interchangeably with *sales*.

Two types of revenue accounts are commonly used.

• Operating revenue is the direct inflow from sales or the performance of services.
• Other income is indirect monies received from areas not viewed as the main part of the company's normal operation.

For instance, a fixed base operator (FBO) derives operating revenue from aircraft repair, whereas the sale of a T-shirt with that FBO's logo is considered other income.

Expense accounts. An expense is the using up of an asset in an attempt to gain revenue. Generally, there are four of these.

• Cash expenses are costs that must be paid in cash at the time of their occurrence.
• Noncash expenses are those that reflect the decline in the value of assets that are consumed during the course of business.
• Interest charges are the result of borrowing money to do business.
• Taxes that are not income taxes are also the cost of doing business. A firm may have to pay state, local, real estate, sales, franchise, or other taxes. Income taxes have their own special place in business.

Internal decisions. Internal decisions will be made at various levels of management, with each level requiring different accounting information. The conclusions to be made from this information can be divided into four categories.

• Financing decisions—Deciding how much capital (money) is needed and whether it is to be obtained from owner investment, borrowed from creditors, obtained by new investment, or financed through internal methods, such as retained earnings.
• Resource allocation decisions—Deciding how the total investment in, or capital of, a business is to be distributed among various types of productive resources, such as buildings, airplanes, or equipment.
• Production decisions—Determining which goods or services are to be

produced, by what means, when, and where, and which elements should be discontinued.

- Marketing decisions—Establishing air fares and advertising budgets; determining marketing techniques and mix; choosing the appropriate means or channels of distribution for the goods or services offered.

External decisions. The many external users of accounting information can be classified broadly into five major categories. The users of this information are, in broad terms, stakeholders of the business. Stakeholders are those impacted by the consequences of decisions made by the organization. Although this may encompass a large category of individuals, the main bodies of stakeholders are

- owners and prospective owners (stockholders, in the case of a corporation) and their financial analysts and investment counselors
- creditors and lenders
- employees and the unions representing them
- customers and consumers
- governmental units and agencies

Types of Accountants

The broad range of accounting activities requires the skills specialists. In our society, accountants typically are employed in public accounting, private industry, or the not-for-profit (government) sector. Within each area, specialization is present. An accountant may, for example, be considered an expert in auditing, systems development, budgeting, or cost and tax accounting.

The best-known type of accountant is the individual employed by an organization to handle in-house accounting procedures. The in-house accountant is not the most common, however. As business becomes more complex, extensive specialization is required. Many in-house accounting personnel, being generalists, cannot address specialized peculiarities. Often extensive specialization falls to an outside concern or accounting specialist. Certified public accountants have met certain experience and education requirements and have passed extensive licensing examinations, providing them with the tools necessary to tackle specialized functions.

More than 40,000 CPA firms are in practice in the United States. Usually CPAs join with one or more other CPAs in a partnership or professional corporation. Some work as individual practitioners. However, five firms (the "Big 5") perform the bulk of large corporations' accounting reviews. They are Arthur Andersen, KPMG Peat Marwick, Ernst & Young, PricewaterhouseCoopers, and Deloitte & Touche. Until the mid-1990s, eight accounting firms controlled the majority of the accounting for large corporations. However, in the accounting industry, as with most segments of the business community, consolidation and merger have reduced the number of major firms. Within a very short time, the Big 8 became the Big 6 and then, in September 1998, the Big 5. This most recent consolidation was the result of a merger between the two firms of Price Waterhouse and Coopers & Lybrand. An indication of the breadth of volume incurred by the accounting firms is that the newly formed PricewaterhouseCoopers will earn more than $13 billion annually and boast more than 135,000 employees. The motive for mentioning this select club of accounting organizations can be determined by the caliber of clients they represent.

- Arthur Andersen's major clients include Texaco, Tenneco, Georgia-Pacific, Colgate-Palmolive, and International Paper.
- KPMG Peat Marwick's major accounts include PepsiCo, General Electric, Citicorp, USAir, Aetna Life & Casualty, Xerox, Union Carbide, JC Penney, and the city of New York.
- PricewaterhouseCoopers represents IBM, USX, Borden, J. P. Morgan, du Pont, W. R. Grace, Hewlett-Packard, Walt Disney, Bristol Myers, Shell Oil, Gannett Advertising, CBS, AT&T, Dow-Jones, Ford Motor Co., Firestone, and Goldman-Sachs.
- Ernst & Young's major clients include Coca-Cola, American Express, Mobil Oil, Apple Computer, Unisys, and Singapore Airlines. The merger of Boeing with McDonnell-Douglas caused Ernst & Young to lose a major aviation client.
- Deloitte & Touche's clients include General Motors, Merrill Lynch, Chrysler, Procter & Gamble, Metropolitan Life, Kohlberg Kravis & Roberts, the New York Times, Sears Roebuck, Prudential, and Boeing.

Just as corporations compete for business, so too do accounting firms. The recent Boeing/McDonnell-Douglas merger has had major implications for two of the present Big 5 firms. Deloitte & Touche has substantially profited at the expense of Ernst & Young's loss of a major client.

While all the Big 5 accounting firms have the heritage of certified public accountants, according to Stevens (1991, p. 18), a close look reveals that they are no longer accounting firms but broad-based consulting practices. As such they serve an interlocking network of corporate, governmental, and institutional clients from Fortune 500 aerospace contractors to Hollywood studios and Congress. Whether the design and installation of massive computer systems, feasibility studies for metropolitan airports, or strategies for shrinking corporate and governmental debt are involved, the Big 5 play a critical role, defining options for managers, politicians, and technocrats. Virtually all CPA firms, whether Big 5 or otherwise, provide three types of services: auditing, tax consultation, and specialized management services.

In mastering the accounting discipline, accountants become aware of the financial problems facing firms or clients. Increasingly, the accountant will advise on courses of action contemplated by a firm.

Auditing. In an audit, the accountant examines a company's accounting system to determine whether the company's financial reports fairly present its financial operations. When a business seeks a loan from a financial institution or seeks to have its securities traded on an exchange, it is usually required to provide statements containing information on its financial affairs. Users of these statements may accept them much more readily and be more willing to rely on them when they are accompanied by an auditor's report. This report contains the professional opinion of a certified public accountant as to whether management has presented a fair report of its financial affairs. To provide an informed opinion, the CPA conducts an investigation (audit) of the underlying accounting procedures and related record keeping, and seeks supporting evidence from external sources (e.g., the company's bank) to verify the company's records.

The audit will determine whether the firm has controls to prevent errors or fraud from going undetected. Auditors also examine receipts such as shipping documents, canceled ticket coupons, flight manifest records, canceled checks, payroll records, and cash receipt records.

While performing these functions, it is an auditor's responsibility to ensure the client's accounting methods adhere to generally accepted accounting principles (GAAP). These rules and procedures govern the what, where, and when of reporting practices. At the end of the audit, the auditor will certify whether or not the client's financial reports comply with GAAP.

Air carriers' accounting information is controlled by a uniform system of accounts and reports (USAR). This system was developed before deregulation under the guidance of the Civil Aeronautics Board (CAB). As many airline activities are unique, several internal accounting controls are peculiar to the industry. The airline accounting policy continues to maintain its accounting requirements to coincide with GAAP. Other industries, having unique accounting methodologies, also attempt to conform to GAAP.

Tax services. Tax services assist clients in preparing their state and federal tax planning and tax returns. A CPA's advice can help a business structure its operation and investments to save tax dollars. Certified public accountants are often called upon for expert advice regarding the preparation and filing of federal, state, and local tax returns. The accountant's objective is to use legal means to minimize the amount of taxes paid. Because of high tax rates and complex tax laws, the area known as tax planning is crucial to the business of the CPA. Proper tax planning requires that the tax effects, if any, of every business decision be fully understood before the decision is made. There may be little opportunity to alter the tax effects of a business decision after it has been made; professional consultation is a wise business practice.

Management services. Professional management services range from guiding personal finances to planning corporate mergers. Services include marketing studies, computer feasibility studies, and design and implementation of accounting systems. Some CPA firms even assist in executive recruitment. Because of insight and knowledge gained in audits, CPAs typically offer suggestions to their clients on how to improve operations. From these as well as other direct contacts, CPAs may be engaged to provide management advisory services. Although such services may include, for example, executive recruiting and production scheduling, they are more likely to involve services related to the accounting process, that is, the design and installation of an accounting system, electronic processing of accounting data, development of an inventory control system, budgeting, or financial planning.

Since accounting has been defined as a comprehensive system for collecting, analyzing, and communicating financial information, it is the accountant's responsibility to keep records of financial transactions such as taxes, sales, incomes, and expenses. But more important is the accountant's analysis of how those transactions will affect a particular business. By sorting, analyzing, classifying, and recording financial events, accountants can determine how well a business is being managed and how financially strong it is. Ultimately, the accumulation and processing of thousands of transactions form the basis for financial reports.

As mentioned earlier, businesses also hire their own private accountants as salaried employees to deal with the company's day-to-day activities. Accountants employed by a single business organization are generally referred to as private or industrial accounts. Private accountants perform an amazing diversity of accounting jobs. Large businesses employ specialized accountants in such areas as budgets, financial planning, internal auditing, payroll, benefit administration, and taxation.

The nature of an accounting job depends on the specific business. For example, the accounting and reporting systems and needs of Trans World Airlines differ considerably from those of American Express Travel or Carnival Cruise Lines. All accountants, whether public or private, rely on record keeping. Because they are intricately involved in the day-to-day operation of a business, company accountants must ensure continuity and procedures in monetary and financial matters and transactions. To maintain this degree of record keeping and consistency, private accountants use journals and ledgers to keep track of business transactions for their company. Underlying these records are the two key concepts of accounting: the accounting equation and double-entry bookkeeping.

Record keeping begins with initial records of the firm's financial transactions. Each penny spent, each cent owed, and each financial transaction must be cataloged daily to develop the basis of any tracking function. Some of the more visible transactions include sales orders, employee time cards, invoices for incoming materials, and customer payments on installment purchases. Unless these and other documents are analyzed and classified daily in an orderly fashion, managers cannot keep track of the business's progress.

Notations of the sorted records are entered into a journal, an intermediate form of record. A journal is a chronological record of financial transactions with a brief description of the transaction. Because of their daily input, some accountants have referred to the daily journal report as the company's financial diary. Some companies keep only a general (single) journal. Others keep specialized journals for each type of transaction. Journals may be maintained solely for cash receipts, sales, purchases, or other individual accounts.

Transactions from a company's journal are then brought together and summarized, usually monthly, in final records called ledgers. Ledgers are divided into categories (accounts) similar to those by specialized journal entries. Unlike journals, accounts in a ledger contain only minimal descriptions of transactions. But they do contain a very important additional column labeled "balance." Because of this column, ledgers enable managers to tell at a glance where the company stands. If the balance is unexpectedly high or low, accountants and other managers can then track backward to the corresponding journal entry to see what caused the unexpected balance.

Finally, at the end of the year, accountants total up all the accounts in a firm's ledger and assess the business's financial status. This summation is the basis for annual financial reports. With the preparation of financial reports, an accounting cycle ends and a new cycle begins.

The Accounting Equation

At various points in the year, public and private accountants balance the data in journals and ledgers by using the following accounting equation:

Assets = Liabilities + Owner's Equity

To understand why this equation is important, you must first understand what accountants mean by *assets, liabilities,* and *owner's equity.* Accountants apply these terms narrowly, focusing on items with quantifiable value. Thus an asset, in the accounting sense, is anything of economic value owned by the firm. Examples include cash on hand, buildings, equipment, land, and payments to the company by others. In contrast, a liability is a debt owed by the firm to others.

Finally, you may have heard people speak of the equity they have in their homes, meaning the amount of money they would get if they sold their houses and paid off their mortgages. In a similar fashion, owner's equity refers to the amount of money a firm's owners would receive if they sold all the company's assets and paid off all its liabilities (i.e., liquidated the company). In this latter context, the accounting equation can be rewritten to strictly show this relationship:

Assets − Liabilities = Owner's Equity

Figure 1-2 indicates the makeup of the accounting equation. If a company's assets exceed its liabilities, then the owner's equity is positive. That is, if the company went out of business, the owners would receive some cash (gain) after selling the assets and paying off the liabilities. If liabilities outweigh assets, owner's equity is negative—there are not enough assets to pay off all the debt. Therefore, the owners of the company receive no cash, and some creditors probably will not be paid what the company owes them.

Owner's equity is helpful not just for liquidation; it is also meaningful in healthy, ongoing business. Owner's equity is made up of what the owners originally invested and what profits the firm has earned and reinvested in the company. Thus, it shows how the owners' financial interests and rights in the company have changed from time to time. For example, in years when a company operates a profitable business, its assets increase faster than its liabilities. As a result, owner's equity will increase (profits flow to the owners). Owner's equity can increase in other ways. For example, the owners may invest more of their own money to increase the firm's assets.

Double-Entry Accounting

The accounting equation must always balance. Thus, if assets increase and liabilities remain unchanged, owner's equity must also increase. If assets decrease and liabilities remain the same, owner's equity must diminish. Changes in liabilities

Figure 1-2. The Accounting Equation

Assets	=	Liabilities	+	Owner's Equity
The resources or properties owned or effectively attached to the firm, including commitments that have little or no independent realizable value but that are significant with respect to future operations.		The rights of all long-term and short-term creditors, including trade creditors, employees, and others to whom the business is currently indebted as well as those holding notes, bonds, and other formal evidences of debt.		The interests of the owners in the ordinary sense. Interest of the proprietor, the partners in unincorporated fields, and the stockholder in the case of the corporation.
What the Company Has	=	What the Company Owes	+	What the Company Owns

have the opposite effect on owner's equity. Thus, a double-entry accounting system requires that any transaction be entered in two ways: how it affects assets and how it affects liabilities and/or owner's equity. Double-entry bookkeeping requires that every "plus" be balanced with a "minus." It is this dual system which provides the basis for accounting practices.

Most businesses and all large-scale enterprises use the double-entry system. It is called double-entry because it is based on the idea that each transaction has an opposite corresponding mirror image. Two entries for each transaction coupled with the need for financial records to balance at the end of the accounting period offer protection against errors.

Transactions and the Accounting Equation

Business transactions affect the elements of the accounting equation. For example, assume that on the first day of March, John White invested $50,000 to open an aircraft painting service in southern Illinois. The business began as John's Aircraft Refinishing Service. After the investment, the one asset of the new business (cash) and White's equity in that singular asset are shown by the following equation:

Assets	=	Liabilities	+	Capital
Cash $50,000.00		Liabilities $0		Owner's Equity $50,000.00

Accounting records are based on the business entity concept. It is assumed that a business is separate and distinct from the person or persons who own it, and the business is treated as though it owns its assets and, in turn, owes both its creditors and its owner the amount of his/her claims.

Another important concept in accounting is the cost principle. When a business transaction is to be recorded, it is the transaction price that sets the accounting value for the property or service acquired. In other words, if the paint White purchased to refurbish aircraft sold for $75 per gallon, but through shrewd bargaining White acquired the paint for $50 per gallon, the lower price is reported as the transaction amount. All properties and services are accounted for at cost. The need for such a principle is obvious: If amounts other than costs were used in recording transactions (e.g., amounts established by estimates, judgments, and appraisals), accounting records would lose a great deal of objectivity.

Continuing with John's Aircraft Refinishing Service, incidental to the operation is the need for tools and the proper equipment and paint library. White found it necessary to invest in aircraft tools. He purchased outright from the Sears Company Craftsman tools for the price of $22,000. He chose these tools because of their guaranteed replacement should they break. This is a good decision for a start-up business, as it may not have enough capital to insure every item. In addition, he purchased a government-required paint and aircraft library for $8,000. His accounting equation now appears thus:

Assets		=	Liabilities	+	Capital
Cash	$20,000		Liabilities $0		Owner's Equity $50,000
Tools	$22,000				
Equipment	$8,000				

Since White began his fixed base operator business at a small airport, he has found it necessary to acquire additional equipment for his office. In an attempt to conserve cash, he purchased office furniture on account from the Better Furniture Company for $450.

Assets		=	Liabilities	+	Capital
Cash	$20,000		Liabilities		Owner's Equity $50,000
Tools	$22,000				
Equipment	$8,000				
Furniture	$450		Better Furniture $450		

Assets were increased by the purchase of the additional office equipment; however, the owner's equity remained unchanged because Better Furniture Company acquired a claim against the assets of John's Aircraft Refinishing Company. The amount owed Better Furniture Company is known as an account payable by John's Aircraft Refinishing Company and is a current liability. Current liabilities are short-term debts that are usually payable within twelve months.

Early in the development of the office structure, White realized he did not need all the office furniture he had purchased. Rather than return the articles for credit from Better Furniture, he sold a desk to another airport concessionaire, Constantine's DoNut Hole Shoppe, for the amount it had originally cost, $150. The head baker, Mr. Blanchard, paid $100 upon delivery to his establishment, promising to pay the balance of $50.00 at a later, unspecified date.

Being very conscientious and frugal in his money dealings, Blanchard paid the amount he owed to John's Aircraft Refinishing Company ($50) within the week.

Assets		=	Liabilities	+	Capital
Cash	$20,100		Liabilities		Owner's Equity $50,000
Tools	$22,000				
Equipment	$8,000				
Furniture	$300		Better Furniture $450		
	($450-$150)				
Account					
Receivable	$50				

Upon receipt of the money, John's Aircraft Refinishing Company immediately turned around and paid Better Furniture Company $200 of the money owed to them for the furniture. The accounting equation now appears as:

Assets		=	Liabilities	+	Capital
Cash	$19,950		Liabilities		Owner's Equity $50,000
($20,100+$50−$200)					
Tools	$22,000				
Equipment	$8,000				
Furniture	$300		Better Furniture $250		
Account Receivable	$0				

As we shall see, the primary objective of a business is to increase owner's equity. John's Aircraft Refinishing Company will try to attain this by selling air service to his clients. This will occur if the income of the company (revenue) exceeds the expenses incurred in making sales and operating the business.

In his first month of business, White sold painting services to one of his creditors, the proprietor of Better Furniture Company. In discussing the price, White advised the charge would be $3,250. Upon hearing this, the proprietor of the furniture company requested that White not only paint the aircraft but also fly it to Hilton Head, N.C. White, a certified pilot, agreed and indicated the cost would now be $3,500, because he would have to buy additional fuel at his airport location.

Upon completion, White flew the plane to Hilton Head, where the owner of Better Furniture took delivery. He was so impressed with the service provided and the quality of work displayed that he told White he would extinguish the outstanding debt White owed to his furniture company. This was, of course, fine with John's Aircraft Refinishing Company. Sometimes jobs well done receive recognition over and above the expected considerations.

The infusion of cash to John's Aircraft Refinishing Service increased the asset account of Cash to $23,450 ($19,950 + $3,500). Since the accounting equation (Assets = Liabilities + Owner's Equity) requires a corresponding offset, the cash infusion increased the value of the business to White. Thus owner's equity increased by a like amount to $53,500 ($50,000 + $3,500).

What happened to the $250 that John owed to the Furniture Company, which no longer is owed, since the owner of Better Furniture, in effect, said forget it? The procedure involved in this instance is convoluted and not easily discernible. In effect, the $250 owed to Better Furniture no longer existed, and the change acted as a credit to the accounts payable; however, since the asset side of the balance sheet was not involved, a like transaction occurred on the liability/owner's equity side. To maintain balance, and since a gift was received, owner's equity increased by $250.

The amount paid for fuel ($250) also worked only on one side of the balance sheet. Effectively there was an exchange of one asset for another. Cash of $250 was paid to obtain fuel of a like value. Therefore, the asset of cash was credited while another asset, that of fuel, was debited for the same amount. The net effects of these transactions would appear as follows:

Assets		=	Liabilities	+	Capital
Cash	$23,200		Liabilities		Owner's Equity $53,500
($19,950+$3,500−$250)					$250
Tools	$22,000				
Equipment	$8,000				
Furniture	$300				
Fuel	$250				
$53,750			$0		$53,750

The amount of money received for this trip is known in accounting as revenue. Revenue is measured by an inflow of cash, accounts receivable, or other assets received in exchange for either goods or services. In one way or another, revenues increase capital.

Expenses, on the other hand, represent the reduction or use of an asset, generally cash. Expenses consist of goods and services (assets) used in the generation of revenue. Expenses deduct from capital. Revenue increases net assets and owner's equity.

Net assets are total assets minus liabilities and thus are equal to owner's equity. Expenses reduce net assets and thus owner's equity.

The scenario used above is both simplistic and conservative. In a real-world setting, the revenues received would be offset by a variety of expenses, such as labor, equipment, and supplies utilized. The totality of the revenues received would very rarely make it to the equity section without having some offsetting costs associated.

Debits and Credits

The system of debits and credits often creates quite a bit of unnecessary confusion for those who are not trained in accounting. Actually, the use of debits and credits is nothing more than a simple shorthand method developed to aid in writing down instructions for making accounting entries. The word *debit* refers to an entry on the left-hand side of an account, while the word *credit* refers to an entry on the right-hand side. Whether a debit or credit has the effect of increasing or decreasing the amount of a particular account depends on the type of account. For example, if the account is an asset account such as cash, the account is a left-hand side account and would be increased by a debit entry and decreased by a credit entry. If the account is a right-hand side account, such as revenue, the opposite is true.

In order to determine the effect of a given entry on the balance of an individual account, one must refer to the accounting equation. The left-hand side accounts (assets and expenses) normally carry a debit balance, are debited to increase, and are credited to decrease. Conversely, right-hand side accounts (liabilities, equities, and revenues) normally carry a credit balance, are credited to increase, and are debited to decrease (see figure 1-3).

Figure 1-3. Debit and Credit Definition

Debit (Dr.)	=	Left-hand side entry
Credit (Cr.)	=	Right-hand side entry

Debit   Increase to assets and expenses or decrease to liabilities, equity, and revenues

Credit   Decrease to assets and expenses or increase to liabilities, equity, and revenues

The use of a debit or credit to increase or decrease depends only on the type of account.

	Debit Side of Balance Sheet *(Asset Side)*	**Credit Side of Balance Sheet** *(Liability/Owner's Equity Side)*
Balance sheet categories	• Assets + Expenses	• Liabilities, equities, and revenues
Actions to increase	• Debit (Dr.)	• Credit (Cr.)
Actions to decrease	• Credit (Cr.)	• Debit (Dr.)
	Normal balance = Debit	Normal balance = Credit

In order for the accounting equation to be in balance, the sum of the debit entries must always be equal to the sum of the credit entries. To determine whether the accounts balance at any given time, one need only add up the sum of the debits and credits. If the two totals are not equal, then an error has been made somewhere and should be located immediately.

The process described above is called "taking a trial balance." The system, of course, is not foolproof. For example, the correct number and amount of debits and credits might be made, but one or more entries may be posted to the wrong accounts. The accounting records will still balance, but they will not be correct. Errors of this type are much more difficult to find.

Some Simple Examples

For illustrative purposes, let's return to John's Aircraft Refinishing Service and assume that one employee, Terry Mechanic, is leaving to start his own business. The new business, Terry's Fixed Base Operation, will be operated as a sole proprietorship beginning June 1. Terry's first "official act" is to open a checking account in the name of his FBO by depositing $10,000 in his bank. The accounting transaction would be recorded as follows:

Debit (Dr.) — Cash	$10,000
Credit (Cr.) — Terry's FBO, Capital	$10,000

As can be seen above, Terry's FBO now has two accounts, one asset account (Cash) and one equity account (Terry's FBO, Capital). If Terry keeps his individual accounts on separate sheets of paper, his accounts will be represented by the following T-accounts:

(10) CASH	(40) TERRY'S FBO, CAPITAL
10,000	10,000

T-accounts are simply representations of particular asset/liability or equity accounts with the left side being a debit and the right side a credit. The mechanics of double-entry accounting are best indicated by the use of the T-account. A title is placed above the T, and debits and credits are entered on the left and right sides, respectively. As indicated earlier, the concept of double-entry accounting is that debits and credits must always be equal. A second concept is that an asset account is increased by a debit entry and decreased by a credit entry. A liability or owner's equity account is just the opposite. It is increased by a credit entry and decreased by a debit entry. As an example, if a fixed base operator borrows money to purchase a new King Air, thus incurring a liability, it must credit a liability account (long-term debt) to offset the asset account that has been debited to reflect the new aircraft.

Note that the T-accounts are numbered. Accounts are often numbered in order to facilitate the recording of transactions in journals if journals are used to record transactions prior to posting the actual accounts. A journal is nothing more than a chronological record of transactions that is to be posted later in the actual accounts. The accounts themselves are kept in books referred to as ledgers. For a small operation such as Terry's FBO, a journal probably would not be used and transactions would be posted directly to one "general ledger." The process of recording transactions in journals is referred to as "journalizing."

The number system used above is not a random process. Each account is assigned a number of at least two digits with the leading digit established according to the order of appearance of the account in the accounting equation. Asset accounts always begin at number one (1) and proceed in balance sheet order. That is, the numbers would correspond to the layout of the balance sheet. Thus, cash would be number 10, accounts receivable 11, inventory 12, and so forth. For a company or organization with an extremely large number of assets, cash might begin with one hundred (100), one thousand (1,000), or even higher. The main focus is to keep consistency in the approach utilized. Similarly, expense accounts begin with 2, liabilities with 3, equities with 4, and revenues with 5. The advantages of using systematic numbering should be fairly obvious.

To continue the FBO example, let us journalize Terry's first month's activities and then post these journal records to his general ledger. Each journal entry will have a number, which will be noted on the simulated ledger sheets so that the reader may examine each transaction. The previous $10,000 transaction will be treated as transaction number 1. Additional transactions during the first month of operation, with appropriate journal notations, are as follows:

2. The FBO purchases a new truck for picking up paint supplies. The price of the truck was $10,000. A down payment of $2,000 in cash was made by the FBO, and Terry borrowed the remaining $8,000 from the local bank and trust in the form of a note:

Debit (Dr.) — Truck	$10,000
Credit (Cr.) — Cash	$2,000
Credit (Cr.) — Notes Payable	$8,000

The T-accounts would appear thus:

(13) TRUCK	(10) CASH	(31) NOTES PAYABLE
10,000		10,000	2,000		8,000

3. Next, the FBO purchases $2,500 worth of paint solvent supplies on open account from Roland's Paint Distributors:

Debit (Dr.) — Supplies Inventory	$2,500
Credit (Cr.) — Accounts Payable	$2,500

(12) SUPPLIES	(30) ACCTS. PAYABLE
2,500			2,500

As with the establishment of T-accounts for asset, liability, and owner's equity purposes, we can similarly develop increases and decreases in the income statement accounts. If an asset increases because the FBO earns revenue, a debit entry increases the asset account and a credit entry must increase the revenue account. If an expense of the business decreases cash (a credit entry to the cash account), the expense must be recorded with a debit entry (an increase in expenses).

4. In the first month of operation, Terry's FBO completes the painting of a Cessna single-engine aircraft for John's Aircraft Refinishing Service, billing the Refinishing Service $6,500:

Debit (Dr.)—Accounts Receivable $6,500
Credit (Cr.)—FBO Revenue $6,500

(11) ACCOUNTS RECEIVABLE	(50) FBO REVENUE
6,500			6,500

5. Aircraft Refinishing Service sends Terry a check for $3,000, which he deposits in his checking account. The remaining $3,500 will be paid at the end of July:

Debit (Dr.)—Cash $3,000
Credit (Cr.)—Accounts Receivable $3,000

(10) CASH	(11) ACCTS. RECEIVABLE
10,000	2,000	6,500	3,000
3,000		

6. With the improvement in cash flow generated by the Aircraft Refinishing Service's partial payment of its bill, Terry now has money to pay off a portion of the debt for paint supplies. Terry pays $1,500 on his account at Roland's Paint Distributors:

Debit (Dr.)—Accounts Payable $1,500
Credit (Cr.)—Cash $1,500

(10) CASH	(30) ACCTS. PAYABLE
10,000	2,000	1,500	2,500
3,000	1,500	

7. Toward the end of the month, the FBO inventories its paint supplies to determine how much was used. It is noted that $500 worth of the original $2,500 inventory is left. Therefore, $2,000 worth of supplies must have been used in painting the Cessna aircraft for John's Aircraft Refinishing Service:

Debit (Dr.)—Supplies Expense $2,000
Credit (Cr.)—Supplies Inventory $2,000

(12) SUPPLIES	(20) SUPPLIES EXPENSE
2,500	2,000	2,000	

If transaction number 7 is the FBO's last transaction for the month, it can readily be seen that Terry now has a total of nine accounts to maintain. If we place them on the side of the balance sheet, according to the accounting equation, and balance each individual account, we can see that

Assets = Liabilities + Owner's Equity

Figure 1-4 takes revenues and expenses into account.

Figure 1-4. The Accounting Equation Applied

Assets + Expenses = Liabilities + Owner's Equity + Revenues			
Assets		**Liabilities**	
(10) Cash	$9,500	(30) Accounts payable	$1,000
(11) Accounts receivable	$3,500	(31) Bank notes payable	$8,000
(12) Supplies inventory	$500	**Equity**	
(13) Truck	$10,000	(40) Terry's FBO, capital	$10,000
Expenses		**Revenue**	
(20) Supplies expense	$2,000	(50) Service revenue	$6,500

The Accounting Cycle

The accounting cycle is a logical series of steps that accountants follow to keep necessary accounting records and prepare financial statements. In this section, the Terry's FBO example will be continued in order to illustrate the steps in the cycle, and a one-month income statement and balance sheet will be presented for Terry.

The first two steps in the accounting cycle are very closely related and are accomplished during the month as transactions occur. Step 1 involves sorting business transactions into an appropriate number of debits and credits to be entered on the accounting records. Thus, in the FBO's first transaction, we conclude that depositing $10,000 in the checking account involves a debit to cash and a credit to Terry's FBO, Capital account.

Step 2 in the accounting cycle involves recording this transaction (as debit and credit entries) in a journal for later posting to the general ledger. As previously noted, a small operation such as this may not even bother with a journal. In this case, one would proceed directly to Step 3 in the accounting cycle and post the general ledger directly.

Posting journal entries to the general ledger, Step 3 in the cycle, is generally accomplished at the end of each month. If no journal were maintained, transactions would simply be posted to the ledger as they occurred. For Terry's FBO, we have already seen examples of journal entries in the previous section, and the general ledger was postings in T-accounts.

Step 4 in the accounting cycle involves making adjusting entries to the general ledger. Adjusting entries involves crediting an asset account for use of an item that may have been prepaid. For example, suppose that Terry's FBO purchased liability insurance to cover any potential mishaps at the shop. The cost of the insurance policy for one year (June through May) totals $2,800 (FBO insurance can be expensive). At the time of purchase of the asset, the appropriate entry would be:

Debit (Dr.) — Prepaid Insurance (an asset)	$2,800
Credit (Cr.) — Cash	$2,800

Because this amount was prepaid, meaning the insurance company was not actually entitled to the money until time had elapsed, when the end of the year arrives and financial statements are drawn up, it will be necessary to "charge" $1,400, or six months' worth, of the policy. The appropriate accounting entry would be:

Debit (Dr.) — Insurance Expense	$1,400
Credit (Cr.) — Prepaid Insurance	$1,400

Thus, $1,400 worth of an asset, prepaid insurance, is "moved over" to the income statement as the year's insurance expense. Adjusting entries, in general, result from the need to match expenses with revenues in accordance with the accrual concept. Adjusting entries are normally prepared at the end of each quarter or at the end of the year, although many firms prepare monthly financial statements. In practice, accountants normally prepare a worksheet showing the current balances for all of a company's accounts and then prepare financial statements from this worksheet. In the simple case of Terry's FBO, financial statements, in all probability, would be prepared directly from the general ledger accounts.

Step 5 of the accounting cycle is commonly referred to as "closing the books." At year's end, all "temporary" accounts are closed out. Temporary accounts are those that begin the new year with a zero balance; generally these include the income statement accounts. All revenue and expense accounts are "closed" into an account called an income summary or profit-and-loss summary. This account in turn is "closed" to the owner's equity account. Expenses are subtracted from revenues to determine net profit (or loss), and this amount is then added to (or subtracted from) owner's equity. Balance sheet accounts are then rectified, and the result is brought forward to begin the new year. The balance sheet accounts are therefore commonly referred to as permanent accounts.

Step 6 in the accounting cycle follows immediately after the closing process. In this final step, financial statements for the period are prepared.

The primary purpose of accounting and its attendant FBO procedures is to summarize the results of a business's transactions. These summaries lead to reports that aid the business stakeholders in making decisions. The more important of these reports are called the business financial statements. They fall into several categories of balance sheets, income statements, and cash flow statements (see figure 1-5.)

Figure 1-5. Accounting and Record Keeping System

Collecting		Analyzing	Reporting
Initial Records	*Journal Entries*	*Ledger Entries*	*Financial Statements*
• Sales invoices • Cash receipts • Equipment purchase • Equipment repair • Revenue received • Misc. expense items	Information logging and cataloging of specific transactions with rationale for each. Example: *'Paid cash for stationary supplies'*	• Cash • Accounts receivable • Accounts payable • Equipment • Notes payable	• Balance sheets • Income statement • Statement of cash flow

Financial statements provide the link between accounting and finance. Preparation and accurate accounting techniques permit analysis of a firm's activities and determination of its financial health. It is for these reasons that financial statements are of interest to all stakeholders (owners, banks, creditors, unions, employees) and, of course, the Internal Revenue Service, a business's silent partner who always wants a share of the company profits.

Suggested Readings and References

Baker, C. R. (1980). *Accounting, finance, and taxation: A basic guide for small businesses.* Boston: CBI.

Bernstein, L. (1990). *Analysis of financial statements.* Homewood, IL: Dow Jones–Irwin.

Booker, J., & Jarnagin, D. B. (1985). *Financial accounting standards: Explanation and analysis.* Chicago: Commerce Clearinghouse.

Davidson, D., & Weil, L. R. (1977). *Handbook of modern accounting.* New York: McGraw-Hill.

Farrell, J. B. (1988). *Accounting perspective.* Gladesville, Australia: Study Panorama.

Gillespie, M. C. (1951). *Accounting systems: Procedures and methods.* Englewood Cliffs, NJ: Prentice-Hall.

Gordon, J. M., & Shillinglaw, G. (1979). *Accounting: A management approach.* Homewood, IL: R. D. Irwin.

Helfert, A. E. (1982). *Techniques of financial analysis.* Homewood, IL: R. D. Irwin.

Larson, D. K. (1989). *Financial accounting.* Homewood, IL: R. D. Irwin.

Larson, D. K., & Pyle, W. W. (1981). *Fundamental accounting principles.* Homewood, IL: R. D. Irwin.

Schroeder, G. R., Solomon, M. L., & Vargo, J. R. (1983). *Accounting principles.* New York: Harper & Row.

Stevens, M. (1991). *The big six: The selling out of America's top accounting firms.* New York: Simon & Schuster.

2

FINANCIAL MANAGEMENT AND SOURCES OF FINANCIAL INFORMATION

After reading this chapter, you should understand some of the forces affecting financial management, the way businesses are organized, and how financial management contributes to the attainment of business goals. You should also know some common financial terminology.

Overview of Financial Management

Financial management consists of three interrelated areas:

- *money and capital markets,* which deal with the many national and international economic, banking, and trade markets
- *investments,* which focus on the decisions of individuals and corporations as they choose their investment portfolio mix
- *financial management or business management,* which involves the actual management of the firm to achieve stated business goals and objectives

Although this text concentrates on financial management, the capital and investment markets will be examined, as they have great influence on aviation and air transport sector share performance. To create a climate of consistency, the airline financial and operational venue will be targeted. Financial realities and intricacies may vary from industry to industry, but the bottom line will be achieved through well-founded and focused financial management. Since financial concepts bridge industry and are applicable whether we are following an airline or a "Big 3" automaker, the use of an airline as our topic is only expedient. Therefore, in the following sections we will use a fictitious airline, Air Atlantis, as a model business.

Financial management methods, practices, and objectives within the air transport sector have evolved over the years, as changes in technology and market emphasis have occurred. In the early days of air transportation, financial management was concerned with forming new airlines, issuing securities (stocks and bonds) to raise operating capital, and developing legal strategies to buy or merge with other airlines.

Financial performance in the air transport sector historically has been linked closely with the domestic economy. As such, business financial performance suffered during the Great Depression of the 1930s. The focus of financial management shifted to bankruptcy, restructuring and reorganization, and aggressive securities regulation.

The federal government mandated the creation of the Civil Aeronautics Board in 1938, with the expressed purpose of developing and regulating the air transport industry. Consequently, the 1940s and early 1950s saw financial management in the air transport sector concentrating on external issues such as government financial regulation, via the CAB, stock and shareholder rights and control, and associated legal issues.

In the late 1950s and 1960s, internalized financial management practices came to the industry. The introduction of extremely expensive turbine transports, the emergence of cost-effective leases on large mainframe computers, and the continued financial regulation by the CAB initiated the movement toward such internal issues as cash flow management, maintenance costs, inventory spare levels control, and capital asset (aircraft) acquisition alternatives. Utilizing theoretical analysis techniques, air transport financial management began to focus on managerial decision making with respect to the choice of assets and liabilities, market capacity, and optimal break-even load factors to maximize the value of the firm.

This focus on valuation techniques continues. Valuation analysis has been expanded from strict asset/liability and capacity break-even load factors analysis. It now includes

- inflation and its effects on business decisions
- deregulation, not only of the air transport sector but of financial institutions and the resulting large and powerful diversified financial service organizations with their attendant impact on financial services availability
- the ubiquity and interconnectivity of the personal computer for both data analysis and data exchange
- the increased importance of the global marketplace as the prime source of new revenue

The most important trend will be the continued pressure to either buy or grow into a global air carrier. This will require adequate market share, decent returns on investment, and finding more rapid and refined ways to utilize computing power for market penetration and exploitation of business advantages.

Globalization of the Air Transport Sector

Several factors make the trend toward globalization virtually mandatory for most air carriers. First is the continued rapid globalization of manufacturing and service sectors. Even in times of domestic and global recession pressure, the demand for international business travel remains strong.

Second, the slow but inexorable reduction in world trade barriers will create markets that have previously been closed to American carriers. The current groups of signatories to all bilateral agreements with the United States are under enormous pressure to open their respective countries' skies. Anticipated pressure will continue to build, and full global open skies will likely become a reality. When this will occur is anybody's guess. However, it will occur, and therefore air carriers must achieve as much global market share as possible to ensure capturing newly emerging markets. This tremendous rush to capture new market share is not just confined to the airlines. It is true of aircraft manufacturers, suppliers, and other related fields within the aviation industry.

Third, the seemingly continuous global economic crisis of the early 1990s has abated, only to be replaced by the monetary problems of the Pacific Rim countries, particularly Asia and the island-nations of the South China Sea, the implementation of the Eurodollar, and a host of other crises. These new monetary exigencies have caused the dollar to become exceedingly strong against most world currencies. As this bullish dollar continues to accelerate, the U.S. air transport sector will undergo an upsurge in global travel and tourism. When the world aviation market gets by these present global economic setbacks, U.S. carriers will be in a formative position to capture more global terrain. Air carriers must position today to snare tomorrow's market share.

The three key factors listed above clearly point to the fact that any and all significant growth in revenue passenger miles (RPMs) and revenue ton miles (RTMs) will occur in the global marketplace. Due to the cost of new aircraft and the oligopolistic nature of the industry, fare prices cannot support financial growth alone. An air carrier will only be able to grow by increasing capacity and ultimately producing more RPMs and RTMs than the competition. Capacities, delivered at the right time in the right market, coupled with a stable long-term price structure, are the keys to global expansion.

There will, of course, always be some purely domestic air carriers. Many of them, to remain competitive, will probably have to negotiate some level of code-sharing arrangements with global megacarriers, as increasingly more passengers travel abroad. Likewise, because some carriers from foreign countries have become megaprofit centers, they will be looking for U.S. code-sharing partners to protect their markets. Lufthansa, the German carrier, has been seeking an American partner. Once-powerful Trans World Airlines fit the profile in 1998 by occupying seventh place in the domestic market while rolling up losses close to $140 million. New airplane purchases, a good feed route to New York, and some international routings would make TWA a likely candidate for a code-sharing partner if it could regain the prominence it enjoyed before deregulation.

Computing Technology in the Air Transport Sector

The air transport sector was one of the first nonmilitary business sectors to embrace and effectively exploit the power of the computer. It advanced telecommunications systems as marketing tools and profit centers. The IBM 360s of the early 1960s were able to manage and communicate crew/aircraft scheduling, maintenance planning, and reservations/ticketing data far more accurately and rapidly than had been previously possible. Today large air transport organizations such as American Airlines, United Air Lines, and British Airways possess some of the most powerful and advanced data acquisition, analysis, forecasting, and communications systems in the world. In the years ahead, the power to analyze past performance, compute present activity levels, and model future trends will be combined with "smart aircraft" capable of "downlinking" operational data on a real-time basis. These "intelligent" real-time computing and communicating systems will ensure rapid identification and exploitation of market opportunities.

Increasing Importance of Financial Management

The historical trends discussed in the previous section have greatly increased the importance of financial management. In earlier times, sales and traffic managers would project city pair bookings for the route system. Flight operations and maintenance personnel would determine the numbers and types of aircraft, flight personnel, and spare parts needed to meet those demands. Financial managers would be charged with the responsibility of raising the money needed to purchase required aircraft, engines, staff, and gate space. That extenuated situation no longer exists. Today's decisions are made in a coordinated manner to maximize shareholder value. The financial manager's massive trend analysis computing power now takes direct responsibility for controlling the process.

Eastern Air Lines and Delta can be used to illustrate both the importance of financial management and the effects of financial decisions. In the 1960s, Eastern stock sold for more than $60 per share, while Delta stock sold for $10 per share. As of January 12, 1993, Delta stock sold for $51 per share while Eastern, after filing bankruptcy, ultimately went out of business. Although many factors coalesced to produce these very different results, financial decisions had a major influence on each airline. Because Eastern had traditionally used a great deal of debt (or high leverage) and Delta had not, Eastern's costs increased significantly, and its profits were decimated when interest rates rose during the early 1980s. These same rate increases had only minimal impact on Delta's performance, since they were not heavily debt laden. At the time of deregulation, because of Delta's traditional frugal nature, the airline was strong enough to expand into developing markets, cut prices, and cross-subsidize new route development. Eastern was not in such a position and, in the vernacular, ended up being flown into the ground by a combination of poor management, poor labor decisions, and mistakes in fiscal accountability.

The Eastern-Delta story and others like it are now well known. Companies today are greatly concerned with financial planning. This has increased the importance of corporate financial management and financial managers. Airline managers no longer concentrate solely on the operative aspects of their responsibility. It is increasingly important for people in marketing, accounting, flight and ground operations, and maintenance to understand finance. There are financial implications in virtually all business decisions, and nonfinancial managers simply must know enough finance to work these implications out in their own specialized analyses. The ability of organizations to balance debt and equity positions, with well-designed forecasting methodology, is imperative to future growth. Being in the right place at the right time is critical in the highly sensitive and volatile aviation arena.

Air Transport Business Structures

Business operation can be conducted in several forms:

- Sole proprietorships
- Partnerships
- Trusts and estates
- S corporations (also known as subchapter-S or sub-S corporations)

The major business entities, or the three main forms of business organizations, are sole proprietorship, partnerships, and corporations. In terms of numbers, about 80 percent of businesses in the United States are operated as sole proprietorships, while the remainder are divided between partnerships and corporations. Based on dollar sales, however, about 80 percent of all business is conducted by corporations, about 13 percent by sole proprietorships, and about 7 percent by partnerships. The distinctions between these forms of business organizations are very important, especially for income tax purposes.

By far, the most popular of business structures in the air transport arena is the corporation. This is not to imply that the corporation is the only form of business structure in the aviation industry. Many airlines as well as fixed base operators and manufacturing support organizations operate under proprietor and partnership arrangements.

Types of Business Organizations

All business owners must decide on a form of legal organization. The decision concerning the type of business entity is often critical, as the choice of ownership and organization structure affects managerial and financial issues. In the choice of a business structure, those concerned must consider their immediate and long-range needs. Each of the following forms of business has advantages and disadvantages. The choice should be well considered.

Sole Proprietorship

Generally, a business owned and operated by one individual who provides the capital to the business and directs all its activities is a sole proprietorship. The owner has unlimited liability for the debts of the business—that is, if the business cannot pay its debts, the owner must do so from personal resources. Although the name implies individuality, this does not mean it can only be a one-person operation. A sole proprietorship may employee hundreds, or even thousands, of employees. As the name implies, an individual owns the sole proprietorship. Many large businesses are sole proprietorships. The Ford Motor Company was for a long time the sole proprietorship of Henry Ford. During his tenure, his organization employed thousands of people as workers and managers, but he totally controlled and owned the business.

Formation of a sole proprietorship is extremely simple. It is usually only a matter of reporting the formation on one's individual tax return. The major advantage of a sole proprietorship is that tax benefits permit the sole proprietor to treat revenue and operating expenses of the business as part of their personal finances. A sole proprietorship is not a taxable entity separate from the individual who owns the proprietorship. The owner of a sole proprietorship reports all business transactions of the proprietorship on Schedule C of IRS Form 1040. The net profit or loss from the proprietorship is then transferred from Schedule C to Form 1040, which is used by the individual taxpayer to report taxable income. The proprietor reports all of the net profit from the business, regardless of the amount actually withdrawn during the year. Thus, a proprietor can cut taxes by deducting any operating losses from individual income earned. Likewise, profits of the business are taxed as sole income. Thus, the owner pays taxes on the business as if the profit or losses were personal income or loss. Income, therefore, may be taxed at a rate considerably lower than that required of a corporation. (See the comparison of corporate and sole proprietorship tax structures following the sub-S corporation section.)

Income and expenses of the proprietorship retain their character when reported by the proprietor. The treatment of income and capital gain (property) is straightforward, unlike other forms of ownership.

A major disadvantage to the proprietorship form of business is its unlimited liability provision. A proprietor is personally liable for all debts incurred in the business. Bills, legal obligations (if the business is sued), and other debts must be paid out of the sole proprietor's own pocket if the business fails to generate enough cash. Creditors may step in and claim the proprietor's personal possessions, including house, furniture, automobile, and other assets if the business is unable to pay its own way.

Major advantages of a sole proprietorship include

- freedom
- low start-up costs
- simplicity
- tax benefits

Major disadvantages of a sole proprietorship include

- unlimited liability
- lack of continuity
- difficulty in raising funds

Partnerships

A partnership is a business owned by two or more individuals who provide the capital to the partnership. Usually these same individuals also direct the partnership activities. Like single proprietors, partners generally have unlimited liability for the debts of the business. A general partnership, as distinguished from limited partnerships discussed later, is really a sole proprietorship multiplied by the number of partners. There is no legal limit to the number of partners in a partnership arrangement.

Partnerships are not subjected to income tax. However, a partnership is required to file an IRS Form 1065, which reports the results of the partnership's business activities. Most income and expense items are aggregated in computing the net profit of the partnership. Any income and expense items that are not aggregated in computing the partnership's net income are reported separately to the partners. Some examples of separately reported income items are interest income, dividend income, and long-term capital gain. The partnership net profit and the separately reported items are allocated to each partner according to the partnership's profit sharing agreement, and the partners receive a Form K-1 indicating their share of the partnership arrangement. Each partner then reports the K-1 items on his or her own tax return.

The major advantages and disadvantages are the same as for the sole proprietorship, except that the exposure is spread over a greater number of people. Like the proprietorship, a partnership is easy to organize, having few legal requirements. The number one concern of a partnership should be to develop agreements concerning the conduct of the partners and how the proceeds of the business will be distributed. As with the proprietorship of business, a partnership by law ceases to exist upon the death of a partner.

Major advantages of a partnership include

- larger talent pool than proprietorship
- ease of formation
- access to more funds
- tax benefits

Major disadvantages of a partnership include

- unlimited liability
- possibility of partner conflict
- lack of continuity
- difficulty of ownership transfer

Limited Partnerships

Limited partnerships are derivations of the general partnership arrangement. In a limited partnership (identified by the word *Ltd.*), someone in the arrangement has opted to assume a limited role, thus limiting their exposure to the potential liability that a partnership and proprietorship may incur. Usually the arrangement is such that one party, the limited partner, provides capital to the business but does not get involved in the active management of the business. The active partners, on the other hand, provide the expertise and time to manage the operation.

Corporations

The corporation is a creation of the law. Subchapter-C of the Internal Revenue Code governs regular corporations. Thus, they are frequently referred to as "C corporations." Unlike proprietorships and partnerships, C corporations are taxpaying entities.

The holding of shares of capital stock proves ownership. In a corporation many stockholders provide capital and in return obtain a portion of the ownership rights. In large corporations, the business may be run with hired managers employed to direct the corporation's activities. Such managers may or may not have ownership stakes in the business.

It is not necessary for a corporation to be a monolithic structure. The nature of the corporate definition is such that the smallest business has as much right to be a corporation as does a giant computer manufacturer. The basic characteristics of a corporation are such that they are a legal entity that has property rights, obligations, and an indefinite life span.

As far back as 1819, Supreme Court Chief Justice John Marshall defined a corporation as "an artificial being, invisible, intangible and existing only in contemplation of the law." Consequently, the Supreme Court defined the corporation as a legal person, almost to the extent that it breathes. As such, a corporation may sue and be sued, commit crimes and be tried and punished for crimes, buy, hold, and sell property, and pay taxes.

With this as a backdrop, the liability emphasis placed on the other form of business enterprises moves from the individual to the business itself. Thus, for an owner or partial owner of a corporation, a limited liability exists only to the extent of one's investment in the corporation. If the business has debts, the business, not the owner, is responsible for those debts. There is, however, a tax disadvantage, which, some say, is a trade-off for the limited liability feature. That is, a corporation pays double income taxes. This double payment occurs first in the form of corporate taxes on profit and then on the personal taxes that the owners must pay when they receive dividends from their ownership rights.

Major advantages of a corporation include

- limited liability
- continuity
- professional managers
- access to money markets

Major disadvantages of a corporation include

- high start-up costs
- regulation
- double taxation

Sub-S Corporations

In 1958, Congress created a hybrid organization whose locus was somewhere between the corporation and the proprietorship forms of business. Its definition is contained in Chapter S of the Internal Revenue Code. A sub-S is a listed corporation whose stockholders have elected to operate under the S provisions of corporate activity. This sub-S status is an elective provision. Failure to make the election will mean that the rules applicable to the taxation of corporations (subchapter-C status, or C-corps) and shareholders will apply. The S election affects only the federal income tax consequences of electing corporations. S corporations are regular corporations in the legal sense.

S corporations enjoy the advantages of limited liability and the easy transfer of ownership, similar to the corporation. As with the proprietorship or partnership forms of business, stockholders are simply taxed. The profits and/or losses of the business are passed through to the sub-S stockholders. This avoids the double taxation of the full corporate entity.

There are, however, some strings attached to these advantages. To qualify as a sub-S corporation, a business must meet some stiff legal requirements. These re-

Figure 2-1. Qualifications for Sub-S Corporation Status

---

1. Is an independently owned domestic corporation (incorporated or organized in the United States).
2. Has no more than 75 shareholders.
3. Shareholders consist of only
    Individuals,
    Estates, or
    Qualifying Trusts.
4. All shareholders are citizens of the United States. No nonresident aliens.
5. Issues only one class of stock.

Source: W. H. Hoffman, W. A. Raabe, and J. E. Smith, *West's Federal Taxation: Corporations, Partnerships, Estates, and Trusts* (New York: West, 1996).

quirements can be found in figure 2-1. It is also important to know that no more than 25 percent of sales revenue may come from dividends, rents, interest, royalties, annuities, or stock sales, and no more than 80 percent of sales revenues may come from foreign markets.

A corporation is a legal entity created by a state. It is separate and distinct from its owners and managers. This separation gives the corporation three distinct advantages:

- unlimited life: Corporations can continue after their original owners have sold out or died.
- easy transferability of ownership interest: Ownership is divided up into shares of stock that can be bought and sold on the open market.
- limited liability: Any shareholder is only liable up to the value of his or her share investment.

These three advantages allow corporations to raise funds in the capital markets easily.

Because the ownership of a corporation is represented by shares of stock, a portion of the ownership can easily be transferred by the sale of such stock. Because these sales can occur as a transfer or as an outright sale, it is necessary to distinguish between two forms of a corporation. In one form, ownership transference is accomplished by simply offering shares of stock for sale to the public. In the other form, difficulties in finding buyers may be common.

In a closed corporation, shares of stock are distributed among the shareholders but are not sold on the open market. In many closed corporations, the owners are tied together along family or friendship lines, enjoying the advantages that the corporate form of ownership provides. Because of this arrangement, the owners of a closed corporation have trouble finding buyers for their shares of stock. According to Gitman (1992), this form of corporate ownership accounts for 99 percent of all corporations.

Publicly traded corporations are those whose stock can be purchased by anyone. It is publicly traded. The shares of thousands of such companies are listed on the stock exchanges or are quoted in the over-the-counter markets. Shares of stock in these large corporations have an extremely high degree of transferability and thus greater ease of sale for the holder of such stock.

Despite the many advantages the corporation has over proprietorships and partnerships, however, there are two disadvantages:

• Corporate earnings are subject to double taxation, first as earnings for the corporation, and then as income to the shareholders from dividends.
• Setting up a corporation requires filing state and federal paperwork and following certain reporting requirements.

A corporate charter and a set of bylaws must be drawn and filed and must include the following information:

• name of corporation
• types of activities it will pursue
• amount of capital stock to be issued initially
• number of directors
• names and addresses of directors

The charter is filed with the secretary of the state in which the firm will be incorporated. Then, after the corporation begins operations, it must file quarterly and annual financial and tax reports with state and federal authorities.

To summarize, the value of any business will probably be maximized if it is organized as a corporation for the following reasons:

1. Limited liability reduces the risk borne by investors, and the lower the risk the higher the value.
2. A firm's value is dependent on growth opportunities, which in turn are dependent on the firm's ability to attract capital. Since corporations can attract capital more easily than other forms of business structures and have various ways of generating cash (discussed in chapters 3 and 4), their ability to invest and move rapidly is enhanced.
3. The value of any asset also depends on its liquidity, which means the ease of selling the asset and converting it into cash. Since investments in the stock or bonds of a corporation are more liquid than an investment in a partnership or proprietorship, the corporation has enhanced value.

Corporate/Sole Proprietorship–Partnership Income Taxes

Since tax savings are a major consideration concerning which business structure to adapt, individuals and partners contemplating owning a business must compare the expected tax rates on the different forms of business. From a financial viewpoint, an individual would be well advised to consider such analysis, as there are situations where the tax savings outweigh the potential business structure benefits. There are times when corporations (sub-S included) pay less than do sole proprietorships. This can occur under anomalies created by the IRS programs. Corporate and individual tax obligations are indicated in figure 2-2.

As can be seen by the table, the tax advantage for a sole proprietorship compared with a corporation occurs in the $75,000 to $278,450 range, where the tax considerations favor the individual rather than the corporation. Although this analogy compares the direct tax advantages or disadvantages, one must remember, in the cases of the corporation, the proceeds or distributed profits (dividends) may again be taxed when the receiver reports them as personal income. To further illustrate this point, consider the following examples:

Example 1: Aircraft Refinishing Services, a closely held C corporation, files a Form 1120, the required IRS income form, and reports a gross profit, or income be-

Figure 2-2. Tax Rates

Corporate		Single Individual		Married, Filing Joint Return	
Taxable Income	Tax Rate	Taxable Income	Tax Rate	Taxable Income	Tax Rate
up to $50,000	15%	up to $25,350	15%	up to $42,350	15%
$50,001 to 75,000	25%	$25,350 to 61,400	28%	$42,350 to 102,300	28%
$75,001 to 100,000	34%	$61,400 to 128,100	31%	$102,300 to 155,950	31%
$100,001 to 335,000	39%	$128,100 to 278,450	36%	$155,950 to 278,450	36%
$335,000 to 10,000,000	34%	over $278,450	39.6%	over $278,450	39.6%
$10,000,000 to 15,000,000	35%				
$15,000,000 to 18,333,333	38%				
over $18,333,333	35%				

Source: Data from Internal Revenue Service tax tables, 1999.

fore income taxes (IBIT), of $100,000. The corporation pays a tax of $22,500 on this amount. The remaining $77,750 is distributed as a dividend to the sole shareholder of Aircraft Refinishing Services, who is in the individual 31 percent tax bracket. He is required to pay $24,103 on his individual income. In total, the combined tax on the net profit of the corporation is in excess of 46 percent, or $46,353.

Example 2: The owner of Aircraft Refinishing Services operates the business as a sole proprietorship. He reports the $100,000 profit from the business on his tax return. He pays a tax of $31,000, the marginal tax rate for an individual with this level of income. As a result of this tax application, the owner of Aircraft Refinishing Services saves over $15,000.

Corporate Goals

Business decisions are not made in a vacuum; decision makers have goals and objectives in mind. We will assume here that management's primary goal is stockholder wealth maximization, which means maximizing the price of the firm's common stock. Firms do, of course, have other objectives. Managers are interested in their own personal satisfaction, in their employees' welfare, and in the greater community good as well as society at large. Nevertheless, stock price maximization is a primary goal of most corporations. Given the air transport sector does not pay dividends on a routine basis, the main reason investors dabbled in air transport stocks is speculative. Stock price appreciation, rather than dividend accumulation, is their primary goal.

Stockholders own the firm and elect a management team. Management in turn is supposed to operate the business in the best interests of the stockholders. We know, of course, that because most corporations are widely held, meaning there are many stockholders from all over the world, most management teams possess great operating autonomy. This gives management wide latitude in determining what goals the business will pursue. However, in the air transport sector, management is faced with an intensely competitive market and constant demands for capital. Therefore, they generally manage operations that are reasonably consistent with shareholder wealth maximization. If they depart too far from this goal, they run the risk of being removed from their jobs through hostile takeovers, proxy fights, or a complete loss of capital markets associated with shareholder apathy accustomed to stock sell-off.

A hostile takeover is the purchase by one company of a major portion of the stock of another, against the wishes of the acquired company's management. Once the opposition decides on takeover, they may generally consider three basic approaches. First, they may contact the firm's management or large shareholders and discuss a possible merger or purchase. Second, they may make a tender offer. A tender is an offer to sell a definite number of shares at a specific price. When a firm selects this method of obtaining voting control, it will solicit tenders from the stockholders. This is done by publishing a notice or by sending letters to all shareholders announcing that the acquiring firm will pay a certain price for shares of stock tendered by the shareholders of the target firm. Normally, a limit is placed on the number of shares and a deadline is specified. Generally, to entice present shareholders to sell, a price per share above the highest price paid for the stock over the last year is offered. If enough shares are tendered, the acquiring firm will be able to purchase voting control of the targeted company. If enough shares are not tendered, the takeover firm is not obligated to purchase them, having agreed on the requirements early in the offer.

The third approach is to solicit proxies from stockholders of the target organization. A proxy is a written power of attorney allowing one person to vote the specific shares of a corporation's stock held by another person. A proxy fight is an attempt to gain control of a corporation by convincing stockholders to vote in a new management team. Tender offers and proxy fights are usually precipitated by low share prices. Both of these actions have occurred many times in the recent past in the aviation industry. Takeovers at Continental, Eastern, and Northwest Orient and a successful proxy fight at United Air Lines to replace former chairman Richard Ferris are just a few examples. It is in management's best interest to keep stock value high through efficient use of assets and liabilities.

Another issue that deserves consideration is social responsibility. Should aviation firms operate strictly in their stockholders' best interests, or are firms also responsible for the welfare of their employees, customers, and the communities in which they operate? Certainly, an aviation firm has an ethical responsibility to provide a safe working environment, to avoid polluting the air and water, and to conduct flight operations with the maximum of safety and security. However, socially responsible actions have costs, and it may be questionable whether a business would take on these costs voluntarily. If some firms do act in a socially responsible manner and incur higher costs, they will be at a disadvantage in the capital markets when compared with those firms not pursuing the greater social good.

With ASM costs and RPM yields reasonably consistent across the industry, the cost of any voluntary commitment to a socially responsible program will become immediately evident in reduced profit levels, lowered yields, and lowered rates of return on investment. This does not mean that firms should not exercise social responsibility. It does reflect the reality that any significant cost increasing socially responsible activities must be enforced on a mandatory rather than a voluntary basis to ensure cost burdens are uniformly spread throughout the sector. A statement often attributed to Shakespeare is that "Beauty is in the eye of the beholder."

The definition of social responsibility also can vary depending on one's viewpoint. In recent years, we have seen the air transport business directly link social responsibility with increased market fervor. In a rush to be responsible, airlines have been underwriting or subsidizing spectator arenas throughout the country. Is this social responsibility or marketing? It may be difficult to differentiate the two. For the people of Chicago, St. Louis, Salt Lake City, and Phoenix, the United Center, the Trans World Dome, the Delta Center, and the America West Coliseum are social concomitants of their respective cities. For others, they may be blatant facades of marketing abuse. Nonetheless, social responsibility is in the eye of the beholder.

Is an aviation firm's attempt to maximize its stock price good or bad for society? In general, it is good. Aside from such illegal actions as attempting to form monopolies, violating safety codes, and failing to meet pollution control requirements, the same actions that maximize stock prices also benefit society. Consider, stock price maximization requires efficient use of assets to produce a high-quality service at an attractive price. Next, stock price maximization requires innovation of service offerings. Finally, stock price maximization requires courteous and safe service with well-timed departures to convenient locations. All these factors are necessary to make sales, sales are necessary to make profits, and competition ensures reasonable fare prices. Therefore, actions that help a firm increase the price of its stock can also be beneficial to society. This is why profit-motivated free enterprise economies have been so much more successful than socialist and communist economic systems.

Business Ethics

Business ethics can be thought of as a company's attitude and conduct toward its employees, customers, community, and stockholders. High standards of ethical behavior demand that a company treat each of these parties in a fair and honest manner. A company's commitment to business ethics can be measured by the tendency of the company and its employees to adhere to relevant laws and regulations and standards of ethical practices.

There are many instances of businesses engaging in unethical behavior. Recent times have seen the destruction of several Wall Street traders, a major Wall Street investment banking house submerged into bankruptcy, a world-renowned British bank decimated by questionable employee derivative trading, and an entire Los Angeles county bankrupt as a result of questionable practices. In spite of these highly visible public relations disasters, most businesses are committed to ethical operations. There is significant evidence of a positive correlation between ethical business practices and long-term profitability. Ethical behavior is perceived to increase profitability because such behavior does the following:

- reduces and/or eliminates fines and legal expenses
- attracts new business
- builds public trust
- attracts high-caliber employees
- supports the economic viability of the communities in which it conducts business

The most significant action a company can take is to demonstrate top management's support for ethical behavior. To reinforce such corporate belief, many companies have adopted written codes of ethics that formally acknowledge the organization's intent to conduct business in an ethical way. Figure 2-3 indicates one former aviation leader's commitment to ethical standards.

Whereas illegal or unethical behavior by managers has caused more problems for companies, firms are taking steps to limit such behavior. According to *Business*

Figure 2-3. Sample Code of Ethics for a Major Corporation

McDonnell-Douglas Corporation is committed to the application of high ethical standards in the conduct of its business and has adopted the following Code of Ethics:[*]

Integrity and ethics exist in the individual or they do not exist at all. They must be upheld by individuals or they are not upheld at all. In order for integrity and ethics to be characteristics of McDonnell-Douglas, we who make up the corporation must strive to be:

1. Honest and trustworthy in all our relationships.
2. Reliable in carrying out assignments and responsibilities.
3. Truthful and accurate in what we say and write.
4. Cooperative and constructive in all work undertaken.
5. Fair and considerate treatment of fellow employees, customers, and all persons.
6. Law abiding in all our activities.
7. Committed to accomplishing all tasks in a superior way.
8. Economical in utilizing company resources.
9. Dedicated in service to our company and to improvement of the quality of life in the world in which we live.

[*]The Code includes an ethics statement, a series of general statements of standards for employee business conduct, and rules governing specific business situations in manual format.

Source: From Ronald E. Berenbeim (1987), *Corporate Ethics,* research report no. 900 (New York: Conference Board).

Week (1988), most firms have very strong codes of ethical conduct and behavior, and many conduct training programs to ensure that employees understand the difference between appropriate and inappropriate conduct. For these programs to achieve success, it is vital for top management to be visibly committed to ethical behavior and to champion the growth of ethical business practices. This is certainly true in the air transport/aviation sector, where any compromise of conduct or standards can place hundreds of customers in harm's way.

Agency Relationships

An agency relationship exists when one or more people (the principals) hire another person (the agent) to perform a service and then delegate decision-making authority to that agent. Important agency relationships exist between (1) stockholders and managers and (2) between stockholders and creditors (debt holders).

Stockholders Versus Managers

A potential agency problem arises whenever the management of a firm owns less than 100 percent of the firm's common stock. If the firm is a proprietorship managed by the owner, the owner-manager will presumably operate the business so as to improve his or her own welfare, measured by increased wealth, leisure time, or perquisites. However, if the owner-manager incorporates and sells some stock to outside parties, a potential agency conflict arises immediately. If the owner-manager now decides not to work as hard to maximize share value, because less of that value will pass to him or her, he/she is flirting with agency conflict. Or should he/she decide to take a large salary increase or more perquisites, knowing part of the cost of these activities will now be borne by the outside shareholders, the owner-manager is in agency conflict with the other shareholders. Agency problems can be the basis for proxy fights and lawsuits.

Agency conflicts between stockholders and managers also arise in a leveraged buyout (LBO). LBOs occur when management, generally with the help of an outside LBO specialist, arranges a line of credit, makes a tender offer to buy all the stock not already owned by the management group, and, when successful, takes the company private and keeps the stock out of circulation. Dozens of such buyouts of major corporations have occurred recently. Some of the most notable were those involving Trans World Airlines and an employee-led buyout of an LBO specialist, Carl Icahn; Air Canada and a Houston-based LBO specialist buyout of Continental Airlines; and Alfred Checci and Gary Wilson's takeover vehicle, "Wings Holdings," which took Northwest Airlines private. The list is long. All of Frank Lorenzo's acquisitions were completed using LBOs. Among these were acquisitions at Texas International Airlines, Texas Air, Continental, and Eastern Air Lines.

In each case mentioned above, there clearly was the potential for an agency conflict. In fact, many people attest that it was agency conflict which allowed LBOs to occur in the numbers that they did. Management tried to pave the way for LBOs in various ways that were decidedly questionable from the stockholders' point of view. If management was trying to take a company private by buying the stock itself, would it not be in the best interest of management to keep the stock price as low as possible, thereby reducing the cost of the buyout to management? Didn't this represent a clear agency conflict of interest between management and the stockholders? If such a conflict did in fact exist, what could be done to ensure that management treated the outside shareholders fairly?

Enter the Securities and Exchange Commission. The SEC regulates the securities markets in the United States. Due to the concern over agency conflicts of interest, the SEC now requires that management disclose all material information relating to a proposed deal. Further, a committee of outside directors must be established to

- seek other bids for the company
- evaluate all bids received and compare them with the management bid
- recommend which offer the stockholders might accept

To ensure objectivity, no outside director on the review committee can have any stake in the reorganized company. This rule eliminates any agency conflict of interest and ensures stockholders will receive maximum share value in a buyout.

Several mechanisms can motivate managers to act in the shareholders' best interest. These include threat of termination, threat of takeover, and compensation packages.

The threat of termination. Until recently, the threat of management being terminated by the stockholders was remote. No longer is this the case. Stockholders are demanding and obtaining more say in the operation of the companies they own. One of the most significant reasons for this involvement has been the power of large investors. In today's economy and market conditions, institutional investors now own large blocks of the common stock of an average firm. These monolithic block shareholders have enormous influence and can thereby influence, if not dictate, operational and financial decisions of the corporation. With these large shareholders leading the way, the true owners of the business (common stockholders) are successfully demanding and receiving increased performance on the part of the management team. Examples of management who have been fired by the stockholders are those at United Air Lines, Disney, and Bank of America.

The threat of takeover. Hostile takeovers, where management does not want the firm to be bought out, are most likely to occur when a firm's shares are undervalued. Where the "book value," or breakup value, of a company is significantly higher than the price the stock is selling for on the open market, a corporation may be vulnerable to takeover. In a hostile takeover, the managers of the bought-out firm are often fired, and those remaining are relegated to smaller operating autonomy. When Trans World Airlines acquired Ozark Air Lines, all vice presidents were summarily reduced, or let go, within the first two years of the changeover. Thus, managers have a strong incentive to take actions that maximize stock prices. In other words, if you don't want to lose control, don't let the stock sell at bargain basement prices.

Actions to increase the firm's stock price and to keep it from being a bargain are obviously good from the stockholders' standpoint. Management may employ other tactics, however, in fending off a hostile takeover. Two examples of questionable tactics are *poison pills* and *greenmail.*

A poison pill is an action a firm can take that practically kills it financially, making it an unattractive investment and an unlikely target for hostile takeover. Examples include Disney's plan to sell huge blocks of stock to friendly parties, Scott Paper's decision to make all of its debt payable immediately if management were forced out, and Carleton Corporation's decision to lay out huge retirement bonuses (golden parachutes) if the firm were taken over. Actions, or intended actions, of this nature make the potential buyer think twice about the possibility of acquiring a company that will be worth less than will ultimately be paid for it.

Greenmail, which is like blackmail, generally occurs when a potential acquirer buys a large block of stock in a target company. If the targeted company's management fears the acquirer will make a tender offer to gain control of the company, management may offer to pay greenmail. This is an offer to buy back the stock from the acquirer at some premium above the market price. Greenmail may occur without offering the same deal to other shareholders. One example of greenmail at work was Disney's buyback of 11 percent of its stock from the Reliance Group at a premium that netted Reliance a quick $60 million profit. However, not all ended well. A group of stockholders sued and forced the Disney and Reliance directors to pay back $45 million to Disney stockholders.

Hostile takeovers depend on one basic fact: A company is owned by its shareholders, not by its management. When you buy stock in a public corporation, you become a partial owner, entitled to your share of its future profits. You and the other stockholders have the right to choose the board of directors, which then hires the managers. These managers are responsible for running the company and maximizing the long-term value of your stock.

This system of means and ends works beautifully in theory, but it is often muddled in practice. Managers usually choose their own bosses, the board of directors. The election of the board of directors is rubber-stamped by their bosses, who are the stockholders. More important, managers tend to run a company as if it belonged to them, which can cause conflicts of interest with the real owners.

Most managers want their company to grow. However, bigger isn't necessarily better. Expanding may just waste money, which will hurt the stock's value. On the other hand, the managers may run the company like a private fiefdom. This, too, will hurt the shareholders' investments. The managers may also receive a bid to buy the entire company, which is usually bad for them but good for the stockholders.

Managers are not very flattered when an outside party believes that it can afford to pay significantly more for a company than its stock market value and still have itself a bargain. A takeover bid tells the world that this company is probably undermanaged, so much so that even at a price 50 percent or more above the current one, better management can make the numbers work. Not surprisingly, most managers resent the implication that they have failed to make the most of a company's assets for the benefit of its owners. They also dislike the thought of losing their jobs. If they reject the takeover bid, however, the story is not over; the final decision rests with the shareholders. In addition, between the first bid and the last tender offer, hostile takeovers can get ugly.

Managerial compensation packages. Firms are increasingly tying managers' compensation to company performance. This motivates management to act in a manner consistent with stock price maximization. There are two basic managerial incentive plans in use today: executive stock options and performance shares.

Stock options allow a manager to purchase stock at some future time at a given price at, or below, current market prices. As the value of the option generally increases if the company's stock price appreciates, it is assumed that these options would cause managers to act to maximize stock price.

The most prevalent incentive program presently in use is a performance share. This involves shares of stock distributed to managers based on company performance as measured by earnings per share (EPS), return on assets (ROA), return on equity (ROE), and other key indicators. The directors of the corporation decide how many shares to allocate to the plan and the performance targets. At the end of a predetermined incentive period, shares are distributed on a percentage basis. In other words, if all performance goals are met, 100 percent of the shares will be released. If 75 percent of the goals are reached, maybe only 50 percent of the shares will be released.

No matter which incentive programs are utilized (such as straight bonuses, performance shares, and options), there are two reasons for their existence. The first is strictly operational: to attract and retain top-flight executive talent. The second is to ensure management acts on issues within their control that will maximize stock price and minimize any potential agency conflict.

Often the intention and the realization of these programs cause employees great distress. It is in the best interest of all concerned that managers meet, or exceed, their goals. Sometimes such bonuses are not exercised in the year awarded but exercised in a year when the stock has exceptionally appreciated. If this happens in a year when the company's profits are not high, or worse, do not exist, the exercise of the option may falsely indicate wage increases for top management at the employee's expense. A company must be cautious of these foibles, as incentive in one year can work as demoralization in another.

Stockholders Versus Creditors

The second area of concern regarding agency relationships and conflicts is the relationship between stockholders and creditors (debt holders). Creditors lend funds to the firm at interest rates that reflect

- the riskiness of the firm, its assets and operations
- expectations of future performance and asset acquisitions
- the capital structure (how much debt the firm is carrying)
- expectations of changes in future capital position

These are the principal factors used to determine the level of risk of a firm's debt, and therefore creditors base the interest rate charged on expectations regarding these factors.

Agency conflicts can arise when management, acting on behalf of the stockholders, or the stockholders acting through management, cause the firm to take on new ventures that carry much higher risk than creditors anticipated. Such increases in risk may lower the value of all outstanding debt held by the creditors. If the venture succeeds, all of the benefit will go to the stockholders, not to the creditors, because the creditors only receive a fixed rate of return on the debt they hold. If, however, the new venture fails, the creditors (bondholders) will have to share the loss with the stockholders. From the stockholders' point of view, this is a classic case of "Heads I win, Tails you lose," which isn't much fun for the bondholders. This ability to increase the use of debt instruments to boost stockholder returns is a common agency conflict and complaint.

During the frenzy of leveraged buyouts (LBOs) in the 1980s, many management and stockholder groups utilized the bond (debt) market to bolster share value while reducing bond values. Several large LBOs, most notably Kohlberg, Kravis & Roberts's (KKR) buyout of RJR Nabisco, caused such losses and disruption in the bond market that bondholders demanded protection mechanisms be included in their credit agreements. The most common bond protection device is the poison put. This provision in a bond agreement permits the bondholder to sell the bond back to the issuer at par value in the event a leveraged buyout takes place.

Can and should stockholders, through their management agents, try to expropriate wealth from the firm's creditors? In general, the answer is no. First, because such attempts have been made in the past, creditors are now protecting themselves against such stockholder actions through restrictive covenants in their credit agreements. Second, if potential creditors perceive that a firm will try to take advantage of them, they will simply not conduct business with that firm. Or they will require very high interest rates on their funds to compensate for the potential risks of sneaky dealings. Therefore, those firms that deal with their creditors unfairly may lose access to the debt markets or be forced to pay high-risk premium interest rates. Both actions reduce the stock value over the long run.

Given this set of market dynamics, fair treatment of creditors is essential to stock price maximization. Stockholder wealth depends on continuous access to the capital markets, and access is solely dependent on fair and equitable treatment. Management, acting as agent for both stockholders and creditors, must act to protect the interests of both parties in a balanced and fair manner. This includes its treatment of, and dealings with, a firm's stakeholders (customers, employees, unions, and suppliers). In short, the goal of shareholder wealth maximization is dependent on the fair and balanced treatment of all the firms' stakeholders.

Maximizing Share Price

The value of the firm's common stock is a matter of primary concern to a management team pursuing a goal of wealth maximization. It is the price of the common stock that is, in effect, being maximized.

If the goal of all corporations is share price maximization, then achieving that goal is simply a function of maximizing profits, right? No, not necessarily. Maximizing share price and value must be viewed from the perspective of earnings per share (EPS), as well as total corporate profits. Maximization of wealth is more useful than the maximization of profits as a statement of the objective of business firms. As such, it properly points out that the profit factor should be considered from a long-term point of view. At the same time, it balances this single factor with relative goals such as growth, stability, risk avoidance, and the market price of a company's stock.

Suppose that a fictitious airline, Air Atlantis, had 100 million shares of stock outstanding and earned $400 million, or $4 per share ($400M ÷ 100M). If you owned 100 shares of Air Atlantis, your share of the total profits would be $400.

Air Atlantis needs to purchase more airplanes. To do so, they issue another 100 million shares of stock. These additional planes produce an additional $100 million of earnings. Total earnings (income) rise from $400 million to $500 million, but earnings per share decline from $4.00 per share ($400M ÷ 100M) to $2.50 per share ($500M ÷ 200M). Now your share of Air Atlantis's earnings drops from $400 to $250. You and the other shareholders of Air Atlantis have suffered an earnings dilution. In the interest of stockholders, management should concentrate on earnings per share rather than total corporate profits.

Timing and risk are important elements in managing share price maximization. Timing refers to the projected payoff date of any venture. Which venture would be better for share price maximization: one that costs $50 million a year for five years, projected to generate $200 million in earnings beginning in the sixth year, or a project costing $200 million immediately, projected to generate $50 million in earnings for six years beginning next year? The answer depends on which of these investments would add the most share value, which is itself dependent on the time value of money to potential investors.

Risk also plays a role in determining which of the two sample projects listed above would be acceptable. In general, risk adverse investors and managers will choose the second project because next year is more predictable and understandable than is the year of first income flows in the first case. The risk included in projected earnings per share (EPS) also depends largely on how the firm is financed. High levels of debt can lead to high rates of bankruptcy. Although the use of debt can boost earnings per share, it also increases the risk inherent in projected future earnings.

The last major issue in share price maximization is dividend policy. Stockholders love to get cash dividends, but they also like to see growth in EPS that results from plowing earnings back into the business. Retaining earnings and investing them in projects and ventures that will generate future earnings streams is a fundamental business growth mechanism. Management must decide how much of the earnings to pay out and how much to retain and reinvest in the growth of the firm. This dividend policy decision can and does have impact on the share price in the marketplace. Some investors want regular substantial dividend payments. Others want rapid growth and are not necessarily concerned about dividend payments. The management team must strike a balance between conflicting interests.

In summary, we can see that a firm's stock price depends on the following factors:

• projected earnings per share
• timing of the earnings stream
• risk of the projected earnings estimate
• use of debt
• dividend policy

Every corporate decision should be evaluated and analyzed in terms of its effect on these factors and on the share price of the firm's stock. These five elements in turn influence consumers, stakeholders, and stockholders' confidence in the company, the ultimate determinant of stock price.

Business Activity and Organization

In order to more fully understand the nature of business activity in the marketplace, particularly the emerging global economy, it behooves us to digress and discuss the American economic system in comparison with economic systems of other countries. In the emerging worldwide economy, it is necessary for the businessperson to know about other cultures and their business environment. This is particularly true of an airline.

The success of the American business system is based on an economic and political climate that allows businesses to operate freely. Any change in the economic or political system has a major influence on the success of the business system. The world economic situation and world politics also have a major influence on businesses in the United States. Therefore, to understand business, you must also understand basic economics and politics.

Factors of Production

Economists use the term *factors of production* to refer to the resources used to create wealth. These factors include natural resources, labor, capital, and entrepreneurs. To some a fifth factor, that of the production of information, is an absolute necessity to the organization.

Natural resources. Natural resources include land, mineral deposits, forests, and water.

Labor. Sometimes called human resources or personnel, labor comprises the mental and physical capabilities of the people of the nation or the company who employ them.

Capital. Obtaining and using material resources and labor requires capital, the funds needed to start up and operate an enterprise. Cash flow, especially positive cash flow, is the lifeblood of any organization. Without capital, it is unlikely that any business can succeed, regardless of how good the ideas, labor, or other factors of production may be.

Entrepreneurs. Many economic systems need entrepreneurs to function. Entrepreneurs are individuals who accept the opportunities and risks involved in creating, operating, and expanding businesses.

Information. In the globalized economy, businesses cannot compete without information about markets and financial conditions. Fax machines, computers and e-mail, cellular telephones, and other communications equipment have added information to the factors of production.

With each of these systems in operation, there is a quid pro quo for their usage. In other words, each has its own inherent costs. The cost for natural resources is the rent to acquire the commodity. With labor, the cost is the wages and benefits the company pays for the service. Capital costs are the cost of money, more commonly known as interest. With entrepreneurs, the cost is the profit of the business.

The factors of production are used to produce goods and services attendant to each economic system in which they fall. The primary questions concerning their usage include the following:

- Who will decide how to allocate these resources?
- What should they be permitted to accomplish?
- Where should they be used?
- When should they be used?
- How should they be allocated?

World Economic Systems

Every society must have some method for making the basic economic decisions that will affect both the goods and services produced. Such decisions impact on the population of that society and, ultimately, the quality of life for the citizenry.

No society in the world operates without the problem of scarcity, whether it is a scarcity of capital, labor, entrepreneurs, or natural resources. In every society of the world, scarcity is a natural phenomenon. A society without scarcity is a society without problems and thus one where there is no need to make economic decisions. Since this perfect environment doesn't exist, all business owners must make some basic economic decisions. The approach each takes toward these decisions is predicated on the type of environment, custom, governmental authority, and market factors. Not all governments concern themselves with all of these modes of adjustment, but all are in one way or another considered.

Almost all economists agree, from a macroeconomics standpoint, that all societies must make three decisions that determine the economic system they will ultimately follow. First, each must determine the amount of goods and services to produce and in what quantities. A second issue confronting society is how goods and services are to be produced. Does the society possess enough resource combinations and production techniques? Last, a society must address the distribution problem. How can the product or services be distributed among the citizenry? Who will receive how much of each good or service produced?

The methodology for making these basic decisions is based on four ideologies or backgrounds: traditional, command, market, and mixed approaches.

Traditional economies rely largely on custom and usage to determine answers for each of these questions. Traditional economies are usually very slow to change and are not well equipped to lead and sustain a society toward continuous growth.

Traditional approaches and systems are found in many third world countries, as well as those heavily indoctrinated in religious beliefs.

Command economies rely on a central authority to make economic decisions. The central authority may be a democratically elected body, a dictator, or a committee charged with the vitality and growth of society.

Market economies are those where the consumer makes buying decisions based on need, desire, and income levels. The fulfillment of self-interest and satisfaction is the rule. Producers of products and supplies decide for themselves what to produce, what price to charge, the resources to employ, and the production methods to use. Producers are motivated by profit, and buyers are motivated by self-satisfaction, which creates a supply and demand system. This very system creates vigorous competition in almost every market.

Mixed economies contain elements of the market, command, and traditional systems. All real-world economies are mixed systems, although the mixture of tradition, command, and market differs greatly. The United States has historically placed emphasis on the market approach. Even so, there is and continues to be a large command sector in action by government activities. Other countries have varying degrees of differences. The former Soviet Union relied on government activity, keeping an eye on the smaller market sector.

In every country, an economic system is in place that uses the factors of production. Each, however, may operate differently. For example, if you live in the United States, the airline you fly, to destinations of your choice, is probably owned by stockholders. The food you eat while in flight was probably grown on a family farm, handled by private middlemen, processed by private companies, and sold to the airline by a wholesaler. The ticket you purchased, like the process involved with airline food, was probably handled by a private middleman, the travel agent, and delivered to you by an independent delivery service. You may have never met the agent who booked your reservation, the supplier of the airline food, or the builder of the airplane you are flying. Nor do you necessarily care to meet them. However, you do care that they keep producing and selling the services you want. In return, they and the companies they work for care that you keep buying the airline services they have to sell. If you and others decided otherwise, the airline, the travel agency, and the others could be confronted with a lack of business. All would be out of business, since no one other than the passenger is paying to keep the airline flying.

The airline that serves Chinese passengers is owned by the Chinese government. The food served on their flight, if they receive any at all, may have been grown on a state or collective farm, processed and moved by state enterprises, and the revenues received from flying the airline inures to the benefit of the state. Should Chinese citizens wish to travel on other airlines, they may be totally out of luck, since the state may require them to travel only on the state-owned carrier. Supply and demand become totally different concepts in Chinese society.

These two simple instances illustrate various ways in which societies operate. An airline, aircraft manufacturer, fixed base operator, or any of a dozen other types of aviation businesses operating in the globalized structure must, by sheer necessity, be aware of the many operative systems if they are to compete technically, operationally, and marketwise within those societies that differ from our own.

From an economic viewpoint, we find three operative economic systems. There are many variations, but for all practical purposes capitalism, socialism, and communism are the triumvirate. Each of these systems has different functional aspects, but its root is in control. A major way in which these economic systems differ is according to the prevailing ownership of productive assets (see figure 2-4).

Wilson and Clark (1993, p. 491) state there are four basic types of economic systems: traditional, market, command, and mixed. In the traditional economy, the questions of what to produce, how to produce, and for whom to produce are answered mainly by social custom. In a market economy, these same questions are decided mostly by individuals in the marketplace. In a command economy, only the government answers production questions. In fact, Wilson and Clark indicate that *social economy* and *planned economies* are other terms for a command economy. A mixed economy is one where the three economic questions are decided by a combination of market decision making and government decree.

Traditional economies have been found to be the least efficient and have tended to evolve into market, command, or mixed economies. Whether defined as mixed, market, or command, they appear very similar to the traditional systems of communism, socialism, and capitalism. None of the three exists in a pure form. Each has one or more of the Wilson and Clark attributes associated with it. In other

Figure 2-4. Comparison of Socioeconomic Systems

Capitalism	**Socialism**	**Communism**
Law of supply and demand determines what, when, and for whom products are produced.	Government owns and operates only the major industries. Examples include airlines, medical, and select manufacturers such as Volkswagen, Air France, etc.	Government collectively owns all resources. A traditional command economy.

words, there is no such thing as a totally capitalist economy, just as there are no true communist or socialist societies.

Today, resource allocation in some countries is largely government controlled. That is the nature of the communist system, in which all resources are collectively owned. The state is the proprietor of all natural resources, and it decides the methods and means of distribution. The state therefore owns and operates all forms of business.

Resource allocation in some countries is left to the individual consumers who bargain in the marketplace and trade goods and services. This is the nature of the capitalist system. In the capitalist economic system, the marketplace decides what, when, and for whom production takes place. In the United States and other capitalistic nations, the law of supply and demand is the great leveler.

Between the communistic and capitalist approaches to resource allocation lie systems based on private exchange and government ownership. In the socialist state (e.g., France), the government owns and operates only the major industries, or those industries that would or could have a major impact on the members of that society. One cannot possibly understand what is happening in business around the world without understanding the changes occurring within each economic system. The magazine *Futurist* says that a unified global economy is emerging that should transform our present world as much as the industrial revolution did in the nineteenth century. To understand these trends, it is imperative to understand those economic terms identified above. Macroeconomics is the study of how society chooses to employ scarce resources to produce and distribute various goods and services. The study of economics was once called the dismal science because it was so pessimistic. This is probably because economics has so often been considered a zero-sum game. A zero-sum game is one where there is only a winner and a loser; if one party gets some resource, the other party must lose or do without. Operating under such a premise, governments have designed systems to allocate most of their scarce resources.

Today, the U.S. economy is an integral part of the world economy. American businesses use labor from other countries, buy land in other countries for their factories and facilities, and receive money from foreign investors. To understand events in the U.S. economy, one must understand the economies of other nations.

Foreign investors have been buying companies, airlines, banks, luxury hotels, and retail chains in the United States. They have also been building new factories and buying U.S. government securities. Because the world has become so interdependent, it is important for everyone entering business to understand the workings of the various world economies. The future of the U.S. economy is directly tied to the economic future of Mexico, Japan, Germany, Canada, the European Union, and the Commonwealth of Independent States. How different economies allocate resources and how they view international trade will determine economic flows among nations, as well as airline routings in the future.

So important is economics to world health that in 1936, Lord John Maynard Keynes, the twentieth century's most influential and noted economist, wrote, "The ideas of economists and political philosophers, both when they are right and when they are wrong, are more powerful than is commonly understood. Indeed the world is ruled by little else" (Keynes, 1936).

All countries of the world, with the exception of those using the most primitive of bartering systems, are represented by these systems. Each have different types of currency in circulation, making interdependence ever more challenging. In the globalized market with airlines, manufacturers, and large FBOs marketing and operating in foreign countries, an awareness of the currency and its values relative to the U.S. dollar is necessary. Since the dollar value and the value of competing currencies respond to the market forces of supply and demand, their currency value is always in a state of flux. If worldwide demand to hold the U.S. dollar exceeds this country's demand to hold other nation's currencies, the value will rise. Stated another way, if other countries of the world seek dollars to buy U.S. goods and that demand exceeds the United States' desire to buy goods or services from those countries, the dollar's value will rise. If the opposite is true, that is, if the United States buys more from other countries than they buy from domestic businesses, the value of the dollar will fall.

Companies operating in other countries must be vigilant of such fluctuations in the dollar's value from the standpoint of goods and services pricing and investments. Consider an airline having a round-trip ticket price of US $900.00 in the St. Louis–Frankfurt market. Now consider, as happened in the late 1980s, that the value of European currencies rose dramatically in terms of dollars. At that time, the German deutsche mark rose from thirty to sixty cents per dollar. In other words, where the U.S. dollar would buy 3⅓ DM, it would now only buy 1⅔ DM. If an individual were traveling on the St. Louis–Frankfurt route and had friends in Germany, it would be cheaper to purchase the tickets in Frankfurt and send them to the party in St. Louis. Such gyrations could save the St. Louis passenger almost 50 percent of the U.S. dollar price. This occurs daily in the travel agency marketplace, especially when foreign students travel back and forth to their homelands. Often, because of fluctuations in the currency market, it is cheaper to purchase the tickets abroad. Of course, wild fluctuations are rare; however, the fact remains that rates do change daily.

The example of a rate change causing grave consternation by a company may be minimal. Just think of a company with operations in foreign countries and the impact that currency trading could have on the financial well-being of that company. If, in the above scenario, a multinational operation, or a flag carrier, had its holdings in deutsche marks rather than the U.S. dollar, it would have doubled its holdings relative to the U.S. currency. Of course, the opposite is true if the holdings were in dollars. Hundred of billions of dollars change hands daily in order to finance international activities. The fluctuations resulting from this trading are always a concern to an international trader.

Several reports are prepared daily in the *Wall Street Journal*, as well as in other financial publications, indicating currency fluctuations. The Currency Trading section of the *WSJ* provides quotations that indicate the dollar's value against other currencies.

From the example shown in figure 2-5, it can be discerned that on Wednesday, May 5, 1993, 1 dollar was equivalent to .99 Argentine pesos and that 1 peso will buy 1.01 dollars. More disparate was the Austrian relationship to the U.S. dollar. In that currency, 1 dollar was worth 11.01 schillings on the Wednesday quote, whereas 1 schilling was worth .09005 U.S. dollars (i.e., 9 cents).

Sources of Financial Information

The world moves too quickly to be captured in a textbook. The fall of governments, currency devaluation, fluctuations in global economy, and the emergence of new markets can make even the most recent books seem out of date. Using

Figure 2-5. Example of Currency Trading Value

Currency Trading

Exchange Rates

Wednesday, May 5, 1993

Example of currency trading values found in the *Wall Street Journal*

The New York foreign exchange selling rates below apply to trading among banks in amounts of $1 million and more, as quoted at 3 p.m. Eastern time by Bankers Trust Co., Telerate and other sources. Retail transactions provide fewer units of foreign currency per dollar.

Country	U.S. $ Equivalency		Currency per U.S. $	
	Wed.	Tues.	Wed.	Tues.
Argentina (Peso)	1.01	1.01	.99	.99
Australia (Dollar)	.7033	.6988	1.4219	1.4310
Austria (Schilling)	.09005	.09022	11.10	11.08

Source: Data from the *Wall Street Journal,* May 6, 1993.

academic theory to analyze the fast-moving financial markets and economies requires immediate knowledge. Such instantaneous information can only be gained through the electronic and news media.

There are five basic sources of financial and economic information: print media, broadcast media, electronic data services, brokerage houses, and shareholder organizations.

The print media includes several major general-interest newspapers, such as the *New York Times, Los Angeles Times, Chicago Tribune,* and *Washington Post.* Several dedicated financial newspapers are also available, including *Baron's, Investor's Business Daily,* and the *Wall Street Journal.* These papers list stock and bond tables for all the major stock exchanges, mutual fund and futures tables, currency and commodities rates, and numerous other indexes and charts. Several industry-specific publications such as *Aviation Week* and *Aviation Daily* contain excellent business articles.

In addition to the newspapers, chart services such as Moody's and Value Line publish detailed analysis charts and evaluations for all stocks listed on the major exchanges. They publish for most large companies sold in the over-the-counter or NASDAQ market.

There are also hundreds, if not thousands, of monthly subscription-based newsletters from fund managers and self-perceived know-it-alls, some of whom actually do. The print media represent the largest body of readily available and economical business information.

The broadcast media present many business programs, some of which are on the Public Broadcasting Service (PBS) or on cable. On PBS, *The News Hour with Jim Lehrer* and *The Nightly Business Report* provide excellent coverage of business news and the related in-depth interviews with the "movers and shakers" in business and politics. These are always insightful. Also on PBS, Louis Rukeyser's *Wall Street Week* analyzes market activities. Cable CNBC, which bought out the Financial News Network, provides open-to-close market coverage each business day.

On the radio, the American Public Radio (APR) and the National Public Radio (NPR) networks present daily economic and business programs. *Market Place,* which airs primarily during morning and evening drive times, summarizes the day's market activities and discusses general business trends.

Figure 2-6 lists a few of the many Internet sites that offer instant access to answers and communications concerning business operations, investment, and personal finance. If you own a personal computer and modem, you can connect to a host of commercial dial-up services. Dow Jones, CompuServe, America Online, and Prodigy access vast amounts of financial data on virtually any topic. Users of Netscape, among other servers, can find commercial services provided by the *Wall Street Journal* such as Wall Street Interactive, Investor's Edge, and Net Worth. Also

Figure 2-6. World Wide Web Sites for Financial Information

Name	Description	Internet Address
Wall Street City	Market information for investors	www.wallstreetcity.com
+Value	Essays that teach aspects of financial planning	www.morevalue.com
Open Market	Detailed information about private and public companies. More than 14,000 companies in database.	www.directory.net
Invest-O-Rama!	Free directory of investing resources with good articles on investing basics.	www.investorama.com
Inc. Online	Resources for small-business owners.	www.inc.com
PrognoSYS Inc.	Forecasts for stock indices, currencies, and interest rates.	www.webcom.com/ ~progsys
The Advisor	American Express newsletter for achieving individual financial goals.	www.americanexpress. com/advisors
Business Resource Center	Essays about starting and running a small business.	www.morebusiness.com
Corporate Financial Online	Information on publicly traded companies. CRO news section includes reports about insider trading, DJIA, and free tax advice.	www.cfonews.com
Dow Jones Business Information Services	Timely business and financial news from the *Wall Street Journal.*	bis.dowjones.com

stock-specific dial-up services, like Big Charts, offer chart analysis and evaluation similar to the printed versions of Moody's and Value Line.

Finding information on the Internet is easy. The hard part is filtering the information obtained. A novice can start by going to the several Internet engines such as Lycos, Infoseek, and Excite to dial up the names of brokers and stock traders. A simpler method is to dial up the Yahoo Finance (yahoo.com) or Motley Fool (www.fool.com) sites.

Brokerage houses are an essential source of information. Full-service stockbrokers will provide annual and quarterly reports of most stocks of interest. They can also provide that brokerage house's research and analysis on a variety of stocks. Brokers are able to check real-time performance of stock and its current bid and ask prices in the market. You can obtain annual reports from most brokerage houses without trouble, but you must open an account to receive more detailed information.

If you are a shareholder of record of any company, you will, by law, receive a copy of the annual report and a proxy card. Even if you do not hold any shares in a particular company, you still can get copies of the annual and quarterly reports by calling the shareholder services department of most major companies. Simply calling the switchboard and requesting assistance is the easiest way. Chances are, they will direct you to someone in the finance department. When that happens, it is always wise to ask as many questions about the financial health of the company as the individual on the other end of the phone will answer. You'd be surprised at how much you can learn this way! People like to talk about their company.

The sources listed above certainly do not represent a comprehensive list, but they are widely used sources of business information.

Suggested Readings and References

Berenbeim, Ronald E. (1987). *Corporate ethics*. Research report no. 900. New York: Conference Board, 24.

Businesses are signing up for ethics 101. (1988, February 15). *Business Week*, 56–57.

Davey, J. P. (1989). *Corporate leveraging and financing plans*. New York: Conference Board.

Development Services Group. (1993). *Business financing and economic development resources guide*. Chicago: Illinois Economic Development Network.

Friedman, M. (1962). *Capitalism and freedom*. Chicago: University of Chicago Press.

Gergacz, W. J., & Whitman, D. (1985). *Other forms of business organization: Sole proprietorships, partnerships, and limited partnerships*. New York: Random House, Business Division.

Gitman, J. L. (1992). *Basic managerial finance*. New York: HarperCollins.

Halal, W., & Nikitin, A. (1990, November 1). One world: The coming synthesis of a new capitalism and a new socialism. *Futurist Magazine*.

Hamilton, W. R. (1989). *Fundamentals of modern business*. Boston: Little, Brown.

Hoffman, W. H., Raabe, W. A., & Smith, J. E. (1996). *West's federal taxation: Corporations, partnerships, estates, and trusts*. New York: West.

Hudson, M. (1992). *Trade, development, and foreign debt: A history of theories of polarization and convergence in the international economy*. Concord, MA: Pluto Press.

Keynes, J. M. (1936). *General theory of employment, interest, and money*. London: Cambridge University Press.

Lazonick, W. (1991). *Business organization and the myth of the market economy*. New York: Cambridge University Press.

Levy, H., & Sarnat, M. (1990). *Capital investment and financial decisions*. Englewood Cliffs, NJ: Prentice Hall.

Moody's Investors Service. (1981). *Moody's handbook of over-the-counter stocks.* New York: Author.

Petty, J. W. (1993). *Basic financial management.* Englewood Cliffs, NJ: Prentice Hall.

Pinches, E. G. (1992). *Essentials of financial management.* New York: HarperCollins.

Rao, D. (1992). *Handbook of business finance and capital sources.* Minneapolis: InterFinance Corp.

Scarborough, M. N. (1992). *Business: Gaining the competitive edge.* Boston: Allyn and Bacon.

Silver, A. D. (1988). *When the bottom drops: How any business can survive and thrive in coming hard times.* Rocklin, CA: Prima.

Silver, A. D. (1990). *Business bible for survival: What to do when your company falls on hard times.* Rocklin, CA: Prima.

Strasser, K. D. (1987). *Business and financial information.* Springfield, IL: Sangamon State University Library.

Wilson, J. H., & Clark, J. R. (1993). *Economics.* Cincinnati: South Wester.

3

GENERAL BUSINESS CYCLES

This chapter examines the external and internal market forces affecting business in general and the air transport sector in particular. It addresses why forecasting future business and economic activity levels is both a necessity and a hazardous undertaking. First examined are the external market forces, consisting of general economic and business cycles. Next scrutinized are the effects that periods of economic growth and periods of economic recession have on business and society. Last viewed are the internal market forces inherent in the oligopolistic structure of the air transport sector and how these cycles impact the oligopolistic market structure and affect air transport financial performance. It will be seen how these market forces cause the air transport sector financial performance to lag, or be out of phase with the general economic conditions.

The volume of economic activity in America has been increasing since colonial days. This has been true not only because population and the number of workers have increased but also because net productivity has improved as methods have been devised to turn out more and more goods and services. This growth activity, however, has not taken place at a steady rate. Growth was very rapid during the 1940s and the early 1980s. Although continuous, it slowed in the 1930s and early 1970s. There have been several periods of decreased economic activity, even in prosperous years. From time to time there have been more serious and protracted interruptions in the forward push of economic progress. This happened between 1929 and 1933 in what became known as the Great Depression. The 1800s, also a time of major economic expansion and industrial change, saw as many as seven depressions. Several of these were more severe than the Great Depression.

The Nature and Significance of Economic Fluctuations

Severe fluctuations in production, employment, prices, and other phases of economic activity are of primary importance in economic, social, and political arenas. They affect not only the economy and society at large but also the lifestyles and living standards of all individuals. These variations can impact the political decision-making process; they can have a major impact on governments.

Economic problems are inherent in any market system. Concomitant problems and their impact on people exist at all times in all societies. The degree to which these fluctuations can be made milder, through informed and enlightened decision making, inherent displacements, and marketplace inconveniences, has to be held to a minimum. This has been particularly true in the United States since the Great Depression. Although the country experienced several severe recessions during the twentieth century, it escaped with only one depression.

The business cycle is nothing new. It's been characteristic of every capitalist economy in recorded history. Nations have endured boom followed by bust, prosperity followed by depression.

Sometimes outside developments, such as war, establish the economy's direction. More often, internal forces establish its direction. And that dynamic, the internally generated causes for the economy's regular and periodic movement through the phases of prosperity and recession, is the subject of the business cycle.

Before we attempt to observe the phenomenon, the never-ceasing undulations of this cyclical motion, we should understand some of the terminology associated with this movement. Several words are always prevalent when movements are discussed: *recession, prosperity, depression, boom and bust, mild,* and *robust.*

The most common term associated with a downturn in the economy, *recession,* is defined by modern standards as two consecutive quarters of declining gross domestic product (GDP). Economists grade a recession's severity by the degree of unemployment. Accordingly, the recession of 1981–82 was the worst since World War II because unemployment exceeded 10 percent.

A *bust period* is defined as a time when there is a severe decrease in business activity leading to high unemployment, low incomes, and low corporate profits. Following these two prognosticators of doom can be the final realization of a full-blown depression.

Many people define a recession as a period when their friends or neighbors are out of work, but a depression occurs when they themselves are out of work. This is a good analogy to defining a depression. Debilitating as a depression can be for some, they can be times of great prosperity for others. Generally, however, a depression is an economic condition in which business activity slows, prices drop, purchasing power is greatly reduced, and unemployment is high.

Prosperity and *boom periods* are harder to define. Some are content with the idea that they are merely the absence of recession. Since that won't work for our purposes, we'll be more specific. A boom, according to the *Dictionary of Business and Management* (1993), is a period of rapidly rising prices and increased demand for goods and services, usually accompanied by full employment. This obviously is the epitome of prosperity. But as there are degrees of recession, so there are gradations of prosperity. Other adjectives used to describe an upward trend in a business cycle are *mild, robust, cautious,* and *bullish.*

Business cycles happen over time; therefore, a study of a cycle must be dynamic rather than static. If economic activity could change instantaneously, the statistics of business activity would look much different. However, most activities take time: time to arrange financing, time to order aircraft, time to hire or lay off workers, time to change route structure and destinations, and so forth. Recognizing time lags of different lengths, for different economic processes, is important in analyzing business conditions.

Market economies have certain characteristics that make them subject to fluctuation. Some of these are desirable, such as growth from technological improvements in production processes and service offerings. Others are not, as they can result in periods of high unemployment and high inflation rates. These variations require a business to have significant market abilities and flexibility to adapt to an ever-changing cyclical environment. Failure to have these components as part of a business acumen has resulted in the death knell for many companies in times of economic stress.

Recession Periods in Economic Activity

While it is difficult to measure how much recessions affect our economic system, it is even more difficult to comprehend the impact on the lives of individual citizens. Those unable to find employment in a recession are forced to curtail consumption of goods and services, sometimes to the extent that real deprivation occurs. The psychological impact implicit with deprivation is difficult to measure. The effect on the attitudes of young people entering the workforce for the first time and unable to find employment can be highly detrimental to the social fabric of a nation. Due to permanent downsizing, corporate reengineering, or general business activity reductions, older displaced workers are often unable to find employment in their field, even after the effects of a recession abate.

Failures increase rapidly during periods of depressed business activity, particularly in deep recessions. Because the business world is so interdependent, the lack of buying and selling of goods and services creates a domino effect that is at length felt by all segments of the community. This depletion ultimately involves losses not only for the owners and stockholders but also for the creditors, or debt holders of a firm. Losses to creditors can be substantial, even in minor downturns. Business failures have an adverse effect on the communities in which the firms are located.

Recessions also create social problems, becoming especially severe during protracted periods of high unemployment. When firms are confronted with declining revenue streams, shrinking capital markets, and banks unwilling to provide loans, they are forced to make difficult choices. Often they have to cut production and reduce the workforce. The consequences of high unemployment rates are almost always negative. Generally and statistically, crime rates increase, marriages are postponed, and birth rates drop. Such conditions further intensify a recession as demand for goods and services are further reduced in the housing and consumer durable goods sectors.

As with the measurement and concern for individuals during periods of recession, the political repercussions of recessions are of great concern and are well documented. History has shown that when large numbers of people are unemployed, they are easily swayed by demagogues who promise methods and approaches to eliminate their agonies. Such political sleight of hand will exacerbate the problems because of the political pressure to make things happen. History has also shown that the more a government tries to fix the problems of recession and depression, the worse the situation becomes. Markets can and will work out the correct solutions more quickly and more permanently with minimal governmental involvement. Governments can and should do all that is possible to shorten the recessionary side of the cycle, but it is important for government to fully analyze and understand all the consequences of any interventionist policies to avoid the possibility of making things worse.

Boom Periods in Economic Activity

It is natural to believe that periods of booming economic growth present no major problems. Unfortunately, this is not true. In periods of rapid growth, even as business revenues are growing and wages and personal consumption levels are rising, problems and fluctuations can and do occur. Rapid growth can cause demand to outrun supply. Any economic system that is experiencing an excess of demand relative to supply is also experiencing an increase in the general level of prices (inflation). It is important to realize that prices do not change uniformly but do so at different rates in different sectors of the economy. Unstable price inflation causes problems that lead to inequities among individuals and groups and thus to a less than optimal allocation of resources. Inflation also creates serious problems for individuals. Although debts may become cheaper to pay off (more cash flow available) and the paycheck may be growing, it does not buy as much as it did before the inflationary period. Insurance, investment, and retirement planning programs become exceedingly unsettled. The face value of insurance policies and vested pension programs may stay the same, but purchasing power declines when adjusted for inflation. Housing costs go up and mortgages become more expensive. Personal budgeting also becomes problematic in any inflationary economy.

Inflation creates complex problems for businesses as well. Even with revenue streams increasing, inflation may cause businesses to raise prices to cover rising costs of their factors of production. As general interest rates rise, businesses are forced to offer higher interest rates on new debt issues and to pay higher interest rates on short- and long-term loans. These higher interest rates can cause businesses to lock in high long-term debt costs that may not be realistic or affordable despite improving revenue streams. Debt, in this instance, can prevent the capturing of additional market share, growth achievement, and maximization stockholder share value.

During an inflation, there is great pressure on government to intercede and mitigate the effects of rapid economic growth. As in recessionary periods, the government, particularly through the intercession of the Federal Reserve Board's fiscal policies, has an inventory of tools that can be employed to address this end. By whatever means approached, movement must be made with caution. Too much control can sow the seeds of a new recession.

Business Cycles

Business economists generally divide the business cycle into four phases. Although there is no particular length of time to a cycle, some economists believe they can last up to fifty years. Exclusive of different schools of thought concerning timing, economists seem to agree on the phases of an economic period. Expressly identified are periods of prosperity, recession, depression, and recovery, as well as punctuated words like *boom* and *bust*.

A period of prosperity becomes evident as production increases, as do employment, wages, and profits. As an upswing in prosperity continues, business partakes in the optimism by increasing and investing in new equipment to satisfy new and increasing orders brought about by the general prosperity, while employees and labor unions demand higher wages to keep pace with the economy. Thus, demand for goods and services begins to outstrip supply or, as indicative in the air transport industry, capacity falls short of passenger demand. It is at this time that new equipment orders are generated for additional and advanced equipment.

There is an old adage, "With the good comes the bad," or as many economists say, "Bad money drives good money out of the marketplace." As an upswing continues, obstacles begin to occur, impeding continued growth. For example, production costs increase as raw materials and labor costs become both more expensive and more difficult to acquire, and interest rates rise because of the greater demand for capital. Meanwhile, consumers retreat from purchasing due to the higher rates for consumer goods and services. As demand declines and consumption falls behind production, inventories accumulate, causing general price decline. When this occurs, a triggering effect is in place, causing a corresponding unthinking reaction. Faced with decreasing demand, manufacturers and service providers begin to retrench and lay off workers. Due to overcapacity created during a period of prosperity, airlines will often sell excess capacity seats at reduced prices, sometimes below cost.

Pessimism about the financial future can cause the most optimistic business leaders to minimize capital spending. When consumer confidence is shaken, investment becomes minimized. As prices and profits drop, production cutbacks and factory shutdowns occur. Carried too far, recession can eventuate into a full-blown depression if the engine of production grinds to a virtual standstill.

It should be noted that all recessions do not necessarily develop into a depression and, in fact, have not done so since the famous stock market crash of 1929.

The duration of recessions and depressions is anybody's guess, but eventually they end. Recovery can be initiated by almost anything from a renaissance of consumer appetites to a nation's involvement in a major conflict or war. The common denominator seems to be a resurgence of consumer confidence in the economy, resulting in demand for goods and services. Whatever the reason for this phoenix, whether it is prompted by government stimulation of the economy, exhaustion of inventories, or monetary availability, the ashes of a downturn are blown away.

During a recovery, prices rise more rapidly than costs as the factors of production are still spellbound by the cold of depression. When companies begin to reacquire profitability, employment increases, providing additional purchasing power to the community; investment in capital goods once again expands; and optimism and investment speculation return to the market structure.

A normal business cycle usually takes several years to complete. When the economy as a whole is slowing down, a recession is under way. Nine recessions struck the United States between 1948 and 1992. They reached their lowest points in October 1949, May 1954, April 1958, February 1961, November 1970, March 1975, the summer of 1980, the end of 1981, and mid-1991. The recession of 1981–82 was the most severe after the Great Depression, but it was followed by one of the most robust expansions in American history.

Figure 3-1. The Typical Business Cycle

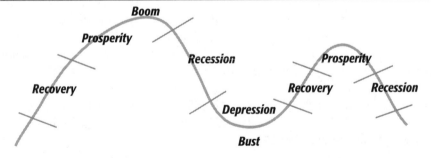

Economists, politicians, and others have been puzzled by business cycles since the early nineteenth century. English economist William Stanley Jevons offered one of the more unusual explanations. He believed that economic ups and downs were caused by sunspot cycles, which affected agriculture and caused cycles of good and bad harvests. This hypothesis is not taken seriously today.

Most business cycle theories fall into one of two categories. Some economists assert that economies have interior flaws which, for some reason, lead to cycles. Other economists insist that only some form of outside interference can cause swings from high to low unemployment. Unemployment and business failures are the most visible and characteristic signs of a recession. Those who accept the flawed-economy theory usually insist that economies are far too large and complex to operate without a significant degree of government guidance and regulation. Those who hold the opposite view believe that economies are not inherently flawed and that there will be no business cycles as long as there is no outside or external interference from governments, banks, or other sources.

All economies undergo stress and shock from time to time. Natural disasters, such as hurricanes, tornadoes, floods, and earthquakes, can do serious economic damage, but the damage tends to be localized. If a severe freeze wipes out the Florida orange and grapefruit crops, the growers lose money, and the consumers are forced to pay more for these goods. A more severe shock, such as the increases in oil prices during the 1970s, can have far-reaching consequences.

Shifts, changes, and temporary fluctuations do not constitute business cycles. They are adjustments that economies have always endured. The question that must be answered is what causes a widespread buildup of prosperity followed by a sudden decline. Since money links all economic activities, the answer must be sought there.

Economies exist because people exchange goods and services for money. This means that economies are consumer-driven. Everyone is a consumer, although not everyone is a producer. Producers spend money for land, buildings, machinery, resources, and workers. Money circulates through the economy as producers pay landowners, builders, machinery manufacturers, resource retailers, and a labor force. Products, when they are sold, circulate money back to the producers to keep production going.

The money that producers use to start a business comes from investment. Investors believe that a product or service will have a good chance of success. Thus they may be willing to invest money in a business. Some invest by buying stock, which is ownership in a company. Others invest by buying bonds issued by the government or an individual company. Once a business is operating, it gets the bulk of its funds for future growth and continued operations from borrowing.

Getting investment money is the beginning of the process called capital formation. Investment money is initial capital. It is used to pay for capital goods indigenous of the start-up of a business: land, buildings, machinery, and labor force. The source of investment money is savings. The money available for investment, especially for loans to business, comes from the savings of all economic units— individuals and organizations.

Because of money's general scarcity, there is competition for it. Like any commodity, money has a price. That price is interest. If savings exceed demand, interest rates will be low. If demand exceeds savings, interest rates rise. However, there is generally a balance between savings and investment in the normal course of economic activity; supply and demand tend toward equilibrium. However, since money is the dominant element of production, demand is always a constant. Its origins are of monumental importance to an economy's well-being.

The Federal Reserve and the Money Supply

Creating a business cycle has never been the goal of the Federal Reserve Bank or any other government agency. On the other hand, controlling a cycle has been an obvious goal of the Federal Reserve Board.

Attempts by the federal government to guide and stabilize the economy began early in the twentieth century, when unemployment first became a political issue. For three-quarters of the nineteenth century, most Americans lived in rural areas and were largely self-employed. About the turn of the century, farmers started to move toward urban areas. Because of this mobility and accompanying city growth, the downturn in the economy put many people out of work and brought unemployment to the attention of social workers and politicians.

The Federal Reserve was very active monitoring the money supply after World War I. Its inflationary policies probably had a great deal to do with promoting the prosperity of the 1920s and that decade's subsequent collapse. After World War II, the federal government deliberately established a full-employment policy to avoid another depression. By then, economists and politicians alike had to accept that the government could fine-tune the economy through adjustments in tax policy, government spending, and control of the money supply. The writings of British economist John Maynard Keynes were extremely influential in spreading this view.

For money to serve as a medium of exchange, both buyers and sellers must agree on its value. The value of money depends in part on its supply, or how much money is in circulation. The Federal Reserve system exercises the greatest influence over the money supply. Managing this supply is the province and responsibility of the Federal Reserve Board (Fed). In short, the Fed attempts to manipulate money without causing either inflationary or deflationary pressures on the economy. It does this by trying to manage both the money supply and subsequent interest rates. This process is identified as the country's monetary policy and the Fed's open market operation.

To accomplish this task, the Fed uses a juggling act to insert and withdraw money from circulation, thus either stimulating or cooling investment. Having too much money in the economy and overemphasizing demand sometimes causes inflation. To counteract this, the Fed may increase interest rates or withdraw money, making less available for spending and discouraging consumers from borrowing. This ultimately works to slow the economy and reduce its inflationary effects.

When the economy is sluggish, the Fed may attempt to jump-start it by putting more money into the economy, thus lowering credit rates. This approach may work to stimulate spending and encourage business growth through borrowing.

In either event, the modus vivendi to accomplish the expansion or contraction of the money supply is the treasury bond market. When the Fed seeks to decrease the money supply in the short run, it may sell treasury bills, bonds, and notes. Offering these instruments at attractive rates of return garners a significant amount of investment because of the security aspect of treasury securities. This money is then effectively "put on ice" until it is returned to circulation.

To increase the money supply, the Fed will recirculate money through the same process identified above except the Fed will buy back outstanding bills, bonds, and notes, enticing the investor to sell securities previously purchased.

Money Supply

If the knowledge of how much money is in circulation is indicative of its value, the measurement of money is germane to the study of fiscal aspects. Unfortunately, it is not easy to measure the supply of money. The most common measure, published weekly in the Federal Reserve section of the *Wall Street Journal,* is called simply M-1, M-2, M-3, and L, each based on liquidity timing.

The characteristics distinguishing these levels are that each successive measure is less liquid than the former. Thus, the money supply is broken down by the immediate ability to spend. This categorization, according to the board of governors of the Federal Reserve system, is as follows:

- M-1. A monetary measure of the money supply that includes only the most liquid forms of money. M-1 consists of currency and coin, travelers' checks, demand deposits, and other immediately usable "checkable" deposits.
- M-2. A measure of money consisting of M-1 plus small denomination time deposits (under $100,000) and agreements that consumers lend money to banks for short periods and the banks put up stocks and bonds as collateral (called repos). M-2 also includes money market mutual funds that service the public and overnight Eurodollar deposits held by U.S. banks.

- M-3. The total amount of M-2 plus large denominations (over $100,000), time deposits, shares in money market mutual funds held by large financial institutions, and large denomination "repos" and term Eurodollars.
- L. The total of M-3 plus nonbank public holding of U.S. savings bonds, short-term U.S. treasury securities, commercial paper, and bankers' acceptances, net of money market mutual fund holdings of these assets.

Other Federal Reserve Controls

In other areas, the Fed works to regulate the economy through controlling reserve requirements in banks, the federal discount rate, and the federal funds rate.

Reserve requirements. Whereas commercial banks accept checking and savings accounts from their customers, the reserve requirement the Fed imposes is that a percentage of such savings be physically retained in the bank, not used for loans or other banking activities. The reserve requirement is the Fed's most powerful tool. When it is increased, banks have less money for loans. Consequently, fewer loans are made, the money supply becomes scarcer, and the long-term effect tends to be anti-inflationary.

A decrease in the reserve requirement increases available funds to banks for loans, and thus money becomes more readily available. This type of increase will tend to stimulate the economy to higher growth potential. It may also act to eventually fuel inflationary movements.

Federal discount rate. When banks, like individuals and business organizations, sometimes become short of capital, they go to a bank for a loan. If a bank is a member bank of the Federal Reserve system, they can borrow money directly from the Fed. The discount rate is the interest rate that the Fed charges for these loans.

An increase in the discount rate can discourage banks from borrowing, thus reducing the number of available loans a borrower bank can offer to its customers. This practice results in a decrease in the money supply. Conversely, a lowering of the discount rate encourages member banks to borrow funds and increases the amount of loans available, resulting in an increase in the money supply.

Federal funds rate. When it is necessary to acquire immediate capital, banks may borrow overnight funds from other member banks. The capital acquired is known as federal funds. Of course, as with any business transaction where borrowing is involved, the cost of obtaining capital is interest. Upon repayment of the overnight transaction, the principal plus interest is due. The interest rate on an interbank loan is known as the federal funds rate. As with the discount rate, the Fed controls the amount of interest charged on interbank loans and, ultimately, the money supply due to liberal or conservative interest policy.

Summary of General Business and Economic Cycles

Economic systems are always in a state of flux. An economy is either growing or contracting but never in a constant state of balance. When an economy is in a contracting period, it is said to be in recession. Increasing unemployment rates, declining or flat production levels, low interest rates, low capital investment, high rates of business failure, and declining share value recognizes periods of contraction. Periods of expansion are recognized by declining unemployment rates, increasing production levels, rising wages, rising prices, increasing interest rates, increasing capital investment, lower rates of business failure, and improving share holder value.

Governments can and do influence rates of growth or decline. Coherent public policy, applied intelligently, can mitigate the negative aspects of both expansion and recession. Incoherent public policy can exacerbate the negative aspects of expansion and recession.

Oligopolistic Characteristics of the Air Transport Sector

The air transport sector is generally described as an oligopolistic market structure. An oligopoly is defined as any industry that has a few firms producing similar products. In addition, it has high entry barriers in the form of high capital costs, patents, or specialized technical expertise required. Oligopolies also exhibit substantial economies of scale. This means that as more units are sold, the long-term average cost of each unit sold goes down. It also means that, to be successful, oligopolies must produce many units for sale to lower their overall unit costs. To accomplish this requires extreme task specialization, exploitation of the latest available technology, and effective marketing of any salable aspects inherent in the primary production infrastructure. Three other characteristics of oligopolies are growth through merger, mutual price dependence, and nonprice competition.

Oligopolistic markets, by their very nature, have few firms competing in the marketplace. To match its market share, each firm optimizes production. Any substantive growth in a firm's market share will generally occur through merger and acquisition. This is due solely to the fact that any attempt to achieve additional market share through price discounting by one firm will be immediately countered by an equal or greater price discount by the other firms.

This inability to price discriminate in oligopolistic markets is the essence of mutual price dependence, and it results in substantive growth occurring only through merger or acquisition. Because competition for market share cannot occur on a price basis, nonprice competition is the last indicator of an oligopolistic market. Firms compete to deliver goods or services first, fastest, most frequently, or most luxuriously. In short, oligopolists compete on a high value-added basis, not on a price basis.

Number and Size of Air Carriers

Clearly, the air transport sector meets the criterion of an oligopolistic market player. As of 1998, there were only nine passenger carriers of national consequence remaining in the United States: American, Continental, Delta, Northwest, Trans World, United, US Air, Southwest, and America West. There were, of course, several large regional and commuter air carriers, but they were principally geared to feeding passengers into the remaining national carriers and major airline route systems.

High Entry Barriers

The entry of new competitors in the oligopolistic marketplace is restricted because huge capital investment is required to enter the industry. This, by itself, precludes many interested parties from venturing into this domain. Thus, oligopolistic industries tend to stay oligopolistic.

An argument could be made that such is not properly the case in the airline industry because, after deregulation, approximately 173 new carriers entered service. Countervailing that argument, however, is the fact that all but a few have since departed the scene.

There are two principal barriers to entering the air transport sector. The first is the significant amount of capital required; the major and single requirement, the aircraft, represents a major investment. Although there are many aircraft available in the United States, the price is still prohibitive. When coupled with the costs of gate space, slots, and the other requisite infrastructure investments, the capital requirement alone is an exceptional barrier to entry.

The second oligopolistic barrier is the high level of technical expertise required to run an airline safely. Flight and maintenance staffs, experienced management and administrative personnel, and maintenance and supervisory employees are necessary in this highly specialized environment. This singular expertise requirement is the main reason that almost all airlines have a "promote from within" policy. Entry-level positions provide the stepping stone to an airline career.

Contrary to the principal definition of high entry barriers, Robert L. Crandall, former CEO of American Airlines, takes a different view of the oligopolistic sector. Crandall (1995) implies that low barriers, witnessed by the influx of new carriers in recent years, have replaced traditional high requirements. At the same time, there exist extraordinary high exit barriers that keep carriers—and the capacity they operate—in the industry much longer than their financial performance would otherwise justify. He sites two requirements for this premise:

• U.S. bankruptcy laws allow failed carriers to continue in operation.
• Airline assets are worth less in liquidation than the present value of the cash flows they generate. (5)

Economies of Scale

Because of their varying size, oligopolies tend toward employee specialization, resulting in more workplace efficiency or economies of scale.

Air carriers must achieve a large volume of output in order to lower their cost per unit. This leads to a low-cost per seat departure or low-cost per available seat mile (CASM). Air carriers utilize three basic techniques to achieve economies of scale in producing a low-cost seat departure.

First, the enormous complexity of providing air transportation is managed effectively and economically through extreme labor specialization. Tasks are divided and subdivided into a series of very small specialized and repeatable tasks that can help highly trained specialization workers perform best. Instead of performing several tasks in the production process, workers may have only one task. This division of labor allows each worker to become exceedingly proficient. This leads to increased productivity through error reduction rates and minimized lost time associated with shuffling workers from job to job.

Large-scale output permits the same level of specialization and efficient utilization of management personnel. With managers and supervisors responsible for performance of only one specialized area, hiring more volume-related workers such as pilots, flight attendants, mechanics, and reservationists can be accomplished with little or no additional administrative cost. Should the level of revenue traffic decline, volume-related workers could be furloughed without cutting the core of essential management talent. This enhanced production efficiency and the flexibility to adjust to changing activity levels allow task specialization to achieve lower unit costs.

The second technique used by the air transport sector to achieve low unit costs is the exploitation of advanced transport technology. The most efficient new transport aircraft, leading-edge maintenance techniques, and advanced computerized inventory management systems all contribute to reductions in the cost of a seat departure. Because of the high cost of such technology, only the large, high-volume air carriers are able to afford to purchase and efficiently operate these advanced systems.

Another technique, employed by air carriers, is the profitable utilization of by-products of their principal activities. Examples of this include selling computer services, performing contract maintenance, selling flight simulator time during off-peak hours, and an array of other less visible projects, such as American's selling of management training and development programs.

Growth Through Merger

A further clear characteristic of oligopolists in general and of the air transport sector specifically has been growth through merger. It is a significant reason for the small number of national air carriers operating today. The motivations for mergers are diverse. The most obvious result is that by combining two or more formerly competing air carriers, the resulting organization can increase its market share substantially and achieve greater economies of scale. Primary motive for mergers is the market power that the new larger airline may acquire. A carrier that is larger may have greater ability to control the market in terms of price and services offered. Another principal reason for merger is that it may bring about tremendous advantage in purchasing power. This advantage may lead to a lower cost structure by forcing suppliers to provide better terms and prices.

Before deregulation, growth through merger was virtually the only way an existing carrier could achieve significant market presence. Of the top ten airlines presently in existence, all are the product of merger activity.

Since deregulation, the industry has been more likely to achieve growth through superior product offerings and carrier management. Mergers are no longer necessary to obtain another carrier's route structure. As routes are no longer protected by government fiat, a carrier able to operate a route may just move in on its competition and attempt to outproduce them. It is now better to beat them on their routes than to buy them when they are down and out.

Merger paranoia seems to occur when the large carriers feel threatened by the number of carriers in the marketplace. Their response to competition has been to buy the competitor out. Since deregulation began, this has been common during industry consolidation. As the market gears up for another probable expansion phase, it will be interesting to observe the workings of this element of a traditional oligopolistic market.

Mutual Price Dependence

Regardless of how an oligopoly evolves, it is obvious that rivalry among a small number of firms will create some fascinating market dynamics. With few airlines in the marketplace, it matters very little what the competition is doing, especially from a fare standpoint. Economists call this concern "mutual dependence." The small number of airlines makes it vital for each to consider the reactions of others when setting their prices. This serve-and-volley relationship has caused knee-jerk reactions to competitors' pricing policies. It has also caused airlines to implement and administer other pricing strategies. An airline that reduces its price is assured that its competitors will follow, thus diluting the elasticity effect that a price reduction can generate. On the other hand, an airline that increases its fares may find itself sitting alone because others will not follow. An increasing fare airline runs the risk of losing passengers to the noncompliance carrier, especially those passengers who seek bargain fares.

In the 1980s, not long after deregulation caused a modification to fare structures, American Airlines president Robert Crandall tried coordinating price increases with Braniff Airlines president Howard Putnam. At the time, both airlines operated out of Dallas/Fort Worth International Airport. The result was that Putnam reported Crandall's approach to the government and the specter of "price-fixing" was raised. Because the cooperative setting of price levels by competing firms which would otherwise be set by natural market forces is in violation of the Sherman Anti-Trust Act, the Crandall attempt was dropped.

In 1992 American Airlines followed a more legal route and attempted to establish a four-tier "value pricing" plan for ticket prices. The program was an attempt to produce rational pricing by simplifying an untenable fare mix created by the freedom of deregulation. The net effect was to trigger a fare war among the U.S. airlines. The results were both disastrous and predictable. Any attempt to increase market share through ticket price discounting in a market (a city pair market or a ticket class) will result in a reduction of affected ticket prices by all competitors in that market. This forces a return to general ticket price equality and a reduction in operating margins for all the affected competitors. It is this inherent oligopolistic inability to compete on price that leads to the last characteristic of air transport sector economics.

Nonprice Competition

With price an ineffective long-term competitive tool, the airlines have turned to value-added services to attract and retain customers. Because ticket prices are set by market structure, additional services are offered to the customer that add value to the price the customer pays for a ticket. Examples of value-added customer incentives targeted at the business flier, the bread and butter of any large airline, are frequent flyer clubs, business class seating, private airport lounges with fully equipped office areas, in-flight telephones, fax services, computer and e-mail access, and a host of other amenities onboard the aircraft to facilitate business. Examples of value-added incentives for the tourist and vacationer are integrated vacation packages that include airfare, hotels, and special ground transportation features. Other less obvious incentives include dominant presence and high frequency to popular vacation locations such as Hawaii, Mexico, and the Caribbean.

Although free or moderately priced to the customer, these value-added services are by no means free to the air carrier. The cost of providing these services runs into millions of dollars per year for each air carrier. The provision of these value-added services raises the cost of a seat departure. Since the costs of these services cannot be passed on to the customer, only the larger carriers can afford them. These value-added incentives do provide some incremental increases in revenue stream, but because all major carriers offer them, eliminating them would result in immediate decreases in traffic and revenues. Like full meal service in the fifties and movies in the sixties and seventies, these value-added services are now expected and demanded by the flying public.

Cyclical Variations in the Air Transport Sector

This section will combine business and economic cycles and the oligopolistic market structure of the air transport sector, examining specific impact periods of recession and growth. Focus is on the financial performance of this sector.

Recession Periods and the Air Transport Sector

The air transport sector is highly susceptible to the most subtle changes in the level of economic or business activity. While the effects of a recession on the air transport sector are not unique, what is different is that, as a service industry, air carriers are much slower in recovering because spending on air travel is discretionary. People have to be working again; businesses have to have expanding revenue streams before airline traffic recovers. This can take anywhere from eighteen to twenty-four months after the sluggish economy rebounds. By virtue of this lag, the financial performance of the air transport sector could be considered a lagging economic indicator. It is always one to two years behind the general economic and business trend when the economy is returning to growth status. Nevertheless, as much as it is a lagging indicator, it also exhibits traits of a leading indicator. Because of the discretionary nature of vacationer and leisure market participants, they tend to reduce their demand for air seats as money begins to tighten. Such economic behavior forces airlines into an unenviable role of being a leading economic indicator, predicting downturns in the economy. Thus, airlines feel the effects of a downturn before other businesses do. Conversely, because of their dependence on a vast majority of passenger discretionary income, they partake in an economic revival after others have experienced its benefits.

Most airlines carry high levels of debt at all times. In periods of growth, there are usually sufficient revenue streams to pay down the debt without undue loss of share value. However, in periods of recession, this high debt load can become fatal. Periods of recession cause airlines to scale back operations and cut volume-related workers and management staff. These expense saving cuts become necessary to help pay down heavy debt burdens. However, when growth returns, carriers often find themselves without the needed manpower to capitalize on the upsurge in traffic, further delaying their return to profitable operations.

When the airlines cut back operations, they find themselves with an excess of capacity (more planes and more seats than passengers are demanding). This anomaly can cause cancellation or delay of new aircraft deliveries. Two principal consequences of these decisions are

- older aircraft continue in service, with associated higher maintenance costs and greater safety risk, and
- when the air transport market recovers and begins to grow again, the airlines will be short on lift (capacity).

Historically, when this initial demand is present, airlines are unable to respond quickly. Demand cannot be met with adequate supply. The cycle begins again.

Periods of recession also cause some airlines to fail. The air-transport sector after deregulation provides a plethora of examples. Among the most memorable are the demise of carriers that had become household names. The end of Braniff Airlines, Eastern Air Lines, and Pan American World Airways saddened employees of those carriers. In addition, bankruptcy protection for America West, Continental, and Trans World Airlines brought recognition to industry observers and participants that the "good old days" of class service and elegance were gone forever. The industry was now recognized as any other "cut-throat" industry.

The ability of an airline to file bankruptcy and continue to operate (Chapter 11) has been a significant issue. In the past when a company or individual applied for bankruptcy, it meant they were "out of business." This is no longer the case. In our postmodern age, when individuals and businesses are not held responsible for their actions and everyone deserves a second chance, regardless of the circumstances, our bankruptcy laws have changed to coincide with these attitudes. Both companies and individuals can now file for protection under bankruptcy, which permits them to continue to operate without creditors being able to demand payment for debts owed. For a designated period, it is protected from its creditors. This means that an airline operating under bankruptcy protection has an enormous cost advantage. Because of the temporary interest savings on massive amounts of capital debt, it can substantially lower seat departure costs. A financially strapped airline can pass the savings of bankruptcy protection on to the passenger in dramatically lowered fares. Since the passenger market, especially the leisure market, has an elastic demand curve, reduced fares actually increase carrier revenues, generating greater cash flow. Unfortunately for solvent carriers, they have no choice but to match or exceed the fare reductions. Failure to do so would result in potential loss of their passenger base and loss of market share.

Another effect of bankruptcy and reorganization is that the firm's debt holders can be forced to take equity positions in the reorganized firm or lose their entire investment. The reorganization at Continental Airlines involved the creditors trading their debt holdings for stock, a highly speculative undertaking even in the best of times. Under its reorganization plan, ownership of Trans World Airlines was transferred from Carl Icahn to the employees and creditors through similar paper "turnover" transactions. More recently, a second bankruptcy led to reduced bond/debt holder numbers, as common stock was offered for debt reduction. Many of today's present TWA owners were former creditors who viewed exchanging debt for equity as the only possible way to recover any of the money owed them.

Boom Periods and the Air Transport Sector

When the economy improves, airlines generally begin to see improving load factors and a return to profitability. The increasing demand allows air carriers to reinstate new aircraft orders and begin to expand operations. However, with growth comes inflation, and the financial performance of the air transport sector is extremely sensitive to any change in inflation rates. High rates of inflation can increase the price an airline must pay for placing bond issues (offered interest rate) and the price they must pay for funds in the short- or long-term debt markets (borrowed interest rate). This can raise debt loads to even higher levels and, at best, cause some degradation in shareholder value and, at worst, create the potential for serious share value decline.

Inflation and general interest rate increases may cause the air transport sector to raise ticket prices. In the short term, revenue flows will increase due to improved load factors. Until load factors hit and exceed break-even levels, a competitive ticket price may not be fully recovering direct operating cost increases due to inflation and increasing cost of supplies. This inability to modulate revenue stream, in an inflationary environment, can be a growth-slowing factor.

Inflation and associated increase in market interest rates also cause increases, and sometimes wild fluctuation, in aviation kerosene prices. The cost of aviation kerosene represents one of the two largest operational expenses confronting any airline. Any increase in the price of fuel creates pressure to escalate ticket prices to recover the increase in direct operating expenses. Because ticket prices are not always possible, extemporaneous uncontrolled cost increases may lead to rapid consumption of internal cash reserves and a negative impact on shareholder value.

Boom cycles and the associated inflationary pressures on general price levels also cause disruption in another major air-transport expense category: labor costs. The air transport sector is highly unionized, and any general rise in prices will lead to new demands for wages or cost-of-living adjustments. Union demands for increased wages and/or benefits can exacerbate an already complex financial position, further delaying or preventing the effective response to dynamic market changes.

Forecasting the Business Cycle

The Need to Forecast

The primary function of management in a business is to maximize shareholder value by determining the objectives for the business, both short and long run. Once decided, management must develop plans to achieve goals by organizing human and material resources, developing and implementing requisite plans, monitoring and controlling resultant activities, and making corrections and adjustments to the ongoing process. General economic analysis and forecasting are involved in each of these management activities. Its usage helps prevent management from either overdeveloping or underdeveloping these plans.

As an example, Air Atlantis wishes to expand into new city pair markets. In determining its objectives (i.e., which markets to enter) Air Atlantis must first determine current and future trends in the general economic activity level of the nation. Subsequently, the current level of regional economic activity and regional trend analysis must be considered. Then Air Atlantis can forecast which markets it believes will grow consistently and thus determine in which markets to invest.

Next, Air Atlantis must determine the type of ticket classes to offer and the amount of lift and frequency to put into a market. Just as important are the competitor's existing fares, the question of whether to cross-subsidize a discount price for market share development, and the potential competitive reaction. Air Atlantis must also determine the equipment needed to support its market penetration, which type, and how many need to be acquired. This list of items needing answers could go on for many pages. Simply, while it is important to know where you are, it is vital to know where you are going and how you are reasonably going to get there. Coupled with these, there must be a reasonable estimation of your chances of getting there with your goals intact!

The basic business objectives of maximum shareholder value and significant market share growth can only be realistic and well balanced if management has analyzed the prevalent trends in the economy. Additionally, it must forecast the demand for its services over time, the prices it can charge, and the cost of the factors of production. An analysis of trends and current developments in the economy and a forecast of the future levels of those activities are necessary to establish sound business objectives and to develop appropriate long-range and short-range plans to achieve them.

The ability to define the direction of future business activity is vital in an industry driven by long lead-time capital goods, extremely costly new route development, and high debt-to-sales ratios. Any significant error in forecasting activity can have severe and immediate financial repercussions.

The Nature and Benefits of Forecasting

What kind of forecasting will be used? There are several approaches a firm can take in forecasting future business levels. It can be accomplished in mechanical ways, such as predicting that sales will increase 5 percent this year. That has been the historical growth rate for several years. On the other hand, relying on one or more of the several series of indicators that have generally led any changes in business activity can do it. Indicators used in this type of analysis have included the stock market, interest rates, housing starts, and the other so-called leading economic indicators. On a more sophisticated level, the mechanical and leading indicator methods can be used with the firm's managerial intuition to develop a complete series of forecasting scenarios.

The scientific approach here is the same as in any other field. It involves knowledge and understanding of what has happened in the past, what is happening in the economy and relevant business sector, and why it is happening. Only when phenomena are understood is it possible to predict, with any degree of accuracy, possible future events. Proper managerial actions based on such predictions may make the difference between corporate success and failure. The adage "They that fail to plan, plan to fail" is apropos in this instance.

The body of knowledge of the causal factors at work in business fluctuations is not yet comprehensive enough to make perfect predictions. However, it is advanced enough to make possible high probability confidence interval assessments of future trends and developments. This allows firms to plan and coordinate activities so they may position themselves to rapidly respond, adapting to changes in economic activity.

The megacarriers of today use very advanced computer-modeled forecasting techniques. These computer systems require input from every sector of the economy. They collate and model data against the assumptions that management provides. From this, they can generate a series of scenarios based on those assumptions. It is management's responsibility to develop plans and activities, effectively maximizing the carrier's ability to respond to market trends indicated in those scenarios.

Leading Economic Indicators as Accurate Forecasting Tools

The *Wall Street Journal* and other business publications track and regularly publish several indices that are commonly called "Leading Economic Indicators." Government and business use these indices as markers of where the economy is, where the economy is going, and how fast it is getting there. It is important to understand what these indicators mean and how useful they are in predicting activity levels in the air transport sector. Those composite indices measure the overall activity level in our economy. The principal indices used in monitoring and evaluating the economic status of the country are interest rates, leading indicators, durable good orders, gross national product (GNP) changes, housing starts, producer prices, and consumer prices.

These seven indices are significant to the air transport sector in that they measure the levels of both business activity and consumer activity. Business activity levels are represented by the key interest rates index, the leading indicators index, the durable goods index, and the producer prices index. Consumer activity levels are represented by the housing starts index, the consumer price index, and the GNP changes index.

Several purely market oriented indices are reported in the *Wall Street Journal* and other business publications. These include the Standard & Poor's 500, the Dow Jones Industrial Average, and the NASDAQ. These also measure activity levels, but they are focused exclusively on the dollar performance of shares of stock or bond issues in the secondary market. These indices can be misleading if applied as exclusive measures of company or business sector performance. It is important to remember these indices measure secondary market beliefs about a company's viability and are not necessarily based on informed and intelligent assessments of true market conditions.

Becoming familiar with items that cover inflation and recession, economic health and market indicators will assist you in understanding the types and uses of the various indices as predictors of economic and business activity.

Economic Indicators

Economists have never agreed on a single economic indicator to predict the future. Some indicators are better than others, but none are consistently accurate; all give false signals on occasion. To deal with this, economists have devised a composite or combination of statistical series drawn from a broad spectrum of economic activity, each of which tends to move up or down ahead of the general trend of the business cycle. These series are referred to as leading indicators because of their predictive quality, and the U.S. Commerce Department has combined eleven into the composite index of leading economic indicators (see figure 3-2).

There are three general criteria for inclusion in the leading indicator index. First, each series must accurately lead the business cycle. Second, the various series should

---

Figure 3-2. Components of the Composite Index of Leading Economic Indicators

- Average weekly hours of production of nonsupervisory workers in the manufacturing sector
- Average weekly initial claims for unemployment insurance, state programs
- Manufacturers' new orders in 1982 dollars, consumer goods and material industries
- Vendor performance—slower delivery diffusion index
- Contracts and orders for plant and equipment in 1982 dollars
- New private housing units authorized by local building permits
- Change in manufacturers' unfilled orders in 1982 dollars, durable goods industries
- Change in sensitive materials prices
- Stock prices for 500 common stocks
- Money supplies—M2—in 1982 dollars
- Index of consumer expectations

provide comprehensive coverage of the economy by representing a wide and diverse range of economic activity. And, third, each series must be available monthly, with only a brief lag until publication, and must be free from large subsequent revisions.

The leading indicators meet these criteria. Weaving these series into a composite statistic provides an indicator that is more reliable and less erratic than any individual component. The U.S. Commerce Department, responsible for tabulating this index, reports the information periodically.

The leading indicators are statistical measures that generally foreshadow movements in the general economy. This is apparent in the indicators that relate to new orders for consumer goods, capital equipment, and housing permits or housing starts. As these indicators move up or down, movements in employment, incomes, sales, and overall production may be expected.

Other indicators contained in the leading group ordinarily have a hypothesis for their particular timing sequence of economic measures. For example, the chairman of the Federal Reserve Board has received great notoriety for his trips to Capitol Hill to discuss short-term economic concerns. Among the indicators adding to his rationale for potential short-term interest changes has been the attention devoted to short-term movement in the money supply (M-3). If the report shows no change or even a reduction in the money supply, the Fed may ease interest rates to promote monetary growth and thereby provide for a flourishing of credit. This reaction may in turn cause stock to rise, which stimulates the economy.

A movement in the money supply is a measure that often can be expected to precede changes in the general level of business. Expansion of money tends to fuel expansion in business activity, while contraction of money tends to have a dampening effect on business levels. As noted above, interest rates play the same role. As the old adage of business goes, "When interest is low, stocks will grow, but when interest is high, stocks will die."

The stock market is sensitive to changes in the confidence level of those holding certificates of stock. Improved confidence about the future usually leads to higher stock prices, whereas degenerating confidence, on the part of consumers, brings prices down.

Changes in sensitive prices of crude material reflect variations in supply and demand for raw commodities or materials. A rise in this index could reflect rising levels of demand, thus creating expectations of increased business activity, whereas a drop in the index could signal the reverse.

The leading indicators are only part of a family of economic indicators. In addition to the leading indicators, there are two supplementary classes of indicators: roughly coincident indicators and lagging indicators.

Roughly coincidental indicators consist of a group of four indices whose turning points usually correspond to the peaks and troughs of general business activity. That is, they move up and down with the swings that pervade most sectors of

Figure 3-3. Roughly Coincidental Indicators

• Number of employees in nonagricultral jobs

• Personal income

• Index of industrial production

• Manufacturing and trade sales

the economy. The economic areas addressed by this group of forecasters are employment, incomes, production, and sales. The apparent rationale for incorporating these four as indicators is that they reflect broad movements of the economy.

The measurement of employment is the monthly report on the number of employees on nonagricultural payrolls. Personal income is the second measurement used in the coinciding indicators. The third is the monthly index of industrial production prepared by the Federal Reserve Board. This index measures activity in manufacturing, mining, and utilities. The final indicator is a combined figure for manufacturing sales and wholesale and retail trade sales. This figure provides a comprehensive report on distribution and consumption activities. These four indicators are combined in a single index of coincident indicators as compiled by the U.S. Commerce Department.

Lagging economic indicators are the third member of the indicator triad. This index consists of a group of six indices whose turning points occur after the turning points for the general level of business activity have been reached. It is interesting to note that since the lagging indicators follow both the leading and roughly coincidental indicators, they turn down before the others turn up. This following nature gives this group a place in the forecasting scheme. Not only is their movement lagging, but it could also portend a leading quality as, presumably, the laggards must turn down before the leaders can begin to prognosticate a resurgence of business or economic activity.

Economic indicators are useful tools in the forecaster's assortment of statistical data. By closely following the business cycle indicators, a business analyst or exec-

Figure 3-4. Lagging Economic Indicators

• Average duration of unemployment in weeks

• Index of labor cost per unit of output in manufacturing (productivity)

• Manufacturing and trade inventories

• Outstanding industrial and commercial loans by large commercial banks

• Ratio of consumer installment debt to income

• Average prime rate

utive may be able to anticipate pending changes in the overall level of business activity. Armed with this knowledge, she may adjust production schedules, levels of employment, inventories, capital goods purchases, such as aircraft orders, and financing to compensate for expected changes in business activity.

So beneficial are these economic variables that many airlines use them not only for financial prognostication but also for marketing. For example, research shows that the GOP is closely correlated with demand for air travel for business people because they are involved with the peculiarities of a robust economy.

Other Measures of Economic Health

Producer Price Index (PPI). The PPI tracks the costs of the raw materials that go into products. Measured in terms of percentage of increase over 1982 dollars, the PPI is a good inflation indicator because consumer prices tend to rise a few months after production costs.

Durable Good Orders. Durable goods are large orders purchased by corporations such as heavy machinery, large aircraft orders, and large computers. Generally, corporations put off buying these items when money is tight. As durable good orders increase, there is a chance that inflation may also increase, because increased costs are usually passed on to the consumer.

Consumer Price Index (CPI). Calculated every month by the Bureau of Labor Statistics, the CPI measurement is the main indicator of inflation. The government monitors prices by shopping for specific goods and services and comparing their prices with a similar set of goods and services in the base year (1982). The difference between the two is the rate of inflation between the base period and the period measured. Commodities compared are food, housing, clothing, transportation, and health care costs.

Statistical Series

One of the most cited indices to judge the vitality of the economy in past years, and one of the most common by name, has been the gross national product. More emphasis has recently been placed on a stricter involvement than provided by GNP. Statistical analysis of the economy has looked more to another measure called the gross domestic product.

Gross National Product. The GNP is the final output of goods and services produced by the U.S. economy in one year. It measures the output and earning of Americans, no matter where they live or work. It also includes the profits of American companies operating outside the United States, but does not include the profits of foreign companies operating within the United States.

Gross Domestic Product. The GDP is the final output of goods and services produced and consumed in the United States in one year. It measures output and earnings in the United States regardless of the earner's nationality. It excludes the profits of American corporations operating abroad, but it includes the profits of foreign companies operating within the United States.

The Gross Domestic Product Indices are an aggregate of four expenditure levels: consumption (C), investment (I), government spending (G), and net imports (X [minus] M). *Net imports* refers to the exports of the country minus its imports. Economists identify GDP by the following equation:

$$GDP = C + I + G + (X - M)$$

Consumption

Consumer demand is the most important component of total expenditures on our economy's output (GNP) and therefore the best place to start in analyzing the forces that shape the economy's performance. This portion of the equation measures expenditures for items such as food, clothing, services, autos, and other durable goods.

Indicators: Personal Income, Retail Sales, Auto Sales, Consumer Credit.

Investment

Investment is the most volatile component of aggregate demand (total expenditures); therefore, economists have traditionally looked to it as a barometer of future business conditions. This area is divided into three areas:

- *Residential investment* refers to the amount spent by consumers on the purchase of newly built homes; it does not include the purchase of older homes.
- *Nonresidential investment* confines itself to the machinery and equipment that companies purchase to continue their operations.
- *Inventory changes* are measured by the accumulation of warehouse inventory fluctuations.

Indicators: Housing Starts, New Orders for Nondefense Capital Goods, Machine Tool Orders, New Contracts for Nonresidential Structures, Business Inventories and Sales.

Government Expenditures

Government expenditures are an important component of total GNP expenditures, just as government borrowing is an important part of total borrowing. You can put both in perspective by learning the conditions under which government becomes a significant stimulus or depressant of economic activity. Not included in this category are transfer payments such as social security and welfare.

Indicators: Federal Expenditures, Revenues and Deficit, State and Local Government Expenditures.

International Transactions

Foreign demand for our goods is part of total expenditures on GNP. Since we have purchased more from other countries in recent years than we have sold to them, this component of GNP actually creates a net reduction in demand for U.S. output.

Indicators: Balance of Payments, Balance of Trade, Foreign Exchange Rates.

Other Important Indicators Not Included in GDP

MONEY SUPPLY AND INTEREST RATES

The money supply grows when banks lend; the interest rate is the price borrowers pay for those funds. Interest rates are determined in the credit markets.

Indicators: Monetary Aggregates, Treasury Bill Rates.

PRODUCTION, COSTS, AND PRICES

Surging expenditures can push the economy's productive capacity to its limit, driving costs upward and generating inflation. Surging inflation brings the economy full circle, depressing consumer sentiment and expenditures and thus generating the recession that ends expansion.

Indicators: Industrial Production, Capacity Utilization, Labor Productivity, Producer Prices, Consumer Prices, Consumer Sentiment (Confidence).

Limitations of Forecasting

All probability-based modeling systems have limitations. In the case of the air transport sector, the statistical modeling limitations may have less to do with the predictability of the customer, the competitors, or the economic trends than with the unpredictability of the elected policymaker. The United States is the only major world power without a coherent national economic policy framework for the air transportation sector. Consequently, any forecasting system must include a multiplicity of possible governmental actions and calculate a variety of possible scenarios.

This lack of coherent national policy greatly complicates the positioning of an airline to best achieve maximal market opportunity and financial flexibility in the U.S. market. Governmental response to foreign investment and the whole issue of continuing operation under bankruptcy protection will continue to complicate forecasting efforts.

The other obvious forecasting limitation is simply one of infallibility. No forecasting system is perfect. None will ever be perfect. There is no single index or formula that provides all the answers to the problem of business forecasting. There is always a calculated level of risk in attempting to predict the future. But a well-developed and economically broad-based analytical modeling system will produce reasonably reliable estimates within a narrow but accurate and financially surviv-able range of possibilities.

Summarizing Economic Indicators

Newspapers and periodicals often show charts capturing the above data. Figure 3-5 is taken from the June 17, 1996, edition of the *St. Louis Post-Dispatch.*

The need for forecasting in all aspects of a business cannot be overstated. Ade-

Figure 3-5. Economic Pulse Reports

Monthly Indicators			
Report and Month Released	Recent Month	Previous Month	Year Earlier
Unemployment rate[1] (May)	5.6%	5.4%	5.7%
Industrial production[2] (April)	124.5	123.4	122.0
Leading indicators[3] (April)	102.1	101.8	101.3
Factory use[2] (April)	83.0%	82.5%	84.0%
Housing starts[3] (April)	1,519,000	1,435,000	1,278,000
Existing home sales[4] (April)	4,220,000	4,200,000	3,470,000
Median home price[4] (April)	$116,800	$115,300	$108,000
Federal surplus or deficit[5] (April)	$72,393,000,000	-$46,275,000,000	$49,720,000,000
Trade deficit[3] (Feb.)	$8,190,000,000	$9,880,000,000	$9,470,000,000
Consumer confidence[6] (May)	101.2	104.8	102.0
Help-wanted advertising[6] (April)	82	84	86
Trade-weighted exchange rate[2] (April)	87.7	86.6	81.6
Consumer price index[1] (April)	156.2	155.6	151.9
Producer price index[1] (April)	130.9	130.4	127.3

Quarterly Indicators			
	Recent Quarter	Previous Quarter	Year Earlier
Gross domestic product[7] (1996-I)	$6,815,600,000,000	$6,776,500,000,000	$6,701,600,000,000
Productivity growth[8] (1995IV)	-0.5%	1.7%	1.7%
Corporate profits[7] (1995IV)	$392,300,000,000	$385,100,000,000	$356,800,000,000

Sources: 1. Labor Department, 1982=100 for price indexes. 2. Federal Reserve Board, 1987=100 for industrial production, and 1973=100 for exchange rate. 3. Commerce Department, 1987=100 for leading indicators; housing starts at annual rate; trade covers goods and services. 4. National Association of Realtors, sales at seasonally adjusted annual rates. 5. Treasury Department. 6. Conference Board, 1985=100 for consumer confidence, and 1987=100 for help-wanted advertising. 7. Commerce Department, annual rate, GDP uses 1987 dollars. 8. Labor Department, annual rate.

quate financial planning is an essential element in the success of any business venture. Conversely, the lack of adequate planning, particularly financial planning, is often a key element in the failure of many business enterprises. The objectives for short-term and long-term planning are the same: both involve the development of financial planning and control systems to guide the organization. According to Droms (1990), short-term forecasts tend to focus much more closely on cash budgeting and cash flow planning than do long-term forecasts. Long-term forecasts tend to focus more on planning for future growth in sales and assets and for the financing of this growth.

Suggested Readings and References

Bails, D., & Peppers, L. C. (1993). *Business fluctuations: Forecasting techniques and applications*. Englewood Cliffs, NJ: Prentice Hall.

Crandall, R. L. (1995). *The unique U.S. airline industry: The handbook of airline economics*. New York: McGraw-Hill.

Cremieux, P. (1992). *The impact of regulatory change on earnings: The case of the U.S. airline industry*. Berkeley: Institute of Transportation Studies, University of California.

Darnay, A. (1992). *Economic indicators handbook: Times series, conversions, documentation*. Detroit: Gale Research.

Dempsey, P. S., & Goertz, A. R. (1992). *Airline deregulation and laissez-faire mythology*. New York: Quorum Books.

Droms, William G. (1990). *Finance and accounting for non-financial managers*. Reading, MA: Addison-Wesley.

Emery, K. M., & Koenig, E. F. (1992). *Forecasting turning points: Is a two-state characterization of the business cycle appropriate?* Dallas: Federal Reserve Bank of Dallas.

Emery, K. M., & Koenig, E. F. (1993). *Why the composite index of leading indicators doesn't lead*. Dallas: Federal Reserve Bank of Dallas.

Eugeni, F., Evans, C. L., & Strongin, S. (1992). *A policy maker's guide to indicators of economic activity*. Chicago: Federal Reserve Bank of Chicago.

Evans, C. L. (1991). *Productivity shocks and real business cycles*. Chicago: Federal Reserve Bank of Chicago.

Holmes, J., & Leys, C. (1987). *Front yard, backyard: The Americas in the global crisis*. Toronto: Between the Lines.

Jenkins, D. (1995). *Handbook of airline economics*. New York: McGraw-Hill.

Kasper, D. M. (1988). *Deregulation and globalization: Liberalizing international trade in air services*. Cambridge, MA: Ballinger.

Kim, M., & Lichtenberg, F. R. (1989). *The effects of mergers on prices, costs, and capacity utilization in the U.S. air transportation industry*. Cambridge, MA: National Bureau of Economic Research.

Link, A. N. (1991). *Mastering the business cycle: How to keep your company on track in times of economic change*. Chicago: Probus.

Mead, K. M. (1989). *Barriers to competition in the airline industry in times of economic change*. Washington: General Accounting Office.

Mead, K. M. (1991). *U.S. airlines: Weak financial structure threatens competition*. Washington: General Accounting Office.

Nichols, D. M. (1979). *Modern money mechanics: A workbook on deposits, currency, and bank reserves.* Chicago: Federal Reserve Bank of Chicago.

Rosenberg, J. M. (1993). *Dictionary of business and management.* 2nd ed. New York: John Wiley.

Roy, R. (1980). *Economies of scale in the airline industry.* Canada: Canadian Transport Commission, Research Branch.

Sellon, G. H. (1984, May). The instruments of monetary policy. *Federal Reserve Bank of Kansas City Review,* 3–20.

Shearman, P. (1992). *Air transport: Strategic issues in planning and development.* London: Pitman.

Youssef, H. A. W. (1992). *Causes and effects of international airline equity alliances.* Berkeley: Institute of Technology, University of California.

4

THE EQUITY MARKETS

This chapter will examine the equity markets used by the air transport sector to generate initial and additional capital. The types of activities discussed are generic and common to all stock-issuing corporations. For illustrative purposes, we will follow the equity market activities of a fictitious airline, Air Atlantis, and examine its motives for those moves.

Most successful new business ventures begin small and grow to a point where large sums of capital become necessary. In their original formation, they may obtain capital from various sources. As businesses grow, capital becomes more and more important. Finding capital and having the ability to pay for it becomes increasingly problematic and costly.

To start a corporation, the owners must arrange financing. In most cases, the owners have adequate cash for immediate business needs when the original venture is entered. They then purchase shares of stock in return for cash they have placed in the company, and the firm begins operations. However, as business progresses, additional capital may be out of their reach. If the owners decide to arrange additional financing, they have two choices: (1) to seek additional owners who will purchase shares of stock (if this approach is used, it means the price for obtaining more capital is a loss of their original ownership amount), or (2) to borrow money from creditors, thus creating debt securities. Both debt and equity securities are used in corporations. The three major financial securities are bonds, preferred stock, and common stock. The debt market, discussed in chapter 5, requires that money be paid back to the lenders.

If a company like Air Atlantis goes public and sells shares of stock to anyone willing to buy them, the company may be able to raise enough money to pay for start-up or expansion without the cumbersome requirements of debt repayment. In what is termed an initial public offering, a company could sell stock and never have to pay the investors their money back, rewarding investors by paying dividends and by growing the business. Investors expect to receive their return primarily through stock appreciation and subsequent trading of the stock on the open market. As long as a company remains profitable and the stock appreciates, the investors will be happy. When a company "goes public," raising additional capital generally becomes easier. As long as the company remains attractive to investors, future projects, expansion, and capital goods acquisition can be financed with new stock offerings.

Common Stock

Common stock is the number one security in our free enterprise system. It is basic to all corporate business, as it is a source of long-term capital for the corporation. If you own a share of common stock in a company, you own part of that company. You and the other shareholders own the company in its entirety and in common. Common stock represents shares whose owners usually have last claim on the corporation's assets but who have voting rights in the activities of the firm.

Common stock is a security representing the residual ownership of a corporation. Residual ownership means that after all debts of the corporation are paid, the remaining value of the company belongs to the common stockholders.

The holding of common stock guarantees only the right to participate in sharing the earnings of the firm if the firm is profitable. Common shareholders usually have the additional right to vote at stockholders' meetings on issues affecting corporate policies. This includes electing the members of the board of directors, inspecting the firm's books, and obtaining a list of the names and addresses of other shareholders.

Common shareholders are entitled to receive dividends when declared by the board of directors. Such dividends may take the form of cash, stock, or property. The most common of these, cash, is expressed in dollars per share and stated in a stock quote under the dividend and yield sections (see Stock Market Quotations following).

Stock dividends occur when the board votes to give each shareholder additional stock on a percentage basis. This method of dividend (stock split) may occur when the organization wishes to place more shares of stock in the marketplace or when fewer shares are wanted (a reverse stock split).

Property dividends are rare but may be a corporation's way of letting the stockholders know of their importance, particularly when other forms of dividends have not been received for some time. An example of a merchandise dividend might be the distribution of chewing gum, as was once a practice of the Wrigley Company. In the air transport section, a discount certificate for a flight may act as a shareholder dividend and a marketing tool at the same time.

Common shareholders have other rights. Of major significance is the right to transfer their ownership by selling their stock without the consent of the corporation. As previously mentioned, common stockholders are entitled to share in the proceeds of a company in a liquidation situation. This occurs only after all other creditors have been satisfied. Of major concern to many stockholders is their right to maintain their share of the earnings and assets of the company. This claim on future stock is embodied in a vested right to purchase proportionate amounts of future stock offerings. This preemptive right, unless waived, is incorporated in the constitution and bylaws of the organization.

So how does common stock come into being? Assume that you have identified a great need for air service between four cities that have lost service due to another airline's route termination. You have negotiated gate space, found suitable aircraft, devised a solid marketing plan, and invented a clever company name to spearhead the advertising campaign, Air Atlantis. You are ready to begin service, except for one thing: capital. You don't have the money to lease the aircraft, hire the required staff, buy fuel, or advertise your service. A well-crafted pro forma, or projected, financial statement and business plan indicates that you need $2 million to start up Air Atlantis. If the banks won't lend this amount, as may be the case, since AirA hasn't been in business long enough for their analysts to determine performance levels, other methods of capitalization become necessary.

Consequently, the present owners of AirA decide to form a corporation and sell shares in the venture. You file the necessary incorporation papers, as required by state law, and Air Atlantis Incorporated comes into being.

In setting up the company, you might find twenty people, each willing to put up an even $100,000 of venture capital. As an indication of ownership identity, then, AirA would have to issue and sell only twenty shares of stock worth $100,000 each. Each investor in Air Atlantis would then own $\frac{1}{20}$ of the company, the ratio of their investment to the total received. But finding investors willing to invest equal amounts of money may prove exceedingly difficult.

While one person might be willing to invest $200,000 in Air Atlantis, another might only be willing to invest $20,000. Thus, instead of issuing twenty shares of stock at $100,000 each, it may behoove AirA to put a lower price on every share of stock and issue more shares. This action enables AirA to issue and sell more shares. This approach may prove more attractive to people interested in buying AirA stock who have limited amounts to invest. Issuing more shares at a reduced price may be more attractive to investors because, if they ever want to sell it, they will probably find it easier to dispose of lower priced shares. After all, more people can spare $10 or $100 than can afford to invest in $100,000 units.

So AirA finally decides to issue 200,000 shares at $10 each. Taken collectively, those shares represent the original common stock issue of Air Atlantis, or in Wall Street terminology, the initial public offering (IPO). All stock issues have a figure of value associated with them called par. A stock's par value can be set at any amount. It is not necessary to establish the par value as the selling price. Many companies issue stock at $1.00 par value, while others are listed for as little as $0.001. Par value is an arbitrary value of a stock set by the company's board of directors. Its primary purpose is for accounting procedures and has little significance to investors. This arbitrary value setting will be explained further in chapter 6.

AirA, through its IPO, sells all 200,000 shares at $10 each and obtains the required $2 million start-up capital. A new airline is in business. Every person who owns a share of Air Atlantis is a stockholder and a part-owner in the company. How big a part of the company each owns depends on how many shares were purchased, in relation to the 200,000 shares sold. Once AirA sells the shares, they are now the chattel of the stockholders and are said to be outstanding.

If an investor buys one share, she owns $\frac{1}{200,000}$ of the company. If an interested party invests $20,000 and buys 2,000 shares, they own 1 percent of Air Atlantis (2,000 shares purchased divided by the total shares outstanding). As evidence of ownership, a stock certificate is issued to each stockholder indicating the number of shares they own.

When all the stock is sold, the company will know how many individuals, groups of individuals, or independent organizations own AirA stock, how many shares each holds, and the percentage of AirA stock each controls. At a selling price of $10 per share, AirA could find it has only 1 stockholder or as many as 200,000.

It would be impossible to operate any airline, even a small start-up like Air Atlantis, if 200,000 owners had to be consulted about every decision. Consequently, for purposes of representation, the stockholders elect a board of directors to oversee the operation of the company. Although there are countless selection and voting procedures indigenous to each stock company, Air Atlantis has selected the most common. Thus the board is selected by the stockholders on the basis of the number of shares of stock each person owns. If there are five people to be elected to the board, each for a set term, the person who owns one share of stock will be allowed one vote for each of the five vacancies, and the person who owns 100 shares will be allowed 100 votes for each vacancy.

This five-man board of directors elects its own chairman, and once organized, it is responsible for managing the affairs of Air Atlantis. Since, in most instances, the board members can't give their full time and attention to the management of the business, they pick a president to be the actual operating head. They may also name other corporate officers. Such officers may or may not be board members, but they are directly accountable to the board. Periodically, generally once a quarter, the officers report to the board on the company's progress and their conduct of its affairs.

Once a year the AirA board of directors will conduct a meeting, open to all the stockholders, and management will make its annual report. The board provides all stockholders, those present and those absent, with a copy of the report.

If any stockholder is dissatisfied with the way things are going, they can speak their minds at the meeting. They may even make a motion that the board adopt some policy or procedure that they think is appropriate. If accepted and the motion is in order, it will be submitted to all stockholders for a vote. In most instances, such issues are decided with a simple majority vote, with each stockholder being allowed as many votes as they have shares.

If an action requiring a vote of the stockholders is scheduled for a meeting or debate, such as the election of new board members, each share owner is notified and afforded the opportunity to attend. If they cannot attend the annual meeting and vote, they usually sign a paper either indicating their vote or authorizing one or more of the officers or directors to vote their shares. Because in the latter case someone is acting in the stockholders' stead, they are acting in their absence with their authority or with their proxy. Sometimes when new directors are to be elected, a dissident group of stockholders will propose a rival slate of candidates in opposition to those picked by management. In such a fight, each side will attempt to solicit enough signed proxies to win the fight and elect their slate of candidates. This type of activity is generally the essence of a proxy fight.

Why should anybody invest his or her money in Air Atlantis? Primarily because they think it has a good chance of making a profit. If it does, they as shareholders stand to make money. That can happen in two ways: first, through the payment of dividends, and second, through the increase in value of AirA stock.

Let's examine the dividend picture first. Suppose in the first year of operation, the airlines has revenues (money received for the airlines product or service) of $5 million. After subtracting from revenues the expenses incurred to generate revenue and taxes it must pay to the government, AirA has earnings, or profits, of $200,000. This profit would amount to 10 percent of its $2 million capitalization base, the money raised by the stock offering. Because this profit was made possible by the initial investment in Air Atlantis, the 10 percent return is called return on investment (ROI).

When a corporation has a profit, it is up to the board of directors to decide how to distribute the money. Although this decision is usually made long before the actual amount is determined, several avenues are possible for its use. It could be distributed to the stockholders in the form of dividends. Or the board of directors could vote to keep every penny of the profit within the company, using it to buy more aircraft or gate space or for other purposes to help generate even more earnings next year. Retention and plowing the money back into the company is called retaining earnings or, on a balance sheet, retained earnings. Because stockholders like dividends or returns on the money they have invested, and most boards of directors know this, the AirA board decides to use their prerogatives and satisfy both the needs of the airline and those of the stockholders. Consequently, they vote to split the earnings, paying $100,000 in dividends and placing $100,000 in retained earnings.

With $100,000 for dividends and 200,000 shares of stock outstanding, each shareholder will receive fifty cents for each share of stock held. The dividend is determined by dividing the amount allocated for distribution (100,000) by the total number of shares outstanding (200,000).

Thus, a shareholder with 10 shares would get $5, and a person with 100 shares would get $50. For each stockholder, that would represent a 5 percent return on investment, regardless of the number of shares they own (dividend [$.50] divided by price paid for each share [$10.00]).

There's also an intangible return that shareholders would obtain through their investment in Air Atlantis. Presumably, the $100,000 in retained earnings will serve to increase the value of everyone's shares in the company, their equity. If an original share of stock in Air Atlantis were valued at $10 when issued, then each of the 200,000 shares outstanding might now be considered worth $10.50, since the company has an extra $100,000 in addition to the original capitalization of $2 million.

So you may ask, what is the value of a share of Air Atlantis or any other company's stock? With all the movement and gerrymandering of earnings, one might feel compelled to maintain elaborate charts to keep track of all that has transpired regarding their stock. The truth is that the marketplace, and thus the value of a share of stock, is subject to the vagaries of the laws of supply and demand. Stock is only worth what someone is willing to pay for it at the time you want to sell it. If, in AirA's situation, the flight offerings aren't adequate or are poorly timed, if there is a general business downturn, if the cost of fuel skyrockets, if union employees strike, if management makes poor decisions, or if any number of exigencies visit themselves, Air Atlantis can fail. Stock values may then plummet and the value may become nonexistent.

But if Air Atlantis proves to be a successful company with a consistent record of good earnings, part of which are paid out regularly in dividends and the rest put back into the company to improve or expand operations, then the stock is likely to be worth more than the $10 the stockholders originally paid. Perhaps a good deal more.

The second way in which stockholders expect to make money on their investments is stock speculation. Through an increase in the value of the stock or rather an increase in the price, which somebody else is willing to pay for it, investors obtain monetary rewards. Such an increase in stock value is known as stock price appreciation.

The price of stock, like any other good, is determined by supply and demand—what one person is willing to pay for a stock versus what another person is willing to sell it for. Because of this trading aspect, stock price is not necessarily a reliable guide to good investing. Some people think that a low-priced stock is a good buy because it is cheap, and they shy away from a high-priced stock because it is expensive. That is simply not true! The stock of a company may sell at a low price because there are millions of shares outstanding, while another equally good company may have a very high-priced stock because of few outstanding shares. The price of any stock has meaning only when it is related to that company's earnings and dividends per share performance.

General Motors, Exxon, and Grand Met may have many millions of shares outstanding. They may even count their shareholders in the millions. But each share of stock in these giant corporations plays precisely the same role as a share of stock in Air Atlantis. The only truly significant difference between buying a share in these giant companies and investing in Air Atlantis is that these big companies have been in business for many years. You know something about them, the reputations they enjoy, and you may know how good or bad their products are. You can look back over many years of financial data and see their earnings, dividends, and stock price appreciation records. Thus you can make a more informed investment choice.

In contrast, the person who buys stock in Air Atlantis has nothing upon which to base a rational decision. Primarily they must concentrate on the quality of the operating plan, how skilled they believe the company will be in managing the venture, and whether sales projections are realistic. A potential investor in Air Atlantis has no history, no benchmarks for guidance, or past records on which to base an appraisal of the future.

As a matter of fact, the Air Atlantis stockholders cannot properly be called investors. They are speculators. An investor is someone who is willing to take a moderate risk to achieve a moderate return over a long period of time. A speculator is someone who takes big risks in the hope of a big payoff in a relatively short time. The equity markets need both kinds of risk takers to function properly. Without speculators, no new businesses would be born. Without investors, corporations would not have the capital required for expansion and growth.

How and Why New Issues of Stock Are Sold

Let's assume that the years have been good to Air Atlantis. As a medium-sized commuter airline, it continues to generate profitable load factors and yields. The high quality of onboard service and on-time performance continues to attract new customers and retain and build a strong and loyal customer base. Good earnings year after year have enabled management to pay a regular annual dividend. It now pays $1 per year per share, 25 cents per quarter. In three good years the directors even declared an extra dividend, one of 25 cents and two of 50 cents.

The company now feels that the time is right for an expansion program that will add new city pairs to the route system and capture a significantly larger market share. In short, the management of Air Atlantis desires to grow the airline into a competitive regional carrier. Management believes revenues and earnings could be doubled with a controlled expansion program, but it needs to purchase or lease more aircraft and gate space while hiring more staff. To begin, management submits its growth plan to the board, which agrees with the basic approach. Now, the question is where to generate the estimated $4 million in required capital.

A bank might advance the money. Possibly several banks would join together, in syndication, and make the loan. The directors, however, don't like the idea of being in debt to the banks. They worry not only about paying the interest on the loan every year but also about paying down the principal in installments. That kind of steady drain on Air Atlantis's treasury for years to come could eat into earnings and result in few, if any, dividends. Furthermore, banks don't usually like to make such long-term loans, and even if they were willing to, they might insist on having representation on Air Atlantis's board to protect their interest, the loan. That is a prospect that none of the directors want to consider at this time.

There is another alternative: the possibility of the existing shareholders putting more money into the company. Maybe there are other people who would like to invest in Air Atlantis, a well-managed and profitable commuter carrier with big plans. And so the board proposes to the stockholders that they authorize the company to issue 300,000 additional shares of stock—200,000 shares to be sold at once and the other 100,000 to be held in treasury for the day when the company may again need to raise capital. Each new share of stock will carry the same rights and privileges as an original share.

To issue new stock requires not only the approval of the board but, foremost, the approval of the present stockholders. The issuance of new securities involves the question of extending the ownership rights to the new security holders. Upon approval, the new issue would be offered to the existing shareholders first and generally on especially favorable terms. This is the traditional procedure for companies that have new issues of stock to sell.

In this instance, the Air Atlantis board recommended existing stockholders be permitted to purchase the new stock issue at a price of $20 per share. This represented a discount of $2 off the current market price of Air Atlantis stock, which is selling at $22 per share. The board also instructed that any shares not purchased by existing shareholders be sold in the market at the prevailing price.

The stockholders approved the plan, and each of them was offered the right to subscribe to the new stock issue in proportion to their present holdings. Although rights are not securities but options to buy securities at a specific price, they do have a market value, and it is helpful to know their characteristics.

State laws or corporate charters frequently provide that stockholders (common) have a prior right to purchase additional common stock, or securities convertible into common stock, which may be issued by the corporation. Such a privilege is known as a "preemptive right" and is theoretically designed to protect a stockholder from losing his proportionate equity in the business when a company issues additional stock. The issuance of new stock by means of privileged subscription rights granted to existing stockholders is a common financial practice, even when stockholders do not possess preemptive rights. In such cases, the new stock is offered at a price substantially below the market price of the old stock. The stockholder may retain his proportionate share in the equity by subscribing to the new stock. He may sell his rights in the market to someone else if he does not want to purchase additional stock.

Every person who owned one of the original 200,000 shares was permitted to buy one of the new shares at $20. In addition, a person with 1,000 original shares could buy 1,000 new shares. The rights had to be exercised within two weeks. Most rights expire quickly. There are similar situations and options that run for longer periods, occasionally up to a year, but these are not called rights; they are more properly called warrants.

Some Air Atlantis shareholders, unable or unwilling to purchase additional shares of the new issue, sold their rights. Often the market for such rights is brisk. Rights and warrants are traded actively on the big exchanges and are reported in the financial press.

In the case of Air Atlantis, each right was worth $1. Here is the way the value of the right was determined. If you owned one share of Air Atlantis worth $22 and you exercised your right and bought one new share at $20, you would then have two shares at an average price of $21 apiece, or just $1 less than the current market price. Hence, the right could be figured to have a value of $1.

The standard formula for figuring the value of rights works this way. First, take the prevailing market price of the stock (in this case $22) and subtract the subscription price of the new issue ($20); then divide this difference ($2) by the number of old shares necessary to purchase one new share ($1) plus an additional one (1 plus 1 is 2, and $2 divided by 2 is 1, the value of the Air Atlantis right).

When the rights expired, Air Atlantis discovered that they all had been exercised except for 5,000 shares of the new issue, and these were readily sold in the open market at $22 per share. The airline had raised $4,010,000 of new capital and had a total of 400,000 shares of stock outstanding, 100,000 shares of stock in treasury, and the money to begin their expansion program.

Had AirA not had a clause in its corporate charter concerning preemptive rights for common stockholders, it might have considered the use of warrants to sell stock. Warrants, like rights, are options to buy other securities, usually common stock, at a stated price. A warrant is a security that permits the holder to buy shares of common stock during a stated period and at a given price. When the option is exercised, the holder must surrender the warrant and pay the firm for the common stock purchased at the option price. For many years, warrants were considered speculative instruments rather than investment securities, since the warrant has no value other than as a right to purchase other securities. In the 1970s, Braniff Airways issued securities with warrants attached.

Warrants arise in a somewhat different manner than rights. They are usually sold in conjunction with other securities that might not be readily marketable without the speculative appeal of an attached warrant. Warrants may be either detachable or nondetachable. Only if the warrant is detachable may the investor resell it separately from the security with which it was issued. Some warrants represent perpetual options, while others expire at a definite time stated in the option. The issue of warrants in connection with the sale of preferred stocks is usually an indication that the securities could not be sold on their own investment merits or reasonable terms. Warrants are not confined only to stock issues; they may also be detachable or nondetachable with bond issues.

By their nature, warrants have a significant effect on the capital structure of the organization. When warrants are issued, the purchaser of the warrant pays additional money to the firm. When the warrants are exercised, the holder of the warrant pays additional money to the firm in return for common stock. Thus, the exercise of the warrants increases the funds available to the firm.

Air Atlantis put its growth plan into action, but because of delays in securing gate space, leasing new aircraft, and getting air and ground crews hired and trained, revenues remained flat. The expenses associated with the expansion plan placed the board in a difficult situation. How were they to keep paying dividends to the stockholders in spite of depressed earnings? In the first year of the expansion plan, the board felt obligated to continue paying the customary $1 dividend, but that put a serious dent in the company's treasury. The second year the directors decided it would be foolish to do that again. They concluded that the only prudent thing they could do was to pass the dividend and keep the full year's earnings in the treasury until the new routes and city pairs started generating revenue.

However, if the company paid no dividend, what would the stockholders say? Passing the dividend would certainly mean that the price of the stock would go down, for those who might be interested in buying the stock could interpret it as a sign of trouble.

The board found the answer in the 100,000 shares of new stock that were authorized but not sold and held in treasury. With the approval of the stockholders, the board took those 100,000 shares and distributed them among the shareholders of the 400,000 outstanding shares on the basis of one-quarter of a share of free stock for each share that a person owned.

Actually, this stock dividend did nothing to improve the lot of any individual stockholder. They were not one penny richer, nor did they own any greater proportion of the company. A person who had one share before the stock dividend owned $1/400,000$ of the company. Now with $1\frac{1}{4}$ shares of the outstanding 500,000 shares of stock, he still owned exactly $1/400,000$ of the company. Yet, in terms of future prospects, the extra quarter share had real potential value. When the company got all the new city pairs and routes on line and revenue generation began, that extra one-quarter share could represent a real profit and extra dividends, too.

That, happily, is exactly what happened, and Air Atlantis prospered. The next year it earned $1 million, or $2 a share, and the directors felt they could prudently restore the $1 dividend on each share. To the person who held 1¼ shares, that meant a return of $1.25. This was 25 cents of pure profit because the ¼ share dividend was free!

Preferred Stock

With its new city pairs and routes on line, Air Atlantis forged ahead. Earnings doubled to $2 million, or $4 a share. Then they doubled again, earning $4 million, or $8 a share. Most of those earnings were, by decision of the directors, reinvested into the business to continue expansion to new cities and continual acquisition of better equipment. Dividends were modest. But the company was growing. Now its assets totaled almost $20 million.

Then another problem and another opportunity arose. Blue Ridge Air, a privately held competitor serving the eastern boundary of Air Atlantis's route system, could be acquired for $7.5 million. It was a good buy at that price and fit very well into AirA's expansion plan. The board of directors agreed to a purchase, but where to get the money?

Negotiations with the owner of Blue Ridge Air indicated that she was anxious to retire from the business. She planned to invest whatever she obtained from the sale of the airline to yield her and her family a safe, reasonable and steady retirement income. Furthermore, it was evident that she had high regard for the management of Air Atlantis and was favorably impressed with the company's prospects. Now, here was the basis for a deal.

AirA directors proposed that they take over Blue Ridge Air and merge it into their existing operations. In return, AirA would pay for Blue Ridge Air by issuing preferred stock. The board proposed an issue of 75,000 shares with a par value of $100 per share in exchange for her company. Preferred stock is a hybrid security that possesses characteristics of both bonds (next chapter) and common stocks. Like a bond, preferred stock is considered a fixed-income investment because it offers a stated rate of return. But because preferred stock represents a type of ownership in a company, it also resembles common stock.

Like most preferred stock issues, this one would ensure the holders a prior claim on all assets of Air Atlantis after all debts had been extinguished. This concern, of course, would only be addressed should it ever become necessary to liquidate the company. In addition, the stock would carry a specific dividend payable every year on every share before any dividends could be disbursed to the common stockholders. To make the deal as attractive as possible for the owner of Blue Ridge Air, the board of Air Atlantis was willing to pay her a good dividend, $6 on every share, or 6 percent.

Sometimes such a preferred dividend is not paid in a given year because the company did not earn enough that year to cover it. To reasonably ensure a dividend payment, Air Atlantis issued cumulative preferred stock. This means that if Air Atlantis could not pay the $6 per share dividend in any one year, the amount due for that year would accumulate, or accrue, to the preferred stockholders and would be paid in the next year or whenever the company had sufficient earnings to pay it. If the company could not make the dividend payments for years, they would continue to accrue and would have to be paid in full before the common stockholders received any dividend payments whatsoever. This meant that the cumulative preferred stockholders would receive all present and missed dividends before the common stockholders received any dividends at all.

On the other hand, it was agreed that Air Atlantis's acquisition of Blue Ridge Air would not be done by issuing participating preferred. This would mean that the holders of the preferred stock would not participate, beyond the fixed annual dividend payment, in any of the extra profits the company might earn in good years. Even if earnings were so good that dividends on the common stock were doubled or tripled, the holders of the preferred issue would still only receive their $6 per share annual dividend and no more. Furthermore, they would have no participation in company affairs and no voting rights except on matters that might adversely affect the rights guaranteed them as preferred stockholders. They were also guaranteed the right to elect two directors to the board if the company should ever pass, or fail to pay, the preferred dividend for eight consecutive quarters.

Although the terms of this issue might be regarded as typical, there is no such thing as a standard preferred stock. About the only common denominator of all such issues is the guarantee that the holders will be accorded preferential treatment, ahead of the common stockholders. As the name implies, preferred stockholders enjoy preferential status compared with the company's common stockholders. A corporation is obligated to pay dividends at the stated rate on preferred stock before paying any dividends to common stockholders. This preference also extends to issues of bankruptcy. Investors don't generally purchase stock with the anticipation that the corporation may declare bankruptcy and possibly liquidate its assets. If liquidation of assets does occur, however, preferred stockholders have a prior claim over common stockholders to the asset residual. Because of these features, the market price of preferred stock usually doesn't fluctuate as much as the price of a company's common stock. In contrast, common stockholders can benefit from a corporation's profit growth through dividend increases and higher stock prices. Declining profits, however, could result in smaller dividends and lower stock prices.

From that point on, specifications vary greatly. Most preferred have a $100 par value, but some are issued as no par stock. Dividends vary from 4 to 8 percent in normal times and can range up much higher during times of tight money when interest rates on borrowed funds are high. Most preferred are nonparticipating, but as always, there are exceptions. Many preferred stocks are issued, as in the case of Air Atlantis, to acquire another company. Most are issued simply to raise more capital for expansion and growth in periods when the company's circumstances are such that its common stockholders and the public at large might not be willing to invest in the company's common stock.

The most common type of preferred stock is perpetual preferred stock. This stock has no maturity date. Consequently, there is no date on which investors can expect to receive par value for their stock. Most perpetual stock issues are callable (redeemable at the company discretion) and may remain outstanding only until interest rates drop sufficiently to make it beneficial for the company to refund or call the issue.

Corporations sometimes issue two or more classes of preferred stock, just as they do common stock. All maintain their degree of priority relationship over common stock, but the priority relationship of preferred stocks to each other may differ.

Corporations sometimes issue a lower priority òf preferred stock commonly called preference stock. The corporation will pay dividends to preference stockholders only after paying higher priority preferred stockholders.

Preferred stocks may be divided into two classes: those with cumulative dividends, and those with noncumulative dividends. Dividends on cumulative preferred stocks accrue to the credit of the preferred stockholder for future payment to the extent that they are not paid on the regular payment date. Legally, these back payments must be paid before dividends are paid to the common stock shareholder.

Cumulative preferred stocks are, by far, the most common. However, as stated above, there are some noncumulative issues in the market. Occasionally, with cumulative preferred the dividends accrue during bad years. Sometimes it becomes impossible for a company to pay them. In such a situation, the company may try to negotiate a settlement with its preferred stockholders on the basis of a partial payment and absolution of the remainder. However, some companies have paid off more than $100 a share in accumulated back dividends due on their preferred stock issued at only $100 a share par.

Another popular kind of preferred issue is the convertible preferred. Such a stock issue carries the provision permitting the holders to convert the preferred into common stock at a specified ratio within a specified time frame. Suppose that a company sold a new issue of convertible preferred at a time when its common stock was selling for $17 per share in the open market. In such a situation, the conversion clause might be structured such that every share of $100 preferred could be exchanged for five shares of common stock any time within the next five years. Obviously, there would be no advantage in exercising the conversion option now with the stock at $17. Only when the open market stock price was at or exceeded $20 would there be any possible incentive or benefit to converting. The key to successfully initiating a deal like this with convertible preferred is the belief by the potential preferred holders that the company is committed to maximizing the price of its common stock through sound and aggressive management practices.

Why? Because the price of convertible issues is apt to fluctuate much more than the price of other preferred, simply because the value of the convertible preferred is tied tightly to the performance of the common stock of the company. This feature has both good and bad points. If the company is successful and the price of its common stock rises, the holder of a convertible preferred will find that the value of his holdings has increased correspondingly, since it can be exchanged for the now more valuable common stock. On the other hand, if the company falls on bad times and the common stock price declines, the holder of a convertible issue is apt to suffer a degradation of value, too. This is because the very feature that makes convertibles attractive has suddenly lost some of its value. Thus other features, such as dividend rates, may not be sufficiently attractive or substantial as those of orthodox preferred.

Most preferred carry a provision that permits the company to call (callable preferred stock) in the issue and pay it off at full value, plus a premium of perhaps 5 percent. A company will usually exercise its right to call down an issue of preferred if it thinks it can replace the outstanding issue with one that carries a lower dividend rate and still be ahead in net dollars.

When a corporation is an investor in another corporation, using its assets to invest in other companies' preferred stock, there are tax provisions for the investing companies. Under present U.S. tax provisions, investing corporations can exclude from federal taxes 70 percent of the dividends received on qualifying domestic preferred stocks. If the investments and the dividends are large enough, this may be a windfall tax shelter for many eligible corporations. Some of the qualified industries include banks, utility companies, railroads, and businesses involved with industrial and financial concerns.

From the point of view of Blue Ridge Air, the Air Atlantis deal looked attractive. So they accepted the offer after the common stockholders of Air Atlantis had approved the plan and authorized the issue of 75,000 shares of 6 percent cumulative preferred stock with a par value of $100 in exchange for the assets of Blue Ridge Air.

With the acquisition, Air Atlantis was on its way to becoming a big business. And in the next ten years, with revenues booming, it strode forward. It bought Small Time Airlines for cash. It acquired SouthAir with another issue of preferred stock, which it called second preferred, because it had to recognize the prior claim to assets and earnings that had been granted the owners of Blue Ridge Air. To make this second preferred issue more attractive to the owners of SouthAir, a conversion clause was included. In other words, it was a convertible preferred issue.

Later, AirA bought East Coast Airlines by authorizing an additional issue of common stock and arranging to trade the East Coast Airline stockholders one share of Air Atlantis for every three shares of East Coast they owned. Finally, it acquired Mid Central Airways on a similar stock swap basis.

Now with an extensive route system, modern aircraft, and a seasoned management team, Air Atlantis began developing and entering new markets. Revenues continued to multiply, as did earnings per share, up to $10 and then $12 per share. Dividends were boosted accordingly, and with the adoption of an annual dividend of $6 per share, Air Atlantis stock was frequently selling at $120 per share or higher.

Stockholders complained that stock was too highly priced; they couldn't sell it easily if they wanted to liquidate their positions. So the board of directors decided to split the common stock 10 for 1. Hence, it issued new stock certificates for ten shares of new Air Atlantis for every single share of old Air Atlantis common stock. Theoretically, each of the new shares should have been worth $12, but since stock splits frequently excite unusual investor interest, it wasn't long before Air Atlantis's stock was selling at $14 to $15 per share in the market. This occurs although there has been no change in the true underlying financial conditions of the company.

As Air Atlantis moved toward becoming a solid national carrier, Best Bargain Airlines was watching. Best Bargain saw the strong growth in earnings and consistent financial performance posted by the AirA management team. Best Bargain had lots of cash, but the markets served by AirA were such that profitable competition was not possible. So Best Bargain decided to propose a merger with Air Atlantis. After many joint meetings and careful examination of the pluses and minuses in the proposal, the directors of Air Atlantis decided that the best interests of their stockholders would be served if Air Atlantis continued to "fly its own airplane." They declined the offer to merge.

But Best Bargain wasn't prepared to take no for an answer. It wanted Air Atlantis's routes, revenues, and customer base to feed into its growing international route structure. Best Bargain then proposed a formal code-sharing agreement in which AirA would remain an independent operation, but all aircraft would be painted in Best Bargain colors. In addition, all Air Atlantis flights would appear in the reservation system with BB flight numbers. The AirA board turned down this proposal, too, because they had ideas about moving into the international markets in the near future.

Needless to say, Best Bargain was both impressed and concerned with Air Atlantis's overseas growth plans and the dilution in revenues and yields that would occur to Best Bargain's international routes. Best Bargain was no longer simply interested in Air Atlantis as a good investment. They were now heading for a potential international revenue traffic fight. Best Bargain turned ugly and initiated a hostile takeover of Air Atlantis. A hostile takeover is an acquisition in which the management of the acquired, or potentially acquired, company fights the firm's buyout by another company. Best Bargain had an eye toward both capturing Air Atlantis's domestic revenue customer base and preserving its own international revenue stream.

Best Bargain began buying all available Air Atlantis stock in the open market and filed Securities and Exchange Commission form 13D, an indication that they were in the process of acquiring stock and had achieved a substantial equity position. Next Best Bargain formally announced a tender offer for control of Air Atlantis. Best Bargain tendered each Air Atlantis stockholder, agreeing to buy all stockholders' shares for cash, at a set date for a set price that was almost 20 percent above the current market price of Air Atlantis's stock. This tender offer was contingent upon enough Air Atlantis stockholders agreeing to sell their shares so that Best Bargain could gain control of the company. If enough shareholders signed up and agreed to sell, they would have to tender their holdings to Best Bargain on demand at the set price and on the given date. Best Bargain would then control Air Atlantis.

The stockholders of Air Atlantis were reluctant to sign on, and Best Bargain upped the tender offer by increasing the price they were willing to pay by a full $20 per share more than their earlier offer. The additional amount would be in the form of BB bonds yielding 13 percent for ten years. This would make the tender offer worth $42 per share, $22 in cash and $20 in bonds. These bond sweeteners were "junk" bonds. Best Bargain was now attempting a leveraged buyout of Air Atlantis.

Air Atlantis fought back. They offered to greenmail Best Bargain by purchasing the block of shares of Air Atlantis stock that Best Bargain held at a premium price higher than the recent tender amount. Best Bargain said no. The board also lobbied the stockholders heavily not to sell out. The board argued that the present management had taken AirA this far, and they could take them farther still. Additionally, they contended the offer from Best Bargain was risky because of the bonds involved.

Best Bargain Airlines is no longer in business today. Unfortunately, neither is Air Atlantis. The shareholders of Air Atlantis accepted the tender offer from Best Bargain. They received $22 cash and a $20 bond yielding 13 percent for each share of Air Atlantis they owned. Air Atlantis was absorbed into Best Bargain. But Best Bargain ran into its own severe trouble. A war in the Middle East drove fuel prices through the roof. A general global recession occurred, and revenues and yields dropped significantly. Best Bargain defaulted on their bond issues, not only to the Air Atlantis shareholders but across the board. Best Bargain filed for protection in bankruptcy court and was unable to develop a satisfactory reorganization plan with the unions, debt holders, and stockholders. It was placed in receivership, and all its assets were liquidated. The sale of these assets was not sufficient to pay off even a portion of the outstanding debts, let alone the shareholders, either common or preferred. The shareholders of Air Atlantis received no money at all for any of the bonds received from Best Bargain. They walked away with $22 per share and not one penny in principal or interest on the bonds. This was only $4 per share more than the stock was selling for when Best Bargain made the original tender offer.

If the Air Atlantis example used in this chapter seems extreme in its rapid growth and then its unhappy conclusion, you should research what happened to the stock price of several real air carriers, such as People Express, Frontier, and Eastern. The equity markets provide the lifeblood of the American air transport sector. Without the broad and deep capital markets available in this country, the air transport sector would not be one of the biggest markets in the world, with the best in services and ubiquity.

The U.S. airline system and scores of air carriers often find themselves in financial trouble. Historically, this has always been the case, and the future holds relevant questions as to any ability to alter this course of events. As bad as this may sound, however, all is not bleak. With the vast pools of capital available and with people still willing to speculate and invest in air carrier stock issues, the future will always be bright for those capable of understanding marketplace idiosyncrasies. New carriers are continually starting up all over the country. Existing carriers are redefining their business goals and objectives. What makes these natural events possible is our equity market and the ability to issue and sell stock.

Mutual Funds

Mutual funds are not a part of the capitalization or equity portion of a corporation's financial structure, but one would be remiss not to mention them as a way to obtain capital investment. Investors buy ownership shares (indirectly) of the mutual fund, which in turn purchases direct securities. Mutual funds differ somewhat in organization form and vary quite widely in terms of the type of direct securities that the fund purchases. These funds offer investors considerable diversification, liquidity, and professional security analysis and selection. They provide an investor with a degree of security due to their diversification feature.

This same diversification feature can be a vital source of capital for a corporation. Recently mutual funds have become the behemoths of the equity investment world. According to the Investment Company Institute (1996), the total value of domestic equities managed by mutual funds in the United States approximates $1.4 billion.

Mutual Funds can play a key role in the success of a corporation's equity offering, as well as in the private placement of stock. It is not surprising that mutual funds loom as large in industry financial centers as do investment bankers. So pervasive have mutual fund investments become that, according to airline annual reports for 1996, all airlines with the exception of Southwest had at least one mutual fund company as a holder of more than 5 to 13 percent of their outstanding shares.

Review

What Is a Stock?

A share of stock represents ownership in a corporation. A corporation is owned by its stockholders—often by thousands of people and institutions.

When people buy stock in a corporation, they become part-owners, stockholders, or shareholders. They immediately own a part, no matter how small, of every building, piece of office furniture, piece of machinery, whatever the company owns.

As stockholders, they stand to profit when the company profits. They are also legally entitled to a say in the major policy decisions, such as whether to purchase new aircraft, issue additional stock, sell the company to outside buyers, or change the board of directors. The rule is that each share has the same voting power, so the more shares owned, the greater the power a stockholder wields.

You can vote in person by attending a corporation's annual meeting. Or you can vote by using an absentee ballot, called a proxy, which is mailed before each meeting (see figure 4-1 for one example). The proxy allows a yes or no vote on proposals. Alternatively, stockholders may authorize votes to be cast consistently with the board of directors' recommendations.

Stock Issuance

When stocks are traded in the market, the company that issued the stock doesn't make any money on the transaction. A company only makes money when a new stock is issued. The first time a company's stock is issued, the company is said to be going public. In other words, the owners of the company are selling part of their ownership to the general public. This process is formally known as an initial public offering.

Typically, a company goes public when it needs to raise cash. In exchange for this cash, the company shares control with the stockholders. A major advantage to the offering of stock is that the amount received in exchange for the stock is not a debt that must be repaid, as the stockholders have not loaned money to the corporation. Instead, they have traded investment for ownership.

When a company goes public, it also benefits from the fact that its stock is trading in the open market. This trading tends to give the company legitimacy. The

Figure 4-1. Example of a Proxy Statement

AIR ATLANTIS-COMMON AND/OR PREFERRED STOCK PROXY
PROXY SOLICITED BY THE BOARD OF DIRECTORS

The undersigned hereby appoints James Koch and Charles Abernathy, as proxy, each with the power to appoint his substitute and hereby authorizes each of them at the Annual Meeting of Shareholders of Air Atlantis Corporation to be held at 10:30 A.M. on December 25, 1997 in the Nativity Ballroom of the Hilton Inn, New York, New York and any adjournments thereof to vote all shares of Air Atlantis Common and Preferred Stock, including full shares held in the Air Atlantis Common Dividend Investment Plan, which the undersigned could vote if personally present as designated below and upon any other matter properly brought before the meeting. **The shares represented by this proxy will be voted as designated below, or if no designation is made, will be voted FOR Items 1, 2, and 3 and AGAINST Items 4 and 5.**

Directors Recommend a vote For the following:
1. Election of Directors—Nominees are: Frank Ips, R.W. Kaps, David NewMyer, Hank Lehrer, Jose Ruiz, Cindy Crawford, O. V. Delle-Femine, Chase Manhattan, Ima Morebucks, Ava Peron, Rube Goldberg, Heime Goldfarb & David Worrells. *(See Pages 7–247 of proxy statement)*
____FOR ALL Nominees
____FOR ALL Nominees EXCEPT:
_____
____WITHHOLD Authority to vote for ALL Nominees

Directors Recommend a vote For the following:
2. Reappointment of Auditors—page 29
FOR ___   AGAINST ___   ABSTAIN ___

Directors Recommend a vote For the following:
3. Amendments (Incorporation & By-Laws) re: limiting liability and providing indemnification for directors, officers, employees and agents. pages 32–38
FOR ___   AGAINST ___   ABSTAIN ___
Directors recommend a vote AGAINST the following:
4. Shareholder proposal for disclosure of board of directors outside salaries and shareholdings. P. 42
FOR ___   AGAINST ___   ABSTAIN ___

5. Shareholders proposal for cumulative voting. P. 44
FOR ___   AGAINST ___   ABSTAIN ___

----

company's performance, financial vitality, and overall operation become visible to everyone interested.

Common Stock

Common stock represents basic ownership of a corporation. Owners of common stock share directly in the success or failure of the business. When the company prospers, common stockholders can benefit through dividend increases and possibly higher stock prices. The latter allows those stockholders concerned with speculation, rather than ownership, to reap rewards due to the stock price fluctuations. The distribution of dividends to a common stockholder are not guaranteed but awarded only after other dividends have been awarded to preferred stockholders. Upon dissolution, the common stockholders are the last in line to receive any residual assets of the corporation. Because of the limited liability of the corporation, the common stockholder's downside exposure is the amount of the investment made for the stock itself.

Preferred Stock

Preferred stock is only issued after common stock has been issued (original issuance). Preferred stock is just what the name implies. Preferred stockholders receive preferential treatment in several areas. Dividends are distributed to preferred stockholders before common stockholders. Should dissolution or liquidation of the corporation take place, the preferred stockholders are entitled to receive the money invested before the common stockholders can make any claim. In exchange for these privileges, preferred stockholders must generally accept a fixed dividend payment, no matter how much the company profits.

Corporation may issue several classes of stock. These are usually labeled in a series (class A, B, C, etc.). Each class has a different market price, different dividend payments, and different restrictions concerning ownership privileges.

Public Offerings

When the corporation decides to "go public," the stock, or bond , offering may be made in one of two ways. First, the stock may be placed directly with individuals who will directly purchase and own the stock. Such agreements can be worked out directly between a corporation and a representative of a direct buyer. This form of placement, called direct placement, does not involve a middleman or brokerage house. The corporation is the beneficiary of all the proceeds of the transaction.

The most utilized are the services of underwriter placement. This form of collateral access requires the services of an investment banker or major stockholder to underwrite or "push" the stock. The underwriter handles the offering. The investment banking division of a securities firm may underwrite all the shares for sale from the company and then sell them on the open market at the best possible price. Underwriting means that the investment banker will buy all the shares of the company and then offer them to the public at the best price possible. In this effort, the investment banker will generally charge a fee for the consultation on the handling, timing, issuance prospectus preparation, and other collateral issues. The money made upon the selling of the stock on the open market over and above the underwriting amount also accrues to the benefit of the brokerage/underwriting house. The activity identified above, before any issuance of stock to the general public, is called the primary market.

Securities that have been previously issued are traded in secondary markets, which are the organized exchanges such as the New York Stock Exchange (NYSE), the American Stock Exchange (AMEX), and the over-the-counter (OTC) markets. When primary market participants sell or place issues, they move to the secondary marketplace. Dealers and brokers aid trading in this market. Dealers act as principals and buy for their own accounts and sell securities from their own inventories. Brokers do not buy or sell from their own inventories. They act as agents for others and receive a commission for assisting a transaction.

To offer the stock to the general public, the underwriter prepares an information bulletin or advertisement that is placed in various newspapers, magazines, and bro-

Figure 4-2. Sample Announcement

SAMPLE
This is neither an offer to sell nor a solicitation of offers to buy any of these securities. This offer is made only by the Prospectus.

January 23, 200X

2,100,000 Shares

Air Atlantis, Inc.

Common Stock

Price $8 per Share

Copies of the prospectus may be obtained from any state from any underwriter who may lawfully offer the securities within such state.

A. G. Edwards Company, Ltd.

Furman Sels Mager Dietz & Birney	Gittem Gottem & Good Peabody Co.
Johnson & Johnson Co., Inc.	Dillion & Dillion
Prudential Capital Funding	LBO Specialities, Inc.
Nicole Kidder Peabody, Inc.	Gabriel & Conway, Inc.
Gecko Ichan, Inc.	First Chicago Corporation
Spectrum Investments	Kennedy Family Investments
Smith Varney, Inc.	Sanford & Sons Investment & Hauling
Ruiz & Worrells Investments, LLC	Bache Buddies Investment Firm Divest, Inc.

kerage firms around the country (see figure 4-2). Contained in the advertisement is the name of the company (Air Atlantis), the type of issue being offered (common stock), the number of shares being offered for sale, where the prospectus can be obtained (this is a brochure required by law that is available to anyone interested that provides detailed financial information about the company, etc.), the names of the underwriters who handle the offering (where more than one underwriting firm is involved, the lead firm has its name displayed most prominently), and a required SEC disclaimer. The disclaimer is required, since the ad is not to be legally used to promote sales. Its purpose is only to announce that the stock is available for trade.

Published Information of Public Stock

Stock market quotations offer a snapshot of a company's earnings activity, its dividend policy, and the willingness of the buyer to purchase the stock. The following information has been taken directly from the *Wall Street Journal Guide to Understanding Money and Markets* (1990).

At first glance, stock listings look like an endless sea of numbers (see figure 4-3). This has more to do with the volume of listings and the use of small type than with the complexity of the information.

Figure 4-3. Example of Dow Jones Stock Report

[1] 52 Weeks		[2]	[2]	[3]	[4] Yld	[5]	[6] Vol	[7]	[7]	[7]	[8] Net
Hi	Lo	Stock	Sym	Div	%	P/E	100s	Hi	Lo	Close	Chg
13¼	3¾	HarBrace	HGJ	....		10	231	12½	11⅞	12¼	+⅛
11½	5¾	HarBrace/pf		1.62		14.9	142	11	10¾	10⅞	−⅛
25¾	16⅜	Harland	JH	.58	2.7	16	792	21⅞	20⅞	21¼	+⅝
27⅞	9¼	HarleyDav	HDI	....		8	444	26⅜	26	26	+½
17⅜	6⅜	Harmanint	HAR	....		11	256	16¼	15⅞	16⅛	+⅛
29¾	8½	Harnisch	HPH	.20	1.2	22	3021	17⅜	17⅛	17⅛	−¼
40⅛	22	Harris	HRS	.88	3.2	17	1020	28¼	27	27⅞	+1
37⅞	23½	Harsco	HSC	1.1	3.6	11	417	30⅞	30½	30⅞	+¼
33¼	18¼	Hartmarx	HMX	1.10	4.2	13	244	26⅞	26⅜	26½	−⅜
19⅜	13½	HattersSec	HAT	1.56	9.8	11	2	16	16	16	+⅛
33⅝	22¼	HawaiiElec	HE	1.92	6.6	12	496	29	28¾	29	...
9½	6¾	HlthRehab	HRP	1.12	12.3	11	901	9¼	9	9⅛	+⅛
29¼	21¾	HlthCare	HCP	2.59	9.5	15	560	27⅛	26⅞	27⅛	+⅛
17¾	10⅝	LandBanc	LBC	.72	4.8	11	365	15	13¾	15	+1⅛

To read the listings, remember that stock prices are given in fractions of dollars. Thus 8½ equals $8.50; 8¼ equals $8.25. The fraction ⅛ refers to 12½ cents; and 8⅛ equals about $8.13.

- Highest and lowest prices of the stock are shown for the last fifty-two weeks. Stocks reaching a new high or low for the year are marked with an arrow in the left-hand margin. These figures show you the volatility of a stock—an indicator of both profit potential and risk. The percentage gain or loss is often more significant than the dollar gain or loss; a $5 change in a $10 stock indicates more volatility than a $5 move in a $30 stock.
- Company names are abbreviated, listed alphabetically, and followed by the ticker symbol. Most symbols are closely related to the name of the company (e.g., HMX for Hartmarx Corp.). Some may be more related to what the company does or produces. CAF, for instance, is the symbol for Furr's/Bishop's Cafeterias (not shown).
- Cash dividend per share is given in dollars and cents. A dividend is a payment to shareholders of part of a company's profit. This figure is an estimate of the anticipated yearly dividend per share. Hartmarx's yearly dividend is estimated at $1.10 per share. If you owned 100 shares, you would receive $110 in dividend payments each year, probably in quarterly payments of $27.50.
- Percent yield is a way of expressing the stock's current value. It tells you how much dividend you get for what you pay. The table calculates yield for you; you could do it yourself by dividing the dividend by the closing price (next to last column). For Hartmarx's yield, divide $1.10 by 26.5 to get .042, or 4.2 percent yield. Think of it this way: you will get 4.2 percent of my purchase price in dividends each year.
- P/E ratio, short for price/earnings ratio, refers to the relationship between the price of one share of stock and the annual earnings of the company. (Since earnings aren't given here, you can't calculate this figure yourself.)

For Harmanint (HAR), the P/E ratio has been derived by dividing the closing price of $16.13 by the company's earnings per share to arrive at 11. It is useful to read the P/E ratio as follows: The price of a Harmanint share is eleven times the company's earnings per share for the most recent four quarters.

The P/E ratio is a critical piece of information because it expresses the value of a stock in terms of company earnings rather than selling price. The P/E ratios of different stocks can be compared to assess their relative values.

It is important to remember that there's no perfect P/E ratio. Some stocks that have lower earnings will have higher P/E ratios; these are usually growth stocks. On the other hand, an income stock that pays consistently high dividends will tend to have a lower P/E ratio.

- "Vol 100s" or "Sales (hds)" refers to the volume of shares traded on the previous day. Just multiply the figure in this column by 100. For example, 49,600 shares of Hawaii Electric stock were traded on this day. Stocks with unusual sales volumes are underlined. Occasionally, a *z* appears before the number in this column. This means you should not multiply by 100; the figure refers to the actual number traded.
- High, Low, and Close tell you a stock's highest, lowest, and closing price for the previous day. These numbers indicate how widely the price has fluctuated in a single day; usually the differences are small. The largest spread seen above is for Harris stock, which traded for as high as $28¼ per share and as low as $27 and closed at $27⅞.
- "Net change" compares this day's closing price with the closing price of the day before. A minus (−) indicates this closing price is lower; a plus (+) means it is higher. Since Harley Davidson's closing at $26 was up half a point, you can infer that the closing price quoted the previous day was $25½. Stocks that show a price change of 5 percent or more are shown in boldface type.

The "Over-the-Counter" Stock Market

Most U.S. stocks are not traded on an exchange at all. Instead, they're traded on the over-the-counter market (OTC), an electronic marketplace.

Traders in the OTC market don't deal face to face. Their marketplace is as large and as wide as the number of desks with brokers at work that day. They see into this marketplace by studying the activity reported on their computer screens, and they trade with other brokers by telephone.

The OTC, however, is far from a chaotic free-for-all. It's a highly sophisticated network called the National Market System (NMS). Its members regulate themselves through an organization called the National Association of Securities Dealers (NASD). Appropriately, the name you see heading the newspaper's over-the-counter listings is the National Association of Securities Dealers Automated Quotations (NASDAQ).

There are so many thousands of stocks traded over the counter that listing them all would require nearly all the pages in the *Wall Street Journal*. Consequently, only the most actively traded issues are listed, and even those are broken down into three tables: the NASDAQ National Market Issues, the NASDAQ Bid and Ask Quotations, and Additional NASDAQ Quotes.

The National Market Issues table lists the most actively traded OTC stocks (see figure 4-4). You can find more detailed information about the stocks in this table than any other OTC stocks. Notice that most companies pay no dividends. In fact, there isn't even a dividend heading on the table. (Dividends are listed, however,

Figure 4-4. Example of NASDAQ National Market Issues

365-day High	Low			Yld	P/E	Sales (hds)	High	Low	Last	Net Chg.
20	7⅝	Minetk	MINL	...	27	147	14½	14⅜	14⅜	−⅛
12	4¾	Minntc	MNTX	...	...	102	8¾	8½	8⅝	+⅛
30	13⅞	Minstar	MNST	...	16	1683	22⅝	21¾	22⅜	+¼
7⅝	4⅜	Mgask	MRGC	...	50	16	5	4¾	5	...
33½	11¾	MoblC	MCGAB	...	176	40	30	29⅝	30	+¼
11	4⅝	MOCON	MOCON	1.9	15	66	10⅜	10⅛	10⅜	+⅛

after the ticker symbol.) Few OTC stocks pay dividends, because they're generally either small or start-up companies that need to put earnings back into the business.

For example, MOCON had high and low prices during the past year of $11.00 and $4.62. Its annual dividend per share is $.20 (1.9 percent of 10⅜); its current yield is 1.9 percent; its price-earnings ratio is 15. Sales volume the previous day was 6,600 shares. During that day's trading, it sold as low as 10⅛ per share and as high as 10⅜ per share, where it closed. This net change was ⅛ point higher than the previous quoted closing price.

NASDAQ Bid and Asked Quotations presents the second tier of most actively traded OTC stocks (see figure 4-5). The information provided here includes the stock name and dividend, sales volume, the highest bid, the lowest ask, and the net change for the day. AA Importing traded 1,000 shares. Buyers were willing to pay $3.75 a share at the close. Sellers were asking $4.25. The price was unchanged from the previous day's close.

Additional NASDAQ (OTC) Quotes show the OTC stocks that are the least actively traded of all stocks listed in the *Wall Street Journal,* yet they are still more heavily traded than thousands of other stocks in the OTC marketplace (see figure 4-6). Information on these stocks only includes the highest bid and the lowest ask of the day. The number of trades actually conducted at these prices is difficult to quote, given the decentralized nature of OTC trading.

Why Do Companies List on One Exchange over Another?

A company able to meet NYSE or AMEX listing requirements gains prestige by listing on those exchanges. Many large and reputable companies, however, choose to stay listed on the OTC; among them are MCI and Apple Computer. In addition, many banks and insurance companies traditionally list on the OTC. Many compa-

Figure 4-5. Example of NASDAQ Bid and Asked Quotations

Stock & Div	Sales 100s	Bid	Asked	Net Chg.
AA Importing	10	$3\frac{3}{4}$	$4\frac{1}{4}$	....
Advatex Assc	60	3	$3\frac{1}{2}$	$+\frac{3}{8}$
Airsensors	58	2	$2\frac{1}{8}$	....

Figure 4-6. Example of Additional NASDAQ Over the Counter (OTC) Quotes

	Bid	Asked		Bid	Asked
AdvDisplay Tec	$\frac{1}{4}$	$\frac{9}{32}$	Creatv Cmptr	$\frac{1}{8}$	$\frac{5}{32}$
AdvMedical Pr	$\frac{1}{32}$	$\frac{1}{16}$	Credo Petrol	$1\frac{3}{8}$	$1\frac{5}{8}$
AFP Imaging	$5\frac{1}{4}$	6	Cryodynmcs	$1\frac{5}{8}$	$1\frac{3}{4}$

nies listed on the NYSE or AMEX are also listed on regional exchanges. None are listed on both NYSE and AMEX, although it is technically possible.

REQUIREMENTS OF THE VARIOUS MARKETS
(TO BE LISTED ON THE EXCHANGE)

New York Stock Exchange. Must have pretax earnings of $2.5 million; 1.1 million shares publicly held with $18 million market value and net tangible assets of $18 million. The type of companies on this market are usually the oldest, largest, and best known. NYSE lists 1,600 companies.

American Stock Exchange. Must have pretax income of $750,000; 500,000 shares publicly held and net tangible assets of $4 million. Generally the companies listed on this exchange are smaller and younger. There are 890 listed companies.

Over-the-Counter Market. There are no requirements for pink sheet listings and minimal requirements for NASDAQ and National Market Systems Issues. Those listed are generally the smallest, youngest companies with many high technology and financial service companies. There are over 31,000 listed companies.

Pink sheets in the OTC market are some low-priced, infrequently traded stocks that are not listed in the papers because they are not on the NASDAQ system. They may trade less than 100 shares a day, and they may trade for literally a fraction of a cent a share. Only brokers receive the daily results for these stocks on a listing called the pink sheets. Attempts have been under way for some time to computerize these listings.

Suggested Readings and References

Bernhard, A. (1975). *Investing in common stocks with the aid of the value line rankings and other criteria of stock value.* New York: A. Bernhard.

Fewings, D. R. (1979). *Corporate growth and common stock risk.* Greenwich, CT: JAI Press.

Financial Accounting Standards Board. (1981). *Criteria for applying the equity method of accounting for investments in common stock.* Stamford, CT: Author.

Financial Accounting Standards Board. (1985). *Yield tests for determining whether a convertible security is a common stock equivalent.* Stamford, CT: Author.

Frank, S. (1987). *The beginner's guide to top no-load and low-commission common stock mutual funds: How to win big in today's stock market.* San Diego, CA: Author.

Goldberg, I., & Gordon, R. S. (1969). *Introduction to methods for buying and selling stock.* New York: Gordon and Breach.

Katz, J. (1992). *Investing for retirement: A successful recipe for the buying and selling of stocks for IRA's and other retirement plans.* Pittsburgh: PTI.

Lasry, G. (1979). *Valuing common stock: The power of prudence.* New York: Amacom.

Lees, F. (1983). *Repurchasing common stock.* New York: Conference Board.

Mangold, M. (1968). *How public financing can help your company grow: A guide to the advantages and ways of securing equity capital through the sales of stock to the public, including twenty-five case histories of actual public offerings.* New York: Pilot Industries.

Rosenberg, C. N. (1978). *The common sense way to stock market profits.* New York: New American Library.

Scott, D. L. (1993). *The guide to investing in common stock: How to build your wealth by mastering the basic strategies.* Old Saybrook, CT: Globe Pequot Press.

Soldofsky, R. M. (1976). *Institutional investor's common stock: Holding and voting.* Washington: Government Printing Office.

Spare, A., & Tengler, N. (1992). *Relative dividend yield: Common stock investing for income and appreciation.* New York: Wiley.

Wurman, R. S., Siegel, A., & Morris, K. M. (1990). *The Wall Street Journal guide to understanding money and markets.* New York: Access Press.

5

DEBT MARKETS

This chapter examines the debt markets used by the air transport sector to supply capital: short-term operating loans and long-term syndicated packages and leases. Again, Air Atlantis is used as a vehicle to discuss the functions, methods, and motives for using bond instruments and leasing techniques in the air transport sector. By necessity, the section on banking will be more generic in nature due to the wide variability of financing options available.

Bonds

Many forms of bonds are available on the market today: government bonds, municipal bonds, and corporate bonds. Due to the limited scope of this book, we will focus on corporate bonds. Principally institutional investors, banks, insurance companies, pension funds, colleges and universities, and charitable foundations buy the kinds of bonds issued by companies like Air Atlantis. Airport managers and some fixed base operators located on or near airport property may have a vested interest in the municipal bond markets. Municipal bonds (Munys) are used to finance a variety of projects in that venue. Airports are major users of municipal bond debt instruments, as will be discussed in chapter 10.

The easiest way to understand corporate bonds is to return to the Air Atlantis example. Let us consider the plight of the treasurer five years after the airline's creation, when it needed to raise $1 million of new capital. AirA needed the money because it had grown somewhat haphazardly, acquiring several types of aircraft, and not all of the gate areas were decorated alike. It was now time to pull the whole operation together and make it function efficiently. An independent consultant had determined just what economies AirA could effect by standardizing aircraft type and passenger gate and lounge areas. In the end, there was no question that the $1 million would be money well spent. But how should AirA raise the money?

If you were company treasurer, you might first discuss the matter with the officers of your regular bank. They have been willing to supply AirA, from month to month, with the credit needed for fuel and payroll requirements. However, they do not want to loan you $1 million to consolidate operations. Instead, they suggest that you contact an investment banker.

Investment bankers specialize in raising the kind of money that businesses need for long-term use, usually in amounts greater than the $1 million needed by Air Atlantis. When a company needs money, it usually hopes to obtain it without too many strings attached and without obligating itself to pay any set returns on the money. In short, it wants equity capital in the form of common stock.

While most companies might prefer to raise new capital by selling stock, this is not the kind of securities issue an investment banker is likely to recommend, especially in the case of a small company like Air Atlantis. They are far more likely to suggest an issue of bonds rather than an issue of common or preferred stock. In normal years, the aggregate value of new bond issues exceeds that of new stock issues by a factor of six to twelve times. In fact, in the modern era, business has raised little more than 5 percent of the money it needs through stock issues. Selling bonds in the bond markets has raised most of the balance. The capital markets for equity stocks are large, but the capital markets for bonds are truly vast by comparison.

Bonds always represent borrowed money that the company is obligated to repay. In short, they are IOUs. They are a debt, which is why they are called obligations. They are a special kind of promissory note. When a company sells bonds, it borrows the money from the buyers, and the bonds stand as formal evidence of that debt. Each bond is an agreement on the part of the company to repay the face value of the bond, usually $1,000, at a specified time (maturity date) and to pay a set annual rate of interest (coupon rate) from the day it is issued to the day it is redeemed.

Anyone who buys stock in a company actually buys a part of the company. People who buy a bond from a company are simply lending their money to the company. They expect to collect dividends, a portion of the company's profits, from their stockholdings. A bondholder expects only to earn a fixed rate of return on his investment in the form of annual interest payments.

There is one other important difference between stocks and bonds. If a company is successful, the stockholder can hope to realize a substantial profit because the price of the stock should go up over time. The bondholder enjoys no such hope. No matter how successful the company is, the price of the bond interest rate is generally fixed. The bond's price does not vary greatly with the performance of the company.

Bondholders don't expect to gain as much on their capital or run the risk of losing to the same extent that stockholders do. Their investment is much better protected. This is because bonds represent debt, and if a company is dissolved, the debt it owes its bondholders must be paid before any of the stockholders get a dime of what is left of the company. The claims of the bondholders come first, then the preferred stockholders, and finally the common stockholders.

Because the element of risk is comparatively slight, bonds are popular with institutional investors. This is the market the investment banker has his eye on when he underwrites a bond issue. Often an issuer may succeed in selling the entire issue to one or two large institutional customers and need not try to sell the issue publicly. This is known as a private placement.

The institutional market for bonds is such a good market that the underwriting and selling commissions charged by investment bankers are usually much lower on an issue of bonds than on an issue of stock. Otherwise, investment bankers sell the two kinds of securities in much the same way.

From the point of view of any company's treasurer, a bond issue has obvious disadvantages as compared with a stock issue. The interest that must be paid on bonds represents a fixed charge that has to be met in bad times as well as good, and the bonds must be paid off when they come due. The stockholder has to be paid only if the company makes money, and even that is not a binding obligation.

On the other hand, if the company is successful, it does not mind having to pay 8 and 9 percent interest on money borrowed from bondholders if it can make a substantially greater profit on the extra capital. Again, bond interest payments are an expense item deducted from a company's earnings before taxes. In contrast, dividends are paid out of what is left after the taxes are paid on its earnings. Thus, it actually costs the company more to pay dividends to stockholders than to pay interest on borrowed funds from its bondholders because it obtains a tax deduction on bond debt but not on dividends. From an investor's point of view, the best bonds are those that have the strongest assurance that they will be repaid in full with the specified interest.

Here the situation is not much different from what it would be if you as an individual sought to get a loan from a bank. If the banker knew you and knew that you could repay the principal and make the interest payments, she might lend money without requiring any collateral. However, if it were a sizable loan, the banker might require some form of collateral. She might insist that you put up your house, life insurance policies, or other property to guarantee the loan. In doing so, the bank might require the borrower to take a mortgage on the property.

It's much the same way with companies when they issue bonds. They would prefer to obtain money without posting property as a guarantee that the contract set in the bond will be fulfilled. In fact, that is precisely the way the Air Atlantis treasurer felt when the investment banker told him the company would have to float a bond issue, not a stock issue.

As long as it had to be bonds, the treasurer proposed that Air Atlantis issue $1 million of debentures. A debenture is a bond that is backed only by the general credit of the corporation. No specific real estate or property stands as security behind it. It is, in effect, a giant IOU. Junk bonds are debentures that pay a very high interest rate and can be high risks for default. Debentures are the most common type of bond issued by well-established companies. Although specific assets do not secure a debenture, its holders have a claim on the corporation's assets if the interest and principal are not made. In some cases, the bond debenture specifies that the claim to assets is secondary to the claims of other bondholders. Such a bond is called a subordinated debenture.

But in the case of Air Atlantis, the investment banker was not disposed to feel that such an issue would be in order because the company, although successful to date, was still relatively small and not well known. He was afraid the debentures would not sell.

Our treasurer then asked if a debenture issue might not be made more attractive by including a convertible provision in the contract. There are many convertible bonds on the market, and their terms vary greatly. However, similar to convertible preferred stock, they offer the bondholders the privilege of converting the bond into common stock at some set ratio and within some set period.

Such a provision adds a certain speculative appeal to the issue, the chance to make an extra profit if the company's common stock appreciates. However, problems could develop. The typical institutional bond buyer may look askance at such "sweeteners." They know you "don't get something for nothing" in a security, any more than you do in any other kind of merchandise. A convertible bond may offer the possibility of price appreciation, but its guarantee of safety may not be quite as substantial.

In Air Atlantis's case, the investment banker did not feel that a convertible bond was feasible, and in light of his attitude, the treasurer did not even raise the question of whether Air Atlantis could issue some kind of income or adjustment bond. These bonds are a kind of hybrid security, something like a noncumulative preferred stock, since they provide that the interest is to be paid on the bond only as it is earned. If earnings are sufficient to pay only a part of the interest on such bonds, the company must make whatever payment it can to the nearest .5 percent. Thus on an 8 percent income bond, a company might pay only 5 or 6.5 percent, depending on its earnings.

The collateral trust bond, which is similar to the income bond, was also deemed unsuitable for Air Atlantis. When a company issues collateral trust bonds, it deposits securities with a trustee as a guarantee that the bonds will be redeemed and that the interest payments will be made. Usually, the securities on deposit are worth at least 25 percent more than the bond issue itself. They are frequently the securities of subsidiary companies.

As the discussion progressed, it became apparent the investment banker felt there was only one kind of bond Air Atlantis could offer with success. It was a first mortgage bond. This is a bond secured by a mortgage on all company property. This includes not only the property it has now but any property it may acquire in the future as well. These bonds are considered to be among the highest-grade security investments, because they offer investors an undisputed first claim on company earnings. First mortgage bonds take absolute precedence over the claims of all other owners of a company's securities, including holders of debentures, adjustment bonds, or secondary mortgage bonds issued after the first mortgage bonds.

Another type of bond suggested by the treasurer was an equipment trust bond, which is secured by a piece of machinery or equipment, such as an airplane, whose title is deposited with a trustee. However, because AirA did not yet have full title to its aircraft, another approach was considered.

Having resigned himself to the fact that Air Atlantis would have to mortgage its property to float the $1 million bond issue, the treasurer next took up with the investment banker the question of what interest rate the company might have to pay. Here the investment banker was in no position to supply an answer because the rate a company has to pay always depends primarily on its credit standing and earnings capacity. The investment banker could not commit himself without a thorough, painstaking investigation of all aspects of the company. All investment bankers, with the help of outside accountants, analysts, and other specialists, perform such detailed investigations before underwriting any new issue of securities for a company.

Bond interest rates vary, not only with the health of the company but also with the bond quality and general business conditions. Whenever a new bond issue is floated, Moody's Investor Service and Standard & Poor's, the two leading firms in the field of securities research, assign it a quality rating. Usually the two companies agree on the rating, but they do not agree on the form of the designation. Thus Moody's grades bonds as Aaa, Aa, A, Baa, Ba, etc., while Standard & Poor's prefers capital letters and uses AAA, AA, etc. Both firms grade in descending order of quality (see figure 5-1).

Figure 5-1. Bond Ratings

Rating Company	High Grade	Medium Grade Investment Grade	Speculative	Poor Grade
Standard & Poor's	AAA AA	A BBB	BB B	CCC to D
Moody's	Aaa Aa	A Baa	Ba B	Caa to C

When money is "tight," home mortgage rates increase, general interest rates on borrowing rise, and the prime rate climbs. Bond interest rates will increase as well. If this happens when stock dividends, expressed as a percentage of the price, have been going down, a situation develops where an investor can get a better rate of return from bonds than stocks, and they are frequently tempted to shift to safer investment, especially if they believe the sag in stock prices will continue.

The interest rate of a bond is referred to as the coupon rate, because traditionally bonds have appended to them a number of detachable coupons, one for each interest payment period of the life of the bond. The owner clips each coupon as it comes due and presents it to the company's paying agent. Coupons were used first because bonds were not registered on the company's books in the owner's name, as are stock certificates. They were property of the bearer. Whoever had them at a given time owned them, so they were called bearer bonds. More and more companies issue bonds registered in each owner's name, just like stocks. On some registered bonds, coupons are still used for payment of interest, but on most others, the bondholder of record gets a check automatically from the company.

Just as crucial as the interest rate of any bond issued by a company is the question of maturity. How long a life will the bonds have, and how soon will the company have to redeem them or pay them off? In general, the stronger the company, the longer the maturity. For a company like Air Atlantis, ten years might be considered the maximum limit. Furthermore, the company would probably be required to establish a sinking fund and put enough money into it every year to provide for an annual repayment of a portion of the issue. A sinking fund bond issue requires the corporation to set aside money at regular intervals, usually payable to a trustee, so that sufficient funds accrue to repay the principal at maturity. This technique increases the chances that the firm has sufficient funds set aside to redeem the issue when the time arrives. The setting aside of money at intervals for the gradual payment of a debt is called amortization.

In view of its good track record and reorganization plan, Air Atlantis would probably get a two- or three-year grace period before it had to start putting money into the sinking fund and calling down the bonds it issued.

Like preferred, most bonds have call provisions, which permit a company to redeem them before the maturity date. The company will pay the holder of the bond the full face value plus a premium of several percentage points as compensation for the call down.

There is a wide variation in how long bond issues run, but a period of twenty to thirty years is common. The maturity of a bond can and does affect the return. You can buy a bond with a coupon rate of 6 percent, but it may yield you something less or something more, depending on how much you paid for the bond and its maturity date.

If you pay exactly $1,000 for a bond and get $60 interest on it every year, you realize a true 6 percent yield. Nevertheless, if you paid $1,050 for that bond, the $60 annual interest payment obviously represents a less than 6 percent yield on your purchase. Furthermore, if you hold that bond until maturity, you will get only $1,000 for it upon redemption, a loss of $50. If the bond has a twenty-year maturity, that would represent an effective net reduction of $2.50 a year in your interest payments. Over the full twenty years, you would also lose the amount of interest you could have earned on that $50.

The net of it all is that if you pay $1,050 for a 6 percent twenty-year bond, you will realize a yield to maturity of 5.58 percent. Of course, if you buy the bond at a discount instead of a premium, $950 instead of $1,050, you will realize a better than 6 percent yield.

When a company like Air Atlantis uses stock or bond issues, which represent new financing, to raise new capital, preferred stocks and bonds are issued as part of a refinancing operation. Thus, when a company refinances, it may seek to substitute some new bond issue for an outstanding one that it issued many years ago, a process known as refunding.

It is to a company's advantage to substitute new bond issues for old ones. As business and investment conditions change, it is frequently worthwhile to call down an outstanding issue of bonds or preferred stock on which the company may be paying a high rate of interest. Floating a new issue carrying the lower prevailing market interest rate can pay off such issues.

When a company has a substantial amount of bonds or preferred stock outstanding, in relation to the amount of its common stock, the common stock is said to have high leverage. This phrase is used because the price of the company's common stock is likely to be disproportionately influenced by any change, increase or decrease, in earnings. Here is why. Suppose Air Atlantis is obligated to pay $500,000 in bond interest and preferred dividends each year. If the company has earnings of $1 million before paying such fixed charges, it has only $500,000 left, to be paid out in dividends to the common stockholders, or retained and reinvested, or split between the two. However, if the company has earnings of $3 million, it will have $2.5 million available for the common stockholders and for retained investment. The bondholders and preferred stockholders would still have received only the $500,000 guaranteed them and no more.

Of course, if the company's earnings decreased to $500,000, there would be no money at all for the common stockholders. Because fluctuations in earnings can have such a magnified effect on earnings available to the common stockholders, highly leveraged stocks are likely to fluctuate much more dramatically in price than the stocks of companies that have relatively small bond and preferred stock floats.

Reading and Interpreting the *Wall Street Journal*

This section will help you understand bond charts, locate and evaluate company information, and interpret the various market and economic indexes that are published in the *Wall Street Journal*. Understanding what these market and economic indexes say and what they mean to the air transport sector are essential steps in appreciating the decisions that confront air carriers today.

Economic trends and overall market health force certain decisions to be made, while creating windows of opportunity of varying risk and growth levels that can be exploited by a well-informed management team to enhance share value. Evaluating and understanding these economic and market indexes will also help you make equally important life and career decisions. The following information has been taken directly from *The Wall Street Journal Guide to Understanding Money and Markets* (1990).

Both the New York Stock Exchange and the American Stock Exchange list a large number of corporate bonds for trading. Quotes for these bonds are listed in daily tables in the *Wall Street Journal*. The table in figure 5-2 is for the NYSE. Tables for the AMEX are read the same way.

The first column identifies the company or organization issuing the bond. These abbreviations can differ from the abbreviations for the same companies in the stock tables. Some are easily guessed (Gdyr for Goodyear) or even fully spelled out (Exxon). You may need a key to help you decipher others.

The second column lists the set interest rate for this bond issue. Many companies, of course, have bonds outstanding from a number of bond issues, floated at different times and with different rates. Bond interest always refers to a percentage of par value, which is the amount the issuer will repay when the bond comes due. The par value of most corporate bonds is $1,000. Thus for Exxon the interest rate of 6 percent means 6 percent of $1,000, or $60.00. The interest payment for this bond will always be $60 per year. The "zr" appearing instead of an interest rate fig-

Figure 5-2. Example of a Bond Listing

(1) Bonds	(2)	(3)	(4) Yld	(5) Vol	(6) Close	(7) Chg
DukeP	9½	05	9.8	45	96⅞	−⅝
DukeP	8⅜	06	9.5	23	87⅜	+⅜
Exxon	6	s97	7.6	98	79¼	+¼
Gdyr	7.35	s97	8.5	20	86⅝	+⅝
MerLy	zr	99	.....	25	74½	.....

ure means that this bond is a zero-coupon bond. Since zero coupons pay no periodic interest, allowing the interest to accrue until maturity, no figure is given here.

Numbers in the third column don't include a fraction and may be confused with the numbers following them. The last two digits show the year in which the bond's principal will be paid off, or mature. It's understood that the first two digits are either 19 or 20. For example, DukeP 9½ percent bond will come due in the year 2005, while Exxon came due in 1997. The *s* that sometimes appears after the interest rate is not a meaningful symbol. It is used simply to separate the interest rate amounts from figures following them in closely set newspaper type.

In the fourth column, the yield is critical because it describes the bond's current value. For example, the yield for the Exxon 6 percent bond listed is 7.6 percent. You can read this as follows: Your interest payments will be 7.6 percent of what you will pay for the bond today. You can see that some yield figures are higher than the bond's interest rate, while others are lower.

In the fifth column, bond volumes are listed not in terms of number of issues sold but in terms of dollar worth. The volume figure tells you how many thousands of dollars were traded on the previous day. You can read the figure by adding three zeros. Thus, $20,000 worth of Goodyear bonds were traded the previous day.

The close, listed in the sixth column, is the amount the bond was trading for when the market closed that day.

In the seventh column, net change represents the difference between the closing price of the previous trading day and the closing price of the day before that. It appears as a fraction and always refers to a fraction of par value. For example, Goodyear was up ⅝ point, which means the closing price given here is ⅝ percent of par value greater than the closing price given the previous day. Since par is $1,000, you know that the closing price shown here is $6.25 (⅝ percent of $1,000) more than the last closing price. This closing price is given as 86⅝ or $866.25; therefore, the last closing price must have been $860.

Figure 5-3. Bond Prices Versus Interest/Coupon Rates

Bond Prices Move in the Opposite Direction to Bond Interest Rates

Examples:

1. $1,000.00 bond with a coupon rate (interest rate) of 10% = $100.00 yield. If the new interest rate drops to 8%, the face value of the bond increases to $1,250.00. (Yield is $100.00 on a bond worth $1,250.00; 100.00 divided by 1,250.00 equals 8%.)

2. If a $1,000.00 new bond issued at 10% thus yielding $100.00 has a rate increase to 12%, the value of the old price of $1,000.00 must drop to $833.33. (Yield is $100.00 on a bond now worth $833.33; 100.00 divided by 833.33 equals 12%.)

Net price changes almost always reflect interest rate changes. If bond prices are up from the previous day, as are the majority shown above, you can guess that interest rates fell. When most bond prices are down, you know that interest rates are up.

Banks

Commercial banks, which are the traditional financial "department stores," serve a variety of customers. Historically, the commercial banks were the major institutions handling checking and savings accounts. It was through these banks that the Federal Reserve system expanded or contracted the money supply. Today, however, several other institutions also provide checking and savings services and significantly influence the effective money supply. Conversely, because of deregulation of the financial industry, commercial banks are providing an ever-widening range of services, including stock brokerage and insurance services.

Note that commercial banks are quite different from investment banks. Commercial banks lend money, whereas investment banks help companies raise capital from other parties. Before 1933, commercial banks offered investment services, but the Glass-Steagall Act, which was passed in that year, prohibited commercial banks from engaging in investment banking activities. Thus, the Morgan Bank was broken up into two separate organizations: the Morgan Guaranty Trust Company, a commercial bank, and Morgan Stanley, a major investment banking house.

Japanese and European banks can, and do, offer both commercial and investment banking services. This severely hinders U.S. banks in global competition, so efforts are under way to repeal the Glass-Steagall Act. This act is responsible for the change in global banking that has resulted in no American bank being on the top ten list of world banks.

Choosing a bank is an important issue for any business enterprise. Individuals, whose only contact with their bank is using its checking services, generally choose a bank for the convenience of its location and the competitive costs of its services. However, a business that borrows from banks must look at other criteria, and a potential borrower seeking banking relations should recognize that important differences exist among banks. A company is well advised to consider a bank's ability to provide the following services.

Willingness to Assume Risk

Banks have different basic policies toward risk. Some banks are inclined to follow relatively conservative lending practices, while others engage in what are properly termed "creative banking practices." These policies reflect the personalities of bank officers and the characteristics of the bank's deposit liabilities. Thus, a bank with fluctuating deposit liabilities in a static community may tend to be a conservative lender, while a bank whose deposits are growing with little interruption may follow more liberal credit policies. Similarly, a large bank with broad diversification over geographic regions, or across industries, can obtain the benefit of combining and averaging risks. Thus, marginal credit risks that might be unacceptable to a small bank, or to a specialized unit bank, can be pooled by a branch banking system to reduce the overall risk of a group of marginal accounts.

Advice and Counsel

Some bank loan officers are active in providing counsel and in stimulating development loans to firms in their early and formative years. Certain banks have specialized departments that make loans to firms that are expected to grow and become more important customers. The personnel of these departments can provide valuable counseling to customers. The bankers' experience with other firms in growth situations may enable them to spot and warn their customers about developing problems or opportunities.

Loyalty to Customers

Banks differ in the extent to which they will support the activities of their borrowers in bad times. This characteristic is referred to as the degree of loyalty of the bank. Some banks may put great pressure on a business to liquidate its loans when the firm's outlook becomes clouded. Others will stand by the firm and work diligently to help get it back on its feet. An especially dramatic illustration of this point was Bank of America's bailout of Memorex Corporation. The bank could have forced Memorex into bankruptcy, but instead it loaned the company additional capital and helped it survive a bad period. Memorex's stock price subsequently rose on the NYSE from $1.50 to $68, so Bank of America's help was indeed beneficial.

Specialization

Banks differ greatly in their degrees of loan specialization. Larger banks have departments that specialize in different kinds of loans, for example, real estate, farm, and commercial loans. Within these broad categories, there may be a specialization by line of business, such as steel, airlines, machinery, cattle, or textiles. For example, some California banks have become specialists in lending to electronics companies, and many midwestern banks are agricultural specialists. A sound firm can obtain more creative cooperation and more active support by choosing a bank that has the greatest experience and familiarity with its particular type of business. Therefore, a bank that is excellent for one firm may be completely unsuitable for another.

Maximum Loan Size

The size of a bank can be an important factor. Since the maximum loan a bank can make to any one customer is limited to 15 percent of the bank's capital accounts (capital stock plus retained earnings), it is generally not appropriate for large firms to develop borrowing relations with small banks.

Merchant Banking

The term *merchant bank* was originally applied to a bank that not only loaned depositors' money but also provided its customers with equity capital and financial advice. Until 1933, American commercial banks performed all types of merchant banking functions. However, a third of all American banks failed during the Great Depression, in part because of these activities, so in 1933 the Glass-Steagall Act was passed in an effort to reduce banks' exposure to risk. In recent years, commercial banks have been attempting to get back into merchant banking, in part because their foreign competitors offer such services. American banks need to be able to compete with their foreign counterparts for multinational corporate business. Currently, the larger banks, often through holding companies, are being permitted to get back into merchant banking, at least to a limited extent. This trend will probably continue, and if it does, corporations will need to consider a bank's ability to provide a full range of commercial and merchant banking services when choosing a bank.

Other Services

Banks can also provide cash management services, assist with electronic funds transfers, help firms obtain foreign exchange, and offer a host of other services. If the firm's manager owns most of its stock, the bank's willingness and ability to provide trust and estate services should also be considered.

Long-Term Loans

A long-term loan is a contract under which a borrower agrees to make a series of interest and principal payments on specific dates to the lender. Long-term loans are usually negotiated directly between the borrowing firm and a financial institution. Generally, these financial institutions are banks, insurance companies, or pension funds. Although long-term loan maturity dates vary from two to thirty years, most are for three to fifteen years.

Most long-term loans are amortized, which means they are paid off in equal installments over the life of the loan. Amortization protects the lender against the possibility that the borrower will not make adequate provisions for the loan's retirement during the life of the loan. Also, if the interest and principal payments required under a long-term loan agreement are not met on schedule, the borrowing firm is said to have defaulted and can then be forced into bankruptcy.

Long-term loans have three major advantages over public offerings such as stock or bond issues: speed, flexibility, and low issuance costs. Because they are negotiated directly between the borrower and the lender, formal documentation is minimized. The essential provisions of a long-term loan can be worked out much more quickly than those for a public issue, and it is not necessary for the loan to go through the SEC registration process. A further advantage of long-term loans has to do with future flexibility. With a long-term loan, the borrower can generally sit down with the lender and work out agreeable modifications to the contract.

The interest rate on long-term loans can be either fixed or floating. If a fixed rate is used, it will generally be set close to the rate on bonds of equivalent maturity and risk. If the rate is floating, it will usually be set at a certain number of percentage points above either the prime rate, the commercial paper rate, the T-bill rate, the T-bond rate, or the London Inter Bank Offered Rate (LIBOR). Then, when the index rate goes up or down, so does the rate charged on the outstanding balance. Rates may be adjusted annually, semiannually, quarterly, monthly, or on some other basis, depending on what the contract specifies. In 1991, about 60 percent of the long-term loans made had floating rate provisions, up from zero in 1970. Banks obtain most of the funds they lend by selling certificates of deposit (CD). Because the CD rates rise when other market rates rise, banks need to increase the rate they charge in order to cover their own interest costs. With the increased volatility of interest rates in recent years, many banks and other lenders have become increasingly reluctant to make long-term, fixed-rate loans and are willing to make only floating-rate loans.

Short-Term Loans

Although banks do make long-term loans, some of them as big as $500 million and above, the bulk of their lending is on a short-term basis. Bank loans to businesses are frequently written as ninety-day notes, so the loan must be repaid or renewed at the end of ninety days. Of course, if a borrower's financial position has deteriorated, the bank may well refuse to renew the note, which can mean serious trouble for the borrower.

When a bank loan is approved, the agreement is executed by signing a promissory note. The note specifies (1) the amount borrowed, (2) the percentage interest rate, (3) the repayment schedule, which can involve either lump sum or a series of installments, (4) any collateral that might have to be put up as security for the loan, and (5) any other terms that the bank and the borrower have agreed on. When the note is signed, the bank credits the borrower's checking account with the amount of the loan, and both cash and notes payable increase on the borrower's balance sheet.

Banks sometimes require borrowers to maintain an average demand deposit (checking account) balance equal to 10 to 20 percent of the face value of the loan. This is called a compensating balance, and such balances raise the effective interest rate on the loans. For example, if a firm needs $80,000 to pay off outstanding debts but it must maintain a 20 percent compensating balance, then it must borrow $100,000 to obtain a usable $80,000.

A line of credit is an agreement between a bank and a borrower indicating the maximum credit that the bank will extend to the borrower. For example, on December 31, a bank officer might indicate to the treasurer of a firm that the bank regards the firm as being "good" for up to $80,000 during the forthcoming year. If, on January 10, the treasurer signs a promissory note for $15,000 for ninety days, this would be called "taking down" $15,000 of the total line of credit. This amount would be credited to the firm's checking account at the bank, and before repayment of the $15,000, the firm could borrow an additional $65,000, or any smaller amounts, as long as the aggregate value of all borrowings did not exceed the $80,000 credit limit. Additionally, a line of credit may be issued for a specific period. Because of this, a company may have to "pull down" funds not necessarily needed at that point to maintain cash availability.

A revolving credit agreement is a formal line of credit often used by large firms. To illustrate, in 1991 Texas Petroleum Company negotiated a revolving credit agreement for $100 million with a group of banks. The banks were formally committed for four years to lend the firm up to $100 million if the funds were needed. Texas Petroleum, in turn, paid an annual commitment fee of .25 percent on the unused balance of the commitment to compensate the banks for making the commitment. Thus, if Texas Petroleum did not take down any of the $100 million commitment during any one year, it would still be required to pay the $250,000 annual fee, normally in monthly installments. If it borrowed $50 million on the first day of the agreement, the unused portion of the line of credit would fall to $50 million and the annual fee would fall to $125,000. Of course, interest would also have to be paid on the money Texas Petroleum actually borrowed. Generally, the rate of interest on "revolvers" is pegged to the prime rate, so the cost of the loan varies over time as the prime rate changes. In this case, the rate charged Texas Petroleum was prime plus 0.5 percent.

A revolving credit line is very similar to a regular line of credit. However, there is an important distinguishing feature. The bank has a legal obligation to honor a revolving credit agreement. For this guarantee, the bank receives a commitment fee. Neither the legal obligation nor the fee exists under the typical line of credit.

The Cost of Bank Loans

Interest rates are higher for risky borrowers, and rates are also higher on smaller loans because of the fixed costs involved in making and servicing loans. If a firm can qualify as a "prime credit" because of its size and financial strength, it can borrow at the prime rate. Traditionally, the prime rate is the lowest rate banks charged. Rates on other loans are generally scaled up from the prime rate.

Each bank sets its own prime rate, but because of competitive forces, prime rates of most banks are identical. Furthermore, most banks follow the rate set by the large New York City banks, who generally follow the rate set by Citibank, the largest bank in the United States. Citibank formally sets the prime rate each week at 1.25 to 1.5 percentage points above the average rate on certificates of deposit (CDs) during the previous three weeks. CD rates represent the "price" of money in the open market, and they rise and fall with the supply and demand of money. CD rates are "market clearing" rates. By tying the prime rate to CD rates, the banking system ensured that the prime rate would also clear the market. Clearing a market means that all demand for that good is satisfied and all supply of that good is used up "at the given price."

In recent years, the prime rate has been held relatively constant even during periods when open market rates were fluctuating. In addition, in recent years many banks have been lending to the very strongest companies at rates below the prime rate. This has occurred because the larger firms have ready access to the commercial paper markets. Use of commercial paper is a method of short-term fund-raising in which a firm sells unsecured notes for less than the set face value and then repurchases them at face value within 270 days or less. Commercial paper is unsecured, so only the more financially stable firms can sell it. It is a way for a firm to get short-term funds for less than bank rates. If banks want to do business with these larger companies, they must match or at least come close to the commercial paper rate. As competition in financial markets increases, as has been happening because of deregulation of banks and other financial institutions, "administered" rates such as the prime rate are giving way to flexible, negotiated rates based on market conditions.

The purchaser of commercial paper profits on the difference between the original price paid and the face value. Since most commercial paper comes due in thirty to ninety days, it is also an opportunity where the buyer can invest cash for short periods to earn interest. People who buy commercial paper are generally looking for a place to put their money for a short time without going through the hassle of dealing with banks.

Bank rates vary widely over time depending on economic conditions and Federal Reserve policy. When the economy is weak, then loan demand is usually slack, inflation is low, and the Fed makes plenty of money available to the system. Therefore, rates on all types of loans are relatively low. Conversely, when the economy is booming, loan demand is high, and the Fed restricts the money supply. This results in higher interest rates. As an indication of the kinds of fluctuations that can occur, the prime rate during 1980 rose from 11 to 21 percent in just four months. Interest rates on other bank loans also vary over time, generally moving with the prime rate.

Leasing

Firms generally own fixed assets and report them on their balance sheets, but it is the use of land, buildings, and equipment that is important, not ownership. One way of obtaining the use of assets is to buy them. An alternative is to lease them. Before 1950, leasing was generally associated with real estate. Today, however, it is possible to lease virtually any kind of fixed asset, and in 1991, about 25 percent of all new capital equipment acquired by businesses was leased.

Leasing takes three basic forms: sale and leaseback arrangements, operating leases, and straight financial or capital leases. We will discuss each type of lease, and then examine how Air Atlantis used each type during its growth.

Sale and Leaseback

Under a sale and leaseback arrangement, a firm that owns land, buildings, or equipment sells the property. It also executes an agreement to lease the property back for a specified period under specific terms. The purchaser of the property or equipment could be an insurance company, a commercial bank, a specialized leasing company, or a private investor. The sale and leaseback plan is an alternative to taking a mortgage loan against the property.

The firm that is selling the property, the lessee (seller), immediately receives the purchase price put up by the lessor (buyer). At the same time, the lessee retains the use of the property just as if it had borrowed and mortgaged the property to secure a loan. Note that under a mortgage loan arrangement, the financial institution would normally receive a series of equal payments sufficient to amortize the loan while providing a specified rate of return to the lender on the outstanding balance. Under a sale and leaseback arrangement, the lease payments are set up in exactly the same way: the payments are set so as to return the purchase price to the lessor while providing a specified rate of return on the lessor's outstanding investment.

Operating Leases

Operating leases, sometimes called service leases, provide for both financing and maintaining the leased equipment. IBM pioneered the use of operating lease contracts on computer systems. Now automobiles, office machines, and computers are the primary types of assets involved. Ordinarily, these leases call for the lessor to maintain and service the leased equipment, and the cost of providing maintenance services is built into the lease payment.

An important characteristic of operating leases is the fact that they are frequently not fully amortized. In other words, the payments required under the lease agreement are not sufficient to recover the full cost of the equipment. However, the lease contract is written for a period considerably shorter than the expected economic life of the equipment, and the lessor expects to recover all investment costs through subsequent renewal payments, through subsequent lease contracts with other lessors, or by selling the equipment outright.

A final feature of operating leases is that they frequently contain a cancellation clause, giving the lessee the right to cancel the lease before the expiration date of the basic agreement. This is an important consideration for the lessee. It means the equipment can be returned if it is rendered obsolete by technological developments or if it is no longer needed because of a decline in the lessee's business.

Financial or Capital Leases

Financial leases, sometimes called capital leases, are differentiated from operating leases in three respects: they do not provide maintenance services, they cannot be canceled, and they are fully amortized. This means the lessor receives rental payments that are equal to the cost of the equipment plus a return on the investment. In a typical financial lease arrangement, the firm that will use the equipment (the lessee) selects the equipment it requires and negotiates the price and delivery terms with the manufacturer. The user firm then negotiates terms with the leasing company and, once the lease terms are set, arranges to have the lessor buy the equipment from the manufacturer. When the equipment is purchased, the user firm simultaneously executes the lease agreement. Financial leases are similar to sale and leaseback arrangements. The major difference is that the leased equipment is brand-new and the lessor buys it from a manufacturer, not from the lessee.

Air Atlantis used these three types of leases to achieve some of its growth objectives. When AirA issued its first stock offering and raised its initial capital of $2 million, all it had was a plan, no aircraft. The management team wisely decided to lease the company's first aircraft and conserve capital instead of purchasing. The question was which kind of lease would best serve the company's interests.

With no maintenance facilities of its own, it was obvious that AirA would need to establish some kind of arrangement to take care of all maintenance needs on whatever aircraft it acquired, no matter how they were acquired. The answer presented itself in an operating lease agreement with a major carrier that had excess aircraft. Therefore, AirA entered an operating lease agreement for two aircraft. AirA would crew and fuel the aircraft, and the major carrier would perform all maintenance work needed, both scheduled and unscheduled. The terms of the lease were set such that AirA would make monthly lease payments for a period of three years. Also, AirA could purchase the aircraft outright at an agreed price any time within the three-year contract, and the leases could be canceled with a small penalty if AirA were unable to continue the arrangement. This agreement gave AirA the use of two aircraft without consuming a large chunk of their small capital pool; it also allowed the company to spend capital on business development, not on equipment acquisition.

Several years later, AirA found itself owning seven aircraft and in need of cash to expand operations. The management and board did not feel the timing was good to float another stock or bond issue. The company was not yet strong enough to get a long-term bank loan on favorable terms. What to do?

Management decided to sell all seven aircraft to a commercial bank that had expressed an interest in generating leasing revenue. Therefore, AirA sold the seven aircraft to the bank for $3 million. This money was immediately put to work expanding and improving AirA's gates, reservation system, and maintenance facilities. They also simultaneously executed a leaseback agreement with the bank, agreeing to pay monthly lease payments that would, over the six years of the lease agreement, provide the bank with their full purchase price and an acceptable rate of return on their $3 million investment in the aircraft. AirA continued to operate the aircraft in revenue service.

Air Atlantis grew, but somewhat haphazardly, and several years later it was operating five types of aircraft, some owned, some leased, and some acquired in the course of purchasing other carriers. The cost of stocking five sets of maintenance spares, the necessity of training multiple crews, and the lack of a unified marketing appearance were eating away at earnings. Something had to be done, or the airline would soon be at a serious cost disadvantage.

AirA management began assessing all available new aircraft that could operate profitably on its routes. It began discussions with RWK Inc., one of the world's largest aircraft leasing organizations. Management's goal was to identify an aircraft that would fit into the existing route structure and still be able to support the ongoing expansion program. Although the company was in a strong financial position, its investment bankers and commercial bankers felt that the company's long-term picture would look better if it leased rather than purchased aircraft.

After careful consideration, AirA selected the Canadair RJ50 and began to negotiate specifications, price, and delivery terms. They also began negotiations with RWK to set the terms of a financial lease agreement that would cover all fifteen aircraft. Management also began discussions about selling all of its existing aircraft to a South American carrier that was looking to expand operations.

Several months later, all the pieces locked into place. Canadair agreed to sell the fifteen aircraft and provide spares and maintenance training support on terms acceptable to Air Atlantis ($10 million apiece, or $150 million). The team of analysts from RWK had verified the financial condition of AirA and agreed to set the lease agreement on terms acceptable to both parties, a fifteen-year lease at $70,000 per month per aircraft. A South American carrier agreed to purchase all five aircraft types, thirteen aircraft, and all maintenance spares from AirA for $7 million.

AirA ended up with a fleet of fifteen brand-new aircraft, $7 million in cash, and a monthly lease payment of $1,050,000 with virtually no expenditure of capital reserves or dilution of shareholder value. With the monthly cash flow generated by existing levels of revenue traffic, AirA would have little difficulty in meeting its monthly lease obligations. With the new aircraft integrated into its route system and with its maintenance costs now in line, AirA was ready for the big time.

Air Atlantis later floated a bond issue of $50 million, purchased outright five more Canadair RJs, and entered operating leases on four more. However, there was one major problem: depreciation write-offs. Air Atlantis did not have many write-offs. It did not own the aircraft and was therefore not entitled to the deduction. Consequently, as its revenue stream grew, so did its tax liability. It was generating enormous revenues, but net earnings per share were low. Now what to do?

A stock issue? Bonds? A syndicated long-term loan from a group of bankers? The board decided that both a stock issue and a bond float were in order. The stockholders were consulted at the annual meeting. Several stated concern about diluting the stock and the wisdom of long-term debt. The chairman responded by indicating that with the debt and depreciation deductions generated by owning rather than leasing some of its aircraft, the net earning per share might actually go up. This, of course, assumed revenues would continue to grow. The matter was brought to a vote, and the motion carried.

Air Atlantis, through its investment banker, floated a $100 million bond issue and offered 500,000 new shares of stock. The existing shareholders purchased 350,000 of the new shares at $12.50 per share, and the rest were sold in the open market at $15 per share. Air Atlantis raised a total of $106,625,000, bought ten more RJs for cash, and used the $6 million remaining to again expand city pairs served.

The preceding examples give a good understanding of the techniques available that business in general, and the airlines specifically, can use to achieve growth and maximize shareholder value. Bonds remain the principal source of new financing for all business, and leases now make up 30–40 percent of all new aircraft acquisitions. Leasing allows an airline to upgrade equipment and service without using up capital reserves. There are, however, several accounting regulations that have made leases more complex than in past years, but again, due to the limited scope of this book, it is not possible to examine these regulations in any depth.

Most of us will never achieve the size of an Air Atlantis when we process our original ideas about going into business. In addition, unless we start our business as a corporation or a sub-S corporation, we may never involve ourselves in some of the intricacies that Air Atlantis experienced. Instead, almost 90 percent of businesses in the United States start out as an idea and become a sole proprietorship. As with any good idea, the idea alone generally will not sustain life. It needs nourishment and help to achieve its full potential.

Some are fortunate to have enough money to do just about anything they so desire, but most must seek out sources of capital to develop the idea, and thus the arduous process of capital development begins. An entrepreneur should carefully calculate and schedule, in as much detail as possible, the income and expenses that can be expected in the first two years of operation.

Methods and Requirements for Raising Business Capital

The amount of capital needed to fund a business should be determined early. The question of how much money will be required should be answered in the "financial plan" section of the business plan. If the business idea is sound and the owner has an established managerial track record and some collateral, the business should have an excellent chance of obtaining start-up capital. In some cases, although slight, credit may be secured even without collateral. Remember that all the people and institutions you may approach for loans want to lend you money if you measure up to their standards. Lending may be the major, or even sole, way they make profits. They look on you, the potential borrower, as a possible source of income. Be aware that professional lenders, in general, are very sharp. They know what their requirements are, and they know whether you meet them. If you meet the requirements, you will get the money. If you do not, try somewhere else.

That does not mean the financing comes without effort. A borrower needs to do a lot of planning, learn about the kind of lenders that might be right, and determine how to approach and present loan proposals. Lenders' requirements may involve personal credit record, type of business, region, prospects for success, potential cash flow, and collateral.

Risk and Reward

One good thing to do at an early stage is to assess the risk that the proposed company poses for a lender. The amount of risk determines not only the likelihood of obtaining a loan but also how much interest will be required. The cost of money depends on risk. If an entrepreneur applies for a loan merely on the strength of his/her ability to make a company succeed, they represent a very high risk for the lender and will undoubtedly pay a high interest rate. On the other hand, some form of collateral lowers the risk coefficient to the lender.

All money sources seek a return on investment in relation to the risk taken. Risk in a financial sense can be divided into two components:

- Liquidity, the ease with which assets can be collected and converted into cash. (Of course, it may already be cash, in which case the liquidity is absolute.)
- Security, the protection required by the lender or investor to ensure that the borrowed money will be returned (or obtained indirectly through sale of an item of collateral). Security may be in the form of a specific lien against a piece of property or any of a number of items of value pledged to the lender in case of default.

Business Plan

An entrepreneur may be able to finance a new business venture, alone or by borrowing from some relative, in which case there is no need to prepare an elaborate loan proposal. On the other hand, chances are good that money will be needed from an outside lender, either at the outset or later, after the company is up and running. In either event, it is a good idea to proceed at this point as if money were going to be required from an institution. The reason is that formal preparation will force a thorough thought process concerning all aspects of the business idea. It brings the entrepreneur down from the clouds and introduces the element of hard reality.

Start-up Money

The small entrepreneur can obtain capital in various ways. Here are some of the most obvious sources:

Yourself. Anyone desiring to start a business must have money. If the planned operation is modest enough, the entrepreneur may be able to supply all the capital. The owner funds about 48 percent of small start-up businesses. However, even if the individual can provide all the money, it is probably a good idea to borrow. For one thing, you do not want to tie up too much of your own funds, and for another, it is good to get experience handling borrowed money. When you borrow money for business reasons, you will almost necessarily have to put up some amount, if for no other reason than that lenders will expect you to do so. If there is insufficient collateral offered as security for a loan, the lenders' main protection against default is the entrepreneur's competence and desire to run the company efficiently. Lenders will therefore expect the borrower to be totally committed to the company. If the venture fails, the entrepreneur loses his/her investment and personal assets before the creditors lose their money. What do you have to offer a lender? The following are looked upon as collateral items. Different types of loans may be secured based on their value.

- Real estate. You can borrow up to 75 percent of its value minus any mortgages.

- Stocks and bonds.
- Late-model automobile (not carrying too much debt).
- Collectibles, such as art, rare coins, and antiques.
- Life insurance policy that has cash value. You can borrow up to 95 percent of its worth, and the interest rate on the cash value is significantly lower than other forms of debt. This is true because the cash value is in effect money that you owe to yourself. Cash value in an insurance policy may be the first place to look for low-interest debt.
- Good credit with a particular bank. On the strength of it, you might get a personal loan. (Establishing that credit is a good reason to borrow and pay back money before you need it.)
- Money in a savings account of the bank you are borrowing from. (It doesn't have to equal the amount borrowed.) You agree not to withdraw it during the term of the loan. The account continues to draw interest, reducing the cost of the loan.
- Cosigner. A wealthy person with an outstanding credit rating can cosign your loan, agreeing to be liable if you default.
- Equity in your business. This is what you offer a venture capitalist.

Friends and relatives. About 13 percent of entrepreneurs obtain start-up capital from friends and relatives. By all means, borrow from people you know. Avoid hassles and misunderstandings by having everything in writing. A written agreement should spell out the amount and date of the loan, the date it will be paid back, the amount of interest, and whether the lender is to play any role in operating the business.

Working partner. One solution to money problems is to take on a working partner who makes an investment and helps run the company. The capital and skills of two people are combined. In an ideal arrangement, the partners' qualities complement each other. One formula teams a money person with someone with expertise in the type of business. Another good combination is one person with administrative skill and the other with operational expertise.

Commercial banks. Any new business is apt to require the services of a commercial bank. There are more than 14,000 banks in the United States, and small businesses rely heavily on them for both short-term and long-term lending.

Banks generally are not crazy about lending to proposed companies. They will do it, but it is up to the borrower to convince them that their money will be safe and that it will be repaid on time and with interest. In most cases, to obtain a bank loan requires collateral, such as real estate or equipment.

Advantages of borrowing from banks:

- They are usually the cheapest source of private funds available.
- In addition to loans, banks offer such services as leasing, financial counseling, tax planning and preparation, investment services, cash management, collections, and credit checks of customers.
- Once a bank lends money, it will pitch in and help to ensure that default does not occur.
- Lots of information is available on banks (their financial condition, which banks lend to which kinds of businesses, etc.).

Disadvantages of borrowing from banks:

- Banks are cautious and conservative; they will insist on collateral (with exceptions we will mention) and will want something close to certainty that the loan will be repaid.
- Banks do regularly turn down loan applicants from smaller firms for reasons that may seem incomprehensible.
- They are under government regulations that hamper the amount and kind of lending in which they can engage.
- While "helping" the client after making the loan, bankers may breathe down your neck, trying to influence decisions, keeping track of everything you do, and recording every check you write.

International (Schedule B) banks. A number of international banks operate in the United States through state-chartered subsidiaries, branches, agencies, and representative offices. They operate just like any other state-chartered bank, offering a full range of services from commercial loans to real estate financing. Other operations are more limited but strive to provide financial links, including import/export financing.

If a small business tends to deal with a particular country, some benefits may be gained by doing business with banks that have roots in particular regions. They usually know their country well, can provide economic updates and other information, can extend business introductions, and can generally pave the way for a small firm to improve its business. Activity focuses on import/export financing and letters of credit.

International banks generally concentrate on commercial rather than consumer banking and therefore have increased competitiveness in the commercial loan market. Most, however, operate in a "middle market," between small-business loans and corporate financing.

By far the most useful part of dealing with an international bank is its knowledge of overseas conditions. It can supply contacts and names of suppliers, customers, and agency representatives. Similar information is also available through some state agencies and the Commerce Department or its regional offices.

In applying for a business loan from an international bank, handle the presentation as you would for any other bank (but, of course, emphasize the international dealings you plan).

Small Business Administration

If you need to borrow money for the business and cannot obtain regular bank financing, do not overlook the possibility of obtaining a loan through the federal Small Business Administration (SBA). Congress set up the SBA in 1953 to help small businesspeople get financing when they cannot get it by any other means. The agency guarantees loans, participates in loans with private lenders, and makes loans itself.

The SBA will not consider you for a loan or a loan guarantee if you can obtain funds from other sources, including banks. Before the agency will consider (but not necessarily grant) a loan or guarantee, you must have been turned down by at least one bank (or two banks in a city with a population above 200,000).

While many small business owners believe it is virtually impossible to obtain an SBA loan unless you are a member of a minority group, this is not the case. Although the SBA does make special efforts to provide financing for minority-owned businesses, only a relatively small percentage of SBA loans are made to solely minority firms. Furthermore, a very high percentage of applications for SBA loans are approved when applications are properly submitted.

SBA loan programs. The SBA guarantees intermediate and long-term loans to small firms and makes direct loans to some small businesses. The SBA is not allowed to grant such financial assistance unless the borrower is unable to obtain private sector financing on reasonable terms. The SBA does not compete with banks or other lenders. Instead, it works with private lenders to ensure availability of capital to potentially profitable small firms.

To qualify for SBA financial assistance, a firm must come within the current definition of a "small business." In general, small businesses eligible for SBA financing include the following:

- Manufacturers with a maximum of between 250 and 1,500 employees, depending on the industry in which the applicant is engaged.
- Retailers (including aviation) with less than $2 million in annual sales (up to $7.5 million for some types of retailers).
- Service firms (which include aviation) with annual receipts of not more than $2 million to $8 million, depending on the industry.

Other definitions apply for businesses engaged in activities such as transportation.

Private lenders that are eligible to make SBA-guaranteed loans or participate in SBA financing packages include banks, savings and loans, small business investment companies (SBICs), and minority enterprise small business investment companies (MESBICs). SBA loan programs include the following:

Guaranteed loans. Most SBA financing actually consists of loans by banks or other lenders that are guaranteed by the SBA, which enables the small business to obtain such loans at reasonable interest rates, since the bank's risk is largely eliminated. Such guarantees are limited to 90 percent of the loan or $500,000, whichever is less, and the borrower must put up a reasonable amount of equity. These loans are usually secured by fixed assets, real estate, and inventory and are limited in term to seven years for "working capital" loans or ten years for purchasing fixed assets. Construction loans can be obtained for up to twenty-five years in duration.

Under this program, the bank or the private lender deals with the SBA. The borrower deals directly with the bank or the lender, not with the SBA. The borrower's involvement with the SBA will consist of the following:

- Define the amount of money needed and the purposes for which the funds will be used. (A well-prepared business plan is very beneficial in this instance.)
- Describe the collateral that will be offered as security.
- Determination from a bank that a conventional loan is not available.
- Preparation of current financial statements. These would include, at a minimum, a relatively current balance sheet and an income statement for the previous full year and for the current year up to the date of the balance sheet. If the business is a new venture, it would need a well-prepared business plan with a five-year plan of financial statements.
- Preparation of personal financial statements for the owners, partners, or stockholders owning over 20 percent of the stock of the company.

Direct loans. If unable to obtain sufficient conventional financing or SBA guaranteed loan funds, a borrower may be able to obtain a direct loan from the SBA for up to $150,000. However, these direct loans are difficult to obtain and can only be made if the SBA has funds available. In recent years, the funds available for lending by the SBA have been limited so that eligible borrowers are frequently turned away. When made, these loans are usually made on a participation basis with a bank or other lender, where the bank oversees the loan payments and loan servicing on behalf of itself and the SBA.

Other SBA programs. New legislation frequently adds to and modifies the number and scope of SBA loan programs. Such other programs include seasonal lines of credit, economic opportunity loans for entrepreneurs who are physically handicapped or members of a minority group, short-term contract loan guarantees, energy loans to small firms to install, sell, service, develop, or manufacture solar energy or energy-saving devices, and disaster recovery loans to firms harmed by natural disasters. Since the nature, scope, and availability of funds under these programs are constantly changing, a bank or local SBA offices should be consulted concerning availability.

- Small business investment companies (SBIC), actually venture capitalists, are licensed by the SBA and provide loan capital or risk investments to small businesses.
- Small Business Innovation Research (SBIR), under SBA supervision, provides grant programs (as opposed to loans), which have to be repaid.
- The Service Corps of Retired Executives (SCORE), a private group with chapters around the United States, provides free counseling and advice to small businesses. Among other things, the group will help you organize and write your business plan at no cost. A separate telephone for SCORE is listed under SBA in cities where a chapter operates. Otherwise, to locate the nearest SCORE office, call the SBA answer desk.
- Procurement center representatives (PCR) aid small firms in landing government supply contracts. They help prepare bids for federal contracts and assist in attaining "certification of competency."
- Small business development centers (SBDC) are based at about four dozen universities, where they link resources of local, state, and federal government programs, university facilities, and the private sector. They provide research and other assistance for small businesses.
- The Small Business Institute (SBI), with branches at more than five hundred American colleges, consists of senior and graduate students plus faculty advisers at schools of business administration. They offer advice and management counseling.
- Business development corporations. These are local development companies (SBA sec. 502) and certified development companies (SBA sec. 503) organized by local residents to promote economic development in their particular communities. These entities do not make working capital loans or loans to purchase free-standing equipment. Instead, they will arrange for SBA-guaranteed bank loans and the sale of SBA-guaranteed debentures for up to 90 percent financing for twenty-five years for land acquisition and purchase of fixed assets such as machinery and equipment.

The SBA's headquarters are in Washington, D.C. It has ten regional offices and about a hundred district, branch, and post-of-duty offices in all fifty states, the District of Columbia, Guam, Puerto Rico, and the Virgin Islands. If a city has an office, it is listed in the telephone book under U.S. Government. If not, they can be reached toll-free at 1-800-827-5722. (Inside the District of Columbia, the telephone number is 205-7715.) The SBA information desk at that number can answer your questions not only about financial help but also on subjects ranging from how to bid on government contracts to how to qualify for state-sponsored small business programs.

Other Government Loan Programs

U.S. Department of Housing and Urban Development. This government agency makes urban development action grants (UDAG) to cities in economically distressed areas. The cities are then able to use these funds to make second-mortgage loans to private developers who are able to leverage these loans by borrowing at least five times such amounts from private sources. The purpose of such loans is to encourage new investment and development in depressed areas.

U.S. Commerce Department. The Economic Development Administration (EDA) of the Commerce Department makes direct loans and offers loan guarantees to businesses in areas with low family incomes or high unemployment, to promote creation or retention of jobs for residents of such areas. To qualify for such financing, a business must be located in an EDA redevelopment area, and the business will directly benefit local residents and not create overcapacity for the industry in question.

Farmers Home Administration (FmHA). The FmHA can be considered an SBA for rural areas. It offers insured and guaranteed loans to develop business and industry in nonurban areas with populations under 50,000. Like the SBA program, the FmHA guarantees up to 90 percent of the total loan and allows up to thirty years for financing real estate acquisition, fifteen years for machinery and equipment, and seven years for working capital. FmHA loan guarantees are not available for agricultural production.

Unlike SBA loan guarantees, there is no dollar limit on FmHA loan guarantees, nor does the FmHA make direct loans. Applicants for FmHA loan guarantees not only must have adequate collateral and good business histories but also must demonstrate that the project will have a favorable economic impact and will create new jobs in the area. Preference is given to business expansions, to projects in open country areas or towns of under 25,000, and to business owners who are military veterans.

Small business investment companies (SBICs) and minority enterprise small business investment companies (MESBICs). SBICs and MESBICs are licensed and regulated by the SBA to provide equity capital, long-term loans, and management assistance to small business. Loans made by these enterprises usually are subordinated to loans from other creditors and are made for five- to seven-year terms. Both types of investment companies are privately owned and thus tend to favor loans to established companies with significant new worth rather than net business start-ups.

State business loan programs. In addition to federal loan programs, each state generally has several small business and business development loan programs.

Credit Unions

Credit unions were established to help people save and to make loans to members at low interest rates. Nowadays they are looking for other kinds of investments, such as loans to start-up companies, where they can realize higher rates of return. They are restricted in how big a loan they can make, but they could be the answer for a small business.

Individual credit unions normally are small, but they know the area and economic conditions well. For this reason they will sometimes take risks or provide loans where other local institutions would not. They are usually run by local businesspersons. Generally, you must be a member of a credit union to qualify, although in some credit unions qualification requirements are not stringent and sometimes are nonexistent. Where there are qualifications for membership, they are not always related to place of employment, but may be based on religious, community, or ethnic considerations. It may well be worth joining a credit union just to obtain a needed loan.

Venture Capitalists

If starting an exciting company that has the potential for fast growth, you might get funding from a venture-capital firm. Venture capitalists are institutional risk takers/gamblers. Venture capitalists scan the horizon for prospects that indicate a huge (40–60 percent) annualized rate of return on investments, and they seek minority positions, often including a seat on the board. If you go after venture capital, make sure your business plan is professionally and concisely written. It probably should be briefer than one you would submit to a bank (say, ten to forty pages).

If you receive funding from a venture capital firm, the arrangements will be very different from those you would expect with a bank. Instead of lending X number of dollars to be repaid in installments at specified times, the venture capitalist will provide seed money for start-up. In return, it will want a share of ownership of the company. The amount of ownership demanded will depend on the percentage of total funding being provided by the venture capitalist and by the amount of risk. A seat on the company board is almost always demanded. This has a positive and a negative side. It will provide a knowledgeable, proven individual to help run the company. On the other hand, there is a loss of independence (which may have been one of the goals in starting the business).

Experienced investors who are familiar with financial markets operate most venture capital companies. They can help in dealing with the bank and with other sources of capital. They also usually have a wide range of contacts and can help in arranging a public issue of stock, in buying or merging with other companies, and in arranging eventual sellouts.

Many venture capitalists focus on high-tech companies. Industry preferences include communications, computers, and related fields, electronic components, genetic engineering, medical/health, and robotics. Among top venture capital firms, minimum amounts invested range from $100,000 to $500,000.

As indicated in chapter 2, you can find venture capitalists via the World Wide Web. Consult *Preztt's Guide to Venture Capital Sources* for a list of nine hundred, including their addresses, phone numbers, fields of interest, and the amounts they like to invest. For other information, contact the National Venture Capital Association, 1655 North Fort Myer Drive, Suite 700, Arlington, VA 22209.

Venture Capital Clubs

If you think your operation may be too small to interest a venture capitalist, but you think it might appeal to one for other reasons, look into venture capital clubs. They have been growing for over a decade, and there are at least two hundred in the United States. Their purpose is to bring together investors, entrepreneurs, consultants, and professional-service providers. These clubs are looking for all kinds of companies, including small start-up ones, to finance.

These organizations can be obtained from the *Directory of Venture Networking Groups and Other Resources,* published by the International Venture Capital Institute, P.O. Box 1333, Stamford, CT 06904.

State Venture Capital Funds

A relatively new source of money for small businesses comes from state venture capital funds, now available in about half the states. Requirements vary. Some provide equity capital. Most offer loans. Some focus on specific areas. Contact state or local chambers of commerce and state industrial development offices for program availability.

Insurance Companies

Some major insurance companies are becoming key sources of venture capital for buildings and equipment. Managers of venture capital units, enjoying autonomy from parent companies, make their own investment decisions and, like venture capitalists, share in the profits. Among insurance companies with venture capital investments are Prudential Insurance Companies of America, John Hancock, Travelers, and Allstate.

Home Equity Loans

If unable to get a start-up loan for a business, you may be able to obtain the money you need through a home equity loan. This is becoming the fastest growing financial product in the United States. It turns every home into an instant bank, ready to be tapped for cash, including funds for developing small businesses. Loans are made primarily through commercial banks or savings and loan associations (or savings banks). Total amounts that can be borrowed depend on equity in a home. Lending institutions generally will lend between 60 and 80 percent of a home's appraised value, minus existing mortgages.

Of course, with a home equity loan, the bank need know nothing about the new business. It is lending money with someone's home as collateral. There is a major drawback with such a loan: the bank or lending institution now holds a lien on the house. Do not take these loans lightly. Loss of a home could follow failure to repay loan amounts.

Credit Cards

Many start-ups have been financed by maximizing out two credit cards, which could yield $10,000 or even more, depending on the person's credit record. It is true that you pay a high rate of interest when you do this, but you are allowed thirty-six months to pay the money back. This action should probably be considered the court of last resort. It is, however, a standard borrowing ground for many entrepreneurs.

Thrifts

Savings and loan associations, despite the scandals and collapses of recent years, are still around. Many of these thrifts today are called mutual savings banks. S&Ls traditionally have been the prime sources of mortgage funds.

Commercial Loan Companies

At some point you may decide to turn to a commercial loan (or finance) company. Generally, it is willing to take more risk than a bank. Because of that, it charges significantly higher interest rates than most lending institutions. It still requires hard assets, but will often make a loan that a bank would not touch.

If you cannot get your start-up money any other way and you are still determined to own your own business, the commercial loan company may be your only choice. However, consider it one of your last resorts.

Summary

There is a lot of money circulating out there, and a deserving businessperson should be able to get money to start a business. As with any constructive venture or engagement, positive groundwork must be laid. In such cases, the best offense is a good defense. When the time comes, preparation is incumbent upon the borrower. Knowledge of everything indigenous to the business and about the potential creditor is an absolute necessity. With traditional bankers, stress the security of the loan and the ability to repay it. In the case of government agencies, stress the good that the business will accomplish for society at large, the cost-benefit aspects of a loan, and the economic and social effects. With a venture capitalist, stress profitability and the return on investment to the lender/investor.

Suggested Readings and References

Altman, E. I. (1989). *Default risk, mortality rates, and the performance of corporate bonds.* Charlottesville, VA: Research Foundation of the Institute of Chartered Financial Analysts.

Financial Accounting Standards Board. (1979). *Accounting for sales with leasebacks.* Stamford, CT: Author.

Fischer, T. G., Gram, W. H., Kaufman, G. G., & Mote, L. R. (1985). *The securities of commercial banks: A legal and economic analysis.* Chicago: Federal Reserve Bank of Chicago.

Greenwich Research Associates. (1986). *Commercial banking.* Greenwich, CT: Author.

Harris, J. G. (1983). *Accounting for leases.* Melbourne: Australian Accounting Research Foundation.

Moss, B. (1989). *The benefits and risks of asset securitization for commercial banks.* Richmond, VA: Federal Reserve Bank of Richmond.

Murphy, J. E. (1990). *The random character of interest rates: Applying statistical probability to the bond markets.* New York: McGraw-Hill.

National Association Insurance Commissioners. (1992). *Insurer's medium and lower quality bond investments.* Kansas City, MO: Author.

Pierce, P. S. (1990). *The Dow Jones investor's handbook.* Homewood, IL: Dow Jones–Irwin.

Robert Morris Associates. (1988). *Lender liability: A special collection from the* Journal of Commercial Bank Lending. Philadelphia: Author.

Shiller, R. J. (1989). *Market volatility.* Cambridge, MA: MIT Press.

Standard and Poor's Corporation. (1984). *Standard & Poor's credit overview international.* New York: Author.

Stephens, R. G. (1980). *Uses of financial information in bank lending decisions.* Ann Arbor, MI: UMI Research Press.

U.S. Securities and Exchange Commission, Division of Market Regulation. *The corporate bond markets: Structure, pricing, and trading.* Washington: Author.

Wainman, P. D. (1991). *Leasing.* London: Waterlow.

Wurman, R. S., Siegel, A., & Morris, K. M. (1990). *The Wall Street Journal guide to understanding money and markets.* New York: Access Press.

6

FINANCIAL STATEMENTS

The analysis of annual and quarterly financial statements of corporations serves two basic purposes. First, these reports are the measure of achievements of the firm's management plan in a given period. Quarterly and annual reports can be used to validate and/or correct management activity and corporate direction. The second purpose is externally focused. Quarterly and annual reports, as well as Securities and Exchange Commission form SEC 10K, are the key analytical tools in determining the investment quality of a firm's stocks and bonds. The annual report of our fictitious airline, Air Atlantis, is the case study for this chapter.

Annual Report Layout

Most annual reports have prose, pictures, graphs, and financial charts. The prose is generally straightforward and understandable. The first item in most annual reports is a summary of the year just ended and an overview of the plans and goals for the coming year. This summary is usually written by the chairman and president or chief executive officer and represents the strategic picture of the corporation. The next section of the typical annual report contains descriptions of the operations conducted by the various regions, divisions, subsidiaries, and holdings of the corporation. These sections are primarily prose but with much greater financial detail and graphic support than the chairman's summary.

The last section of a typical annual report contains the statements of consolidated operations, consolidated financial conditions, cash flows, common shareholders' equity, and endnotes or footnotes. These financial position charts and footnotes represent the legally required and audit-certified results of all operations of the firm in the year ended. The footnotes are very detailed explanations of specific entries in the financial charts and contain essential information for correctly interpreting the charts.

Figure 6-3 consists of the financial charts of Air Atlantis. These charts are typical of many annual reports in that they contain a statement of consolidated operations, financial highlights and operating statistics, a balance sheet, also known as the statement of consolidated financial position, and a cash flow chart. Augmenting each of these statements is an explanation of their containments.

The Balance Sheet

A business is always in a condition of equality: what it owns equals what it owes to either its creditors or its owners, thus the familiar equation mentioned in chapter 1:

Assets = Liabilities + Owner's Equity

Assets are those resources that the business owns. Liabilities are obligations owed by the business to persons other than its owners. Owner's equity is what the business owes the owners. The balance sheet shows all of these elements at the last day of an accounting period.

Air Atlantis's balance sheet represents the financial picture as it stood on December 31, 1997, as though the activity of the company were momentarily halted. Air Atlantis's balance sheet includes not only 1997 financial performance but 1996 performance as well. This permits the reader to compare how the company fared in its last two years.

The balance sheet is divided into two primary parts: the first assets, the second liabilities and stockholder equity. Both sides of the balance sheet, as indicated in chapter 1, must always be in balance. On the asset page are listed all the property and equipment owned by Air Atlantis as well as any claims against others that remain to be collected. On the liabilities and shareholder equity sheet are listed all the firm's debts and the amount the stockholders hold in equity. Essentially and theoretically, this is the value the shareholders would receive if Air Atlantis were liquidated at its balance sheet value.

Assume that Air Atlantis goes out of business on the date of the balance sheet. Assume also that the assets, when sold, bring exactly what is shown in the balance sheet. (This will never happen!) If that occurs, the common shareholders of Air Atlantis would expect to divide the amount shown in the following chart.

Total assets (less amortized intangibles)	$987,625,000
Amount required to pay all liabilities	
(includes preferred stockholders)	$827,946,000
Common stockholder distributions	$159,679,000

In the sections that follow, we will examine each category appearing in the balance sheet and determine where the numbers come from and what they mean.

Asset Sheet

Current Assets

Some assets are of greater utility than others are. Financial analysts recognize this greater utility, and a special category of assets, called current assets, has been established for inclusion in the balance sheet. Current assets include cash and other assets that can reasonably be expected to be converted to cash or sold or consumed in the near future through the normal operation of the business.

Cash

This is just what you would expect—bills and silver coin in petty cash and funds in demand deposit (checking) accounts at the firm's bank. Air Atlantis has $44,900,000 in cash and equivalents available.

Short-Term Investments

This asset category represents temporary investments of excess cash that is not needed immediately. It is usually invested in T-bills and commercial paper. Because these funds may be needed on short notice, it is essential that these securities be readily marketable and subject to minimal price fluctuation. The accepted method of reporting these investment values is to list them at cost, not current value. Air Atlantis has $72,744,000 in short-term investments.

Accounts Receivables (A/R)

Here we find money owed to the firm but not yet received. The figures listed by Air Atlantis for receivables are $91,218,000, but the actual amount due to Air Atlantis is more than this. The reason the receivable category appears understated is due to the historical experience of not being able to collect all money owed. Firms that owe funds may go bankrupt or suffer other *force majeure* incidences and be unable to pay. Consequently, all firms reduce their actual receivables by making an allowance for bad debts or doubtful collections. In Air Atlantis's case, management believes uncollectable funds will total $1,308,000 for 1998. Uncollected funds totaled $1,312,000 in 1998.

Aircraft Fuel, Spare Parts, and Supplies

This asset category reports the current value of all aircraft fuel in the airline's tank farms, the value of all spare parts, tooling used to maintain aircraft, ground service equipment, and the value of all general supplies of the firm. However, because of production changes or technological improvements, a credit for obsolescence is taken against the value of these items. Air Atlantis reported $91,218,000 in fuel, parts, and supplies with an obsolescence allowance of $6,730,000 for 1998. The obsolescence allowance for 1997 was $5,740,000.

Refundable Income Taxes

Air Atlantis expects to get a refund of $16,693,000 from the IRS this year. This represents overpayments of estimated taxes and appears as an asset because it is cash back into the business.

Prepaid Expenses

Air Atlantis has already paid for some services, and if it were liquidated, these funds would be counted as assets and returned to the company. Items in this category can include property insurance, building rents, and service contracts on things like personal computers and copiers. Air Atlantis has prepaid $29,013,000 in 1998.

Total Current Assets

The value of all of the current assets of Air Atlantis for the year ended December 31, 1998, are $288,186,000. The assets are working assets in the sense that they are in a constant cycle of being converted into cash and used to pay debts and running expenses.

Operating Property and Equipment

The next items, operating property and equipment, are also known as fixed assets. They represent those assets not intended for sale, which are used over and over to produce the goods sold to the customers, in our case, a seat departure. Accordingly, this category will include aircraft, maintenance base facilities, terminal facilities and headquarters, and reservation buildings. The generally accepted and approved method for valuation of these assets is cost minus the depreciation, discussed in the next section, accumulated by the date of the balance sheet. Also included in this category are aircraft and other fixed assets under capital lease to Air Atlantis. When an item is under capital lease, there is no depreciation credit. Instead, the firm takes a credit for accumulated amortization that represents the accrued equity paid into the leases by the firm. The booked values of Air Atlantis's own fixed assets are $940,146,000. The booked value of equipment under capital leases to Air Atlantis is $78,265,000.

These figures do not reflect the present market value or replacement cost of those items in the future. While it is recognized that the cost to replace plant and equipment at some future date may be higher, that cost is variable. For this reason most firms have followed the general rule of acquisition cost less the accumulated depreciation based on that booked cost.

Depreciation and Amortization

Depreciation has been defined, for accounting purposes, as the decline in useful value of a fixed asset due to wear and tear from normal use and the passage of time. Fixed assets may also suffer a decline in useful value from obsolescence or technological innovation that renders the asset noncompetitive or out of date. For tax purposes, any asset, except land, used for the purpose of generating revenue may be depreciated.

The cost incurred to acquire the property and equipment must be spread out over its expected useful life, while taking into consideration the factors mentioned above. There are four basic methods for calculating depreciation, each providing the business with a different set of benefits. These methodologies are straight-line depreciation, units-of-production depreciation, and two accelerated methods called sum-of-the-years-digits and double-declining-balance depreciation.

Straight-line depreciation is generally the easiest method to figure. As the name implies, it is simply writing off a depreciated amount at an even rate over a selected number of years. Therefore, if a depreciable amount of $100,000 were to be written off over twenty years, each year would have a deduction amount of $5,000.

Units-of-production depreciation, like the straight-line method, is based on some predetermined criteria for reduction. In the case of straight-line depreciation, that criterion is years of service. In units of production, the depreciable balance is simply allocated according to the number of units the capital asset is expected to produce. In the airline industry, that measure may be revenue passenger miles (RPMs) or available seat miles (ASMs). For a fixed base operator (FBO), that measure may be the number of aircraft painted or students receiving instruction.

The remaining depreciation methods are forms of accelerated depreciation. Under sum-of-the-digits method, the numbers of years of depreciation are summed. Should the number of years of depreciation be twenty, a sum of the total years would be made. For example, the sum for twenty years would be two hundred and ten, figured by totaling the sum of each year $(1 + 2 + 3 + 4 + 5 + 6 + \ldots 20 = 210)$. The depreciable balance of the asset is then figured by establishing a series of depreciation fractions that have the sum of the year's digits as their denominator and the depreciation year as the numerator. For example, the $100,000 of depreciation used in the straight-line method would be reduced to $20/210$ for the first year, $19/210$ for the second, $18/210$ the third, down to $1/210$ for the twentieth and final year of depreciation. The first year's depreciation under this accelerated method would provide a greater write-off when the item is newer and more costly.

The fourth most commonly used procedure of depreciation is the double-declining-balance method. Under this method, a firm may write off up to double the straight-line depreciation rate. This methodology permits a company to accelerate its depreciable amounts at a far more rapid pace than any of the other methods. The depreciation rate allowed is applied to the declining balance of the cost of the asset rather than the depreciable balance. The firm, however, may not write off more total depreciation than the amount of the depreciable balance.

As an example of depreciation calculation, a new aircraft costs $50 million and is expected to have a useful life of twenty years. Using the "straight-line" depreciation method, it will decline in value at a rate of $2.5 million each year. The balance sheet at the end of the first year for that aircraft would show

Aircraft (cost)	$50,000,000
less accumulated depreciation	$2,500,000
Net Value	$47,500,000

The balance sheet at the end of the tenth year would show

Aircraft (cost)	$50,000,000
less accumulated depreciation	$25,000,000
Net Value	$25,000,000

In the Air Atlantis balance sheet a figure appears for accumulated depreciation. This amount is the total of accumulated depreciation for all owned property and equipment. Land is not subject to depreciation and is listed at acquisition cost. Air Atlantis's accumulated depreciation on owned property and equipment for 1998 is $388,743,000.

Amortization has been defined for accounting purposes as the increase in equity accrued to the lessor of a fixed asset under a capital lease contract. Under capital lease contracts, as the lessee makes payments to the lessor, a portion of that payment is applied to the principal value of the leased equipment. Each payment then reduces the lessor's equity in the equipment. The lessor, over time, releases 100 percent equity in the leased equipment, and title and ownership then transfer to the lessee. Accumulated amortization then represents the equity position the firm has released in capital leased equipment on the date of the balance sheet.

Air Atlantis has a total of $78,265,000 in equipment under capital lease contracts. Because they have been paying the leases over a period of time, they also have increased their equity position in equipment by $30,126,000. This is Air Atlantis's accumulated amortization (equity release) under the capital leases.

Net Fixed Assets

Net fixed assets are the valuation, for balance sheet purposes, of the total investment in property and equipment by a firm. As stated above, it generally consists of the costs of the various assets reduced by the accumulated depreciation and amortization as of the date of the balance sheet. Air Atlantis's net fixed asset valuation is $551,403,000 in owned equipment and $48,139,000 in capital lease equity for a total net fixed asset valuation of $599,542,000.

Other Assets

This category includes all assets that cannot be classified as current assets or operating investments. It includes investments in stocks and bonds of other companies, real estate and intangibles such as franchises, patents, trade names, copyrights, trademarks, and goodwill.

Intangibles represent a somewhat nebulous sounding asset category but of great importance. Intangible assets, in the air transport sector, take the form of route authorities, code share valuations, and high customer recognition items like slogans such as United's "Fly the friendly skies" and Air Atlantis's "We're number six to the sticks." Goodwill also comprises what may also be called an intangible. Goodwill can be an attitude generated toward you for a variety of reasons. Trans World Airlines has, in its name alone, a value that is immeasurable. Being one of the first airlines around the world, it has developed a name synonymous with international travel and recognized the world over. An upstart airline would do well to capture the name of TWA alone. It could bring instant marketing recognition. Thus the name, or the goodwill generated by the name, is of marketable value. Other assets are just that, items of value that cannot be logically placed in any other category. Total assets are the dollar book value of a firm's assets on the date of the statement. In the Air Atlantis's case, the figure for total assets as of December 31, 1998, was $987,625,000.

Liabilities

Current Liabilities

Current liabilities include those owed to creditors that must be paid within the current fiscal period (the same period used for current assets). Current liabilities incurred on open credit are called accounts payable. When a business is aware that it owes money to someone other than owners but has no bill, or the amount is not payable for another few weeks, it is said to have accrued liabilities. These can include such items as salaries and wages earned by employees but not yet paid, interest due on obligations and sales, and payroll and income taxes not yet payable.

Current liabilities include all debts that fall due within the coming year. It can be said that current assets are the companion of current liabilities because current assets are the source of payment for current liabilities. Let's examine each line item on Air Atlantis's current liability sheet.

Short-Term Borrowings

Air Atlantis has $44,857,000 of short-term loans. Short-term borrowings most often take the form of operating lines of credit and bridge or float loans. Loans of this type generally mature within ninety days and are constantly being renewed or rolled over. Short-term borrowings help a firm stabilize its cash flow requirements over days, weeks, and months. Many firms also issue short-term commercial paper in the open market, borrowing funds from investors for thirty, sixty, or ninety days and paying them prime or sometimes lower interest.

Long-Term Debt Maturing in the Current Year

Long-term debt payable in the current period can take the form of bonds and/or fixed installment syndicated bank loans that run for many years. This category recognizes the installment payments or bond redemption that will have to be made in the current year. In Air Atlantis's case, $6,866,000 in long-term debt obligations is due in the current period.

Current Obligations under Capital Leases

This category recognizes the installment payments due on capital leases in the current period. It is similar to the previous category. Air Atlantis will make $3,932,000 in capital lease payments in the current period.

Advanced Ticket Sales

This category, also known as air traffic liability, recognizes money received from passengers for flights that they have not yet taken. It is a liability because the passsenger could cancel and request a refund. Funds received by Air Atlantis for flights not yet taken by passengers totaled $88,259,000 in the current period.

Accounts Payable (A/P)

This category represents goods and services purchased by the firm in the normal course of business, on an open account basis and not yet paid. Air Atlantis's accounts payable is $58,014,000 for the current period.

Accrued Salaries and Wages

This category accounts for all payroll costs that have been accrued, or accumulated, but have not been disbursed to the employees. This can happen when the closing date for the annual report does not coincide with a normal payroll period because of accumulated vacation time not yet taken by employees, for which the company is liable. Air Atlantis has $77,493,000 in accrued salaries and wages due in the current period.

Accrued Aircraft Rent

This category reports rent due in the current period on aircraft rentals. The amount reported by Air Atlantis that is due in the current period is $52,638,000.

Accrued Taxes and Other Liabilities

Taxes owed to the IRS and any other money owed by the firm on the day the balance sheet is closed are listed in these two categories. Air Atlantis has accrued $76,271,000 in expense liabilities for the current period.

Total Current Liabilities

Total current liabilities include all categories and all the money that Air Atlantis will have to pay out in the current period, in this case $408,330,000.

Long-Term Liabilities

All liabilities that are not due to be paid in the current fiscal period are called long-term liabilities. Businesses are often financed through the use of long-term credit. When the amount due is for money borrowed on a note from a bank or another lender and is not due within the current year, the liability is termed *notes payable*. When the amount due is from money borrowed from a group of investors under a bond indenture contract, the liability is called *bonds payable*. When the amount due is for money borrowed to complete purchases of property, and that property is used as security to insure payment, the liability is called *mortgage payable*. A problem that is always present in establishing this part of the balance sheet is the determination and classification of the portion that is due in the current period separately from the part not due in the current period. Remember that current liabilities are due within one year, and long-term liabilities include everything else due after one year.

Long-Term Debt

Long-term debt represents bonds and loan commitments due over many years and not payable in the current year. The value of these long-term obligations for Air Atlantis is $182,658,000.

Long-Term Capital Lease Obligations

Long-term capital lease obligations represent the contractual commitments of the firm to equipment under capital lease. In this case, Air Atlantis is committed to $59,660,000 of capital leases.

Other Liabilities and Deferred Credits

Listed and recognized as other liabilities and deferred credits are such things as pension fund liability, undistributed gains, and any other miscellaneous obligations. The figures for Air Atlantis in this category are $62,276,000 in pension liability, $112,674,000 in undistributed gains, and $2,237,000 in miscellaneous liabilities.

Total Liabilities

Adding up current liabilities, long-term debt, and capital lease obligations and the total of other deferred liabilities derives the total liability figure. The total liabilities of Air Atlantis are $827,835.

Capital Stock (Owner's Equity)

The third section of the balance sheet tells what the business owes its owners. In the broadest sense this represents shares in the proprietary interest in the company. These shares are represented by stock certificates issued by the firm to its shareholders. Firms issue several types or classes of stock, and each class has attributes slightly different from those in another class.

Preferred Stock

Preferred stocks have some preference over other shares as regards dividends or the distribution of assets, in case of liquidation, or both. The specific provisions of any issue of preferred stock are spelled out clearly in the firm's prospectus and or charter. Air Atlantis has a small float of redeemable preferred stock still outstanding with a value of $11,100,000. Having issued 111,000 shares with a par value of $100 each represents this.

Common Stock

This category represents the value of the shares of common stock outstanding at par value. On the closing date of Air Atlantis's balance sheet, there were 2,524,420 shares of common stock with a total par value, at $5 per share, of $12,622,000.

Capital Surplus

Capital surplus is the amount paid by the shareholders over the par value of each share. It represents the market premium over par the stock was originally sold at, not the current market value of the stock. Recall that par value is only a value assigned to the stock for accounting purposes. In the case of Air Atlantis, the additional capital invested is $30,403,000.

Retained Earnings

This category recognizes not all earnings that are paid out to debt holders or shareholders. Funds that are not released to debt service or to shareholder dividends are said to be retained. Stockholders benefit from this income form, just as with dividends, as its retention of profits increases the value of the firm. Air Atlantis had accumulated retained earnings of $108,133,000 in 1998.

Reading the Balance Sheet

The balance sheet is the starting position to get a sense of the company's financial position (i.e., what assets are owned and how they are financed as of the date of the statement). The first look should be toward the major totals and subtotals, which indicate the size of the company, its largest assets, and how either debt or equity finances those assets. Since most financial reports show comparative data for several periods, observe how these balances have changed over the periods shown. If total assets have changed, determine whether this trend has occurred because of a significant increase in current assets, fixed assets, or other assets. Also, compare these trends with the movement or changes in total liabilities and total equity. This will indicate whether the company is financing with debt or equity. Then examine the level of current liabilities versus long-term debt.

The balance sheet allows for the observation of trends and logical relationships between accounts. For example, if you know Air Atlantis's ticket sales are growing, you probably should see a proportionate increase in accounts receivable (outstanding accounts due to credit card purchases and Tele-Mail ticketing and ARC time lag). Similarly, an increase in accounts payable (due to advance purchase holdings), cash, and travel agent commissions should be evident. Inconsistencies, such as a decrease in operating equipment accompanied by an increase in accounts payable, warrant further investigation.

The assets are carried on the books of the company at their historical cost. Market value may be significantly different than what is reported on the balance sheet. This may be especially true for any real estate holding that the company maintains.

Cash flow projections and information are the province of the cash flow statement. However, the balance sheet can also provide significant data. Having evaluated the balance sheet accounts for consistency, you should look at the same accounts from a cash flow standpoint. See if changes in assets have created or consumed cash. The same procedures should be used for liabilities and equity. To perform such function, two accounting truisms should be kept in mind: Increases in asset accounts consume cash, whereas decreases generate cash, and increases in liability and equity accounts generate cash, whereas decreases consume cash.

Close observation of a company's balance sheet should provide the observer with a general understanding of the following:

- the size of the company
- the major assets
- the major liabilities and long-term debt
- major changes that have occurred in the debt and equity areas
- methods of financing (with either debt or equity)
- any major changes occurring in debt and equity in recent report periods

Ratio Analysis

Evaluating and interpreting specific financial ratios is a commonly used tool of financial statement analysis. Ratios are primarily used in two ways. First, by using standard accounting ratio analysis, the financial and managerial members of the organization can compare their activities with those of similarly situated companies within a particular industry or with business in general. Industry standards may be obtained through commercial services, such as those provided by the Dun and Bradstreet reports or industry trade associations. A second use of ratio analysis is to compare trends that a company has experienced. It is often useful to track key ratios through economic boom and bust periods to determine how well the company financially operates during periods of economic prosperity and adversity. Such knowledge can be used as a major forecasting tool.

Figure 6-1 lists some of the more commonly used measurements of analysis. As we read through the Atlantis Airlines financial statements, we will utilize several of the ratios listed.

Key financial ratios are generally grouped into three major areas, according to the particular financial condition being considered. Many of these are used in the following sections to analyze balance sheet and income statement information. For the benefit of the reader, each is discussed below with an indication of how each measurement is calculated.

Liquidity ratios are commonly used to indicate whether a firm has sufficient working capital (the excess of current assets less current liabilities) to pay its current obligations. The two that are used most often are the current ratio and the quick ratio, or acid test.

The current ratio is a ratio of the firm's total current assets to its total current liabilities. A low ratio is an indicator that a firm may not be able to pay its future bills. A high ratio may indicate an excessive amount of current assets and management's

Figure 6-1. Breakdown of Ratios and Measures by Analysis

Area of Analysis	Ratios and Measurements	
Liquidity	• Current Ratio • Average Collection Period • Payable Turnover	• Days Sales in Inventory • Quick Ratio • Inventory Turnover
Operating Efficiency	• Sales to Inventory • Sales to Working Capital • Sales to Total Assets	• Sales to Fixed Assets • Sales to Equity
Capital Structure	• Debt Ratio • Times Interest Earned Ratio	• Debt/Equity Ratio • Bond Cap Ratio • Preferred Cap Ratio • Common Cap Ratio
Profitability	• Return on Sales • Return on Investment • Income Before Tax Margin	• Return on Equity • Return on Assets • Profit Margin

failure to utilize its resources properly. As a rule of thumb, a current ratio of 1.5 to 1 is considered acceptable.

The quick ratio or acid test ratio is a more stringent measure of liquidity. This measure indicates the company's ability to pay its debts immediately. It is figured by subtracting inventories from current assets and dividing the difference by current liabilities.

Two ratios are used to measure the liquidity of a company's account receivables: accounts receivable turnover, calculated by dividing sales by accounts receivable, and average collection period, calculated by dividing accounts receivable by the company's daily sales. These two measurements are useful in a manufacturing business, FBO operations, and organizations such as the Boeing Company. Here they take on more proportions than with an airline where the inventory is rolling. However, they may be used in terms of available seat miles to provide a comparable relationship.

The accounts receivable turnover is a comparison of the size of the firm's sales and the size of its uncollected bills from customers. When an organization is having trouble collecting from its clients, it will have large receivables and a low ratio. The average collection period compares the receivables with the daily sales required to produce the balance.

Another liquidity measure is the inventory turnover statistic. The liquidity of a company's inventory may be calculated by dividing the cost of goods sold by the organization's inventory. The significance of inventory turnover is that it helps the financial accountant measure the adequacy of goods available to sell compared with the actual sales. Because management must compromise between running out of goods to sell and investing in excessive inventory, either a high or low ratio may be an indication of poor management. A high turnover may indicate future shortages, whereas a low turnover may indicate overstocking of inventory. The cash, receivables, and inventory ratios should be used together to gain an overall grasp of the liquidity of Air Atlantis, using the balance sheet and income statement provided.

Profitability ratios are used in two major areas: profits in relation to sales, and profits in relation to assets. Profit margins are an indication of the company's ability to withstand both adverse and favorable conditions such as rising and falling prices, costs, and sales. The most widely understood of the profitability ratios is that of the profit margin. The company's profit margin is calculated by dividing operating income by sales. These figures are both derived from the income statement.

A second ratio linking sales to profits is the gross profit margin, calculated by dividing the gross margin (sales less cost of goods sold) by sales. The difference between profit margin and gross profit margin lies in the expenses that are not directly related to the operation of the business. In some basis for argument, this may be the difference between the line and staff organizations. In an airline, the difference between the actual cost of flying a route, the direct operating cost, and the total absorbed cost of flying the same route is the fully allocated cost.

Highlighting the amount of assets that the organization uses to produce its total sales is the ratio called asset turnover. When you divide sales by the organization's total assets, or by the operating assets, depending on the measurement desired, this ratio indicates the ability of the organization to produce sales vis-à-vis its asset base. Idle or improperly used assets increase the organization's need for costly financing and the expenses for maintenance and upkeep. Achieving a high asset turnover, a firm reduces costs and increases the eventual profit to the owners.

Return on investment is a ratio of concern to everyone in the organization. It is the indicator of return for the money invested in the organization. This singular ratio may be the most important for future growth of the organization. Return on investment may be calculated in two ways. First is a ratio of operating income to the assets used to produce the income. This is calculated by dividing the earning before interest and taxes (EBIT) by assets. The second method is to multiply the profit margin times the asset turnover. In either event, the return on investment is the key indicator of profitability. It matches operating profits with the assets available to earn a return. Firms that are efficiently using their assets have a relatively high return. Less efficient firms have a lower return.

Another of the liquidity measurements is that of return on equity (ROE). This measurement is very important to shareholders because it indicates the degree to which the firm is able to convert operating income to an after-tax income that can be claimed by shareholders. This is a useful measurement for analyzing the ability of the firm's management to realize an adequate return on the capital invested by the owners of the corporation. It is figured by dividing net income by total equity. Earning power is the after-tax return on investment.

Finally for this treatise but obviously not for all liquidity calculation is the measurement of times interest earned. This statistic provides a useful measure of profit that does not link return to resources. It is calculated by dividing the firm's operating income by the interest that it must pay on its debt. It relates operating profits to the fixed charges created by the company's borrowing.

The times interest earned ratio indicates the margin of safety between financial obligations and the net income. A firm may have an operation profit but may face difficulty in making excessive interest payments. If a drop in operating profits confronts it, it may be unable to meet its debt obligations. In either case, its net income will decline or vanish. A satisfactory guideline for this ratio is that EBIT should be five to seven times interest charges. Thus, a firm could experience an 80–88 percent drop in EBIT and still cover interest payments.

Ownership ratios primarily assist the stockholder in analyzing investment potential. Of the ratios identified in the table, probably the most viewed is that of the earning per share. This ratio is calculated by dividing net income by the number of shares outstanding. Shares authorized but not issued or authorized, issued, and repurchased (treasury stock) are also omitted from the calculation.

Another of the ownership ratios, the price/earnings ratio, is used as a method of valuing stock. It is calculated by dividing earnings per share into the market price of the stock, or the price listed on the particular stock exchange. Many investors consider this the most important measure to evaluate stock.

The debt/equity ratio is calculated by dividing the total debt of a company by the total equity, whereas the debt/asset ratio considers dividing the total debt by the totality of assets. These ratios indicate how much of a firm's assets are financed by debt and how much are financed by equity. Each of these measures provides significant insight into the workings of the company. If a company has excessive debt, it will experience difficulty in locating additional debt financing, whereas if debt is unknown, it may indicate a failure to use lower cost borrowed funds to raise the return earned on the common stock.

The book value of a firm's common stock is the reflection of the firm's accounting records rather than a strong measure of the assets' real value. Depending on whether assets are evaluated high or low, the book value is of limited use as an ownership ratio. Although it is nice to know that the book value of a stock is $21 per share and selling in the market at $7 (as was the case with Ozark Air Lines stock in 1985), its value is only valid at the time of liquidation. The book value of a firm's common stock is calculated by dividing the stockholders' equity by the number of shares outstanding.

Finally, two ratios of concern to the common stockholder relate to the return on their stock investment: dividend payout and dividend yield. Dividend payout is a ratio of dividends per share to earnings per share. It is figured by dividing dividends per share by earnings per share. This ratio indicates what percentage of earnings is being paid to the stockholder.

Dividend yield is a ratio of dividends per share to the market price per share. It is calculated by dividing dividends per share by the present market price of a share of common stock. It indicates a return on the stockholders' investment at the time quoted. This information is calculated daily and is included in stock quotes contained in the major securities markets.

Some of this ratio analysis will be used in the following sections.

Balance Sheet Ratio Analysis

Net Working Capital

This ratio measures the difference between total current assets and total current liabilities. You will recall that current liabilities are due and payable within one year from the date of the statement. The source of funds to pay those liabilities is current assets. Therefore, net working capital is the amount left over after all current debts are paid. For Air Atlantis, this appears as follows:

Current assets	$288,186,000
less Current liabilities	$408,330,000
Net working capital	($120,144,000)

Clearly Air Atlantis has serious cash flow problems and will have to borrow heavily in the short-term markets to meet its obligations.

Current Ratio

An easier and faster way to determine the working capital position of a firm is to find its current ratio. This is derived by dividing current assets by current liabilities. By using ratios you will be able to compare several firms within the same frame of reference. The current ratio for Air Atlantis is

Current assets	$288,186,000	
divided by	$\overline{\hspace{3cm}}$	= .705 to 1
Current liabilities	$408,330,000	

This translates that for every $1 of liability there is only 70.5 cents of assets to cover it.

Book Value of Securities

Another important observation that can be found in the balance sheet is the net book value or net asset value of the company's securities. For bonds or shares of preferred or common stock, this value represents the amount of corporate assets backing these securities.

Net Asset Value per Bond

In order to state this figure correctly, the intangible assets are subtracted as though they had no value upon liquidation. Current liabilities are subtracted, which assumes they would have been paid off at liquidation. This leaves net tangible assets to back the bonds. For Air Atlantis, the valuation works out as shown below:

Total assets	$987,625,000
less Intangibles	$66,629,000
less Current liabilities	$408,330,000
Net tangible assets	$512,666,000

Accordingly, the net tangible assets value indicates the company has $512,666,000 available to pay its bond debt of $182,658,000.

Stated another way, for each $1,000 AirA bond outstanding there is $3,135 to cover it. This is derived by dividing net tangible assets by the total number of bonds outstanding.

Net tangible assets	$512,666,000
divided by	
Outstanding bonds @$1,000 ea.	$82,658
Net asset value per bond	$3,135

Air Atlantis has a strong bond asset valuation ratio.

Net Asset Value per Share (Preferred)

This ratio reveals the asset valuation per share for the preferred stockholders. It is calculated similarly to net bond value above with one change. Debt holders get paid before any shareholders in liquidation. Therefore, it is necessary to subtract all long-term debt figures to accurately derive this valuation. AirA's preferred share valuation is

Total assets	$987,625,000		
less Intangibles	$66,629,000		
less Current liabilities	$408,330,000		
less Total long-term debt	$419,505,000		
Net tangible assets	$93,161,000		
divided by	_____	=	$839
Shares of preferred stock	111,000		
Net asset value per share of preferred stock	$839		

Thus, for every share of preferred stock outstanding, valued at $100, there are technically assets in excess of eight times the stock price to cover repayment.

Net Asset Value per Common Share

This ratio reveals the net asset value per share of common stock and can be viewed as the amount of money a share of common stock would be worth if liquidated at balance sheet values. Because common stock is the last in line for distributions at liquidation, all outstanding obligations must be paid off before any money goes to the common shareholders. The common shareholders' asset value for Air Atlantis is

Total assets	$987,625,000
less Intangibles	$66,629,000
less Current liabilities	$408,330,000
less Total long-term debt	$419,505,000
less Preferred stock	$11,100,000
Net tangible assets	$82,206,000
divided by _____	$32.56
Shares of common stock	2,524,420
Net asset value per share of common stock	$32.56

A word of caution is in order. Do not be misled by book value figures, particularly of common stocks. Many profitable companies often show very low net book value and very substantial earnings. Airlines, on the other hand, may show very high book values but have such low or erratic earnings per share that the market price can be less than book value.

Capitalization Ratios

Capitalization ratios indicate the proportion of the capitalized base that issued securities represent. There are three capitalization ratios: bond cap ratio, preferred cap ratio, and common cap ratio. Air Atlantis's ratios are listed below along with the items that make up the capitalization base.

```
Capitalization base:
     Bonds                                        $182,658,000
     Preferred stock                               $11,100,000
     Common stock                                  $12,622,000
     Additional capital                            $30,403,000
     Retained earnings                            $108,133,000
     Total cap base                               $344,916,000

Bond cap ratio              $182,658,000
divided by                 _____          = 52.96%
Total cap base              $344,916,000
Preferred cap ratio         $11,100,000
divided by                 _____          =  3.22%
Total cap base              $344,916,000
Common cap ratio            $151,158,000
divided by                 _____          = 43.82%
Total cap base              $344,916,000
```

Because retained earnings theoretically belong to the common stockholder and additional capital is surplus over the common stock par value, both are included in the common capitalization makeup.

The Income Statement

The owners and other interested parties want to know how much profit or (loss) was generated by the operations of the company. In other words, did running an airline this year prove profitable? What were the sales and expenses? The profit and loss statement or income and expense statement answers these questions.

The net increase in assets due to operations (sale of airline seats, computer reservation services, etc.) is called income (or revenue). Because a business has sold goods or rendered a service, assets in the form of cash, accounts, or notes receivable are increased. In all businesses, income is produced while the business is burdened with certain expenses. Expenses are the costs expired during the period to produce income. The concept of cost expiration is best explained on the basis of its effects. One effect is that equity is reduced. When the equity of business is reduced because it is necessary to produce income, there are expired costs. It may be the result of a single event (e.g., the replacement of landing gear) or a continuing event (e.g., labor costs). The second effect may be that assets are reduced in value, because cash has been paid out or asset utility has been decreased, or that liabilities are increased because equity has been decreased.

If income is measured when cash is received, and expenses are measured when cash is spent, the company is operating on a cash basis. If income and expenses are measured when the transactions occur, the business is said to be operating on an accrual basis.

The income statement, also known as the statement of consolidated operations, shows how much the corporation made or lost in the period. While the balance sheet shows the fundamental soundness of a company by reflecting its financial position, the income statement may be of greater analytical interest because it shows the record of its operating activities for the entire year.

The income statement serves as a guide in anticipating how the company may do in the future. The figures given for a single year are not the complete story. The historical record for a series of years is far more enlightening, and therefore most firms include the previous year's figures for comparative purposes.

The income statement matches the amounts received from the sales of goods and services against all the costs associated with providing those goods and services. The result is a net profit or loss for the year. The costs incurred usually include the cost of producing the salable items (in AirA's case, the costs of providing a seat departure). Overhead expenses such as salaries and wages, rents, supplies, depreciation, interest on borrowed funds, and taxes also fit into this category.

Now let's examine Air Atlantis's statement of consolidated operations and see how the firm fared from an income and expense standpoint.

Operating Revenues

The most important source of revenue always appears as the first item on the income statement. Air Atlantis's primary revenue source is passenger ticket sales. In 1998 Air Atlantis generated $1,029,579,000 in passenger ticket sales. This is a substantial increase over 1997 passenger revenues. Air Atlantis also experienced increased cargo sales over 1997, generating $70,406,000 in cargo revenue in 1998. The firm did, however, experience a decrease in contract service revenue in 1998, generating $66,271,000 as opposed to $81,097,000 in 1997. Total operating revenue for Air Atlantis in 1998 was $1,166,256,000, which represented a $62,509,000 increase in total revenues from the previous year.

As globalization of the air transport sector moves forward, one of the income areas likely to see tremendous growth is contract services. In a recently completed negotiation, AMR, the parent of American Airlines, entered into a series of agreements with Canadian Pacific International, which included not only an equity investment in CPI by AMR but also a twenty-year support services contract with an estimated value of $2 billion. For a fee, AMR will provide virtually all of the support services, including maintenance planning, computer reservation services, and aircraft route planning and scheduling. Extensive service support contracts sold by a major carrier to smaller operators will become a significant revenue generator in the next three to five years.

Operating Expenses

Operating expenses represent the costs incurred by the firm to provide seat departures and cargo ton-mile departures. Air Atlantis, like all airlines, is strictly an intangible service industry and as such has no cost of goods sold. There is no inventory or raw material used to produce a seat departure. Airlines don't buy each seat they sell; they buy seats and constantly resell them. Therefore, all expenses incurred in generating revenue are operating expenses only. The actual cost of any given seat is accounted and expensed under the depreciation and amortization category.

The operating expense categories are intuitively obvious, and so we will not discuss each line item separately. The most important analytical point in reviewing operating expenses is a comparison between figures for the current year and previous year. This will illuminate any particular line item that either increased or decreased significantly as a function of changes in revenue stream. The salient fact that emerges from an analysis of Air Atlantis's operating expenses is that although revenue grew by $62 million, the expenses incurred in supporting that revenue growth increased by $108 million. In short, Air Atlantis went $49 million in the hole to support the revenue growth. Where did that money come from? Retained earnings from previous years.

Operating Profit or (Loss)

Subtracting all operating expenses from operating revenues derives operating profit. Because expenses exceeded revenues, Air Atlantis experienced an operating loss of $49,404,000 in 1998 compared with an operating loss of $3,624,000 in 1997.

Other Income or Expense

It is important to realize that we have not yet arrived at net profit or loss for the firm. Net income is a firm's gross profit less its operating expenses and income taxes. Net profit, net loss, and net earnings are synonymous in the method of obtaining them. There are still income and expense items that must be reported and charged to the operating profit or loss. In the case of Air Atlantis, $20,985,000 was expensed on interest charges on bonds and other long-term debt service. Air Atlantis also capitalized $9,121,000 in interest received and took in an additional $8,541,000 in noncapitalized interest income. The firm also had a $4,871,000 gain on the sale of property and equipment, a $733,000 equity increase in their CRS participation and a charge (expense) of $3,628,000 for miscellaneous expenses. The income or loss from all of the adjustments in this category for Air Atlantis totaled a loss of $1,347,000.

Earnings Before Income Taxes (EBIT)

Air Atlantis's EBIT totaled a negative $50,751,000. This represents the total of all sources of income minus the total of all expenses incurred in generating that income. In the previous year, Air Atlantis had an operating loss of $3,624,000, other income adjustments totaling a positive $20,064,000 and a positive EBIT of $16,440,000.

Provision (Credit) for Income Taxes

When a firm has generated a negative EBIT (a loss), it pays no taxes and in fact is entitled to a tax credit. This credit is applied to the losses incurred and reduces them by the value of the tax credit. In 1998, Air Atlantis was able to reduce its loss by taking a tax credit of $17,561,000. In 1997, however, Air Atlantis had to pay taxes totaling $6,990,000 because the firm had a positive (taxable) EBIT.

Net Earnings (Loss)

In 1998, Air Atlantis experienced a net loss of $33,190,000, or a loss of $14.31 per share. In 1997, Air Atlantis generated a net profit of $9,450,000, or net earnings per share of $4.34. The figures of earnings or loss per share are calculated on the average number of shares outstanding during the fiscal year. To do otherwise would mislead the reader, especially if most shares were sold near the end of the fiscal period. Although AirA issued a total of 2,524,420 shares by the end of fiscal year 1998, it averaged 2,320,00 shares over the same period. This later figure accounts for the net loss of $14.31 per share.

Reading the Income Statement

Reading the income statement starts with the big picture, that is, addressing the (top line) revenues and the (bottom line) net income. Here, trends are of major significance. Next, observe important subtotals such as gross profit, operating income, operating expenses, other income and expense and taxable income, observing dollar amounts, percentages, and trends. Notice also the availability and usage of product (available seat miles [ASM], revenue passenger miles [RPM], load factor, and yield).

With this basic knowledge and the resulting effect on profits for the periods, look at the statement in more detail. Review the operating expense against the company's sales and load factors, noting any inconsistencies that may require further examination.

Keep in mind that revenue is recognized when the ticket is sold or the ARC reports such sale to the airline. Expenses are recognized when they are incurred, regardless of when they are paid. This is the accrual basis of accounting, which complies with formal accounting principles but does not clearly reveal cash flow. To review the income statement from a cash flow perspective, add back to net income the depreciation expense. This provides a primitive version of "cash income," since depreciation is a noncash expense, carried on the balance sheet as a negative asset.

From this brief observation of the income statement the following can be ascertained:

- size and trend of airline capacity (ASM)
- size and trend in seats utilized (RPM)
- amount of revenue generated for each mile a passenger is carried (yield)
- capacity of the carrier's equipment utilized (load factor)
- size and trend in sales
- major expense totals and trends
- net income or loss
- cash income generated from the business

Analyzing the Income Statement

The income statement, like the balance sheet, will tell us a lot more if we make a few detailed comparisons. One key index is changes in operating profit margin. Below are the operating profit margins for Air Atlantis for 1998 and 1997.

1998	Operating profit	($49,404,000)	
	divided by	————————	= (4.23%)
	Operating revenues	$1,166,256,000	

1997	Operating profit	($3,624,000)	
	divided by	————————	= (0.328%)
	Operating revenues	$1,103,747,000	

This means that in 1998 a gross loss of 4.23 cents was incurred for each dollar of revenue. In 1997 the figure is .328 cents loss per dollar of revenue. Changes in profit margin can and do reflect changes in operating efficiency as well as changes in service offerings. Another way of saying this is that in 1998 it cost AirA $1.0423 to make $1.00 in revenue. In 1997, it took $1.00328 to produce $1.00 in revenue.

We can also compare Air Atlantis with other companies in the air transport sector. To do this we develop an operating cost ratio. It is the complement to operating profit margin. Operating cost ratio indicates how much of the revenue stream was consumed by operations. Air Atlantis's operating cost margin is listed below.

1998	Operating costs	$1,215,660,000	
	divided by	─────────────	= 104.23%
	Operating revenues	$1,166,256,000	
1997	Operating costs	$1,107,371,000	
	divided by	─────────────	= 100.328%
	Operating revenues	$1,103,747,000	

Net Profit Ratio

Net profit ratio is still another guide to indicate how satisfactory the year's performance has been. Air Atlantis's net profit ratio is shown below for 1997 and 1998.

1998	Net profit	($33,190,000)	
	divided by	─────────────	= (2.84%)
	Operating revenue	$1,166,256,000	
1997	Net profit	($6,990,000)	
	divided by	─────────────	= (0.633%)
Operating revenue		$1,103,747,000	

This means that for every dollar of revenue generated in 1998 the company had to spend 2.84 cents in retained earnings. In 1997, the figure was .633 cents in retained earnings.

The operating profit margin, the operating cost ratio, and the net profit ratio, like all those we examined in connection with the balance sheet, give us general information about the company and its prospects for the future. All these comparisons have significance for the long term, since they tell us about the fundamental economic condition of the firm. But one question remains to be answered: Is the firm a good investment? Such analysis is crucial, not only to future investors but also to management so that future investors can be obtained. For these answers we must look at several more factors.

Interest Coverage

The bonds and long-term loan packages of Air Atlantis represent a substantial debt, but they are due and callable many years from now. The yearly interest, however, is a fixed charge, and one of the first things we would like to know is how readily Air Atlantis can meet its interest obligations. More specifically, we would like to know whether the borrowed funds have been put to good use generating enough earnings to meet interest obligations.

The source of funds to service these obligations is total income before interest on bonds and provisions for taxes. It is there that money will be required to meet required payments. In the case of Air Atlantis, this is obtained by adding the operating revenues and other income category (less interest expense) together. Air Atlantis's total income figure is $1,166,256,000 in revenues, plus $19,638,000 in other income, to equal $1,185,894,000. The interest on bonds and long-term loan packages is $20,985,000. The ratio for interest coverage for 1998 and 1997 is listed below.

1998	Total income	$1,185,894,000	
	divided by	———————	= 56.51
	Interest expense	$20,985,000	
1997	Total income	$1,143,033,000	
	divided by	———————	= 59.46
Interest expense		$19,222,000	

Clearly Air Atlantis is in good position to service its annual interest obligations.

Preferred Dividend Coverage

To calculate the preferred dividend coverage, the number of times the preferred dividend was earned, we must use net earnings as our base, since taxes and all interest charges must be paid before anything is available for stockholders. Air Atlantis has 1,110 shares of cumulative preferred stock outstanding paying a dividend of 6 percent ($6.00 per share). The total dividend requirement is $6,660 per year. Dividing net income of $33,190,000 by this figure, we arrive at approximately 49.8. As absurd as this result sounds, in a strict sense, Air Atlantis cannot pay the dividend and must therefore accrue it for payment in another period. The dividends will be added to any other passed payments and will accumulate until they are paid.

Earnings per Share

The buyer of common stocks is often more concerned with earnings per share than dividend payments. Usually earnings per share, or the potential earnings per share, influence the stock price in the open market much more than dividend payments. Air Atlantis's income statement shows earnings per share of common stock of minus $14.31, or ($14.31).

Because of the ever-increasing significance placed on the results of the year's operating activity, earnings per share are required on the income statement. It is improvement in earnings per share that drives stock price appreciation in the marketplace.

Extraordinary Items

Events or transactions during one year, which are significantly different from customary activities, are now separated from recurring items and called extraordinary items.

What is an extraordinary item? An example of these may be the sale of route authorities to another airline, termination of service to a previously significant destination, or possibly recognition of the total value of pension liabilities as required by government pension specialists. All of these events are onetime occurrences whose costs are above and beyond the normal conduct of business.

They are recognized as separate items because of their uniqueness and nonrecurrence. Their impact on the financial condition of the company can vary from very positive to very negative, but the investors must be made aware that any impact is strictly temporary and a onetime adjustment. By recognizing these extraordinary items as separate financial transactions, the company will not inadvertently mislead an investor into believing the finances of the company are significantly better or worse than their true positions.

Primary Earnings per Share

Now we come to the most difficult problem in the earnings report: deciding how much a share of common stock actually earns. One tool used to determine this is called primary earnings per share. This is determined by dividing the earnings for the year not only by the number of shares of common stock outstanding but also by the common stock plus common stock equivalents.

Common stock equivalents are securities, such as convertible preferred stock, convertible bonds, stock options, warrants, and the like, which enable the owner to become a common stockholder by exchanging or converting his security. These are deemed to be but one step short of common stock because their value in large part stems from the common stock to which they relate.

As to convertible preferred stock and convertible bonds, they offer the holder a specified dividend rate or interest rate return coupled with the advantage of being able to participate in the increased potential earnings of common stock. They do not have to be converted to common stock for these securities to be called a common stock equivalent. This is because they are equivalent to common shares, enabling the holder at his or her discretion to cause an increase in the number of common shares by exchanging or converting. This dilutes the earnings per share.

How do accountants determine a common stock equivalent? A convertible security is considered a common stock equivalent. Based on its market price when issued, its rate of return is less than two-thirds of the prime rate at that time.

As an example, assume SIU Airlines has 100,000 shares of common stock outstanding plus another 100,000 shares of convertible preferred stock outstanding, convertible on a one-for-one ratio. We add the two together and get 200,000 shares of common stock equivalents. Assume also that SIU Airlines has earnings of $500,000 for the current year. With these facts, the primary earnings per share computation is easy:

Earnings per share $500,000
divided by   _____ = $2.50
Common stock equivalents   200,000
Primary earnings per share is $2.50

Now let's assume that the preferred stock paid a dividend of $1 per share and was not convertible into common stock. Our earnings per share would then be $4 per share. Why? Because we would subtract the total preferred stock dividends—$100,000—from the total earnings, leaving $400,000. But we would also divide that $400,000 by only 100,000 shares of common stock.

Earnings per share $400,000
divided by   _____ = $4.00
Common stock   100,000

Fully Diluted Earnings per Share

The primary earnings per share item, as we have just seen in the preceding section, takes into consideration common stock and common stock equivalents. The purpose of fully diluted earnings per share is to reflect dilution in earnings that would result if all contingent issuances of common stock had taken place at the beginning of the current year.

This computation is the result of dividing the earnings for the year by common stock and common stock equivalents and all other securities that are convertible (even though for valid reasons they are not considered common stock equivalents).

How does this work? First, remember from the last section that we have 100,000 of convertible preferred outstanding as well as 100,000 shares of common stock. Now let's say SIU Airlines also has $10 million in convertible bonds outstanding. These bonds pay interest at 6 percent and are convertible to common stock at the ratio of 20 shares of common stock for every $1,000 bond. These bonds are not common stock equivalents, but we have to count them in determining fully diluted earnings per share. If all 10,000 bonds were converted into common stock, there would be another 200,000 shares of common stock outstanding. We would have to add these 200,000 shares to the existing 100,000 shares of common stock and to the 100,000 shares of convertible preferred for a total of 400,000 shares. But converting the bonds to stock, we would also not have to pay the $600,000 in interest payments. This gain would be credited toward gross earnings. The final calculations for fully diluted earnings per share look like this:

Earnings for the year	$500,000	
Interest on bonds	$600,000	
less Deduction for taxes	($300,000)	
Adjusted earnings	$800,000	
divided by	_____	= $2
adjusted shares	400,000	

In this example the fully diluted earnings per shares is $2.

The most important point to remember is that you should always be aware of what type of earnings per share you are analyzing. Based on the examples given here, earnings of $500,000 per year can have several different meanings on a per common share basis:

Before allowing for conversions	$4.00 per share
Primary earnings per share	$2.50 per share
Fully diluted earnings per share	$2.00 per share

Price/Earnings Ratio

Both the price and the return on common stock vary with a multitude of factors. One such factor is the relationship that exists between the earnings per share and the market price. This is called the price/earnings (P/E) ratio. It is calculated in the following manner. If a stock is selling at $25 and earning $2 per share, its P/E ratio is 12.5 (25 divided by 2, or selling price divided by earnings per share), and the stock is said to be selling at 12.5 times earnings. If the stock rose to $40, the P/E ratio would be 20. If the stock dropped to $12, the P/E ratio would be 6.

When a company is in a loss situation, as much of the air transport sector has been in the recent past, the P/E ratio is negative and therefore meaningless. This is why companies in loss situations have no P/E ratio listed in their stock report lines in the newspapers. Just remember one important fact when reviewing P/E ratios: in the real world, no stock will ever keep its same P/E ratio from year to year. The historical P/E multiple is only a guide to potential performance, not a guarantee.

Statement of Consolidated Cash Flows

This final statement for Air Atlantis indicates changes in working capital and presents the flow of funds through the business or, if you prefer, how the cash flows were used during the year. There are five categories of cash flows on the Air Atlantis statement: (1) cash and equivalents at the beginning of the year; (2) cash flows from operating activity; (3) cash flows from investing activity; (4) cash flows from financing activity, and (5) cash and equivalents at year end.

Cash at the Start of the Year

Air Atlantis started 1998 with $22,140,000 in cash and equivalents. This represents net operating, or working, capital available from 1997.

Cash Flows from Operating Activities

Air Atlantis had net additions to working capital from operating activities of $33,799,000, which included the $33 million net operating loss and $60 million in depreciation. Why does depreciation, which was first listed as a cost on the income statement, now appear as a source of funds? Because if you'll remember the balance sheet definition of depreciation, it is the decline in useful value of a fixed asset due to wear and tear over time. A company has to place this depreciation figure in its books as a cost of doing business during the year.

But to whom do they pay this money? They've already paid, or are paying, for whatever it is that they are depreciating: aircraft, engines, ground equipment, etc. Therefore, this is money that is deducted and paid to them. Obviously there is no actual payment. It's only a bookkeeping entry. But it does free up this money to be included on the asset side of the books. It isn't new money but "found" money. They can either put it in the bank or add to it up until the day when they must replace the equipment being depreciated, or they can use it elsewhere in the business. It is important to realize that depreciation is the single largest source of internal funds in highly capitalized industries like the air transport, rail, and ocean shipping sectors.

Air Atlantis also took a $25 million hit in accrued taxes, but an increase in accounts payable of plus $35 million offset this. This accounts payable increase implies Air Atlantis is not timely in paying its bills. It is stretching out payments to creditors. The net position from cash flows in operating activity is plus $33 million.

Cash Flows from Investing Activities

The principal activities in this category were the sale of owned assets for $128 million, which was offset by acquisitions totaling $212 million. Air Atlantis bought more than it sold for net changes of negative $95 million.

Cash Flows from Financing Activities

There are two principal activities in this category, both with net positive effects on working capital. First, Air Atlantis sold its long-term debt instruments, raising $68 million, and it also issued common stock, which raised another $24 million.

Cash flow from financing activity generated a total of $84 million in net additions to working capital.

Total Increases (Decreases) in Cash and Equivalents

By summing up the category totals, we can see that Air Atlantis, in spite of a $33 million net operating loss, actually had an increase in net working capital of $22 million for 1998. When added to the cash and equivalents available at the beginning of the year, we can see that Air Atlantis increased its working capital to $44 million.

Reading a Statement of Cash Flow

The statement of cash flow reveals not only the increase or decrease in the company's cash for the period but also the accounts, by category, that caused change.

Armed with knowledge of the company's cash balance and how it changed during the periods presented, look next at the total change in cash caused by the three major cash activities presented on the statement: operating, investing, and financing.

To fully comprehend the company's cash flow from daily operations, look at the increase or decrease in cash caused by changes in the working capital accounts as well as from the revenue and expense accounts. Revenues and expenses cause most of the daily cash flows in business, but the flow of this cash is frequently postponed by credit transactions. Consequently you must examine changes in the current asset and liability accounts, the working capital, to accurately trace daily cash flow.

Cash flow from operating activities can be presented using either the "direct method" or the "indirect method." Under the direct method, cash inflows and outflows are summarized for major categories, including the following:

- cash received from customers
- cash paid to employees and suppliers
- cash paid for interest
- cash paid for taxes

Although the direct method is a more intuitive approach to understanding cash flows from operating activities, it is the indirect method that is seen in most annual reports. Under the indirect method, net income is listed, followed by a series of adjustments to remove the effects of accrual accounting. The first adjustment is to add back depreciation expenses. This is because it is a noncash expense that was subtracted when determining net income. To this simplified subtotal of "cash income," referred to earlier, add or subtract the cash that was created or consumed by the working capital accounts—current assets and current liabilities—that are used in the company's daily operations. It is in these accounts that cash seems to appear or disappear mysteriously. The resulting cash flow from operating activities is one of the most important indicators of the company's performance.

Fortunately, understanding the investing and financing activities on the statement of cash flow is much simpler. Investing activities include the acquisition or disposal of fixed assets. Since most companies buy more fixed assets for growth or replacement than they sell, the effect of investing activities on cash flow is usually negative.

Cash flow from financing activities includes the effect on cash from transactions with creditors and investors. Positive financing cash flows include loan proceeds or shareholder investments, while negative financing cash flows are caused by repayment of these loans or dividend payments.

Look for a relationship between the investing and financing activities. For example, a major acquisition of aircraft is frequently accompanied by an increase in liabilities or equity to finance it. As you look for these relationships, also look for similarity between the expected life of the asset and the length of the financing for it. Trucks and other vehicles are seldom owned for more than five years, so they usually would be financed with debt of five years or less.

From this brief review of the statement of cash flow, you should have a general sense of the following:

Figure 6-2. Effects of Certain Changes on Cash Flow During a Report Period

Change	Possible Reason	Result
Accounts receivable increase	Sale of more immediate travel tickets by travel agents causing lag time for ARC to clear and forward payment to the airline	Negative
Accounts receivable decrease	Collection of amount owed by customers sooner or less credit extended	Positive
Cash on account increases	Airline holdings of PFC money increases	Positive
Prepaid expenses increase	More money paid in advance for airport gates, taxes, insurance, etc.	Negative
Prepaid expenses decrease	Less paid in advance for above	Positive
Employee payroll costs increase	Employees receive general cost of living adjustments or salary increases	Negative
Accounts payable increase	Purchasing more goods on credit or pay debts at a later than normal date	Positive
Accounts payable decrease	Pay creditors sooner than normal date or purchase equipment with cash	Negative
Accrued payable increase	Take longer to pay taxes, employees, and others than is normal	Positive

- the amount of cash created or consumed by daily operation, including the cash effect from changes in working capital accounts
- the amount of cash invested in fixed or other assets
- the amount of debt borrowed or repaid
- the proceeds from sale of stock or payments for dividends
- the increase or decrease in cash for the period

Footnotes and Auditors' Reports

The annual reports of many companies contain this statement: "The accompanying footnotes are an integral part of the financial statements and are incorporated by reference herein." The reason is that financial reports by themselves are kept concise and condensed. Therefore, any explanatory matter that cannot be abbreviated is set out in greater detail in the footnotes.

Most people do not like to read footnotes because they may be complicated and they are almost always hard to interpret. Read them anyhow! They sometimes can contain dynamite. Even if they do not reveal that the company is being forced into bankruptcy, footnotes can and often do reveal fascinating sidelights on the financial picture. They are most definitely worth the effort.

The last area to be addressed is the certification of the financial reports by the company's independent auditors. This certification says auditing steps taken in the process of verifying the company's statements were conducted in accordance with acceptable methods and practices of the accounting profession. The second thing covered by the auditor's certification statement is financial statements, which have been prepared and presented in conformance with generally accepted accounting principles.

When you see the auditor's certification statement, note two important items. One is that the annual report contains financial statements that have been given the stamp of approval from an independent public accounting firm, and the figures are fairly and conventionally presented. The second is that even with this certification stamp, the audit is only as good as the books on which it was based. In other words, an auditor's stamp of approval does not, under any circumstances, guarantee an unscrupulous management has not doctored the books. As in all things financial, *caveat emptor!*

As an example for this chapter, the financial report for Air Atlantis is shown in figure 6-3.

Figure 6-3. Sample Business Annual Report

Air Atlantis, Inc.
Statement of Consolidated Operations
Year Ended December 31, 1997

(In thousands, except per share)	1997	1996
OPERATING REVENUES:		
Passenger	1,029,579	963,362
Cargo	70,406	59,287
Contract Services or Other	66,271	81,097
TOTAL OPERATING REVENUE	1,166,256	1,103,747
OPERATING EXPENSES:		
Salaries and Related Costs	405,666	354,998
Commissions	204,648	171,890
Aircraft Fuel	167,405	181,141
Rentals and Landing Fees	108,461	82,931
Purchased Services	78,381	65,978
Depreciation & Amortization	60,378	55,958
Aircraft Maintenance	36,290	38,813
Food and Beverages	29,158	24,158
Personnel Expenses	23,885	21,217
Advertising & Promotion	20,844	20,321
Other	80,546	91,066
TOTAL OPERATING EXPENSE	1,215,660	1,107,371
EARNING (LOSS) FROM OPERATION	(49,404)	(3,624)
OTHER INCOME (EXPENSE):		
Interest Expense	(20,985)	(19,222)
Interest Capitalized	9,121	7,132
Interest Income	8,541	12,261
Net Gains on Disposition of Property	4,871	28,584
Other, Net	(3,628)	(10,313)
Equity in CRS System	733	1,622
TOTAL OTHER INCOME (EXPENSE)	(1,347)	20,064
EARNING (LOSS) BEFORE INCOME TAX	(50,751)	16,440
PROVISION (CREDIT) FOR INCOME TAX	(17,561)	6,990
NET EARNINGS (LOSS)	(33,190)	9,450
NET EARNINGS (LOSS) PER SHARE	(14.31)	4.34

Figure 6-3 *continued*

Financial Highlights & Operating Statistics
Year Ended December 31, 1997

(In thousands, except as indicated)	1997	1996
FINANCIAL HIGHLIGHTS		
Operating Revenues	1,166,256	1,103,747
Operating Expenses	1,215,660	1,107,371
Earnings (Loss) from Operations	(49,404)	(3,627)
Net Earnings (Loss)	(33,190)	9,446
Net Earnings (Loss) per Share	(14.31)	4.34
Average Number of Common Shares	2,320	2,178
OPERATING STATISTICS		
Revenue Passengers	6,200	5,759
Revenue Passenger Miles (RPMs)	8,229,028	7,613,746
Available Seat Miles (ASMs)	12,410,038	11,499,509
Passenger Load Factor	66.30%	66.20%
Break-Even Passenger Load Factor	69.50%	66.50%
Revenue per Passenger Mile	$.1250	$.1260
Cost per Available Seat Mile	$.0980	$.0960
Revenue Ton Miles (RTMs)	979,219	903,169
Available Ton Miles (ATMs)	1,700,940	1,561,165
Cargo Load Factor	57.57%	57.85%
Average Fuel Price per Gallon	$.71160	$80.40

Figure 6-3 *continued*

Balance Sheet (Assets)
Year Ended December 31, 1997

(In thousands, except per share)	1997	1996
ASSETS		
Cash and Cash Equivalents	44,900	22,140
Short-Term Investments	72,744	97,369
Receivables, Less Allowance for Bad Debt		
(1997–6,730; 1996–1,312)	91,218	91,266
Aircraft Fuel, Spare Parts, Less Obsolescence		
Allowance (1997–6,730; 1996–5,740)	33,618	32,286
Refundable Income Taxes	16,693	
Prepaid Expenses	29,013	20,943
TOTAL CURRENT ASSETS	288,186	264,004
OPERATING PROPERTY & EQUIPMENT		
Flight Equipment	671,004	567,742
Advances on Flight Equipment Purchases	78,459	64,128
Other Property & Equipment	190,683	174,746
TOTAL	940,146	806,616
Accumulated Depreciation & Amortization	(388,743)	(356,559)
TOTAL EQUIPMENT LESS DEPRECIATION	551,403	450,057
Capital Leases		
Flight Equipment	68,232	42,045
Other Property & Equipment:	10,033	10,033
TOTAL LEASEHOLD	78,265	52,078
Accumulated Amortization	(30,126)	(27,239)
TOTAL NET LEASE VALUE	48,139	24,839
OTHER ASSETS		
Intangibles, Less Accumulated Amortization		
(1997–9,139; 1996–5,502)	66,629	12,888
Deferred Income Taxes	2,716	4,913
Other	30,552	41,550
TOTAL OTHER ASSETS	99,897	59,351
TOTAL ASSETS	987,625	798,251

Figure 6-3 *continued*

Balance Sheet (Liabilities/Owners Equity)
Year Ended December 31, 1997

(In thousands, except per share)	1997	1996
LIABILITIES AND SHAREHOLDER EQUITY		
Current Liabilities		
Short-Term Borrowing	44,857	44,276
Long-Term Debt Maturing During Year	6,866	6,160
Current Obligations Under Capital Leases	3,932	2,717
Advanced Ticket Sales Obligation	88,259	84,266
Accounts Payable	58,014	55,278
Accrued Salaries and Wages	77,493	67,554
Accrued Aircraft Rent	52,638	38,077
Accrued Income Taxes Payable		8,694
Other Accrued Liabilities	76,271	68,251
TOTAL CURRENT LIABILITIES	408,330	375,273
Long-Term Debt	182,658	87,650
Long-Term Obligations—Capital Leases	59,660	36,124
Other Liabilities and Deferred Credits:		
Deferred Pension Liability	62,276	36,795
Deferred Gains	112,674	92,286
Other	2,237	2,449
TOTAL LONG-TERM DEBT	419,505	255,304
TOTAL LIABILITIES	827,835	630,577
OWNER'S EQUITY		
Preferred Stock		
6% Cumulative @ $100 Par Value	11,100	15,900
Common Stock—$5 Par Value		
12,500,000 Shares Authorized		
Issued: 2,524,420 (1997); 2,346,788 (1996)	12,622	11,733
Excess Paid in Capital	30,403	5,239
Retained Earnings	108,133	136,399
Unearned Compensation	(1,725)	(805)
Common Stock Held in Treasury		
Shares: 148,610 (1997); 158,290 (1996)	(743)	(792)
TOTAL EQUITY	157,790	167,674
TOTAL LIABILITIES & EQUITY	987,625	798,251

Figure 6-3 *continued*

Consolidated Statement of Cash Flow
Year Ended December 31, 1997

(In thousands, except per share)	1997	1996
Cash and Equivalents at Beginning of Year	22,140	46,518
Cash Flows from Operating Activities:		
Net Earnings (Loss)	(33,193)	9,446
Adjustments to Net Cash Operating Activity		
Deferred pension Expense	7,518	417
Depreciation and Amortization	60,376	55,958
Foreign Exchange (Gains) Losses	1,974	723
Gain on Disposition of Property	(4,871)	(28,584)
Provision (Credit) for Deferred Income Tax	2,208	2,165
Undistributed Earnings From CRS	(366)	
Change in Receivables	47	(2,464)
Increase in Other Current Assets	(9,067)	(13,951)
Increase in Advanced Ticket Sales	3,992	18,202
Change in Accrued Income Taxes	(25,387)	2,428
Increase in Accounts Payable	35,255	32,067
Amortization of Accrued Gains	(8,208)	(4,663)
Other, Net	3,521	(163)
TOTAL CASH FLOWS FROM OPERATIONS	33,799	71,581
Cash Flows from Investing Activities:		
Additions to Property and Equipment	(212,242)	(257,592)
Proceeds from Disposition of Property	128,131	173,756
Changes in Short-Term Investments	24,839	(1,080)
Acquisition of Intangibles	(35,837)	(3,444)
Other, Net	(58)	874
TOTAL CASH FLOWS FROM INVESTING	(95,167)	(87,486)
Cash Flows from Financing Activities:		
Proceeds from Issuance of Long-Term Debt	68,743	
Repayment of Long-Term Debt	(6,662)	(6,795)
Principal Payments on Capital Lease	(3,154)	(2,286)
Proceeds from Issuance of Common Stock	24,716	
Increases in Short-Term Borrowing	131	98
Other, Net	355	507
TOTAL CASH FLOWS FROM FINANCING	84,129	(8,476)
Increase (Decrease) in Cash and Equivalents	22,761	(24,378)
CASH AND CASH EQUIVALENTS–YEAR END	44,901	22,140

Suggested Readings and References

Bernstein, L. A. (1993). *Financial statement analysis: Theory, application, and interpretation.* Homewood, IL: Irwin.

Bukics, R. L. (1991). *Financial statement analysis: The basics and beyond.* Chicago: Probus.

Coughlan, J. D., & Strand, W. K. (1969). *Depreciation: Accounting, taxes, and business decisions.* New York: Ronald Press.

Finnerty, J. E. (1993). *Planning cash flow.* New York: Amacom.

Fridson, M. S. (1991). *Financial statement analysis: A practitioner's guide.* New York: John Wiley.

Gibson, C. H. (1991). *Financial statement analysis: Using financial accounting information.* Cincinnati: College Division, South-Western.

Internal Labor Office. (1998). *How to read a balance sheet.* Geneva: Author.

International Accounting Division. (1992). *Cash flow statements.* London: Author.

Lalli, W. R. (1990). *Checklist and illustrative financial statements for personal financial statement engagement: A financial accounting and reporting practice aid.* New York: American Institute of Certified Public Accountants.

Lamp, G. E. (1968). *Dispersion effects in industrial property life analysis.* Thesis, Iowa State University of Science and Technology, Ames.

Livingstone, J. L. (1992). *The portable MBA in finance and accounting.* New York: John Wiley.

McMeen, A. R. (1992). *Debt repayment capacity: Cash flow forecasting for borrowers and lenders.* New York: Amacom.

U.S. Small Business Administration. (1992). *Cash flow analysis.* Washington: Author.

Worthington, P. R. (1993). *Investment cash flow and sunk costs.* Chicago: Federal Reserve Bank of Chicago.

7

AIR TRANSPORT SECTOR REVENUE GENERATION

This chapter will examine techniques of generating revenue. By its very nature, revenue generation in the air transport sector means one thing: marketing. Marketing and market power are the keys to any successful service industry, and no example more clearly makes this case than the air transport sector. Failure to correctly identify exactly what an airline is selling, and to whom, has caused many otherwise excellent airline service offerings either never to get off the ground or to cease to exist after a short and turbulent life. Proper utilization of marketing techniques means more than just adequate revenue generation for an airline; it means existence.

Regulated Revenue Generation (1938–1978)

Before 1978, the airline industry in the United States was, de facto, a regulated public utility. Various fare categories were available, but their costs were regulated with only incremental differences. Fares were identical from carrier to carrier. Price competition was not allowed. In addition, the government suggested an airline rate of return and thus the profitability a carrier could experience. This interventionist policy created problems for airline management.

Without price competition, any marketing efforts designed to capture more market share and more revenue had to be targeted at strictly intangible value-added services. Such services as jet engine instead of piston transports, meals on china rather than plastic, onboard movies, convenient gate locations, desirable departure/arrival times, modern computerized reservations systems, and ease of booking were advertised. In that bygone era, the airlines were buying anything and everything to differentiate their service offerings. These services were the marketing hook to increase load factors and grow revenue streams. There were, however, two fundamental problems with this approach.

First, being a regulated oligopoly, whatever one carrier did, others in that market very quickly duplicated. This was not just good business. It was survival. If TWA put jets on its Los Angeles–New York route with no response in kind from American or United, they would eventually haul most of the traffic. What customer would want to ride a DC-7C for eleven hours when, for the same basic fare with a premium surcharge added, they could do the trip in six hours? It should be obvious that the other carriers quickly negated any unique service offering by one airline before deregulation. The result was an ever-escalating war to provide the latest, best, fastest, and most luxurious services that could be bought, no matter what the cost. Carriers bragged in their advertising that they were the first to do this or that. They were first to offer in-flight movies, first to be an all-jet airline, first to provide on-board meals—all to capture the public's attention.

The other fundamental problem was the escalating cost of these value-added services. The federal government, acting through the Civil Aeronautics Board (CAB), in essence guaranteed the airlines a slight profit over and above their costs. Airlines bought jets by the hundreds, increased frequencies, put movie systems on board, expanded or built new terminal facilities, improved their onboard meal and drink services, and hired new staff by the thousands. How could the airlines spend these enormous sums of money and still be guaranteed a profit?

They simply asked the CAB to increase their fares to cover these diseconomies of scale. After lengthy deliberation, the CAB routinely granted these demands. This false economic base, over years, created an air transport system that, in terms of service and traffic levels, was the envy of the world. However, in terms of fiscal prudence, the industry was an unruly and irresponsible child.

The airlines were not overly concerned with a new service offering or new aircraft costs to operate. They did not have to be. It was not their primary concern. The CAB had granted them a de facto exemption on cost control management. The only thing that mattered was the kind and type of marketing hook generated by a new service offering and how much revenue it would generate. Thus, marketing and revenue generation in the regulated days were relatively simple procedures. Find and buy something new, publicize it to the maximum, sit back, and reap the improved load factor revenues until other carriers catch up. Then repeat the process.

The CAB's restrictive control of new airline entrants and the constant upward climb in fare prices granted to existing carriers to pay for all these new services did not go unnoticed. These two actions made deregulation a virtual certainty.

Deregulated Revenue Generation (1978–1988)

Deregulation brought two fundamental changes to the U.S. air transport industry. The first was open price competition, and the second was aggressive cost and capacity control measures. The advent of these two essential changes significantly altered the marketing and revenue equations familiar to airline management.

The domestic open-sky policy directives inherent in the Deregulation Act of 1978 allowed many new airlines to begin service. New entrant start-ups had a tremendous advantage over existing carriers. They were, from day one, geared for and focused on profit maximization and cost control. They had no huge infrastructure consuming large chunks of their revenue streams. They were able to purchase only the equipment and facilities that their traffic would support. Generally, because of limited labor contracts, they were able to outsource other requirements. Without huge infrastructure costs, new start-up carriers were able to achieve and maintain reduced available seat mile (ASM) costs. These diminished costs provided significant ticket price advantage, generating better yields and profits than old-line carriers.

These huge disparities in ASM costs precipitated price wars in the early days of deregulation. New carriers initially, and predictably, reduced fares to build market share and market presence. Thus began a slow escalation to what airlines perceived as long-term profitable pricing levels based on their leaner cost structures.

Economically, deregulation could not have arrived at a worse time. Inflation and interest rates were at very high levels, and the country was heading into a severe recession. The industry was also experiencing extreme instability in the price of aviation kerosene, and fuel allocations were being cut back. These factors would have been sufficient to disrupt the labor-management relationship; however, an even more pervasive event shook the very foundations of organized labor.

The public policy goal of the Deregulation Act was to "encourage development and attain an air transportation system that relies on competitive market forces to determine the quality, variety, and prices of air services." Regulatory changes were intended to promote more competitive pricing, establish greater flexibility of changing market demands, and improve overall efficiency of the industry.

The framers of the act paid little attention to the underlying reality that all collective bargaining agreements in the airline industry were also based on that very same regulatory system. The unions had captured a portion of, and were equally slaves to, the monopoly profits generated by the CAB regulatory process. Consequently, deregulating the airlines also meant deregulating the air transport collective bargaining process, a reality that was evidently ignored by the framers.

These new market entries triggered a series of "fare wars" that would have disastrous consequences on income and profitability and would directly influence the collective bargaining process. These fare wars would force the airlines to negotiate aggressively for lowered labor costs in the future.

The year 1979 saw the beginning of a massive profit decline driven by this fare competition. In 1978, the trunk carriers generated operating profits of $1.2 billion. By 1981, the trunk carriers had suffered operating losses of $672 million, a swing of $1.9 billion.

With new low-cost, nonunion carriers entering the market place, competition in the area of lower fares became increasingly disastrous to the unionized carriers. Price wars became common. Price cutting of as much as 75 percent of preregulation fares became the norm. With wages established by contract, existing carriers were forced to match the prices of the new carriers without the ability to lower costs. These fare wars, promulgated by the new entrants' lower cost structures, caused the unionized carriers to seek immediate solutions. The fare wars set the stage for demands of wage and benefit concessions. Several carriers even formally asked their unions to open negotiations in advance of established contract amendment dates.

As the fare wars continued, market analysts were seeing airline losses so catastrophic that they questioned the ability of some airlines to recover. In an article for *Forbes,* Harold Seneker wrote, "So what this game is really about is: Who will have to draw back from the brink first? Who will have to choose first between owning the routes and owning the more fuel efficient planes the airlines must have in the future? It is a trench war whose Verdun is New York–California. If it long continues without some sort of de facto truce, even winners may be bled white."

Aside from the price wars that developed, incumbent carriers were forced to adopt new managerial strategies. They now had to manage costs and generate revenues to achieve a profitable return, instead of collecting monopolistic revenues guaranteed by the CAB to return an acceptable profit irrespective of costs.

During the initial years of deregulation, the airlines were faced with the challenge of new entrants in the marketplace and had to develop new plans for future viability. No particular approach was followed by all airlines, nor were the questions of expansion, maintenance of market share, fares, and route structure answered similarly. Instead, each airline followed its own path based on its own management capabilities, experiences, capital structure, and the conservative or liberal policies held by its management and boards of directors.

While the depressed economic conditions and fuel crisis of 1979 were beyond direct control of the airlines, many members of the industry made crippling strategic errors. The most prominent example was Braniff International.

Braniff International Airlines saw deregulation as an opportunity to expand its route structure. Braniff was the first airline to apply for "automatic market entry" of unused routes made available by the sunsetting Civil Aeronautics Board. Although others (Texas International, Continental, Pan American, and North Central) would also follow an expansion philosophy, no one did so with the same vigor as Braniff. This monomaniacal approach, without consideration for costs, market surveys, and equipment, would end in the nation's first casualty of deregulation. Braniff filed for a Chapter 11 bankruptcy two years later.

Another option pursued by many airlines was to use the financial mechanism that became the trademark of Texas International. The airlines began to form holding companies. This financial restructuring allowed the carriers to start up a low-cost nonunion airline, owned by a holding company that also owned a union carrier. This is what Texas International did in 1980 with the start-up of New York Air.

To compete both economically and pragmatically, existing carriers began to develop new marketing hook approaches to their former customers when they realized how price sensitive the flying public had become. New marketing devices were developed to reacquire their original customer base and acquire new customers. The business traveler had long been recognized as the core customer for the airlines. With prices at such low levels, what could be done to retain the business passenger?

Frequent-flyer programs were established during the 1980s as a means of instilling passenger loyalty to a given airline. In many ways, frequent-flyer programs are similar to the "Top Value" and "Eagle" stamps programs of the 1960s, which were designed to produce customer loyalty to grocery stores, drug stores, and service stations.

Frequent-flyer programs cater to the business traveler by offering rewards for repeated travel on a given airline. After a designated number of trips, the frequent flyer is eligible for free airline tickets, not only to domestic locations but also to destinations in many parts of the world. In addition to free airline tickets, awards include free hotel stays, free use of rental cars, class of service upgrades, and other onboard amenities. Some of the more recent upgraded programs even include free Caribbean and Greek island cruise trips.

By creating incentives to repeatedly fly on one airline, frequent-flyer programs make it difficult for new carriers to enter a given market. These programs have proved to be very effective marketing tools with which to capture passenger traffic and increase market concentration. Because most frequent flyers travel on their employers' business, their demand for service is highly inelastic. Their employers normally pay for their fares, so passengers are less responsive to lower or incentive fares. With inelastic demand, the high-profit segment of the airline industry is strengthened. This program thus keeps a specific segment of the traveling public at defined high rates as opposed to the leisure or vacation traveler who is cost-conscious.

In addition, marketing shuttle service between selected city pairs increased flight frequencies. In one instance, United changed its name to Alegis and began buying into hotels and car rental companies to offer full door-to-door service for the business traveler. Most major carriers initiated advanced boarding pass and seat assignment programs. On-time performance was also marketed aggressively.

The tourist and vacation passengers were not ignored either. The best surviving examples of marketing and revenue generation in the tourist and vacation segments are United's virtual dominance of the Hawaiian market and American Airlines' AA Advantage vacation packages. Tourist load factors climbed steadily during the early days of deregulation because prices were so low. As prices began to escalate to realistic levels, the smart and customer-responsive carriers began to build loyalty among the tourist passengers with these marketing techniques. This had never been done before.

All of these marketing tools were designed to do one thing: increase load factors and generate increased revenue streams in the face of severe price prostitution by the new entrant carriers. The existing major carriers, financially speaking, had very deep pockets, but they also had very big infrastructure bills to pay. They had to increase revenue growth or lose ground and cease to exist. The list of airlines, both old and new, that are no longer in business is far longer than the list of those that are still operative.

Deregulation forced all carriers to become extremely intelligent marketers. The age of enlightened customer marketing had arrived in the air transport sector with a resounding revenue crash. The major carriers began to recognize the tremendous databases at their disposal in the form of their computerized reservation systems (CRS). Before deregulation, such systems were principally used for flight and route management, overbooking estimates, and static revenue stream and returns analysis.

Deregulation forced the majors to reexamine these computerized reservations systems. They discovered that they could fine-tune their seat departures by creating a variety of "managed yield" fare offerings based on the customer behavior data available. In short, aggressive yield management systems came into their own. The majors also realized that these systems were a marketable profit center in and of themselves, and they began to sell access for profit to the new carriers. They, of course, did not provide full access to all the data, and this created a series of price fixing and unfair competition concerns that continue today. This also provided fertile ground for litigious carriers to seek remedy through the courts.

The automated reservation system has provided several major airlines with a powerful tool to reduce competition. Automated reservation systems are vast computer networks that large carriers, such as United and American and the consortium of Northwest, Delta, and Trans World, use to provide up-to-date flight information to travel agents. Each day, hundreds of thousands of fares change in the airline industry, which high-speed computers can constantly update to assist travelers in purchasing, assist travel agents in selling tickets, and enable airlines to allocate seats.

The travel industry has come to rely not only on automated reservation systems but also on the airlines that own them. It is estimated that nearly 90 percent of all flights are now booked through carriers with computerized networks. American Airlines has the largest system and is used by approximately 14,000 agencies to track some 45 million fares. In 1988, this system produced more than $100 million in profits for American Airlines.

Critics of automated reservations systems claim that airlines employ them to reduce competition. The Transportation Department has charged that American and United provided information that is more prominent for their own system than for competing carriers. It also charged that airline-owned automated reservation systems each profit more than those that would be expected in a competitive market do. In addition, the automated reservation system creates a barrier to entry. Should competitors enter a market, airlines owning the reservation system charge a booking fee for each ticket purchased. This has had the effect of raising a new competitor's cost relative to such airlines who own reservation systems. Consequently, booking fees can reduce prospects for a new carrier's profitable entry.

As the first decade of deregulation ended, many carriers, both new and old, disappeared. Principally, they either merged with stronger operators or experienced bankruptcy. As the industry sorted itself out, fares began to escalate upward reflecting two fundamental facts. First, fewer competitors existed to drive the price downward. Thus, in some markets a classic monopoly developed and price gouging was experienced. Second, increasing operating costs led by high fuel costs and exorbitant fleet replacement costs pushed ticket prices higher. With market consolidation and increased fare structures came profitability, at least for a while.

Frequent-flyer programs were well established and expected perks. The enhanced utilization of CRS capabilities allowed very precise market offerings to specific groups of customers. The travel and tourism market segment was growing significantly. It was too good to be true. The euphoria had to subside. Ultimately it did, as the U.S. and global economy headed toward recession. This downturn started pushing load factors down as businesses were laboring under their own heavy debt loads, the consequence of which is reduced business travel. With the reduction in load factors, airline fleet replacement costs and debt loads were escalating. Some U.S. carriers were operating under bankruptcy protection, again driving fares to unprofitable levels, and foreign carriers were knocking at the door wanting to buy into the largest revenue market in the world.

No amount of marketing could overcome these fundamental market changes. But clearly something had to be done.

Global Revenue Generation (1988–Present)

Domestic Market

Revenue generation and marketing efforts have taken a decidedly different direction since 1988, due to fare wars driven by some carriers operating under bankruptcy protection, which provides them with legally derived but unrealistically low costs and false economies of scale. Competition for domestic passengers remains intense. Partnering with second- and third-level carriers (regional and commuters) has reached new levels of sophistication with shared flight numbers, paint schemes, logos, and interior colors. Many second- and third-level carriers are wholly owned subsidiaries of the surviving major carriers.

The goal is to market seamless service to the customer—one airline from origin to destination. The revenue impact is obvious: all of the fare stays within one organization. The number of interline tickets cleared through the Airline Reporting Corporation (ARC) is still high, but the customer only sees one airline name on the flight coupon, reflecting this trend toward seamless service offerings.

The domestic market has not yet returned to profitability because of the inability to maintain adequate fare levels. This may change in the near future, but if it does, it probably will not last. New carriers are emerging who are able to lease modern equipment and contract services and operate at substantially reduced costs relative to the surviving majors. What can they offer to attract customers? Point-to-point service, instead of connecting through a hub, and low fares for that point-to-point service—in a word, niche markets.

The majors have reduced or eliminated much of their point-to-point service due to low profits or high costs. They prefer instead to let their second- and third-level partners haul the traffic to one of their hubs. The major will then move passengers to their final destination or to another hub to be hauled to the final destination by another of the major carriers supporting partners.

This type of service offering allows a niche player to succeed. Although annoying and troublesome, the majors will probably not choose to compete with a niche player unless that niche player begins to hub and spoke their traffic as well. Should this occur, the majors would probably react rapidly and aggressively.

There is, however, a much more serious domestic market share loss potential than market losses to the emerging niche players. That threat could come from foreign carriers wanting to collaborate and expand into the United States. This potential is immutably tied to U.S. carrier operations in the international markets and will be discussed next.

International Market

The international market remains strong and growing in spite of the global recession. It is the key source of revenue growth in the decade to come in terms of both passenger traffic and cargo. The international market is, however, an extremely complex and politicized market, and it presents some truly significant strategic management problems. By comparison, marketing efforts in the international sector are straightforward. Due to the highly charged political issues involved, let us first examine the historical role of U.S. carriers in the international venue and then move forward to the market and revenue opportunities extant today and in the near future.

To understand the international market requires an appreciation of the bilateral agreements this country has entered into with all foreign nations serviced by or flown over by U.S. carriers. They directly influence marketing and revenue generation in the international venue.

For many years, the dominant carrier in the Pacific was Pan American World Airways. In Europe and the Middle East, it was Pan Am and Trans World Airlines. Both of these carriers operated with full five freedom rights within these regions.

The "five freedoms" of air travel originated in 1944, when fifty-two countries met in Chicago and signed an agreement ostensibly designed to promote a free market philosophy toward the development of relatively unrestricted operating rights in the world marketplace. The participants agreed to the following:

- A civil aircraft of one country has the right to fly over the territory of another country without landing, provided the overflown country is notified in advance and approval is granted.
- A civil aircraft of one country has the right to land in another country for technical reasons, such as refueling or maintenance, without offering any commercial service to or from that point.
- An airline has the right to carry traffic from its country of registry to another country.
- An airline has the right to carry traffic from another country to its own country of registry.
- An airline has the right to carry traffic between two countries outside its own country of registry as long as the flight originates or terminates in its own country of registry.

Since the original five freedoms were identified, three others have been discussed, although not necessarily agreed to by all countries or even by the original parties to the Chicago accord.

- An airline has the right to carry traffic between two foreign countries via its own country of registry.
- An airline has the right to carry traffic from one point in the territory of a country to another point in the same country. This is more commonly known as "cabotage" and is forbidden in many countries by virtue of legislation and bilateral agreements.
- An airline operating entirely outside territory of its own country of registry has the right to fly into the territory of another country and there discharge, or take on, traffic coming from, or destined for, a third country.

These rights and routes were held over from the cold war when the United States aggressively expanded its presence in these regions through the North Atlantic Treaty Organization (NATO) and the Southeast Asia Treaty Organization (SEATO).

The politically free nations of the world did not object to the U.S. presence during these years. In fact, they generally welcomed enhanced air transport services. It meant the nations did not have to invest heavily in the sector themselves. They could devote their capital to other objectives such as industrialization.

The 1960s and 1970s saw these unrestricted fifth freedom operations become more restricted as the flag carriers of the various foreign nations grew into successful operators in their own right, demanding and receiving political action to secure market share for themselves. Understandably, they wanted a bigger piece of the action within their own country. Generally, they received it. However, the American carriers were still the dominant players overall. Foreign carriers operated point-to-point service into selected U.S. cities under bilateral agreements that granted them very little flexibility. U.S. carriers other than Pan Am and TWA also operated point-to-point services to foreign destinations with the same levels of restrictions.

Bilateral agreements are negotiated between the governments of the nations involved, not between the airlines themselves. Airlines file route and rights requests with their respective governments. It is the governments of the two involved nations that negotiate the details of how many flights per week, to what destinations, from what origins or gateways, and any continuation and enplanement privileges. These negotiated agreements remain valid until both parties agree to amend them. Consequently, both governments tend to take somewhat defensive long-view positions when negotiating the agreements.

Bilaterals became a political hot bed of negotiation when deregulation arrived. The foreign carriers wanted into the U.S. market in a big way, but did not want to grant substantive additional rights and routes to the U.S. carriers in return. After all, they had operated under the market dominance of Pan Am and TWA for twenty years. This was their day in the sun.

The result was price wars in the lucrative North Atlantic market, with some of the foreign carriers' losses being absorbed by their respective governments. Price wars and explosive growth in the Pacific Rim by Cathay and Singapore Airlines, Japan Air Lines (JAL), and Air Nippon Air (ANA) were fueled by the tremendous economic growth of the Gang of Four, as they have become known. Throughout the 1980s, Pan Am and TWA took a beating in the international marketplace. Prompted by fares at low yield levels, routes and rights being lost in revised bilateral agreement negotiations, and little cash to upgrade or modernize fleet and service offerings, the outlook for U.S. carriers in the international market was bleak. In Pan Am's case the beating was fatal. TWA survived but lost or was forced to sell much of its foreign operations just to stay in business in the domestic arena. The glory days of American airline international firsts had come to an abrupt end.

In the late 1980s, the surviving U.S. carriers acquired all of the route authorities that remained valid under the revised bilaterals by purchasing them from Pan Am, TWA, and Eastern. United bought all of Pan Am's remaining routes and rights in the Pacific as well as Eastern's South American routes and rights. American Airlines and Delta each bought routes and rights to the European Community from Pan Am and TWA. These actions caused a new round of protestation from the foreign flag carriers and their governments.

The principal reason for these new complaints centered around the wave of privatization that was occurring within the foreign flag carriers. Their governments, strapped for cash, were selling the airlines to their citizens and disengaging from financial support. After all, it would not look good for the British government to raise 3 billion pounds by selling British Airlines (BA) to its citizens and then have BA get run over by American Airlines or Delta, who were not only operating their original route authorities but had acquired the rights and routes of other carriers, which increased their market power significantly.

The situation today is still highly charged. Even as financial support is withdrawn from the various flag carriers in Europe and the Pacific Rim, the governments of these nations have increased their political support of bilateral rights and authorities for their carriers, and so has the U.S. government.

Neither side wants to grant too many new routes and rights, which would cause financial hardship and market share loss to their own carriers. But both sides realize that they will have to grant something to obtain something. Quid pro quo is the basis for bilateral negotiations in the coming decades. Reciprocal rights between countries are considered the minimum bargain. Completely open skies between countries with all carriers in the two countries permitted to fly as frequently as the market will bear and to provide any intracountry continuation services is considered the most attainable and the maximum expectation.

Until recently, the only country to offer an open sky bilateral was the Netherlands. Why did they do this? Purely political reasons. The Netherlands market is not very large relative to the rest of the European Union, and most traffic hauled by KLM, the Netherlands flag carrier, is international in nature. In short, they have nothing to lose at home but something to gain abroad.

The primary reason the Dutch government offered "open skies" is they did not want any political obstacles to surface regarding KLM's equity investment in, and code and equipment sharing arrangements with, Northwest Airlines. Whatever market share KLM loses at home will be more than recovered by coordinated flight operations and joint marketing efforts with Northwest Airlines. In short, this open sky bilateral will mean much more revenue for KLM with incremental increases in operating expenses.

"Open skies" accords allow airlines of two countries to operate air services from any point in one country to any point in the other and from those points to and from third countries. The Clinton administration signed accords in 1995 with about thirty countries but was unable to make any inroads with Great Britain. Most of the agreements reached were with smaller nations, nine in Europe and several in

Asia. In addition, the United States reached an agreement with Canada to liberalize aviation between the two countries. Progress has been made in cargo talks with Japan, and an agreement was reached with China to allow the first nonstop direct U.S. service to Beijing. Accords were also signed with the Philippines, Hong Kong, and Thailand.

The European Union has mixed emotions about "open skies." Although long an advocate of free-market economics, Great Britain has repeatedly refused to ease its highly restrictive relationship with the United States for service into Heathrow Airport, London's premier airport and homebase for British Airways. The United States has attempted to negotiate domestic carrier rights into Heathrow. Domestic airlines argue they need the additional runways that Heathrow provides if they are to compete for the British market and stage planes for flights to continental Europe. Britain, however, refuses to open the skies over Heathrow, for to do so would eliminate a left-handed way of subsidizing that nation's flagship airline. While Britain denies U.S. carriers additional space at Heathrow, British Airways has many gateways into the United States and has a marketing pact with USAir that gives it added access to hundreds of other American cities. With such an arrangement, is it any wonder that the British want to keep Heathrow away from the open sky snowball that is beginning to roll downhill?

The European countries presently participating in an open sky agreement with the United States are the Netherlands, Belgium, Iceland, Austria, Luxembourg, Switzerland, Finland, Denmark, Norway, Sweden, and, most recently, Germany and Spain. The French and Italians, however, are adamant against opening their highly restricted aviation markets.

What does all this have to do with revenue generation and marketing in the international venue? Everything! International enplanements, RPMs, and RTMs are growing steadily. Access to foreign destinations is essential to any carrier that wants to grow. All carriers want to grow! From a U.S. point of view, the existing hub-and-spoke domestic market structure feeds passengers into international routes and feeds international arrivals into the domestic market. The ability to provide seamless passenger service from domestic to international and back to domestic flights will be the key to significant growth. Due to the highly political nature of bilateral negotiations and the strong nationalist movements abroad, it may be quite some time before other nations adopt the open sky policy of the Dutch. If this is the case, and it certainly appears to be, how can carriers achieve the levels of market penetration and load factors to support a massive international investment? There are two methods available today: code and equipment sharing agreements, and direct equity investments.

Code and equipment sharing agreements allow two carriers to book (from the U.S. point of view) passengers on domestic, international, and foreign domestic flights with return on one ticket and one airline code. When passengers arrive for their flight, they could find themselves flying on an aircraft owned and crewed by either carrier. This would be true for all flight segments—domestic, international, and foreign domestic—on that ticket. The distribution of revenue is complicated in this arrangement.

The revenue from a U.S. passenger on domestic flight segments is accrued to the U.S. carrier, no matter which airline carries them. The international revenue could be split between the two carriers, each taking the revenue from one of the international flight segments, both outbound to the U.S. carrier and return to the foreign carrier or the other way round. The foreign carrier would take the portion of the fare attributable to foreign domestic flight segments.

Why go through all this rigmarole? Equipment utilization and operating economies of scale are the major reasons. Both carriers can gear their marketing efforts, highlighting the seamless nature of the service offering. Reduced baggage loss, convenience of transfers, consistency of quality, transferability of frequent flyer miles—all become marketing "hooks" to bolster their respective products. Each carrier can also better use their equipment inventory by combining flight and maintenance planning and coordination, thereby achieving reduced operational expenses with increased load factors.

By coordinating flights and bookings, carriers can fully use their respective bilateral route authorities. This provides for maximum revenue generation and market share impact. Additionally, this duality provides passenger feed into and out of the domestic route systems. Difficult to achieve? Yes. But the additional revenue available at only incremental cost increases makes it a worthwhile exercise, particularly for two carriers who do not have a great deal of investment capital.

The second method is direct equity investment and profit or loss participation. This method is the most frequently utilized, but there are some political problems associated with equity investments. A foreign carrier cannot own more than 25 percent of the voting stock of a U.S. carrier and cannot hold more than a 49 percent equity position in any U.S. carrier. The level of voting stock ownership and total equity investment by a U.S. carrier in a foreign carrier varies widely from nation to nation.

Equity positions and voting rights give the investing carrier strong input into the management decision-making process—but not without risk. These invested positions are open to downside losses as well as upside profits. The synergy achievable under equity partner positions can be more fully exploited due to the high levels of operational and financial input granted to the investing carrier. Fleet replacement orders can be combined and negotiated to terms that are more favorable. The entire system schedules of the two carriers can be melded to achieve maximum utilization, coordination, and therefore enhanced market penetration opportunities. There will still be some segregation of revenues, but not to the same extent as non-equity sharing agreements.

The goal of equity participation investments is to generate revenue streams from air transport service offerings and growth in capital investment value without violating any agreements. Equity participation will remain the principal source of collaboration and market penetration for the next five to ten years at least. Open skies will come, but not for a while.

The easiest way to understand the political and business implications inherent in bilateral route authorities and rights agreements is to return to our dauntless Air Atlantis. We shall examine AirA's international routes and rights requests to serve three equally fictitious countries. AirA is interested in serving New Capitalland, East Ablished, and the island nation of Maple Keys, which is located in the middle of the ocean.

To get to either New Capitalland or East Ablished requires flight through airspace claimed by Maple Keys. Consequently, Air Atlantis needs permission from the monarch of Maple Keys, King Mediator, to overfly his airspace. Although Air Atlantis does not believe there would be a market for air service either to or from Maple Keys, it would also like permission to land at MKY in an emergency. Maple Keys has never signed the Bermuda Agreement permitting the five freedoms of the air.

After lengthy deliberation, the monarch grants these rights for Air Atlantis and asks for nothing in return. Yet!

New Capitalland has two major cities that Air Atlantis wants to serve. Presently AirA does not service New Capitalland. East Ablished has three major cities, and AirA presently services two of these cities. The two countries are located next to each other, and AirA wants to be able to fly into any of the five cities with deplanements and the ability to enplane traffic. AirA would like to haul New Capitallanders' traffic back to the United States and, on a continuation basis, to any of the other four cities in either country. In short, AirA desires full five freedom rights and routes in and between New Capitalland and East Ablished.

The two countries could not be more different. New Capitalland is an emerging capitalist democracy struggling to life after decades of communist rule. It has virtually no inter- or intracountry air transport service. Consequently, New Capitalland welcomes the overtures of Air Atlantis.

East Ablished, on the other hand, is the economic powerhouse of the region with well-developed air transport services provided by its flag carrier, Nocomp Air. Nocomp Air does not want any competition and views the AirA request with a jaundiced eye. In fact, Nocomp Air would like to expand its own service offerings into U.S. markets. It presently serves only two cities in the United States. Nocomp Air is well connected with the government, and it lobbies vigorously to prevent any rights or routes from being given to Air Atlantis. Instead, it seeks more rights and routes for itself into the United States. The battle lines are drawn.

Air Atlantis files its routes and rights requests with the U.S. government. The government contacts New Capitalland and East Ablished. The negotiations with New Capitalland move forward rapidly. The U.S. government supports the emerging democracy and favors the AirA proposal. The negotiations are almost completed when the head of the New Capitallander government, President Milikin, announces there will be no agreement unless Air Atlantis agrees to provide scheduled air service to and between five other New Capitalland cities. He has targeted the cities for massive economic investment and development. This announcement pleases the U.S. government but scares the AirA management team.

Air Atlantis has no desire to be locked into an agreement providing air service to essentially the entire country of New Capitalland. The resultant losses associated with serving an untested market could be fatal. The AirA management team does, however, start analyzing potential cost and revenue models with their CRS database. They also quietly poll the Fortune 500 companies to determine the levels of big business commitment to New Capitalland investment. The results of the poll and the cost and revenue modeling are very encouraging. Many businesses are gearing up to invest in New Capitalland, and the government, under Milikin, is very serious about developing the nation. Air Atlantis has walked into a market lockup. Or has it? Both governments quickly ratify, Air Atlantis agrees to the bilateral terms, and full five freedom skies open.

Air Atlantis announces the start of service and begins training the indigenous staff. In-country load factors in the first full month of operation exceed 90 percent, with fully half of the passengers coming from the United States. The future of AirA revenues and operations to, from, and in New Capitalland is bright indeed.

The negotiations with East Ablished, on the other hand, are at a virtual standstill. The head of the East Ablished government, Chancellor Lozenge, is incensed by the open skies agreement between New Capitalland and the United States. The flag carrier of East Ablished, Nocomp Air, has provided air service to New Capitalland for over twenty years and has increased its frequency to support the democratic revolution. Chancellor Lozenge and his government feel that the United States has played a political end run on them. The position of the East Ablished government has solidified. They will only grant route or rights requests to a U.S. carrier if Nocomp Air gets the same level of access to the U.S. market. Otherwise, there is no deal, and the current bilateral agreement will not be revised.

The management team at Nocomp Air is equally perturbed by the developments in New Capitalland. They inform the government that they adamantly oppose granting any new routes and rights to Air Atlantis. They do, however, recommend granting new routes and rights to another U.S. carrier, BrokeAir, which is seeking and filing for new route authorities to East Ablished. This change of attitude toward a U.S. carrier is not surprising given the fact that Nocomp Air has taken a $500 million equity position in BrokeAir. BrokeAir, a former trunk airline decimated by price wars and the victim of a leveraged buyout, is struggling to emerge from bankruptcy restructuring. It is seeking both an international partner and cash infusion to remain a viable carrier.

Chancellor Lozenge and the government agree to relax their full reciprocity demands. They are willing to grant new operating authorities to BrokeAir to serve the three cities and grant one additional round-trip per week to each of the cities requested by Air Atlantis—provided the United States will grant Nocomp Air access to one more city and open frequency privileges to all three of those cities. Air Atlantis screams at the obvious political retaliation, but its protests are ignored. The U.S. government still wants everybody to be friends and, in the spirit of goodwill, accepts the East Ablished offer. Air Atlantis lobbies Congress to block ratification of the revised bilateral, but to no avail.

Air Atlantis ends up with one additional round-trip per week to the two cities it serves in East Ablished. The additional revenues generated do not cover costs, and Air Atlantis does not continue these authorities. It sells all its operating authorities a year later to Big Brother Airlines for $100 million. The combined marketing power of BrokeAir and Nocomp Air dominates the market within East Ablished and the transatlantic link routes between the two countries as well. Air Atlantis could not compete successfully.

Although it started on a much more positive note, the situation for Air Atlantis in New Capitalland ended up much the same. The country grew very rapidly. Progress was evident all across New Capitalland. Money was flowing into the country in vast quantities. The standard of living was increasing across the board, and many individuals were accumulating great wealth. President Milikin resigned, alluding to health reasons, and for the first time in its history, the government committed to the economic development of New Capitalland.

Milikin evidently started feeling a heck of a lot better after resigning, because he started a new airline in New Capitalland called Krazo Airlines. He first leased new and efficient short- and medium-capacity transports to serve the burgeoning intracountry traffic. Krazo competed head to head with Air Atlantis. Krazo had a solid marketing hook. Milikin marketed Krazo as the national airline of New Capitalland. Krazo advertising even hinted, none too subtly, that it would be downright disloyal to the country not to fly Krazo. Within a year, Air Atlantis quit hauling traffic within New Capitalland. They concentrated instead on further development of the transatlantic feed routes into the New Capitalland market and New Capitalland departures into Air Atlantis's domestic route system.

The former president had other ideas. Krazo leased six intercontinental transports and five additional medium-capacity transports and began service not just to the United States but within the United States as well. In short, Krazo began using

its full rights granted under the open skies bilateral agreement, which was negotiated several years earlier. The U.S. government, pressured by every U.S. carrier, requested new negotiation of the open skies bilateral. New Capitalland politely but
firmly refused. With a full open skies agreement in place, Milikin developed Krazo
from nothing into the dominant carrier in New Capitalland, the dominant carrier
between New Capitalland and the United States, and now an up-and-coming air
service provider within the United States, offering excellent service with modern
aircraft and convenient point-to-point service to the principal business centers
from Krazo's gateway cities. These actions caused AirA's transatlantic load factors
to drop below breakeven. Air Atlantis exited the New Capitalland market as quickly
as it had entered. They couldn't even sell the routes to another competitor, because
under open skies bilateral agreements no route or rights authorities are needed. If
a carrier wants to fly to an open skies country, all that they must have is terminal
facilities and landing slots. That's it. No other permission is needed.

There is one bright spot for Air Atlantis. The AirA market development staff took
a hard look at the island nation of Maple Keys. They discovered an island paradise
with pristine beaches, friendly people, and no tourism development at all. Air Atlantis teamed up with Motel 6 and developed plans for several blue-collar economy
resort complexes on Maple Keys. They requested an audience with King Mediator
to explain the benefits to him and to the island of building such complexes.

When he became aware of how much money Motel 6 and Air Atlantis were willing to put squarely into his hands, King Mediator signed on the dotted line and
threw a big party. Motel 6 built several complexes, and soon several other resort developers discovered the island paradise. The tourist trade soared.

Air Atlantis is the dominant operator to the island from all of North America
with high-density wide-body load factors averaging a consistent 80 percent month
after month. They have a solid marketing hook with a high customer recognition
marketing campaign built around "cheap vacations in paradise." Tom Bodett does
all the radio and TV commercials. No other carrier has been able to make a dent in
AirA's traffic. In short, it is a tremendous success for all parties involved. King Mediator now resides in Atlantic City. He occasionally calls home for more money.

Although somewhat frivolous, the story of Air Atlantis's ventures into the international market represents the range of opportunities and hazards involved in
playing in the international venue. Politics, subterfuge, and graft are common. The
rules can change at any time, for any reason, and in any direction. The rewards are
enormous. But, as with any financial venture, so are the risks.

Although the above story makes for interesting reading, it does fail to take into
account some of the facts of the modern air transport world. Most specifically it
glosses over the important role cabotage plays in the world marketplace. Cabotage

is the right of a foreign carrier to transport fare-paying passengers between two points in a country other than its own. As an example, cabotage rights could permit Japan Airlines, after flying into Chicago from Tokyo, to pick up passengers in Chicago and transport them to St. Louis and then pick up St. Louis passengers and transport them to San Francisco. This is not permitted, however, under present legislation.

Legislation opposing cabotage has given U.S. airlines the exclusive carriage of fare-paying domestic traffic between points in the United States. The Federal Aviation Act of 1958 contains language prohibiting foreign carriers from transporting persons, property, and mail for compensation between two points in the United States. Most countries have similar legislation.

The U.S. Subcommittee on Aviation hearings in 1979 contains a brief history of the origins of cabotage. In the International Air Transportation Competition Act of 1979, the following notation is made:

> Cabotage in aviation matters was apparently first recognized in 1910. The French, who became concerned with German free balloons flying over French territory, convened what was probably the first diplomatic conference to consider flight regulation. While nothing came of the Conference at that time, the later Paris Convention of 1919 provided that contracting states could establish restriction in favor of their national aircraft in connection with the carriage of person and goods for hire between two points in its territory.

The Carter administration developed its own version of "open skies," giving foreign carriers access to an unlimited number of new gateway cities. Before this time, most foreign carriers only had access to the traditional gateways, including New York, Chicago, Los Angeles, San Francisco, and Washington. In spite of their ubiquity, they are still precluded from carrying revenue passengers between two U.S. cities.

Recent "open skies" advocates desire to incorporate the original five freedoms of the air with the three additional ones later promulgated. Combination and acceptance of this arrangement would vitiate any preemption of foreign carriers to cabatoge.

Suggested Readings and References

Airline Deregulation Act of 1978, 49 U.S.C. 1302 et seq.

Curtain, W. (1986, June). Airline labor relations under deregulation. *Monthly Labor Review 109*, 30.

Fradenburg, L. G. (1980). *United States airlines: Trunk and regional carriers, their operations, and management.* Dubuque, IA: Kendall/Hunt.

Goodall, B., Radburn, M., & Stabler, M. J. (1988). *Market opportunity sets for tourism.* Reading, England: Department of Geography, University of Reading.

Great Britain Civil Aviation Authority. (1984). *Deregulation of air transport: A perspective on the experience in the United States.* London: Author.

Heins, C. L. (1991). *To what extent do the various domestic, international, and foreign airlines utilize creative management, incentive, and motivation plans to increase sales?* Chicago: Chicago State University.

McMullen, S. B. (1993). *Profits and the cost of capital to the U.S. trunk airline industry under the CAB regulation.* New York: Garland.

Oster, C. V., & Pickrell, D. H. (1986). *A study of the regional airline industry: The impact of marketing alliances.* Washington: U.S. Department of Transportation.

Robertson, T. S., & Ward, S. (1983, January-February). Management lessons from airline deregulation. *Harvard Business Review.*

Schumann, H. O. (1986). *Oligopolistic nonlinear pricing: A study of trading stamps and airline frequent flyer programs.* Evanston, IL: Northwestern University, Transportation Center.

Seneker, H. (1980, September 1). Fare wars. *Forbes,* 37.

Shaw, S. (1990). *Airline marketing and management.* London: Pitman.

Taneja, N. K. (1982). *Airline planning: Corporate, financial, and marketing.* Lexington, MA: Lexington Books.

U.S. Congress. House Committee on Public Works and Transportation. Subcommittee on Aviation. (1991). *Review of U.S. international aviation policy and bilateral agreements: Hearings before the Subcommittee on Aviation of the Committee on the Public Works and Transportation.* 102nd Cong., 1st sess. Washington: Government Printing Office.

U.S. General Accounting Office. (1990). *Airline competition: Industry operating and marketing practices limit market entry.* Washington: Author.

U.S. Transportation Department, Office of the Secretary. (1990). *Airline marketing practices: Travel agencies, frequent-flyer programs, and computer reservation systems.* Washington: Author.

Yang, C. (1989). The impact of new equity financing on firms' investment, dividend, and debt-financing decisions. (Doctoral dissertation, University of Illinois, Urbana-Champaign.) Available through University Microfilms Vita.

8

AIR TRANSPORT OPERATING COST MANAGEMENT

This chapter examines the cost side of the air transport operations equation. Like revenue generation, cost management and cost control systems evolved in a somewhat haphazard fashion over time. We will first examine a brief history of cost management under CAB regulation. Then we will discuss cost management systems in the industry today with special emphasis on five primary negotiable operating costs incurred by the airlines: labor, commissions, fuel, landing fees, and rentals.

Cost Management (1938–1978)

From 1938 to the late 1960s, cost management under federal regulation was a two-step-backward, one-step-forward process. For example, airlines first had to determine whether they had sufficient financing to purchase a new airport. If they could, they made the purchase, absorbed higher cost profiles, filed a rate increase with the CAB to pass higher operating costs on to passengers, and only then figured out ways to reduce the operating cost of the new equipment to achieve better rates of return.

A hazard to this reverse engineering cost management approach during regulations was that if an airline did achieve significant operating cost reductions, thereby increasing profits, the CAB was almost certain to deny further rate increases. This was done to ensure balanced returns on investment and equity throughout the industry. Through industry regulations, the CAB almost ensured that no particular airline would generate profits more than the return rates of all airlines. In short, well-managed cost-conscious airlines were penalized for being too efficient. Poor cost management practices at some airlines were then subsidized, giving returns to investors throughout the industry.

It wasn't as if airlines and their management could not keenly control costs and profitability. With the advent of powerful data processing and financial modeling systems of the 1960s, the major airlines became supremely capable of "defining" the cost of new equipment and service offerings. However, the safety net of CAB cost pass-through did not create airline impetus to proactively "define cost or reduced operating modalities." All cost reduction efforts were reactive, developed after the equipment introduction or service implementation. In addition, generally, this occurred only if traffic and revenues failed to meet projected expectations.

These philosophies of both regulated rates of return and of operating cost increase pass-throughs, in the form of fare increases, began to change in the early 1970s when vocal critics of the agency charged that its policies had the effect of reducing efficiency, discouraging innovations in service, raising prices, and causing a severe misallocation of resources. This vocalization coincided with the passage of the CAB chairmanship, first to James Robson and then to Alfred Kahn. Both of these gentlemen advocated a more realistic "sink or swim" attitude. Both believed the industry had matured to a point where financial protectionism was no longer necessary. Their laissez-faire policies, coupled with the activity in Congress, led to the passage of legislation that would forever change the complexion of the industry. In 1978, Congress passed the Airline Deregulation Act (ADA), which called for an end to all price changes and route controls by 1983 as well as the termination of the CAB itself in 1985. In the interim, airlines could reduce fares by as much as 50 percent or raise them by as much as 5 percent without CAB approval. Deregulation was not received with universal enthusiasm. Some of the major (previous trunk) airlines vigorously opposed it. Among other things, ADA stopped the practice of passing costs on to the customers through the medium of regulations. After 1978, the airlines would operate as a business devoid of economic protection.

As the move toward deregulation began, the airlines found themselves in a Catch-22 situation. In the early 1970s, the oil-producing countries, represented by OPEC, drove fuel prices to record highs. An aging, non-fuel-efficient fleet, coupled with these high fuel prices, placed the airlines in an untenable position. The question became one of survival economics, and the choices were to keep the old aircraft and lose any market edge due to high fuel costs or to purchase new fuel-efficient transports. Unfortunately, the latter was not easy, as the economy was in recession and capital investment was on the wane. Traffic levels, feeling the effects of recession, were deteriorating. Airline labor unions of the trunks and regionals were demanding their usual 10 percent increases in salaries and benefits. There was also a situation of massive overcapacity and financial losses, and no effective, proactive cost reduction programs were in place. The existing airlines were concerned with survival and found themselves trapped. Too much capacity, inefficient fleets, depressed traffic and revenues, unrealistically high union wage and benefit demands, and uncertain capital market financing commitments made problems that were insurmountable.

The Deregulation Act of 1978 exacerbated this situation by removing all barriers to new carriers. In a tentative marketplace complete with high costs conditioned by years of regulation, the new airlines obtained a tremendous cost advantage. They were immediately able to initiate air service without the weights of the huge infrastructure and high costs of existing carriers. Some argue that this singular aspect put the prederegulation carriers at a distinct disadvantage, and they blame the policies of the CAB for subsequent airline failures and loss of jobs. The old carriers, efficient in the operations of an airline, were inefficient in the game they had been playing, as a new set of regulations changed the ground rules. The new entrants were able to offer the same or better services at noncompetitively lower prices and still make a reasonable return on their investment.

This had not been the experience of the prederegulation carriers. The smart new entrants were cost managed from the outset. The existing majors had to become cost centered overnight. They also still had to replace fleets, deal with union demands, and be price competitive with new carriers. Not an easy task, especially given the conditioning the prederegulation airlines had received for more than fifty years. With the increased mobility of existing airlines and the entry of new firms into the industry, intense price competition was inevitable.

Downward pressure on airfares was exacerbated by the entry of cut-rate carriers, such as People Express, New York Air, and Air One, as well as decisions on the part of several existing carriers, such as Braniff, Frontier, and Continental, to become exclusively discount-fare airlines. Introductory low-fare service was also prevalent wherever major trunk carriers such as American, Delta, or United entered new markets. On long-haul flights, aggressive price cutting occurred as airlines sought to deal with excess capacity resulting from CAB regulation. Competition served to keep a lid on price increases, and discount fares had become so widespread and accessible that by 1986 it was estimated that over 90 percent of all paying passengers were flown at an identified discount rate (i.e., a rate different from the traditional F [First Class], Fn [First Class Night], Y [Coach], and Yn [Coach Night] rates of prederegulation). Lower prices necessitated lower costs, and existing carriers looked to labor as the area to subsidize lower cost implementation. This resulted in slashed labor costs wherever feasible.

The net result of all of the changes was four solvent major carriers (American, Delta, United, and Southwest), three majors who had to use bankruptcy protection law to survive (Continental, America West, and Trans World), Northwest, and USAir. Many carriers either merged or disappeared.

The principal reason for the shape of the current U.S. air transport system is the need for severe cost reduction and cost management practices. Such cost control practices have taken the form of mergers and acquisitions (buying up the competition), outright service reductions (hub-and-spoke operations or parking aircraft and furloughing staff), bankruptcy (eliminating debt load, which creates a reduced cost operating basis), and contractually negotiated cost reductions (union wage reductions and givebacks, long-term fuel commitments and hedges, and negotiated travel agent commission plans).

The following pages concentrate on cost management through negotiated contractual cost reductions for labor, commissions, fuel, and an emerging high-cost area, rentals and landing fees. All of these negotiated areas play directly to service reduction programs of which they are an integral part. Discussion of mergers and bankruptcy is a book unto itself, and we have already examined these areas from a topical perspective in previous chapters.

Labor Costs

Salaries and benefits generally make up 30 to 40 percent, and sometimes more, of an airline's total operating expenses. This should not be surprising given traditionally high levels of task specialization employed in the air transport sector. However, this extreme task specialization has led to an inordinately high level of unionized workers and a plethora of unions. Some of these unions are specific to one craft at one airline alone. Labor relations in the air transport sector are made more complex by being governed by a well defined and yet ambiguous act of labor legislation, the Railway Labor Act of 1926. This labor-management regulation act, amended in 1934 to cover the then emerging air transport sector, is the only area that the Deregulation Act of 1978 failed to address.

In effect, airlines labor relations is no different today than it was in 1958 when jet aircraft first entered service. The reason for this is that the act has never been amended to bring it into the modern day. It still operates under guidelines and procedures defined in 1926. Its sister act, the National Labor Relations Act, which addresses all other forms of labor except for railroads, airlines, and government employees, has been amended several times to more adequately compensate for changes that have occurred. This Railway Labor Act anomaly has created a great impediment to the established carriers' ability to react to the expense side of their operations.

Contractual Environment

A full history and analysis of the implications of the Railway Labor Act is beyond the scope of this course. There are, however, two salient points that must be recognized under the RLA. First, once a craft is unionized at an airline, the employees of that craft must remain represented for as long as the craft exists. For example, if the mechanics of our fictitious airline, Air Atlantis, succeed at gaining representation by the International Association of Machinists and Aerospace Workers

(IAMAW), from that day forward the mechanics at Air Atlantis will remain in a represented state. If, after several years, the Air Atlantis mechanics decide to oust the IAMAW, they will be allowed to remain IAMAW members or to replace that union with another. The new representative does not have to be a certified, bona fide union, as individuals may be certified as employee representatives. The Railway Labor Act, unlike its sister act, gives no indication that a representative can be decertified without replacement. In short, once unionized or represented, they are always unionized or represented.

Because of this, a labor agreement or a contract is valid in perpetuity. Essentially, labor contracts under the RLA never expire. They can be and are amended, generally every three years, but they can never expire or be terminated, and they remain in force until modified by the negotiation process. Therefore, the original labor contract negotiated between management and a union back in the 1930s is still valid today. It has simply been amended over the years to reflect the changes occurring in the world and within the process. This rather bizarre contractual twist makes for some interesting situations. A craft union may strike a carrier, after the government (the National Mediation Board) has released the parties from negotiation responsibilities. Should a union strike a carrier, the carrier may, under certain circumstances, hire replacement workers. These replacement workers are, however, by legalese peculiarities future members of the union they are replacing. This is so because the striking union or representatives have rights to the job or the work involved. Consequently, the replacement workers are covered by the very contract the striking workers are seeking to affect, excluding the particular contract items for which bargaining remains open. Thus, these individuals are not replacement workers at all but additional hires to the existing craft workforce, who just so happen to be on strike.

This type of regulatory system omnipresent in a "deregulated" industry provides shtick for comedy teams like Bud Abbott and Lou Costello, who made famous the "Who's on First?" routine. In a fight for their economic life, the preregulation carriers have had to contend with mixed signals, changing environments and antiquated labor relations regulations.

Because of these two unique contractual labor situations, labor employees over the life of an airline service fared extremely well in terms of wage and benefit increases. Where the company could not control costs at the bargaining table, the CAB provided necessary relief by increased fare levels. Wage and benefit levels became bloated, and inordinate increases outstripped productivity and growth. Over the years, as the union represented employees and to a lesser degree management, members grew complacent, expecting and anticipating large increases in wages and benefits with little or no offsetting improvements in productivity.

The Deregulation Act of 1978 changed that expectation. The most profound internal impact of deregulation has been its effect on collective bargaining labor contracts and labor cost versus productivity equation. Before deregulation, virtually all productivity improvements in the air transport sector came about through improvements in technology, not in labor productivity. The air transport unions were just as unprepared for deregulation as management. However, due to a pro-business Republican administration in the early postderegulation period, management found a new and powerful set of cost management tools and began correcting the excessive labor cost structures accumulated over the forty years of CAB regulation.

Labor Cost Management in the 1980s

The responsibility for improving labor cost structures fell solely to the existing majors as the new carriers avoided unionization. The existing majors attempted to redress the errors of past overinflated industry wage levels. To accomplish this without affecting the present employee population, the industry attempted to lower entry-level wages. This approach to future wage controls would ensure future cost reductions. These so-called B scale or two-tiered wage plans were contested vigorously by the transport unions. The original intent of the B scale plan was to remain unlinked with the A scale wages then in effect. However, over time the unions successfully negotiated linkages back to the A scales, and the B scales have ultimately faded from the labor scene because the unions have been successful at negotiating them out of existence.

The original B scale concept would have provided immeasurable cost reductions for the beleaguered industry. Had the Railway Labor Act been impacted by the Airline Deregulation Act, B scales might still be in place. However, the inordinate amount of power provided by present labor procedures inuring to the unions eliminates a necessary ingredient to cost control, the inability to manage.

A more effective and pervasive technique to cost control was to negotiate temporary wage reductions; such reductions were to be given back plus some level of additional increases on the condition of significant craft productivity increases and business improvement. This technique challenged the unions to become part of a solution by improving performance and working with management to help the airline prosper.

Grudgingly, the unions agreed to such contractual agreements. Such introspection was probably due to the realization that the only other choice available to management was massive service reductions coupled with deep furloughs. The unions, in their zeal to seize some of management's responsibilities, negotiated adequate protection for any concessions. Some of the early concessions, however, were lost forever. This brings us to the present labor environment.

Labor Cost Management in the 1990s

Until recently, the U.S. air transport industry suffered from massive overcapacity, depressed revenues, fleet upgrade and replacement requirements, and high cost structures. Consequently, they sought union wage and benefit concessions, improvement of craft level productivity, and the unequivocal use of cross-utilization abilities. The unions were again faced with agreeing to these concessions or experiencing large workforce reductions.

This time the unions agreed to wage and benefit reductions only on the condition that they be given significant input into the business decision-making process by obtaining equity offsets for productivity gains. Unions' counterdemands exhibited themselves as seats on the board of directors and on various long-range planning committees, as well as substantial equity positions in the company. Experience had taught them to respond, "We'll give you millions of dollars in wage and benefit reductions over the next so many years, but there must be a quid pro quo, a return."

Where many were predicting the demise of unions in general and in the airline industry specifically, the tail is now beginning to wag the dog. Just as the unions were uncertain how to view management proposals of the early 1980s, management is now uncertain and skeptical about union proposals. Are the unions disciplined enough to reduce their own memberships through layoffs and workforce reductions if those steps become necessary to save their employer? Do union equity positions in a carrier create a legal conflict of interest between union management and rank-and-file members? These and many more complex questions have yet to be answered.

Although management has been successful at achieving substantial labor cost reductions in the last ten years, the unions have come to realize they must become proactive in dealing with legitimate management cost concerns. In this tenuous and uncertain market, a stable, long-term, equitable, and viable contractual labor environment and collective bargaining process has yet to be found. The RLA remains virtually unchanged from the 1930s and in many ways is debilitating to both management and labor. One might say that the act designed to promote harmony in the industry actually seems to promote adversarial relationships. The parties in deep need of each other's help may be restricted by the very act that allegedly helps them.

Commissions

Commissions paid by the airlines to travel agencies generally represent the second or third largest operating expense for most carriers. Again, because most airline costs are variable, any of the items of labor, agency commissions, and fuel can change swiftly and thereby alter the ranking of the big three costs.

Given the fact that travel agencies generate well over 80 percent of airline ticket sales in the United States, any attempt to reduce or reformat commission payments to these agents can be akin to making nitroglycerin. It's a very simple, straightforward process to reduce commission payouts, but if even the slightest error in judgment or procedure is made, a significant piece of the surrounding real estate can be converted into a smoking hole in the ground. The dangers of attempting to fiddle with travel agency commission programs have not prevented some airlines from trying. In 1997, Delta Airlines proposed a commission reduction to agencies such that they would continue to pay agency commissions at the prevailing 10 percent rate. However, the maximum amount would be capped at $50 per ticket sold. This means a ticket of $1,000 whose normal commission generation would be $100 would now only garner $50. With a leader in the field, other airlines who would not consider taking such a chance jumped on the bandwagon. In a knee-jerk fashion, the American Society of Travel Agents (ASTA) filed a lawsuit against all participating carriers charging restraint of trade, price fixing, and other charges. Since this filing, several airlines have backed away from the suit and reinstituted the standard 10 percent commission rate without any cap. The most notable of these carriers has been Trans World Airlines, who as a result had the ASTA charges dropped.

The net result of attempts to reduce agency commissions was a completely legal and very effective boycott of that airline by the travel agents. Agents would not refuse to book tickets on the affected airline, but they offered their customers other airline services and connections. The response to Delta's commission reduction was not dissimilar. Some agencies went to such extremes of charging surcharges when their clients booked on airlines participating in the commission reduction.

Given the power that the travel agencies have in funneling customers to airlines, how and what can be done to reduce the cost of commissions? In a typical airline industry fashion, the answer lies in another reverse engineering cost reduction solution reminiscent of the 1940s and 1950s.

Most airlines are now owned by holding companies with the airline itself being only one part of the holdings. Another part of the holding company assets are their computerized reservations systems (CRS) and the attendant massive data gathering and processing capabilities these systems possess. The holding companies of most majors have split off the CRS and have made them stand-alone profit centers. How? By requiring travel agencies to purchase or lease the computers, monitors, and keyboards used to access the CRS or to pay a monthly user access fee or a volume-related activity-based-on-usage fee to the computer company.

In this scenario, the airline leaves the commission structure alone but charges the travel agencies to access its CRS. The net increase in CRS usage revenues can offset commission payouts to travel agents. The result is a net reduction of the commission rate. It would be logical to assume the travel agencies realize what is transpiring and will complain. They do. But the travel agents are dealing with their own kind of nitroglycerin access to CRS. Without access, a travel agency is virtually noncompetitive. The major airlines of today have constantly expanded the capabilities of their reservations systems, making it harder, if not impossible, for the travel agencies to operate efficiently without them. So, like the airlines who scream about commissions, the travel agencies complain about CRS access fees, but not too loudly.

The Deregulation Act saw a rapid rise and then a shakeout in the number of airlines in the United States. It also saw a rapid rise in the number of travel agencies. Approximately 32,000 travel agencies presently operate in the United States, compared with 5,000 before deregulation. Because of this huge increase and the competitive nature of the industry, the trend has been toward consolidation and franchise. Many of the extremely large agencies, including Maritz, Carlson Travel, and IVI, have been absorbing smaller agencies. Large franchisers have entered the market, causing a proliferation of new agencies. The largest of these organizations are Uniglobe Travel and Travel Agents International. Franchising permits individuals to buy into a known name and sell agency services registered with the franchiser. Basically, a franchised travel agent is an independently owned travel agency using the franchiser's name, travel packages, management procedures, and training expertise. In return for the franchisers' expertise, the franchisee pays a percentage of the agency sales to the franchiser.

The 32,000 agencies can be grouped into three general classes: very large franchised national agencies catering almost exclusively to business or tourism, the local full-service mom-and-pop agency, and a niche agency catering to a specific type of client or travel.

In terms of the cost of access, the large national agencies, because of their huge sales volume, can and do receive favored nation access rates and privileges from the major reservation systems and substantial perquisites such as free trips, preferred seating, and direct access to the lowest fares for any category of ticket. The local mom-and-pop has to pay the going rate, as determined by the CRS, without any special privileges. The niche player can pick and choose which access level and CRS best suits its type of sales categories.

Figure 8-1. Airline Reservation Systems

Airline Computer Reservation Systems	Owners/Participating Carriers
Apollo	United Airlines
Sabre	American Airlines
System One	Continental Airlines
Worldspan (formerly PARS)	Delta, Northwest, and Trans World Airlines

There is, however, a problem. Because there are only four or five fully capable reservation systems available, any attempt by an airline to cut CRS access rates to capture market share will be met with equal or greater cuts by the other reservation systems. Such attempts could also generate lawsuits of unfair pricing and collusion. Just as ticket price reductions trigger fare wars, CRS access fee reductions can trigger CRS wars. Another market share acquisition technique used by the big four CRS operators is to offer to buy out an agency's existing CRS contract with another system and install their system at favorable rates.

This is done in the hope of generating not only additional CRS revenues and agency loyalty but also additional bookings on the new CRS's airline. This technique has been used extensively at locations where a competing airline and its CRS have a dominant hub presence, such as American Airlines attempting to buy out Worldspan contracts in St. Louis where TWA is the main carrier.

If there has been a sacred cow in the airline industry, up to this point it has been the travel agency commission structure. As with all things, this too is beginning to pass. Predictably, airline concern about supply channel and the desire to minimize its cost impact will ultimately be the unraveling of travel agencies, as they are known today. Ultimately, because of the lower and lower margins, a vast number of the 32,000 agencies will depart the scene. But for now commissions remain, and the only way to mitigate the cost of commissions is to charge the travel agencies for CRS access or attempt the present Delta strategy. But the airlines are still working on new ways to reduce their commission costs through technological innovations.

Many of the reservation systems have opened access to individuals with personal computers through links with such on-line software as Prodigy, Netscape, America Online, and CompuServe. This positions the airlines to capture more non-travel-agent bookings as personal computers continue their surge to ubiquity and people become more comfortable utilizing on-line services. Airlines are also placing automated ticketing machines (ATMs) at various locations throughout a city. These ATMs also book flights directly into the CRS, bypassing the travel agencies and their commissions.

Maintaining commission and CRS fee structures and innovating new non-travel-agency booking techniques work well, but obviously only for those airlines that have reservation systems. Airlines that don't have systems of their own pay not only commissions to travel agents for tickets sold but also "listing fees" to the airlines that do have the CRS. Additionally, they pay a "booking fee" every time a travel agent books a non-CRS airline passenger ticket or changes information in that passenger's record locator. This fact has led to several more lawsuits charging unfair competitive practices and collusion. Several of these suits are still in litigation.

In summary, travel agency commissions are negotiable but only over an extremely narrow range and only with the largest of travel agencies. All other agencies receive the going rate of approximately 10 percent net after applicable taxes and the rate for CRS access. The airlines reduce their commission costs by charging access fees on their CRS, again only over a narrow range so as not to trigger a CRS access fee war. Mom-and-pop travel agencies and non-CRS airlines get hammered the hardest by having to pay the most for access to CRS listings and bookings. Advanced technology access methods like on-line links with personal computers and ATMs directed at the customer are in initial stages of development. However, as the industry continues to move toward globalization, commission structures, access fees, and nonagency ticketing methods, like every other negotiable operating cost, will be affected.

Fuel

Fuel represents the most significant item in an airline's operating budget and is the single highest direct operating cost for many carriers. The best way for an airline to save fuel, and ultimately fuel cost, is to modernize its fleet, converting to newer, fuel-efficient aircraft. However, for many carriers, the practicability of this approach is lost in the cost of such an endeavor. In 1990, Perry Flint wrote an article for *Air Transport World* entitled "A Fuelish Problem," which has distinct applicability to the carriers' cost dilemma. Its message was valuable then and is so today, when fuel prices are again on the increase. By special permission of *Air Transport World*, the main thrust of that article is reprinted below.

> Next to the cost of employing the thousands of workers that it takes to operate a large airline, fuel is the single greatest operating expense facing any carrier. But unlike wages and benefits of these employees, which are fixed over the life of a contract and relatively predictable even over the long term, changes in the price of fuel can and often do occur with little or no warning. Furthermore, although airlines can exert a good deal of influence over labor expense, they have little control over the price of oil, which in turn largely determines the price of jet fuel.
>
> Given these realities, it is somewhat surprising that so many airlines take a laissez-faire approach to dealing with the cost of purchasing fuel, preferring to focus only on controlling consumption as a way of reducing fuel expense. . . .
>
> It is not as if airlines are unaware of the existence of financial-market mechanisms intended to reduce their vulnerability to rapid shifts in the price of fuel. It's just that the carriers prefer not to use them. Their reasoning runs from the theoretical to the practical.

One of these mechanisms, known as *hedging*, consists of counterbalancing a present sale or purchase with a purchase or sale of a similar or different commodity, in this case fuel. The desired result is that the loss or profit on the future purchase or sale offset the profit or loss on a current sale or purchase.

For example, one executive with a major U.S. airline recently explained that airlines do not need to hedge their fuel costs, because they can pass increases along to the paying customer in the form of higher ticket prices. That strategy works in theory. Of course, it assumes that there are enough passengers willing to fork over extra money for tickets and not enough airplanes to carry them on or, in industry lingo, that traffic demand is strong and capacity is tight. Any other situation could result in consumers declining to play the part of industry safety net. . . .

Another commonly accepted rationale [for not considering hedging approaches] is that all airlines suffer equally when oil prices rise and benefit equally when prices fall, so why bother hedging? A corollary to this argument is that unless everybody hedges, the tactic actually could destabilize the industry, since those who hedged [their fuel costs] would be tempted to use it as a weapon to their own advantage: Having locked in cheap fuel for a few months, they could keep fares low, forcing nonhedgers to match those fares—despite higher fuel prices—or risk losing market share. Better that all remain equally vulnerable to fuel-price hikes, the reasoning goes, so that none is tempted to exploit the situation and start an all-out fare war. . . .

As to whether higher fuel prices affect all carriers equally, no doubt it has occurred to some carriers that as they operate a larger percentage of aircraft powered by fuel-efficient, high-bypass engines, they will see a measurable difference in the total amount of fuel they consume. . . . It is an advantage that will occur slowly but inevitably. As they consume less fuel, so will they be less affected by higher fuel prices—and they can be expected to turn this advantage into a marketing weapon.

Airlines can also utilize advanced route planning and navigational systems to fly more direct routes that consume less fuel. Using advanced routing and navigation systems does require permission and cooperation from federal and international air traffic management authorities. Not all air traffic control systems are capable of supporting these advanced route planning and navigation requirements.

While fuel hedging is available to all carriers, only carriers with superior financial resources can afford to buy new fuel-efficient transports and improved navigation systems. They are not cheap. So why haven't the airlines utilized fuel hedging more aggressively? Flint explains:

Beyond the theoretical arguments against fuel hedging, there are the practical ones: It's still too new a concept; it's risky; it's expensive and it requires additional employees and a large in-house trading department.

. . . Fuel hedging is new to the airline industry, says Elizabeth Reed of Phibro Energy, a subsidiary of the investment banking firm of Salomon, Inc. . . . According to Reed, airlines only began using financial mechanisms to protect fuel expenses [during the late 1980s] and no market yet exists for the trading of jet-fuel futures contracts. Instead, airlines that hedge on their own must try to find benchmark oil products that behave in a manner similar to jet fuel, such as heating oil.

The first carriers to begin hedging were European charter airlines. Because they cater to package-tour operators who need to have fixed airfares well in advance of actual tour dates, charter carriers are especially vulnerable to rapid swings in the price of fuel. On the other hand, charter airlines have the advantage of knowing what their revenues will be months in advance, thus making it easier to budget expenses.

Says Reed: "The charter airlines had fixed-price ticket sales, so economically it was easier for them to go out and lock in their fuel prices because then they'd locked in their margin." Being relatively small and operating limited numbers of routes, charter carriers also could hedge fuel expense on a route-specific and aircraft-specific basis. Today, charter airlines are still the ones most likely to be found using fuel hedges. . . .

Certain European flag carriers also have admitted that they hedge their fuel expenses, including Aer Lingus, KLM and SAS. One European airline executive told *ATW* that his company has been hedging for two years and expects to save in excess of $10 million, thanks to its hedging efforts this year. The executive suggested that European airlines are more comfortable with fuel hedging because they have relatively more experience in dealing with currency swaps because so much of their traffic is international.

Beyond the newness of the concept, other arguments used by some airlines—that it's risky and costs too much—suggest . . . that many airlines are not completely clear on what hedging is supposed to do for them. In the first place, "hedging is not supposed to make you money," states [Phibro Energy's Chris] DeMarco emphatically. And rather than increasing risk, it is supposed to reduce it, assuming airlines are not tempted to try to turn hedging into an income tool by playing the market.

"Airlines should know up front that hedging is a negative-net-present-value investment. You go into it expecting to lose a little bit of money, the same way that you don't insure your home expecting to make money on the insurance.

Most people insure their home knowing that, year after year, they throw away the premium. You don't invest hoping to make money as a result of the disaster. You pay a little bit of money this year and a little bit of money next year, and when a catastrophe does happen, you are protected. . . ."

And rather than adding an element of risk to the operating equation, "the whole idea of a hedge is to stabilize cash flows, standardize the budget and control costs and hopefully make the airline's profitability slightly more predictable," he explains. Airlines that are only trying to safeguard their fuel prices do not need a full-fledged trading department, either, says DeMarco.

DeMarco outline four basic hedging strategies . . . which also can be used in combination with one another.

The simplest hedge is a swap transaction. "That means fixing the price of jet fuel, relative to an established benchmark and then exchanging cash payments throughout the terms of that contract so that the customer effectively is made whole to that fixed price," explains DeMarco.

For example, says DeMarco, Phibro and an airline might agree on a price of $200 per metric ton [fuel is purchased in tons, not gallons]. If the price of fuel goes over that figure, then Phibro Energy must make up the difference. But if the price falls below the established benchmark to $190 per metric ton, then the customer must pay Phibro the difference. . . .

The risk in this sort of transaction for the airline, in addition to the up-front fee to purchase a swap, is that if jet-fuel prices fall dramatically, its competitors may be able to lower fares to reflect the savings that a hedging carrier might not enjoy. Acknowledging this risk, an executive with a major European flag carrier says the time to think about a swap is when the upside risk exceeds the downside risk—that is, prices are likely to rise faster and further than they are likely to fall.

The second hedge technique is known as price insurance. The airline pays an up-front fee for the right to cap its maximum exposure to increases in the price of fuel. The only cost to the airline is the up-front premium it is paying for the privilege of limiting its exposure to an increase in fuel prices.

Another hedging technique is called a collar and does not involve an up-front fee. In this case, the airline and Phibro agree to both a maximum and a minimum price of fuel. If the price of fuel climbs above the maximum price, Phibro must absorb the excess. But if the price falls below the minimum, Phibro pockets the savings. In effect, the airline hedges its upside risk in exchange for giving away some of the benefits from a decline in the price of fuel.

The fourth hedge is known as a participation hedge. With no up-front fee, the airline can establish a level above which Phibro must absorb an increase in fuel expense. In exchange, it agrees to share with Phibro a percentage of the savings, should the price fall below that level.

In each case, the goal of the hedge is to allow the airline to know what its maximum fuel cost will be and to plan accordingly. "I often wonder," says DeMarco. "You do a margin analysis and factor in the cost of hedging and what it means to the bottom line. Certainly, you lose something on margin but it makes the margin less volatile. And it means that in times of high prices, such as these, at least with respect to jet fuel, airlines can maintain their profitability."

For the most part, the U.S. carriers have not yet accepted hedging as a viable cost control tool. Instead, they prefer the more conventional methodologies of acquiring new fuel-efficient transports and improving flight route planning. However, as the pressures of globalization mount, particularly in the face of depressed traffic and uncertain capital market access, hedging fuel costs will become a widely used and accepted cost containment tool. When is anybody's guess, but certainly not until the U.S. carriers can learn to avoid devastating and self-destructive fare wars and begin to focus on the offshore threats to market share. Foreign flag carriers are already hedging fuel and achieving substantial gains in operating cost stability and flexibility.

Landing Fees and Rentals

Cost management and legalized control of competition have become a significant concern and strategy for airlines in regard to airline-airport operations. Limited airport resources constitute a significant barrier to entry for airlines seeking to establish new service. The two most important airport resources are gate space and takeoff and landing slots. Many preregulation carriers have negotiated long-term leases with airports that serve to lock out new airlines, preventing them from serving select markets. With long-term leases existing at many airports on most gate spaces, new carriers are impeded from securing a foothold in the market, and existing smaller carriers find it difficult to expand services. The market value of gate space to airlines is evident whenever an ailing airline seeks to leave a given market.

Takeoff and landing slots are also sources of barriers to entry. These slots are usually allocated by administrative decision. At four major airports—O'Hare (Chicago), National (Washington), La Guardia (New York), and Hartsfield (Atlanta)—these slots can be bought and sold at market price.

One of the most radical changes relative to airport operations abetted by deregulation has been the manner in which airlines have restructured staging areas to increase market share. In the preregulation environment, most trunk carriers flew linear route structures or mostly point-to-point between cities. After deregulation they initiated hub-and-spoke systems. This system allows for increased service between smaller cities and permits a carrier to feed itself rather than rely on another carrier to act as a prederegulation local carrier.

The hub-and-spoke system provides important advantages to both passengers and airlines. First, the system generates more service, allowing passengers to select flights closer to their preferred departure times. Second, travel time is reduced. Passengers departing from the hub are better able to fly nonstop to their destinations, while passengers located in spoke cities are usually faced with no more than a change of planes at the hub. With this system, the need to change airlines is sharply reduced. Third, a major advantage to airlines from the hub-and-spoke systems is an increase in the average load factors.

Airline domination of certain airports has led to the terminology of "Fortress Hub," a location where a dominating carrier has established operations that make competition virtually impossible or impractical for another carrier. So dominant have such carriers become that their monopoly routes have caused increased ticket prices, rather than the reduced prices that the framers of deregulation had promised. The rise in ticket prices at hub airports has led to investigations by the federal government's General Accounting Office. In 1989, the GAO indicated that thirty-eight airports dominated by one or two carriers had airfares that averaged twenty-seven more revenue-per-passenger miles.

Landing fees have escalated steadily as airport authorities try to generate funds to ensure modernization and expansion in the face of uncertain federal, state, and local funding commitments. Most airports are public institutions and as such are free of taxation and eligible for federal and state funding. Over the years airlines have become financial partners with the major airports in the United States. The airlines have invested heavily in terminals and hanger facilities, and they operate under virtually permanent leases. Existing airports are now either at or beyond physical operating limits and in desperate need of replacement or substantive expansion.

As the need to expand or replace has become critical and funding sources have become uncertain, existing transport airports had to seek self-help funding methods for expansion. Federally allowed PFCs are one new method. Escalating landing fees and lease rates are another.

All major transport centered airports have increased landing fees substantively over the last ten years. Initially these increases were due to higher levels of operational activity spurred by the new carriers. More takeoffs and landings caused runway, taxiway, and apron maintenance costs to rise, justifying the increases. Then, as the industry sorted itself out through consolidation and bankruptcy, flight activity began to drop. But the airports, which were by now very attached to the new income generated by increased activity levels, began to see revenue decrease. To compensate, they increased landing fees further in an effort to preserve their expansion plans.

The airlines also began to hub and spoke their operations, which increased their activity levels and costs at hub airports and decreased them at spoke airports. The spoke airports raised landing fees. The airlines who, through hubbing and merger, became the dominant operator at an airport sought negotiated relief, and they generally got it with favored nation landing and lease fees, in return for capital improvement programs in terminal and hanger facilities.

Today the picture is still very unclear. The airlines are reducing service offerings and flight frequencies in an effort to cut costs and return to profitability. This reduces the airport revenue stream and can trigger another round of fee escalation and negotiation sessions. Any such fee escalation could cause the airlines to further reduce activity levels in an effort to save their way back to profitability. The problem is circular and can and will only be managed through active and forthright negotiation with the airport authorities.

Also at issue is the potential privatization of some public airports. If the privatization movement gains momentum, landing fees and lease rates could rise to unaffordable levels at privatized airports. A delicate balance of airport funding and the airlines' ability to pay may well have to be struck. In this case there is no reason for the airport to exist, and it would probably be sold off to developers. The United States needs more transport airports, not fewer. This potential privatization and closure could be severely restrictive to the successful continuation of the world's best air transport system. A coherent and well-funded federal transportation policy would be an excellent first step.

The airlines are suffering from massive overcapacity, aging fleets, an uncertain economic outlook, and the requirement to meet Stage III noise objectives on time. With all the excess capacity and an uncertain economic outlook, why would airlines aggressively rent more transports? They do so because they can rent more efficient aircraft that are better suited for use on selected routes and city pair markets and park older, more costly aircraft. By tailoring their rental of new aircraft and retiring older aircraft, they can generate the same or greater revenues at considerably lower unit costs. By judiciously using rental and leasing options, an airline can achieve the goal of more efficient and less costly operations without having to purchase capital equipment.

Renting also allows the airlines to add appropriate equipment to their inventories and to support even short-lived promotional activities such as charters and onetime or short-term ticket promotions. By requiring advanced purchase, the airline can identify the level of traffic needed to be carried and quickly rent the most cost-effective transport to accomplish the task.

In summary, landing fees will continue to increase as airports try to maintain revenue streams and expansion programs. The airlines will negotiate favored nation rates wherever they have the power to do so. The federal government needs to establish a coherent transportation policy for both the airports and airlines to build on. As market perturbations continue and globalization inches forward, airlines will seek the best price rental opportunities to capitalize on unit cost operating advantages for even short-term market-specific activities and promotions. Rental activity will decline when the industry is able to see stable profits returning and it begins to make capital plant investments for the long term.

Suggested Readings and References

Air Transport Association. (1980). *Fuel: The most critical problem facing the U.S. airline industry*. Washington: Author.

Allen, R. (1979). *Capital financing and re-equipment of the world's commercial airline fleets in the 1980s*. London: Economist Intelligence Unit.

Doganis, R. (1992). *The airport business*. New York: Routledge.

Flint, P. (1990, December). A fuelish problem. *Air Transport World, 27*, 56–57.

International Civil Aviation Association. (1986). *Manual of airport and navigation facility tariffs*. Montreal: Author.

International Civil Aviation Association. (1991). *Airport economics manual*. Montreal: Author.

International Civil Aviation Association. (1992). *Statements by the council to contracting states on charges for airports and air navigation services*. Montreal: Author.

Koelsch, R. K. (1978). *Gear-up and throttle-down to save fuel*. Ithaca, NY: Northeast Regional Agricultural Engineering Service, Cornell University.

Richardson, D. J., & Rodwell, J. F. (1990). *Essentials of aviation management*. Dubuque, IA: Kendall/Hunt.

Saunders, L. (1987). *Wages, work rules, and cost-efficient firms in the deregulated airlines industry*. Berkeley: Institute of Transportation Studies, University of California at Berkeley.

Smith, J. (1981). *Trends in energy use and fuel efficiency in the U.S. commercial airline industry*. Washington: U.S. Department of Energy, Office of Policy, Planning, and Analysis.

Stratford, A. H. (1967). *Air transport economics in the supersonic era*. New York: St. Martin's.

U.S. Federal Energy Administration and U.S. Small Business Administration. (1975). *Handling fuel and fuel problems: An energy handbook for small businesses*. Washington: Author.

9

AIR TRANSPORT YIELD MANAGEMENT SYSTEMS

Airline yield management is an attempt by the airline to maximize revenue (RPMs and RTMs) on a given city pair route with the minimum capacity (ASMs and ATMs) needed to achieve that objective. Yield measures the effectiveness of route and system revenue generation efforts. The advent of powerful data processing systems has driven airline yield management to new levels of sophistication and responsiveness.

In this chapter we will discuss what airline yield management is and what it is designed to accomplish. Then we will examine three components of modern airline yield management systems: (1) air traffic demand and capacity supply characteristics, (2) national and international business and economic conditions and trends, and (3) competitive forces.

Yield Management Definition

Yield management is a mechanism of pricing management and market segmentation. Airlines use this to continuously monitor and analyze traffic demand and regulate the number of seats offered at various prices. This allows them to fill seats with traffic paying the highest price, maximizing revenue generation.

The standard equation for deriving passenger yield is

$$\frac{\text{Passenger Revenue}}{\text{Revenue Passenger Miles}}$$

The standard equation for deriving cargo yield is

$$\frac{\text{Cargo Revenue}}{\text{Revenue Ton Miles}}$$

Yield is a direct measure of retail sales activity. It is not a measure of profitability. The result of these two equations is a measure, in cents per mile, of the total value of the sales generated (tickets sold) on a particular route segment across the airline's entire system. There are no cost factors included in the yield equations, only revenue. Therefore, yield is a tool for measuring the effectiveness of marketing and pricing strategies and not a direct measure of profit or loss. Although the annual and quarterly financial reports of the airline indicate yield as calculated for the entire system, internally airlines utilize track yield by a variety of breakdowns, including service class, ticket type, city pair, time of departure, and day of week.

The yield levels generated by any particular route are used to identify problems or opportunities that airlines can address. Low yields on a route can point to problems such as ineffective marketing, unpopular frequency patterns, highly elastic traffic demand, or some combination of these factors. Low yield can also be caused by a deep discount fare war among the carriers in that market. Routes with high yield can point to market dominance due to effective promotional efforts or a market with low but inelastic traffic demand.

Yield, when matched with load factor, can help further identify marketing or pricing problems or opportunities. It is possible to generate extremely high yields with very low load factors when traffic demand is inelastic. It is equally possible to generate extremely low yields with load factors approaching 100 percent when traffic demand is highly elastic. Either can point to capacity, frequency, pricing, or competitive problems. The following examples will help clarify this apparent paradox.

A 100-seat aircraft is flying on a 500-mile route segment, and the baseline one-way fare for this route segment is $200. The discounted one-way fare is $100.

Example 1:	Full fare	
	Load factor	50%
	Revenue (50 × $200)	$10,000
	RPMs (50 × 500)	25,000
	Yield (Rev ÷ RPM)	$0.40
Example 2:	Discount fare	
	Load factor	100%
	Revenue (100 × $100)	$10,000
	RPMs (100 × 500)	50,000
	Yield (Rev ÷ RPM)	$0.20

With these two extreme examples as a backdrop, let's examine the input factors of a yield management system.

Yield Management Factors

There are three basic components to any yield management system: traffic demand, capacity supply, and the general business climate. The first two factors, coupled with business and economic conditions, are used to establish the baseline, or full fare, ticket prices. Traffic demand and the varying elasticity of demanded traffic set the baseline fare pricing.

The baseline fare is designed to capture the inelastic portion of the traffic demand that represents the core revenue source for the airline, the business traveler. The fare prices for the discounted fare discretionary travelers are calculated from the baseline fares and are designed to capture the highly elastic portion of the traffic demand. The prevailing economic and business conditions regulate these fare prices over the range of elasticity in that market. The competitive factor enters the equation due to the oligopolistic nature of the air transport sector. Air carrier ticket pricing, load factors, and yield levels are greatly influenced by competitive actions in a given city pair market or customer segment.

Although we will be discussing each of these factors separately, it is important to realize they are all interrelated and intertwined in a complex web of cause and effect. It is this complex interdependency of these endogenous and exogenous variables that are the typical markets.

Traffic Demand: Passenger Market

The traffic demand falls into three segments:

- the highly price elastic discretionary travel segment
- the highly price inelastic small and medium business travel segment
- the negotiated price unity of the large business travel segment

Discretionary travelers. Yield management allows airlines to tap the high elasticity of demand of the discretionary traveler by offering discounted fares. These discounts encourage individuals who might not otherwise fly to purchase tickets. These discounted fare purchases by discretionary travelers allow the airline to fill seat departures that would otherwise go unfilled and be lost forever at pushback.

However, the airline does not want to sell these discounted seat departures to passengers who would normally fly, particularly the price inelastic business travelers who often fly on short notice. Therefore, the discounted fares contain restrictions such as fourteen-day advance purchase, weekend stayovers, and specific departure and return days. They are either wholly or partially nonrefundable. These restrictions serve the discretionary travel market and allow the airlines to target discounts and promotions directly to the discretionary market without disrupting or threatening their primary source of revenue, the business traveler.

Small and medium business travelers. This segment represents the largest revenue base for most airlines. Small and medium business enterprises are the most numerous consumers of air travel, and they generally purchase tickets on short notice. Due to this immediacy of demand, small and medium business travelers are price inelastic, in that they are willing to pay a higher fare to ensure they get to their destinations on short notice. Yield management for this segment of the traffic market means ensuring adequate seat departure capacity and fare levels to capture the maximum percentage of this high revenue demand.

Large business. This final segment of the passenger market uses air travel regularly and heavily. One would think that this segment would be the prime revenue-generating business segment. It is, and then again, it isn't. It is, because large business air travelers are steady customers. This allows airlines to predict, with reasonable accuracy, a stable revenue stream. It isn't, because many large business enterprises realize they represent significant market share. The huge dollar volume of air travel generated by these big business consumers allows them to negotiate contracted fare prices. These contracted travel agreements also eliminate the restrictions normally associated with discounted tickets, permitting big business customers both very low fares and short notice flight privileges.

As with the small and medium business segment, yield management for the big business segment focuses on ensuring adequate seat capacity and fare prices to capture this lower yielding revenue stream.

Traffic Demand: Cargo Market

Yield management of cargo traffic demand is virtually identical to that described for the passenger markets, with one notable exception. There is no discretionary, deep discount fare for advanced purchase of cargo transportation. The cargo market consists of two classes of customers and rates: contracted freight rates for government and heavy-use customers, and straight market rates for everybody else. A fare structure associated with cargo operations, different categories of shipments, and different freight rates for these different kinds of shipments.

Most airlines are passenger oriented, and cargo represents a "value-added" revenue source in city pairs that are primarily passenger markets. However, air cargo is a significant growth segment, particularly in and out of the Pacific Rim. Many airlines are aggressively seeking cargo customers. The principal goal in cargo operations is getting as much of the cargo traffic as possible onboard in the principally passenger-oriented markets and developing a sufficient cargo customer base to add cargo-only operations in those markets that justify such activities. Yield management on cargo-only operations is directed at obtaining a profitable mix between contracted rate customers and market rate customers.

Yield management is designed to ensure that as many seats and cargo container spaces are sold at the highest prices possible. So it brings us to a question of how many seats and cargo container spaces should an airline put up for sale in any given market?

Capacity Supply: Passenger Market

Capacity, the number of seat departures or "lift" an airline offers in a city pair market, is one of the most important decisions made by an airline. The amount of lift offered in a city pair market takes several forms. The first form of lift is cabin space allocation for first class, business class, and coach class seating. The second is aircraft size and type. The third is seat pitch, which measures the density of seating in each class of service. The fourth is frequency, or the number of departures per day. The final form of lift is seat blockout allocations, for heavily discounted fares, and frequent flyer redemption traffic.

The combinations and permutations of lift affect the number and type of aircraft needed, flights, seats, customer service and ground personnel, gate spaces, and landing slots required. In short, lift decisions affect every operational department. Lift, therefore, has a direct impact on yield because it determines levels and types of fare categories associated with seat departures.

Even though each form of lift will be discussed individually, it is important to realize that calculating the market lift equations is an extremely integrative and relational exercise, and no one type of lift can be manipulated without affecting all the others. Due to the integrative nature of these factors, the order in which we discuss them is arbitrary.

When preparing to enter a new market or when preparing to modify service offerings in an existing market and before an airline can begin calculating any lift equations, it must develop a traffic demand model of the market in question. This traffic demand model must include the anticipated levels of origin and destination (O&D) traffic, the principal economic and business base of the city, the projected mix of discretionary and business traffic, and the business and economic growth trends of the market. Other prime factors in the traffic model are the airport terminals, gate facilities, and runway and taxiway weight limits, which could affect aircraft type selection. Existing market competition is also factored. Once the model is complete, the airline can begin to project fare pricing, load factors, and yield levels. Thereafter, the airline begins to analyze various lift equations with a reasonable level of accuracy.

Cabin space allocation. Using the traffic model, airlines can decide whether to offer one, two, or three classes of service in the market. The traffic model will also allow the airline to determine how much cabin space to devote to each class of service to be offered. Furthermore, it permits the airline to evaluate different cabin configurations for load factor, revenue, and yield generation. The final decision will be optimized for the anticipated levels of traffic type.

Aircraft selection. Each carrier must determine what type of aircraft best meets the planned traffic and yield levels of a particular market. Not all aircraft are capable of being configured for multiclass service. Each must be able to operate within an airport's weight, noise, and size limitations. And each must be able to operate at an ASM cost level allowing for profitable returns, given traffic demand model assumptions of fare levels, load factors, and yields.

Seat pitch. Seat pitch is defined as the distance from the front edge of a seat to the front edge of the seat directly in front of it. The tighter the pitch, the more seats will fit into a given cabin space. Seat pitches range from over 40 inches in first class to a practical safe emergency-egress minimum of about 32 inches in coach class. Seat width is also a factor and can vary from about 16.5 inches for six abreast to about 18 inches for five abreast on a typical narrow body aircraft.

From a yield management standpoint, seat pitch is a double-edged sword. Seats in first class will always be arranged to reflect the significant fare premium paid and yields generated. In coach class, tight pitch means more seats available for sale at reduced incremental cost. Tight pitch, however, can mean unhappy passengers flying in cramped quarters. This could lead to their decision to select another carrier in the future.

The seat pitch and yield equations in business class do, however, possess some market flexibility. Over recent years, several airlines, notably Continental and British Airways, generated strong marketing campaigns and experienced good results by aggressively advertising a spacious business class configuration with an upgraded first-class seat. Although business-class fares do carry a small premium over the baseline full coach fare, they are gaining acceptance and justification by businesses that have a large number of middle and senior management traveling frequently. The advent of in-seat telephone service and sufficient room to allow these passengers to be productive en route has made this class a significant traffic growth segment.

Airlines are able to generate improved yields in this market segment by increasing pitch, upgrading seat types, and improving both in-seat and onboard services. By aggressively marketing upgraded services, airlines are able to achieve higher load factors in business class without increasing fares. The net result of reducing the number of seats in the business section, improving services, and aggressively marketing this concept has resulted in higher load factors and yields for the business-class section on the flight. With well-planned marketing efforts, reducing lift in business class can increase the business-class yields significantly.

Frequency. The traffic demand model will also help the airline define the flight frequency needed to capture the anticipated traffic demand. The traffic model will point out not only how many flights to offer per day but also the time for those departures and arrivals. Frequency and timing are critical to capturing the maximum percentage of demanded traffic. Poorly chosen departure and arrival times, regardless of frequency, can result in depressed load factors and yields. Inadequate frequency may result in high load factors and yields, but it may also mean that traffic is being left on the ground, either uncaptured or diverted to the competition.

Frequency, anticipated load factors, and yields must be played against the increased operating costs of that frequency. Obviously, if load factors and yields were not sufficient across all the projected flights, it would be self-defeating to offer a high level of frequency. However, some situations require an airline to offer unprofitable frequency in a city pair and cross-subsidize the loss from other profitable routes in an effort to maintain market share and presence.

Frequency decisions also impact the airline system schedule. Departures from a city must be aligned and coordinated with interconnecting flight schedules, particularly those interconnect schedules to the key business locations. It does little good to have sufficient departure frequency in a city to capture maximum originating traffic if that traffic cannot connect and get to its ultimate destination in a timely and convenient fashion. Conversely, the inbound traffic to a city must be able to pick up destination traffic on the return legs of their travels with the same timeliness and convenience. Failure to achieve both of these essential features will result in poor load factors and yield levels.

Seat blockout allocations. The necessity of allocating seat blockouts for deep discount fare promotions and for redemption of frequent-flyer coupons can have significant impact on revenue and yields. As mentioned earlier, deep discount fares and frequent-flyer flight coupons have restrictions placed upon them. These restrictions are designed to provide the airline with sufficient lead time to control the seat allocations for this class of low-yield or, in the case of frequent-flyer flight coupons, no yield traffic. Before the deep discount promotions are released for advertising, the airline will project discount load factors and block out enough seats to handle the anticipated traffic. Then, as tickets are sold or free flight coupons are redeemed, the airlines can quickly adjust the seat inventory to match sales activity. They are able to achieve this level of precision due to the restrictions on the tickets and coupons.

The advance purchase and notification requirements permit the airline to remove from the salable seat reservations inventory a sufficient number of seat departures. The day-of-week restrictions allow the airline to block out only the number of seats necessary on that day and that flight to carry the traffic. By carefully regulating and adjusting the seat allocations for this discount fare and frequent flyer traffic, the airlines are able to keep the maximum number of seat departures in the CRS inventory and available for sale at higher yield levels.

It is important to realize that determining and regulating capacity in a market is not a step-by-step process. Nor is it a onetime undertaking. The airlines are constantly monitoring traffic levels and adjusting fares, service offerings, and frequencies to match fluctuations in traffic demand. The process of determining seat departure category and capacity is an exercise in passenger market dynamics.

Capacity Supply: Cargo Market

Capacity determinations for cargo operations fall into two basic categories: ATMs on principally passenger route markets and ATMs of dedicated cargo routes.

Capacity issues and yield management decisions on cargo-only routes are identical to those of passenger capacity. The differences are so obvious as to not need further elucidation. No, there are no cargo frequent-flyer programs. There are, however, contracted cargo rate breaks for shippers achieving and exceeding certain tonnage levels. These reduced rate cargo shipments do need to be factored into the cargo traffic demand model.

Cargo rates and yields are an interesting challenge and profit opportunity, especially on passenger-oriented routes. However, recall that one of the components of the traffic demand model was the economic and business base of the city being evaluated. If that city's revenue base were principally derived from industrial and manufacturing activities, then the airline could reasonably anticipate active levels of O&D component cargo shipments.

This industrial orientation could generate additional "value-added" low incremental cost revenue sources that could aid in the generation of profitable revenue streams and high yields. It could also help support and subsidize passenger-related operating costs. If the cargo revenue were sufficient, it could even allow reduced load factor profitability requirements and thus affect the type of aircraft allocated for service in that city.

In cities whose principal economic base is nonindustrial, the cargo opportunities are certainly lessened but by no means absent. There is always cargo traffic demand for fresh seafood, produce, mail contracts, and same-day, counter-to-counter, small package express services. The ability to generate cargo revenue with adequate yields in markets that are principally passenger oriented is limited only by the willingness of the airline to innovate. They must be willing to develop service offerings that match the traffic demand model assumptions and then market these value-added services aggressively to grow the revenue stream and yield levels over time.

Business and Economic Conditions and Trends

As stated in chapter 3, the air transport industry is a countercyclical business sector, and so it is very sensitive to fundamental changes in overall business and economic conditions. Chapters 3 and 4 illuminated the necessity for the air transport sector to have timely and reasonable access to the capital and debt markets. Access to these markets is the lifeblood of any capital-intensive business.

These economic factors are important in the yield management equation. When an economy is growing quickly and market trends are pointing toward continued growth, generally interest rates are also rising. This rise in interest rates reflects increased demand for money. The supply of money becomes "tight," and interest rates reflect the degree of tightness.

The airlines are active users of debt instruments: bonds, syndicated loan packages, and lines of credit. As the cost, or interest rate, of debt increases, it must be recovered by revenue increases in the form of higher fares. Higher yields will be necessary. Traditionally, periods of high economic growth have been accompanied by increased load factors. Airlines will offer a variety of discount fare promotions, but the depth of the discount is less and restrictions on ticket usage remain in force. Most promotions during periods of high economic growth are targeted at increasing the load factors of the high-yield core revenue base, the small business traveler.

Conversely, periods of either recession or slow but positive economic growth present a more complex set of yield management decisions. In periods of low economic growth, load factors drop as discretionary and business travel demand contracts. In response, airlines generally adopt a two-pronged market modification.

First, to preserve their overall financial health, airlines initiate severe cost reduction programs. They start canceling or delaying fleet replacement orders, reducing service, and furloughing or eliminating staff. They also attempt to reschedule or roll over their debt instruments to capture the lower interest rates extant in a recessionary period. These actions will bring their cost structures into closer alignment with declining traffic and revenue streams.

Second, airlines will attempt to maintain positive cash flow and preserve yield levels by either initiating baseline fare reductions or increasing discounted fare promotions and easing the discounted fare restrictions. In short, they reduce both discretionary and business fares in an attempt to dramatically increase their load factors and preserve yield and cash flow. When an airline initiates fare reductions in a market that it dominates, the reductions will generally result in increased load factors. However, when initiated in intensely competitive markets such as hub-to-hub routes, reductions will precipitate a fare war among the competitors.

The two sets of economic recession or slow growth management decisions discussed above — cost reduction and fare reduction — are not designed to turn a profit during these difficult periods. They are designed to hold losses to a minimum and avoid forced bankruptcy restructuring or dissolution of the airline. They are, in short, survival strategies.

Yield, as a measure of retail sales activity, is a key indicator of successful or unsuccessful market penetration efforts and pricing strategies. Yield levels are greatly influenced by prevailing economic and business conditions. Periods of economic growth drive fares and yields up. Periods of economic recession, or very slow growth, drive fares down. Often the latter culminates in fare wars on competitive routes. This forces carriers to market and promote heavily to preserve yields and cash flow.

Competition

The ability to generate high yields and profitable revenue streams, sell tickets at or near the baseline fare level, and sell enough tickets to pay all operating costs and have something left over for the shareholders is the dream of every airline executive. Unfortunately, in the airline industry, that's all it is—a dream. The recent recession and the continuing slow economic recovery have depressed traffic demand, yields, and revenue streams, and this has generated tremendous losses. These losses have caused the airlines to cancel or reschedule necessary fleet replacement orders, lay off or terminate staff, and initiate destructive fare pricing. All of these factors create challenges to the airline management team to maintain adequate yield levels, but none more so than the oligopolistic nature of competition in the industry.

As discussed in chapter 7, in the forty years of CAB-regulated fare levels prior to deregulation, competition and yield management was centered on innovation, onboard service, and frequency. All of these factors are still viable yield management tools, but they have become secondary. Price is the primary competitive weapon today, and fare wars have become the principal manifestation of price competition since deregulation.

Although fare wars have been directed at all classes of service and all categories of traffic, most fare wars are targeted at the discretionary traffic market. There are two principal reasons for this target fixation. The first is that even in periods of recession, businesses still have to put people on the road selling products and negotiating deals. Since this market segment is more or less stationary, less need exists to reduce fares to entice travelers, because they must fly.

The second reason is that the core revenue business traffic pays for the bulk of the operating cost of a given flight. Tapping potential demand elasticity by discounting discretionary traffic fares will increase load factors but will lower yield. Price reduction of the discretionary ticket has less absolute impact on the cost recovery and profitability of that flight. Revenue generated from discretionary traffic becomes incrementally additive in paying for the flight. These bargain tickets can be discounted deeply with less impact on overall yield. This approach to reduced rates does not pervert core traffic fares and yields.

There is another way to look at this pricing issue. It may be classified more as a marketing approach than as a pricing attitude. First-class and business traffic yield is driven by frequency, service, and then price, whereas discretionary traffic yield is driven by price, frequency, and then service. These two fundamentally opposing sets of priorities are at the root of normal competition between carriers. Airlines will offer increased pitch, better seats, and upgraded onboard service to attract first-class and business-class traffic without enormous adjustment to these fare prices. Carriers are competing for first- and business-class traffic utilizing the prederegulation marketing strategies of service and frequency. They resort to outright price competition only when all competitors in the market have achieved equal service and frequency offerings or when they are initiating new and innovative service offerings that require price promotion.

Discretionary traffic does represent an extremely elastic traffic source. A $100 reduction in business fares will not generate much additional traffic. Conversely, a reduction of $100 in the discretionary fare level can generate significant additional load factor. Discretionary traffic is highly price elastic and responds positively to fare reductions. Airlines take advantage of this elasticity of demand by pricing discretionary fares at low levels.

Due to the incremental cost additions and the significant profit contributions of discretionary traffic, competition for discretionary traffic is both pervasive and intense. Even in the absence of competition, carriers will price discretionary traffic fares at low enough levels to capture maximum available demanded traffic. With competition, carriers will reduce discretionary fare levels to a point where the reduced fare level will just equal or slightly exceed the incremental short-term costs of producing the seat departure.

In short, airlines will price discretionary fares at levels to just recover any costs not funded by the existing first- and business-class traffic model assumptions in that market. This cost recovery discretionary fare level will be calculated on the historical discretionary traffic load factors for the market in question. Therefore, any seat sold at a fare higher than the discretionary fare level is pure profit to the airline. This type of pricing is not a "fare wars" type of pricing determination. It is simply a method of matching price to the average long-term cost of a seat departure in the discretionary traffic class based on the historical load factor generated by this category in that market.

The most damaging form of fare wars occurs when an airline reduces the price of a fare category below the cost of production. When this situation occurs, airlines competing with the discounting carrier must match the price reduction by either funding the subsequent losses from more profitable routes or absorbing the losses. The alternative of not competing will certainly destroy market share. Yields are severely depressed on a fare war route, although revenues may be flat or slightly increased.

Competition and fare wars are healthy and necessary when they serve to mitigate the effects of monopoly pricing practices and generate a fair price for a fair service. Competition is unhealthy and destructive when it drives price below the long-term cost of producing that service. The ability of an airline to continue to operate under bankruptcy reorganization protection, thereby operating under a legally entitled but unrealistic cost structure and under a false economy of scale, further exacerbates this situation. A bankrupt carrier, who is not obligated to service the bulk of its debt, has a phenomenal cost advantage over fiscally responsible airlines that are attempting to provide equitable service to their customers and their debtors.

A carrier enters into bankruptcy proceedings for poor management decisions. Bankrupt carriers are allowed to provide service, and their unrealistic cost structures allow them to prostitute fare prices to an extreme degree. This forces fiscally responsible carriers to lower fares just to maintain market share.

These unrealistic fares drive down yields and revenue to significant loss levels and create a long-term "no win" situation for all classes of traffic demand for the fiscally responsible air carriers. Then, after the bankrupt carrier either ceases to exist or emerges from bankruptcy, fare levels snap back, exceeding pre–fare war prices as the surviving carriers try to recoup their losses.

It is this kind of deep discount and then snap-back fare pricing that has left the American traveler and the financial community in a quandary. Revenue streams and yields are too unstable to support the necessary fleet upgrades and service improvement programs. Lack of stable revenue streams and yields causes the financial community to be less than enthusiastic over new equity and debt offerings by the airlines at the time they most need access to fresh capital.

Denial of capital causes the airlines to operate inefficient transports on unprofitable routes and to continue fare wars to generate cash flow. This complex chain of events degrades the financial integrity of the entire industry as well as long-term service levels to the flying public.

The ability of an airline to operate under the legally entitled but false economies of scale of bankruptcy is one of the fundamental flaws of U.S. air transportation policy. Air transportation has become essential in this nation's economy. Any issue or legislative loophole that compromises the ability of our air transport sector to provide stable, timely, and price-responsive service to the American public, over the long term, must be viewed with a jaundiced eye.

Suggested Readings and References

Busnar, G., & Putnam, H. D. (1991). *The winds of turbulence: A CEO's reflections on surviving and thriving on the cutting edge of corporate crisis.* New York: Harper Business.

Davis, J. E. (1989). *Airline market share modeling in originating city markets.* Cambridge: Massachusetts Institute of Technology, Department of Aeronautics and Astronautics.

ESG Aviation Services. (1988). *The airline monitor: A monthly review of financial and traffic trends in the airline industry.* Cos Cob, CT: Author.

Gialloreto, L. (1988). *Strategic airline management: The global war begins.* London: Pitman.

Hall, S. A. (1993). *Aircraft financing.* London: Euromoney.

Hansen, M., & Kanafani, A. K. (1985). *Hubbing and airline costs.* Berkeley: Institute of Transportation Studies, University of California.

International Air Transport Association, Economics and Industry Finance Division. (1984). *Total market passenger traffic forecasts.* Geneva: Author.

International Air Transport Association, Industry Automation and Finance Services Department. (1987). *Scheduled passenger traffic forecast.* Geneva: Author.

International Air Transport Association. (1992). *Air transport in a changing world: Facing the challenges of tomorrow.* Montreal: Author.

Lynch, J. J. (1984). *Airline organization in the 1980s: An industry report on strategies and structures for coping with change.* New York: St. Martin's Press.

Mathaisel, D. F. X. (1983). *Optimization of air transport yields and capacity.* Cambridge: Massachusetts Institute of Technology.

Michaels, S., & MilSal, T. (1987). *Points: A guide to frequent flyer bonus programs.* New York: Hippocrene Books.

Wells, A. T. (1989). *Air transportation: A management perspective.* Belmont, CA: Wadsworth.

Wells, A. T. (1990). *A casebook for air transportation.* Belmont, CA: Wadsworth.

10

AIRPORT FINANCING

As **airports** are major players in the aviation industry, they rely on capital to keep the avenues of transportation open. Unlike others, however, airports face a different capital market than their industry contemporaries. Due in part to the regulated public domain environment, the approach to revenue generation and debt markets varies significantly. Airports are key to the transportation policy of both the United States and the international community. This chapter explains the need for airport funding by delving into the basics of airport operating and capital costs and revenues. The chapter ends with an exploration of alternative capital finance strategies, including privatization.

Airport Revenues

Revenue generation in the airport business is derived from a broad base. Depending on the size of airport operations and the infrastructure supporting that airport, major revenue sources may vary considerably. Besides deriving a portion of their revenue stream from airlines, airports collect revenues from a large contingency of concessions not related to aviation, including rents for parking areas, restaurants, gift shops, rental car agencies, hotels, and industrial parks located on airport grounds. In some cases, airports collect a portion of a business's gross revenue as compensation, over and above standard rates.

Smaller airports even collect rent and fees from farmers who either sharecrop with the airport land or rent areas for farming purposes. For the most part, however, most airport operating revenues are derived from rates, fees, and charges made by the airlines.

Airports are a unique breed of capitalist structure, and they face tremendous needs for capital. The Deregulation Act of 1978 removed barriers of entry and exit for airlines, permitting airlines to refine and change existing route structures. This served to increase air service to many airports while decreasing service to others. Ease of entry and exit left some airports bewildered as former lifetime tenants vacated the premises. For airports enjoying increased demand, new facilities and modifications to existing facilities were required. While deregulation changed the airlines' operating environment, a concomitant change occurred in the airport environment. A new era of revenue generation and bottom line results was ushered in and thrust upon the airport manager. Airports had to become more dependent on the fiscal elements of their operation than on federal, state, or local subsidization. Airport managers were forced to find new or modified ways to finance capital projects.

As with all businesses, an airport must rely on its ability to attract capital to remain viable. In some respects, an airport's ability to obtain capital, other than through revenue generation, comes from either the debt or quasi-equity markets, with one major exception. We know from our previous airline and fixed base operator discussions that an equity market does not exist per se in the airport terminology. This is so because private capital has not been infused into the system. The financing of airports has been a public concern. If an analogy can be drawn between stockholders of a corporation and citizens of a locale where an airport is located, airport stockholders are the citizens of the community served by the airport. Citizens enjoy airport viability and community embellishment rather than dividends in the form of money for their equity holdings. As most airports are publicly owned, private investment is not a consideration. Instead, federal, state, and municipal moneys work as a traditional equity infusion. Should there be a return on this investment, it becomes not the province of the stockholders but an increase to the general fund, which is ultimately a benefit to the citizenry.

Air travel is one of the fastest growing global industries. Airport planners around the world have found it virtually impossible to keep pace with the growing numbers of passengers and the demand for additional facilities. Airport capacity problems arise in virtually every developed country. In 1995, the administrator of the Federal Aviation Administration (FAA) predicted that air travel in the United States would increase by 60 percent within ten years. He also stated that within fifteen years airports would be faced with accommodating as many as one billion passengers annually. In 1998, there were 615.8 million passengers.

The need for airport financing in the United States is driven by the users of the airport system, which are the scheduled airlines, general aviation (including corporate/business aviation, nonscheduled air taxis, flight instruction, and pleasure flying), and the military. The FAA's National Plan of Integrated Airport Systems (NPIAS) 1990–1999 (February 1991) estimated the total cost of federal, state, local, and private airport development under the Airport Improvement Program (AIP) to be $40,544,000,000 between 1990 and 1999. This estimate included $6,153,000,000 for new airports, including $4,742,000,000 for new primary airports such as the Denver International Airport, which opened in February 1995. The FAA estimated the DIA project at $2,400,000,000, which was half of the actual cost.

So one can see the total costs noted above were underestimated. In addition, the costs estimated for the other primary airports in the NPIAS (Austin, Texas; Chicago; Lake Havasu, Arizona; San Diego) were for nominal planning and land acquisition costs. They did not include development costs. It should be noted that the new primary airport construction estimates amount to less than a fourth of the total costs estimated for the NPIAS from 1990 to 1999.

Another aspect of domestic U.S. need for airport finance are the huge costs involved in reconstructing and/or expanding the existing airport system. For example, several airports are planning to add runways to their current layouts as a way to increase capacity without building all-new airport sites. Examples are Dallas/Ft. Worth International (DFW), Los Angeles International (LAX), and St. Louis Lambert International (STL). In fact, LAX is in the midst of a $14 million airport master planning and environmental planning effort considering the possibility of adding two runways to the two that now exist at LAX. Similarly, STL is planning to add a third east-west runway, for which preliminary FAA approval was granted in December 1997. When these plans are finalized, the need for additional airport financing will be acute, since these airports are all planning multibillion dollar projects.

In the United States, rules, regulations, politics, and public outcry can inhibit financing abilities and accomplishments. Justifying expenditures that exceed some countries' entire gross national product can prove difficult. Whitlock (1992, 99) states, "Professionals working together to plan expansion of existing and new airport facilities must be aware of the constantly changing aviation industry in order to be accurate and effective with their numbers in projecting costs and income to support the feasibility of improvements." A definitive need as well as a plan that ensures financial integrity is necessary before the public as well as private entities will consider backing airport improvements. Because of such huge financial considerations, correspondingly colossal national debts, and budgetary shortfalls, one trend in airport development is toward privatization. Privatization may mean different things to different bureaucrats, but part of the thinking implies that money, other than that of the government, with some return on investment, is utilized in airport financing.

It has been demonstrated that private concern can develop and control airports with a greater degree of efficiency, safety, and possibly concern than can government agencies. Other countries have set precedent.

In the Far East, airport development has surged forward due to the popularity of the Pacific Rim products and religious travel to Mecca. Massive population and an explosion into the industrial age have forced many countries in the Orient to drastically improve their modes of transportation.

China is one such country. According to the National Bureau of Statistics, passenger volume in China increased over 300 percent between 1987 and 1997 and maintained that growth in 1998, reaching 1.06 trillion person-kilometer (Fu 1999; China's Passenger 1999).

By 2010, passenger traffic levels in this region are expected to more than triple to 137.4 million passengers (Mecham 1995). As a result, China needs foreign investment for its transportation infrastructure. One slight problem exists, however. With the demise of the USSR, China is now the guardian of communism. Consequently, the Chinese are reluctant to allow any sort of private involvement in such a large industry. It is interesting to note, however, that the architect of modern China, Deng Xisopong, suggested that the Chinese civil aviation administrative system was incompatible with the development of the country's "reform and opening up." In a 1980 speech, Deng stated that "civil aviation must adopt the road of enterprise" (Fu 1999). Since then, the Chinese government has undertaken development ventures with Singapore, Japan, and even the United States. In fact, Lockheed is involved in building a terminal at the Beijing Capital Airport.

To accommodate this steady increase in air traffic, Beijing Capital Airport is transforming from a domestic to an international hub. In 1997, the airport handled 16.9 million passengers of which 11.6 million flew domestically and moved 458,000 tons of cargo on 141,185 flights (Fu 1999). The current $1.1 billion expansion is the sixth in the airport's history. The airport was originally designed to accommodate 118 flights.

Hong Kong, before the reversion to Chinese control from Great Britain, undertook a major airport construction project. Financing the HK$115 billion project was split almost evenly between private and government sources. The airport construction was mostly financed through private sector enterprises like export agencies and commercial banks. Projects such as roads, ATC, and land reclamation are the province of the government.

Once basking in 35–42 percent annual growth rates, Vietnam's airports are now facing their first crisis since the country's economy was opened in the late 1980s (Citrinot 1999). Because of the war, the country has 297 airport facilities but only three international airports: Noi Bai in Hanoi, Than San Nhat in Ho Chi Minh City (Saigon), and Da Nang.

The refurbishment of Than Son Nhat is estimated to cost $3.6 billion, and the first phase of construction for Noi Bai is expected to cost $150 million (Citrinot 1999). Although the funds have not yet been secured, work has begun on airports (Four Years 1999). The Civil Aviation Authority of Vietnam received German funding in November 1996 to build a two-story terminal in Hanoi, but problems with the main contractor have slowed construction (Citrinot 1999).

Vietnam was seriously affected by the Asian economic crisis of 1998. Because of the drop in tourism, Vietnam airlines reported a loss of $4.5 million, their first loss in ten years. The appointed general manager, Dao Manh Nhuong, predicted a $38 million deficit for 1999. Since Vietnam relies on long-term foreign loans to finance their endeavors, the infusion of money from private concerns and other governments acts not as a direct private investment but as loans. In this way, the sanctity of the communist doctrine remains sacrosanct. However, repaying those loans is becoming a great problem.

Japan's Kansai International Airport is suffering problems of a different nature. The Japanese are in the midst of a 75 billion yen expansion of Kansai International Airport at Osaka. According to Mecham (1994), a 1,260-acre man-made island was created three miles from the shoreline in Osaka Bay, and plans for new runways and an additional terminal will require an enlargement of the island. The second phase of construction will add 542 hectares of land, a 4,000-meter runway, a cargo complex, and a supply management facility. These improvements will double the airports' capacity. Unfortunately, the world's first offshore airport is sinking into the sea faster than expected.

This poses a problem for all the Japanese governments involved in the project. They have raised more than 80 percent of the funds required, but that is now in jeopardy. Revenue for the cost of construction and maintenance of Kansai is derived partly from landing fees. In fact, landing fees in Japan are two to ten times higher than those charged in other countries (Airport Fees 1998). Landing fees at Kansai can reach 850,000 yen for a Boeing 747-400. By comparison, Washington Dulles International charges the equivalent of approximately 75,000 yen for the same airplane. Japanese airlines have been urging the government to lower the landing fees, arguing that the added costs make them less competitive against international airlines. The Transport Ministry did decide in 1998 to reduce landing fees overall by 30 billion yen at twenty airports for fiscal year 1999 (Airport Fees 1998). However, this excluded fees at the four international airports. Kansai's overall declining profitability and the withdrawal of international airlines may curtail the future development or limit the current expansion efforts.

Airport Ownership

Airport finance is a function of the operating and ownership environment of the airport system. Since the passage of the Air Commerce Act of 1926, it has been the policy of the United States to relegate the ownership of the nation's civil airport system to state and local government entities and to private entities. The federal government has been excluded from such ownership, with the exception of the Washington Capital Airport System. So who owns the airport system of the United States? In figure 10-1, it can be seen that in December 1996 there were 18,292 total airports in the United States. Of these, 5,389 were open to the pub-

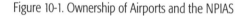

Figure 10-1. Ownership of Airports and the NPIAS

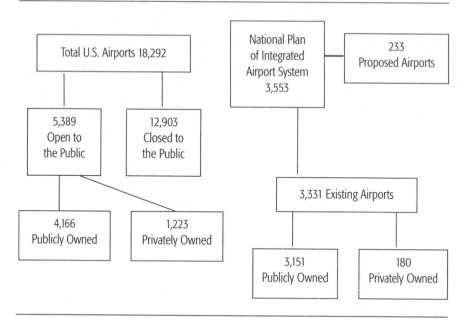

lic. Within those open to the public, 4,166 were publicly owned and 1,223 were privately owned. Of the 4,166 publicly owned airports that were open to the public, about three-fourths were owned by local governments and the rest were owned by states. Only Washington National and Washington Dulles were owned by the federal government.

Public airport ownership can occur in several ways, and each method can have its own peculiar limitations or advantages for airport finance. For example:

- In the instances where states own airports, such as in Alaska or Hawaii, this grew out of a time when the state government was the only government capable of handling such an investment. In the case of Rhode Island, the state airport system might possibly be sold to local governments as the state rethinks its role.

- Cities, counties, townships, and other forms of general-purpose local governments are major stakeholders in airports nationwide. Where the local airport is doing well, airport ownership has been viewed as quite an advantage to the local economy. Where there are economic or environmental questions, the airport can often be a source of strife in a general-purpose government's council or board chambers. Also, there is competition for operating or expansion dollars (when needed) with other branches of the city, county, or township government. The airport might be viewed as a rich man's playground in some cases, making the effort to get these dollars even more difficult. On the other end of the spectrum, if the airport does very well financially, the city or county government might want to divert airport revenues to other needs in the city or county. This revenue diversion is banned by FAA regulations for any airport that has received federal grants (which is virtually any significant airport in the United States).

• Port districts and port authorities are normally known for their operation of ports and harbors across the United States. However, a number of such government bodies also operate airports. Some of the best-known examples are the Port Authority of New York and New Jersey (operators of John F. Kennedy International, La Guardia, Newark, and Teterboro Airports) and the Port District of San Diego (operator of San Diego Lindbergh Airport). One of the distinct advantages of a port district or authority operating an airport is the insulation of this form of government from the general-purpose government bodies. There is less competition for operating and capital funds, although there still is some, since the port district or authority has other responsibilities to fulfill with its budget. This insulation was critical to the Port Authority of New York and New Jersey in the 1970s when the city of New York was virtually bankrupt. The Port Authority was financially healthy and quite separate from the problems that the city government faced.

• Park districts or boards also can operate airports. An example of this is in Illinois. Canton, Decatur, and Joliet all have park district–operated airports. Insulation from the general-purpose government body is again an advantage of this form of ownership. A disadvantage is that the primary focus of a park district is not on transportation but on recreation. In addition, a park district's mandate to operate open lands for outdoor use can sometimes run in conflict with their simultaneous operation of a large open area for airport use.

• Airport authorities are special-purpose units of local government with the singular task in the law to own and operate airports. At least twenty-five of the fifty states have an airport authority law. An important advantage of this form of airport ownership is the focus on the airport alone. Another advantage is the one already mentioned, which is the budgetary insulation from other forms of local government. This means that the airport authority has its own taxing power and its own ability to raise funds for capital improvements separately from the local government units surrounding it.

See figure 10-2 for specific examples of government bodies that owned airports in the United States.

Figure 10-2. Examples of Public Airport Ownership

Federal Government Owned Airports

Ronald Reagan/Washington National
Washington Dulles
Aside from the civil portion of joint-use airports, these are the only federally owned civil airports in the nation.
Both are on long-term lease to the Washington Metropolitan Airport Authority.

State Government Owned Airports

Baltimore-Washington in Maryland
Providence, Rhode Island
Most airports in Hawaii; all are state operated
Most airports in Alaska, except in large cities such as Anchorage and Juneau

Local Government Owned Airports

County Ownership

Palomar and Gillespie Airports in San Diego County
Brackett Field and El Monte Airport in Los Angeles County
Shonomish County/Everett Paine Field, Washington
DuPage County, Illinois
DeKalb-Peachtree near Atlanta, Georgia
Detroit Metropolitan, Michigan
Las Vegas, Nevada
Greater Pittsburgh International, Pennsylvania
Westchester County, New York

City Ownership

Chicago O'Hare and Midway
Phoenix Sky Harbor
Los Angeles International
Kansas City
Oklahoma City Will Rogers
Charlotte-Douglas International, North Carolina
Philadelphia International
Houston Intercontinental, Hobby, and Ellington Field
Atlanta Hartsfield International
Dallas Love Field

Port Authority

Port Authority of New York and New Jersey: Kennedy, La Guardia, Newark and Teterboro
San Diego Lindbergh
Waukegan Memorial, Illinois
Jacksonville International, Florida
Portland International, Oregon
Seattle-Tacoma International

Figure 10-2 *continued*

Cleveland-Hopkins International
Toledo-Lucas County, Ohio
Boston Logan International

Airport Authority, Airport Commission, or Airport Board

Indianapolis, Indiana
Minneapolis-St. Paul, Minnesota
Nashville, Tennessee
Lansing, Michigan
Tulsa, Oklahoma
Raleigh-Durham, North Carolina
Bradford and Allentown, Pennsylvania
Charleston, West Virginia
Salt Lake City International
Port Columbus International, Ohio
Great Falls International, Montana
Lincoln Municipal, North Platte Regional, and Omaha-Eppley, Nebraska
Greater Cincinnati/Northern Kentucky International
New Orleans International
Sioux Gateway, Iowa
Several of these airport authorities operate more than one airport including general aviation reliever airports.
There is airport authority enabling legislation in at least 25 states.

Park Districts
Canton, Decatur, Joliet, and Schaumburg Airports in Illinois

Airport Usage Categories and the Scope of Airport Finance

As already noted, there are 18,292 airports in the United States. Of this, about 600 are served by the scheduled airlines as well as general aviation. The rest are served by general aviation only. Whether or not an airport is served by an airline has a lot to do with its ability to finance itself, both operationally and for capital projects. Airlines and their passengers provide a daily flow of revenue to the airport based on the scheduled airline service that is provided by the airlines. The airlines lease facilities, rent space, and pay for fuel. The passengers rent cars, pay parking fees, purchase items from concessionaires, and so forth. All of this airline-related activity generates revenue for the airport operator.

At general aviation airports, on the other hand, there is no fixed schedule for the coming and going of aircraft. Since the activity at a general aviation airport is unscheduled, the flow of revenue from it is relatively unpredictable. In addition, general aviation is just now recovering from a nearly twenty-year downward spiral in national activity. There are still, of course, some critical and highly utilized general aviation airports, particularly in major metropolitan areas. However, without airline service, the general aviation airports are missing a key ingredient for airport funding—a consistent source of daily revenue. In addition, general aviation airports are ineligible for the passenger facility charge (PFC) revenue, which is also derived from airline passenger volume.

Therefore, airport finance options for general aviation airports are somewhat more limited. For example, many very small general aviation airports are almost totally dependent on Airport Improvement Program funding for capital development due to their lack of local funding options.

Financing Airport Operations

Before an airport operating body can consider expansion or replacement plans, it must first consider how its daily operations are financed. The following are key operating cost categories:

- salaries of airport employees, including management/administration, operations, maintenance, and, where applicable, security, police, and airport rescue/firefighting
- airport utilities, including the operation on any on-airport plants, substations, etc.
- equipment costs, including mowers, snow removal vehicles, airfield maintenance/operations vehicles, and, where applicable, airport police cars, airport security vehicles, and airport rescue/firefighting trucks
- materials costs including paint, building materials, snow removal salt, fuel spill clean-up agents, lighting items, etc.
- other costs that pertain to specific airports such as airport owned and operated air traffic control towers or aircraft fueling facilities

To finance these operating costs, airports must consider a wide range of revenue generation possibilities for their airport, including the following:

- airfield or airside user charges. These are charges related to the use of runways, taxiways, ramps, hangars, and any other airport facilities on the operational side of the airport. Examples of such charges are aircraft landing fees (by weight, by aircraft type, by common fee for all, etc.), aviation gas/jet fuel charges or fuel flowage fees, hangar rentals, aircraft parking/storage fees, etc.
- concessionaire fees. These are landside lease or rental charges that companies wishing to operate at the airport must pay to use the terminal, the fixed base operator building, or any other airport building. Companies providing services such as airlines, air taxi/charter operators, flight schools, aircraft

fueling, car rental, food service, business services, banking services, gift shopping, or newspapers can all expect to pay such charges. Charges can be assessed in terms of space used on the airport or in terms of units of business or sales volume or some combination thereof.

- local tax revenues. These can be general-purpose municipal taxes allocated to the airport by a city or county council. They can also be taxes assessed directly for the airport by an airport authority or district based on the assessed valuation in the area covered by the taxing unit's voter-approved boundaries.
- agricultural fees. These are fees collected from farmers who harvest crops on airport-owned lands. This is a special form of concession or lease fee.
- industrial park fees. Many airports have encouraged the development of industrial parks as a way to add revenue streams as well as a way to provide compatible land use near runways. This is also a special form of concession or lease fees.
- mineral or mining fees. These are fees collected by the airport for oil, gas, or minerals pumped or mined from beneath the airport. This can be an important source of income in certain parts of the nation.

At air carrier–served airports, the major tenants of the airport are the scheduled airlines. These tenants are key to financing the operating and capital needs of airline-served airports.

Revenue Generation

A major consideration to be made by airport personnel at airline-served airports in forecasting their projected revenues is that of how to charge the airport's major tenants, the airlines. Because such charges impact heavily on the airport's revenue stream, it is important to be fair to the tenants as well as to gain sufficient revenue to operate the airport and make related major purchases.

Airports use two techniques to set airline rates and charges: the compensatory and the residual methods of rate making. Each of these methods has a variety of subdivisions and approaches to their usage. The most prominent are the standard/commercial compensatory plans, the cost center residual, and airport/airline system residual methods. Each of these will be briefly discussed.

Standard Compensatory

This approach to ratemaking considers the airlines as the ultimate user of the terminal and all other airport facilities. Rates and charges are calculated so that the airport fully covers the airlines' share of operation and capital costs of the entire facility. These costs are only those necessary to operate the airport as a landing and take-off location. Costs incurred by the airport for the maintenance of public areas and concessionaires are excluded from these charges to the airline. In this case, should Air Atlantis fly into XYZ and be the only carrier operating out of that airport, the entire costs of the airport and its operation, except for operations not involving an airline, would be borne by Air Atlantis. The airport under this arrangement must ensure that the profits made from its nonairline operations exceed the nonairline costs. Otherwise, the airport will not profit.

Commercial Compensatory

Under this method of rate/rent making charges, all are calculated by pro rata charging the airlines, the concessionaires, and all rent-paying tenants for concession space and public area costs. Whereas, in the previous method, airline costs excluded those for maintenance of public and concession areas, under this method they are included. Under both the standard and the commercial compensatory methods, the airport assumes the risk associated with vacant rental space, but can, and often does, receive a portion of the concessionaires' gross revenues.

Cost Center Residual

This approach to rate setting establishes a cost center mentality. It allocates the cost of operating an airport to a particular area, as opposed to an all-encompassing approach of the entire operation. In other words, accounts are established for operational areas such as terminal, ground transportation, airfield, parking, staging areas, and other buildings and grounds operations. Rates and charges, particularly airlines charges, are set to recover the costs of this cost center. Charges are based on the usage of this area and any offset or credit that may be received due to non airline revenue generated by the area. The net costs are then prorated to the airline or airlines involved.

Airport/Airline System Residual

This is an all-encompassing assumption of airport financial risk by the airlines. Under this arrangement, the airlines pay landing fees large enough to ensure that the airport breaks even. Under residual methods, the airlines primarily assume financial risk of airport operations. Because long-term leases may run twenty or thirty years, airlines may subject themselves to paying costs of undefined future facilities. Generally, as quid pro quo for their financial solvency, an airline obtains lease arrangements satisfactory to their market share. Often, these arrangements create majority-in-interest clauses in their lease agreements, whereby airlines obtain sufficient influence to gain control over airport financial and investment decisions. Majority-in-interest arrangements may go so far as to permit the airlines to review, approve, or veto airport capital projects.

Much consternation exists over the establishment of airport fees. In recent court cases, the court affirmed an airport's right to set rates and charges through a compensatory method. In 1995, Congress established new rate, fee, and charge guidelines; 14 CFR part 302 highlights that the rates established must be "fair and reasonable," may not unjustly discriminate against aeronautical users or other groups, must be set so that the airport is financially self-sustaining as possible, and that airport revenues must be expended for aeronautical facilities within that airport.

Once the method of cost allocation is chosen, the airport director must determine the difference from anticipated revenues versus the cost of operation. As we all know, under traditional accounting methods, revenue minus expense equals profit or loss. Under the airport equation, revenue minus expense equals either costs covered or an inability to cover costs. If costs are covered, revisions to scheduling or scope of proposed master projects might have to be made to keep the tight balance of costs to expenditures. In the alternative, where revenues do not cover airport costs, a shortfall exists. When a shortfall is either experienced or anticipated, a break-even need is created. This need creates the necessity for airports to seek other arrangements to secure required capital.

Airport Funding

Obtaining funds over and above the traditional revenue sources to support an airport's operation generally falls into two categories: grants or debt. Grants are the receipt of money conferred by a fund for the purpose known to the fund. The exceptional benefit of having a grant conferred is that fulfillment of the duty associated with such grants acts as payment of the principal amount conferred upon the recipient, in other words, free money. The debt market, on the other hand, confers money to the borrower but expects to have the principal returned with interest. Before one goes to the debt markets for additional financing, all avenues of "free" money should be exhausted. The avenue of approach should then be grants, other possibilities, and then the debt markets. Airports, according to FAR part 150, have one additional predebt option after the grant route has been exhausted. The passenger facility charge may provide additional sources of revenue. Each of these areas will be briefly discussed.

Because the national infrastructure is dedicated to the support of the transportation system, particularly the air transportation system, the federal government has historically provided airport developmental funds. This funding is provided primarily through the Airport Improvement Program.

The Airport and Airway Trust Fund

The Airport and Airway Trust Fund, which began as part of the Airport and Airway Revenue Act of 1970, supports the nation's aviation infrastructure. Zorn (1990) indicates the purpose of the fund was to support capital development of the nation's air transportation system and support part of the FAA's operating and maintenance costs.

The Trust Fund relies on user fees and taxes assessed on those who use the air system for development of its funding mechanism. Fund revenues are derived from

- taxes levied on all domestic airlines tickets (10%)
- taxes levied on all freight airway bills (6.25%)
- international departure taxes assessed per passenger ($6.00)
- general aviation gasoline taxes ($0.15 per gallon)
- commercial and jet fuel tax ($0.17 per gallon)

The principal advantage of the user approach to generating the trust funds was that it provided predictable and increasing sources of income commensurate with need. This permits more effective and long-range planning. It was estimated that in fiscal year 1996, airline ticket purchases alone contributed more than $5 billion to the fund. More could probably have been collected had it not been for the government shutdown during the Democratic and Republican debates over balancing the federal budget. Because of an oversight, the Trust Fund fees were not extended into early fiscal 1997 and were not collected by the airline community. This provided windfall fares for the traveling public and a competitive edge for some airlines, but it did little for the fund itself. Early in 1997 Congress reestablished the user charge and trust fund approach.

The Airport Improvement Program

The Airport Improvement Program (AIP) was established by the Airport and Airway Improvement Act of 1982. Its funds, derived from the Airport and Airway Trust Fund, are used for four general purposes: airport planning, airport development, airport capacity enhancement, and noise compatibility programs.

AIRPORT PLANNING

Funds received for airport planning may include grants for integrated airport systems addressing the current and future air transportation needs of a region as a whole. Individual airport planning needs can be funded for the current and future needs established through the airport master plan for aviation requirements, facility requirements, and compatibility with environmental and community goals.

AIRPORT DEVELOPMENT

Grants issued in this area may include funds for repair and improvement construction on airport grounds, which excludes routine maintenance. The following may also be included: land acquisition, improvement and repair of navigational aids, terminal building construction, site preparation, and development and repair of roadways, runways, and taxiways. Specifically excluded is the construction of hangars, automobile parking lots, terminal art objects, decorative landscaping, and building improvements not related to the safety of persons on the airport grounds.

AIRPORT CAPACITY ENHANCEMENT AND PRESERVATION

Funds may be used for projects that significantly enhance or preserve airport capacity. Consideration for these types of funds rests on the airport's desire to improve upon these areas and the project's cost and benefit, the project's effect on overall national air transportation system capacity, and the financial commitment of the airport sponsor to preserve or enhance airport capacity. Rationale and commitment would be evidenced by the airport master plan.

NOISE COMPATIBILITY PROGRAMS

The 1982 Airport and Airway Improvement Act contained a provision to make funds available for noise compatibility planning and program implementation as authorized by the Aviation Safety and Noise Abatement Act of 1979. The specificity of this program is contained in FAR part 150. Owners and operators of a public use airport and local governments/communities adjacent to an airport are eligible for such funds.

Fund Eligibility

To be eligible for AIP funding, the airport must be a part of the National Plan of Integrated Airport Systems (NPIAS). According to Wells (1992), the criteria for inclusion in the NPIAS are minimally restrictive. They include the following:

- The airport has at least ten permanently based aircraft.
- It should be at least a thirty-minute drive from the nearest existing or proposed airport currently in the NPIAS system.
- There is an eligible sponsor willing to undertake ownership and development of the airport. As noted in figure 10-1, there were 3,554 airports in the NPIAS as of December 1996 out of 18,292 airports in the nation.

Additionally, an airport must be of the public-use variety and be characterized by one of the following criteria:

- have at least 2,500 passenger enplanements each year,
- serve the general aviation community, or
- be designated as a reliever airport by the FAA.

Both publicly and privately owned airports qualify for AIP funds, provided these conditions are met. Airports that receive AIP funds fall into five defined types. The first of these is that of commercial service airports that enplane 2,500 or more passengers annually from scheduled service carriers. Airports with fewer than 2,500-

passenger enplanements are classified as general aviation airports. For the general aviation airport to be eligible for AIP grants, it must be either publicly or privately owned and designated as a reliever airport by the FAA. The third type, primary airports, are those used primarily by commercial carriers. Their annual enplanements are well in excess of 10,000. The fourth and fifth categories are those of reliever airports and cargo service airports. As their names imply, these airports are specific to some type of operations. Reliever airports are those designated to relieve congestion at commercial and primary airports. Cargo service airports must have a total aggregate landing weight in excess of 100 million pounds per year and be dedicated to cargo/mail services. Passenger or scheduled passenger service is not a major portion of the airport's operation.

Fund Allocation

Allocation of AIP funds fall into four broad types. The first are called entitlement or apportionment funds. Otherwise known as formula grants, they are based on airports' annual passenger enplanements. The more traffic an airport handles, the more money it is eligible to receive. In the cargo service area, apportionment funds are based on an aggregate landing weight of all landed aircraft.

The second category of funds is designated for congressional "pet" projects. Called set-aside funds, they are available to any airport sponsor according to congressionally mandated requirements deemed necessary for the furtherance of the aviation community.

The third category is that of discretionary funds. These are funds that enhance capacity, safety, security, or mitigate noise.

The fourth category is called letters of intent (LOI). Essentially, LOIs are signed by the FAA as a commitment of long-term AIP funding of a specific project, or series of projects, at a specific airport. The word *intent* is used to indicate that the federal government intends to commit AIP funds if they are available. The LOI is important to large, long-term airport development, since the commitment of the federal government can help the airport sponsor obtain other types of financing, in addition to the AIP money that is being committed. The downside of the LOI is that there can be substantial commitments made to LOIs nationally by the FAA, which then would have top priority in the annual allocation of AIP funds to the detriment of other categories of AIP projects.

State Block Grant Program

The FAA State Block Grant Program was authorized in 1987 by an amendment to the Airport and Airway Improvement Act of 1982. It became effective in October 1989. That amendment authorized the FAA to initiate a pilot program using state block grants to provide AIP funds to nonprimary airports. The participating states receive funds directly from the AIP and are able to choose, within federal restrictions and guidelines for such funding, which airports will receive funding. The state will also perform the FAA's inspections and oversight role at these airports (GAO/T-RCED-96-86, 1).

The State Block Grant Program has specific regulations concerning the use of the funds distributed through the program. The participating states must use the monies distributed for airport development and planning, for airport noise compatibility planning, or to carry out airport noise compatibility programs in accordance with the Airport and Airway Improvement Act of 1982, as amended. The participating states may not use funds distributed under the program for integrated airport system planning, projects related to any primary airport, airports outside the states' boundaries, or airports inside the states' boundaries that are not included in the National Plan of Integrated Airport Systems (FAR 156.4). In addition, the FAA's regulations determine that participating states cannot use AIP funds to finance the cost associated with administering the program unless granted a waiver by the FAA (GAO/T-RCED-96-86, 3).

In participating states, the block grant program transfers the responsibility for administering AIP grants from the FAA to the states. The states take on the FAA's responsibility in four key areas: planning, grant administration, safety and security inspections, and project construction oversight. The states join airport officials in long-range airport planning, approving changes to airport layout plans to reflect construction plans, and conducting environmental assessments. By performing grant administration, the states help airports select projects that qualify for AIP funding, award AIP grants, issue grant reimbursements, and provide grant oversight. Also, the participating block grant states conduct safety inspections at small airports and investigate compliance issue and zoning concerns. Finally, the states provide technical assistance, including guiding airport sponsors in soliciting bids for construction, approving AIP constriction change orders, and monitoring the progress of the project through preconstruction, interim, and final construction inspections (GAO/T-RCED-96-86, 6).

The FAA State Block Grant Program authorizes the secretary of transportation to select qualified states to assume administrative responsibility for all airport grant funding available under this program. To qualify, states submitting applications to participate in the State Block Grant Program must meet certain criteria:

- have an agency or organization capable of administering effectively any block grants made under this program
- use a satisfactory airport system planning process
- use a programming process acceptable to the transportation secretary
- agree to comply with federal procedural and other requirements for administering any such block grant

• agree to provide the secretary with such program information as the
secretary might require (Title 49 U.S.C. 47128)

The first three states to meet these criteria were Illinois, Missouri, and North
Carolina (GAO/T-RCED-96-86, 3).

The Aviation Safety and Capacity Expansion Act of 1990 extended the State
Block Grant Program expiration date from September 30, 1991, to September 30,
1992 (Pub. L. No. 101-508, sec. 9114). The Airport and Airway Improvement Act
Amendment of 1992 then extended the effective date of the program from September 30, 1992, to September 30, 1996 (Pub. L. No. 102-581, sec. 116). This legislation contained the following new sentence: "The seven states to be selected for
participating in the program in fiscal years 1993, 1994, 1995, and 1996 shall include
the three states selected for participation in the program in fiscal year 1992 (Illinois,
Missouri, North Carolina)" (Pub. L. No. 102-581, sec. 116). Michigan, New Jersey,
Texas, and Wisconsin were selected on the basis of the same criteria as the three
original states (GAO/T-RCED-96-86, 3).

The FAA Reauthorization Act of 1996 made the State Block Grant Program a
permanent part of the AIP. This act also made provisions for two more states to
be included in the program. Pennsylvania was added for 1997 and Tennessee for
1998 (NASAO; Pub. L. No. 104-264, sec. 147).

The states and the FAA have different views about the purpose of the State Block
Grant Program. The FAA views the program's purpose as identifying administrative functions that might be shifted to or shared with the states. Also, the FAA sees
the program as a means of giving the states more discretion in selecting and managing projects and testing their ability to improve the delivery of federal funds. On
the other hand, the states view the program as a means of putting funding decisions
into the hands of those with firsthand knowledge of the projects competing for
funds (GAO/T-RCED-96-86, 8).

It appears that the State Block Grant Program has been successful in terms of
both the FAA and state officials. The FAA has benefited from the program because
it has been able to shift regional staff resources to deal with other pressing priorities. This has helped the FAA to partially compensate for a 12 percent reduction
of its airport staff in the affected regions. It has also allowed the FAA to assign a
larger portion of its remaining staff to emerging priorities at larger airports, such
as reviewing passenger facility charges and environmental compliance issues
(GAO/T-RCED-96-86, 8).

The officials of the participating states also feel that the State Block Grant Program has been successful. It has allowed the states to expedite project approvals because they may now approve the project's scope and financing, which formally
required FAA approval. This has produced a quicker turnaround time, which has
enabled airports to use their contractors more efficiently, saving time and money.

Also, the states have been able to reduce the paperwork required to apply for federal grants by using their own forms instead of both their own and the FAA's. Another benefit of the program is that the duplication of airport oversight activities has been reduced or even eliminated in some cases.

Although the State Block Grant Program has provided the participating states with more flexibility on how to spend their AIP funds, it has not necessarily provided them with increased funds. When compared with the amount of funds received before they became block grant participants, only Illinois, North Carolina, Michigan, and Texas have received a higher percentage of AIP funds. Missouri, New Jersey, and Wisconsin received a smaller percentage (Kirchoff).

The participating states, airports, and the FAA believe that the State Block Grant Program has been an overall success. The states have been able to streamline the AIP project approval process, reduce paperwork requirements, and eliminate the duplication that occurred when state and federal activities overlapped. Airports have benefited from the states' efficiency, allowing them to obtain project approvals and to change projects more quickly. Finally, the FAA has been able to shift its resources to other high-priority tasks, allowing them to partially offset the reductions in field staff that have occurred in recent years.

Allocation of AIP Funds

Nothing in the funding process is automatic. Irrespective of an airport's need and/or eligibility for funds, the operator must submit an application to the FAA. Additionally, even if an airport is eligible for set-aside or discretionary money, it must submit an application for FAA review.

The AIP program is not a free ride. Just because an airport is eligible for funding does not mean that its request will be either honored or filled to the degree of total funds required. Applicants for grants must show that they are active partners in the proposed venture by having available capital of 10–25 percent of a project's cost. This advanced requirement must be in place before the FAA opens its checkbook.

Figure 10-3 indicates the amount of money provided by AIP for the select airport projects. Should the revenue stream of the airport not provide the additional capital to venture into the AIP arena, funds from other sources may become a necessity. Moreover, since the flow of funds from AIP has been anything but stable, it is important for airports to have other sources of funds for capital development. As noted in figure 10-4, there has been a discrepancy between congressional authorization of AIP via airport funding laws and actual appropriations via budget bills passed each year. There was a $700 million gap in these figures in recent years, which was reversed in fiscal year 1998. Still, the $1.7 billion authorized in FY 1998 does not address the tremendous airport capital improvement need identified in the NPIAS. This is especially true for nonpassenger facility charge, "AIP-dependent" airports served by very little air service or by general aviation only. Such airports were heavily affected by the changes in AIP funding by Congress in the early 1990s.

Passenger Facility Charges

In 1990, Congress passed the Aviation Safety and Capacity Expansion Act. A portion of this act established ability on the part of publicly owned commercial service airports to assess airport user charges on passengers utilizing their facilities. Passenger facility charges (PFCs) were developed to address critical shortages of airport capital to finance future airport development.

Those airports eligible to assess PFCs are permitted through the federal aviation administrator (FAR part 158.5) to assess a charge of $1, $2, or $3 on all domestic or international passengers enplaned at an airport. There is currently legislation before Congress to raise the PFC charge to a maximum of $6. These fees are collected by the airlines, travel agents, and any other airline ticket-issuing office at the time of travel purchase.

Project Eligibility

Virtually all airports seeking PFC revenue streams have been approved by the FAA. Originally established to address definitive projects requiring additional capital, virtually all airport projects have been declared eligible for PFC financing without regard to either the need or cost-effectiveness of the project (Delgado 1998). The statutory requirement for fund usage is contained in FAR part 158.15, which

Figure 10-3. Percentage of Project Monies Provided by AIP

Project Type	Large Primary Category of Airports	All Other Categories of Airports
Airport planning	75%	90%
Airport development	75%	90%
Noise compatibility programs	80%	90%
Terminal development (relievers and hub airports)	75%	75%
Terminal development (commercial, non-primary airports)		85%
Terminal development (military airport programs)		90%

Figure 10-4. AIP Funding, 1982–1998

Fiscal Year	Authorizations (millions)	Appropriations (millions)
1982	$450.0	$450.0
1983	800.0	804.5
1984	993.5	800.0
1985	987.0	925.0
1986	1,017.0	885.0
1987	1,017.0	1,025.0
1988	1,700.0	1,268.7
1989	1,700.0	1,400.0
1990	1,700.0	1,425.0
1991	1,800.0	1,800.0
1992	1,900.0	1,900.0
1993	2,050.0	1,800.0
1994	2,105.5	1,694.0
1995	2,161.0	1,450.0
1996	2,161.0	1,450.0
1997	2,161.0	1,460.0
1998	1,740.0	1,700.0

Sources: Data from FAA (1996), *Aviation forecasts 1997–2002* (Washington, D.C.: GAO); Darryl Jenkins (ed.), (1995), *The handbook of airline economics* (New York: McGraw Hill), 111.

Figure 10-5. Selected Airports Collecting Passenger Facility Charges, 1992

Airport	PFC Amount	Effective Date	Collection Total
Huntsville, Alabama	$3.00	6/1/92	$20,831,051
Las Vegas, Nevada	3.00	6/1/92	428,054,380
Muscle Shoals, Alabama	3.00	6/1/92	104,100
Minneapolis–St. Paul, Minnesota	3.00	6/1/92	23,408,819
Springfield, Illinois	3.00	6/1/92	682,306
Stapleton, Colorado	3.00	7/1/92	2,330,743,321
Gulfport, Mississippi	3.00	7/1/92	384,028
Portland, Oregon	3.00	7/1/92	17,961,850
Hattiesburg, Mississippi	3.00	7/1/92	119,153
Savannah, Georgia	3.00	7/1/92	39,501,502
Buffalo, New York	3.00	8/1/92	189,873,000
Columbus, Mississippi	3.00	8/1/92	1,693,211
Lawton, Oklahoma	2.00	8/1/92	334,078
Memphis, Tennessee	3.00	8/1/92	26,000,000
Tulsa, Oklahoma	3.00	8/1/92	6,450,000
Lake Tahoe, California	3.00	8/1/92	928,747
Missoula, Missouri	3.00	8/1/92	1,900,000
Charlottesville, Virginia	2.00	8/1/92	402,000

Source: Data from Aviation Daily, June 26, 1992.

enumerates the requirements for usage and eligibility for PFC funds. To be eligible, a project must do one of the following:

- reserve or enhance safety, security, or capacity of the national air transportation system,
- reduce noise or its impacts resulting from the airports operations, or
- facilitate competition amongst air carriers.

Presently PFC revenues provide the nation's eligible airports with approximately $1 billion in windfall funding money. This money, because it is not tied to airline terminal usage or majority in interest clauses, strengthens an airport's ability to make spending decisions without the influence of participating airlines.

Uses and Future of PFC Funds

Within the confines of the three prescriptions outlined above for PFC usage, PFC funds can finance an entire project or can be used to pay debt or related expenses for bonds issued to fund an eligible project. Interestingly, PFC revenue may be used to meet the percentage requirement or airport share of projects funded under the Airport Improvement Plan (AIP).

Between 1992 and 1996, PFC funding of airports grew to over $1.1 billion per year in funding for airport construction projects. As noted in the National Civil Aviation Review Commission's 1997 report, this funding grew as follows:

1992	$0.085 billion
1993	$0.485 billion
1994	$0.849 billion
1995	$1.046 billion
1996	$1.113 billion

However, the controversy remains regarding the appropriate use of PFC funds and the possibility of raising the $3 cap on PFC funding. Airports would like to see the cap in PFCs raised, and in 1996 Rep. James Oberstar contemplated amending the FAA authorization bill to raise the PFC cap by $1. Oberstar decided not to submit the idea due to limited support. The idea to raise PFCs had little political support, as other issues were in the forefront. The National Civil Aviation Review Commission recommended that the cap on PFCs will also need to be raised to meet capital demands while coincidentally recognizing the strong political disparity between interest groups. Several attempts have been made to take the Trust Fund off the federal general budget to prevent it from being caught in the political game of masking the national deficit. Since all parties have recommended that an AIP minimum annual funding level of $2 billion should be reached, it is unlikely to see any movement toward an increase of PFC monies, since taking the budget off status would possibly allow a fully funded AIP.

While almost all parties agree to the idea of funding AIP to the $2 billion mark, ATA strongly opposes raising the PFC cap. ATA's position is that PFCs "when used wisely, have also been a useful tool in meeting aviation infrastructure needs. However, there are too many examples of airports which have sought to build projects more driven by local politics, than by a desire to enhance safety or capacity. After all, of the current $18.5 billion authorized for PFC collection, only a little over $3 billion is earmarked for inside safety and capacity projects such as runways, taxiways, aprons, and lighting" (Merlis 1998).

Bonds

After funding options such as AIP grants, the use of PFCs and other federal sources has been exhausted. Airports and municipalities usually finance capital improvements and additions through the issuance of debt. Most such debt is in the form of bonds. Bonds in the airport venue are operative and technically similar. The major difference is the way bonds are backed, the taxability of such instruments, and the methods of responsibility for repayment.

Airport bonds come in a variety of types. The most common are the General Airport Revenue Bonds (GARBs), General Obligation Bonds, Self-Liquidating General Obligation Bonds, and Revenue Bonds. Since these are only titles, it is important to recognize that most bonds work similarly and only the method of repayment, interest rates, maturity dates, usage purposes, and responsibility for repayment may differ. Face value, percentage payment, yield, and yield to maturity are all the same.

Markets for Airport Bonds

Airports raise billions of dollars annually in the debt/bond markets. This is not a new phenomenon. The first airport revenue bond in the United States was issued for $2.5 million in 1945 by the city of Miami, Florida. It was backed and was to be repaid by revenues from what is now Miami International Airport. During the 1950s, the city of Chicago, in seeking finances for improvement of O'Hare International, took a historic step in revenue bond underwriting. In the O'Hare Agreement, airlines operating into the airport agreed to back the repayment. The airlines pledged that should O'Hare Airport income fall short of repayment capabilities, the airlines would make up the difference by paying larger landing fees.

Airport bonds are primarily a municipal undertaking that is exempt from taxes. Therefore, the buyer or owner of such bonds is not obligated to pay any taxes, either federal or state, on interest obtained through holding such debt instruments. To purchasers in high income tax brackets, this tax-free instrument can provide income security without elevating them to increased tax brackets. They may permit them to obtain greater earnings than those investments paying higher returns but requiring a percentage to be paid to the Internal Revenue Service.

Of course, the tax-exempt status of municipal bond issues makes financing less expensive than other debt instruments. Because the tax-exempt nature of the bond saves investors tax money, the bonds can be issued at lower interest rates than normal debt instruments. Predictably, most airport debt capital is raised in the tax-exempt bond market.

An interesting element to airport bonds is that since their inception, not one bond had been defaulted. This, unfortunately, cannot be said for those bonds discussed in previous chapters.

Types of Airport Bonding Issues

General Obligation Bonds

General obligation bonds are issued by states and municipalities. Sometimes other subdivisions of states and municipalities have authority to issue this type of debt instrument. All bonds are agreements to repay a specific amount of money borrowed (IOU) at a certain time (maturity) with periodic (usually yearly) payments of interest. General obligation bonds are the responsibility of the citizenry of a particular locality to repay the amount borrowed. The repayment to bondholders is secured by the full faith, credit, and taxing power of the issuing government agency. Thus, to have permission to undertake such a debt financing measure, the community usually must approve by vote any potential bond issues, or community indebtedness.

In addition to general obligation bonds being utilized for airport construction and improvements, many compete with other local necessities for improvement and building of such programs as schools, roads, and other essential public works.

Because the bonds are backed by a community guarantee to repay them at maturity, they are generally issued at lower interest rates than competing methods of securing debt. However, because of this advantage, many states have set by statute the maximum amounts of general obligation debt that a municipality may incur.

Self-Liquidating General Obligation Bonds

Self-liquidating general obligation bonds are secured by the full faith and credit of the taxing power of the local citizenry, just as are general obligation bonds. The difference, however, is that the cash flow from the project being financed is adequate to repay the amount of debt plus the costs to operate the project. Because of this ability to repay, the debt is not legally considered a part of the community's limitation set for the general obligation bond. A strange anomaly occurs here, however; because the project's performance and ultimate risk lie with the local government, which is appointed by the community, the community bears the ultimate responsibility for repayment. Due to this convoluted method of risk application, the self-liquidating general obligation bond method of financing means a higher rate of interest than the general obligation bond.

REVENUE BONDS

One may infer that the term *revenue bonds* means that they are issued to obtain revenue. That is their purpose, but in this case the word *revenue* applies to the way the bond is to be repaid. Repayment of bond indebtedness is payable solely from the revenue derived from the operation of the facility, road, or other project that was constructed or acquired with the bond proceeds. Financing with revenue bonds provides an opportunity to obtain airport improvements without directly burdening the taxpayer.

Some examples of revenue bonds are those issued to finance and build major highways. Generally, such highways turn to toll roads, where fees are collected to repay the debt. Often when the debt is repaid, the toll is extinguished and the highway becomes free to all.

GENERAL AIRPORT REVENUE BONDS

General airport revenue bonds (GARBs) are secured solely by the operation of the airport and are not backed by any additional governmental subsidy or tax levy. In short, the community is not responsible for the debt service or payback of the borrowed amount.

In addition to GARBs, airports may issue a hybrid bond, or special facility bonds. These are designed to address one particular undertaking, such as an industrial development bond (IDB). These may be issued to finance some specific facility, such as a new hangar or gate jetway installation on behalf of a specific carrier. The carrier in turn directly secures the debt.

Bond Ratings

The methodology of getting bonds to market is almost the same as bonds in the corporate venue. Investment bankers also specialize in the airport bond market, and their approach does not vary considerably.

Bonds issued to finance improvements at municipally owned airports are granted tax-exempt status by the U.S. Internal Revenue Tax Code. This allows bonds issued for these purposes, whether they be general obligation, revenue, general airport revenue bonds, or some other derivation, to borrow at lower interest rates than corporate bonds. The precise level of the interest associated with these bonds is a direct function of the bond rating.

As with bond ratings for corporate issues, airport bonds are rated by either Standard & Poor's or Moody's according to investment quality. In the airport bonds market, ratings vary between the top and medium grades issued by the rating agencies. A medium grade means that rating firms see the investment as carrying a measure of speculative risk. General obligation bonds usually draw the best ratings. Under this form of security, ratings are determined by the economic vigor of the issuing municipality. Because of this, the airport has no influence on the general obligation rating. Revenue bonds, since they are directly tied to the airport, draw ratings according to the airport's financial and fiscal responsibility and vitality.

Credit analysts at the major bond rating services rank airport bonds according to various factors. These include financial and operational comparables, the nature of airline rates and charges, the local economic base, the airport's current financial situation, the strength of the airport management cadre, and the airport layout.

Financial and Operation Comparables

In chapter 6, financial analysis and comparative ratio analysis were discussed concerning balance sheet and other operating statements. In terms of airport ratio analysis, bond rating agencies will evaluate a series of ratios that address the vitality of airport operations. These may consist of the following:

- debt per enplaned originating passengers
- debt per enplaned transfer passengers
- ratio of originating and departing passengers to transfer passengers
- percentage of traffic generated by the primary carriers serving the airport
- annual traffic increases
- debt service coverage
- revenue per enplaned passenger
- concessionaire revenue per enplaned passenger
- demographics of metropolitan area

Rates and Charges to Airlines

Since these charges generate the major portion of an airport's revenue, they are strongly considered in the rating methodology. The type of rate setting (discussed earlier) employed by the airport can give the bond rating agency a bird's-eye view of the airport's control over its spending decisions. As airport revenues are the sole backing for a GARB and other revenue bonds, the nature of the airport's ability to control these revenues has a considerable impact on a bond rating.

Economic Base of the Community

Demand for air transportation is a function of the economic characteristics of the community served by the airport. Airports located in areas insulated from economic hardships or those in economic boom locations may receive higher bond ratings than those in depressed communities.

Current Financial Situation

All interest rates, from IOUs to bond issues, are predicated on the risk involved in the transaction. The higher the risk of having the money returned, the higher the interest rate to borrow that money. Conversely, the greater the possibility of having the money returned, the lower the charge for that money. To discern risk, you only need to look at the way and method an airport or city operates and maintains its financial house. Ratios, similar to that of the current ratio in standard accounting, should provide means of determining risk.

Strength of Management Team

Traditional management values should prove beneficial to the airport seeking funding ratings. Analysts review both the managerial and administrative performance of airport operators in determining rating outcomes. Evidence of success of sound management techniques in the areas of planning, operating, controlling, and directing the airport environment is a positive factor in ratings.

Airport Layout

The landside and airside arrangements and setup can have a significant impact on the rating agency determination. An example of an airport layout that may engender a decision on the part of a rater to provide superior analysis would be one where all the concessionaire facilities are located in the main terminal, away from the connecting or transferring passengers. This may indicate a less than opportunistic ability on the part of the operator to achieve profit maximization.

Whatever methodology is employed in determining bond ratings and ultimately interest rates on bond issues, a finalized rating will eventually develop. In this venue, the ratios deemed worthy of consideration are listed as best grade, high grade, upper medium grade, and medium grade.

- best grade: A strong capacity to pay both interest and principal with the lowest degree of risk to the bondholder.
- high grade: A strong capacity to return both principal and interest but judged just a little less exciting than the best grade.
- upper medium grade: Usually well protected in relationship to ability to return both medium principal and interest but susceptible to the potential fluctuations in grade economy, etc.
- medium grade: The protection is deemed at the time of rating; however, the presence of grade speculative elements could impact upon the ability to pay interest or principal should economic conditions change.

Any grading below these would be very questionable and costly to the seeker of funds.

Figure 10-6. Airport Bond Ratings

Rating Company	Best Grade	High Grade	Upper Medium Grade	Poor Grade
Standard & Poor's	AAA	AA	A	BBB
Moody's	Aaa	Aa	A	Bbb

Airport Privatization

The prospect of owning and operating an airport is appealing to many individuals and companies alike. An airport is the Mecca for worldwide travel. It is also a pivotal point in international commerce. Although the process for establishing an airport is arduous, the results can be quite rewarding to a private concern.

Supporters of airport privatization, according to Haririan (1994), are in favor of transferring responsibility of the system to a for-profit, user-owner corporation. Airport owners, under this system, would be free to charge market-driven prices for their services, using rationale and market-oriented pricing systems. With privatization, airports could avoid using federal grants, instead seeking economic solutions, such as peak-hour pricing, user fees for weather briefing, and other services.

Private ownership has been tried in recent years. President George Bush promoted privatization. In 1992, he signed an executive order allowing for the privatization of airports. This activity culminated years of the Transportation Department's admonitions under Secretary Skinner that a new relaxed method to financing must be developed.

Airport privatization can be accomplished in several ways. The most obvious would be the outright sale of either the whole or parts of the airport to a private enterprise. Other ways include the establishment of contracts that provide for private management of the airport or segments such as particular gates, control towers, concourses, etc., or long-term leases to accomplish various privatization objectives.

There are examples of cooperation between private parties and the government where partial and complete privatization has proved beneficial. One is the Teterboro Airport in New Jersey. The ownership of the facility belongs to the Port Authority of New York and New Jersey; the airport is operated by a private for-profit company, Johnson Controls, Inc. Under this arrangement, Johnson Controls is responsible for airport operation and design of capital development programs. In return, the port authority receives a revenue share and usage fee from the income experienced by Johnson Controls.

In Great Britain, a pure example of private ownership exists. The British Airports Authority (BAA) owns and operates British airports. The company was established by a public stock offering on the London Stock Exchange. Although the BAA is completely private in its operation of airports under its jurisdiction, the British government periodically reviews its fees. All profits flow to the BAA. Another example is an airport development in the Portuguese colony of Macao, a short distance south of Hong Kong, which has also evolved through the control of a private concern. Concessionaria de Aeroporto de Macao has contracted the construction and operation of the Macao International Airport for the next twenty-five years. The financial plan involved a variety of loans, with more than half coming from the Macao government itself. Airport finance by other developed countries outside the United States seems to be handled in a generally consistent manner. In this regard, it appears that the cost of developing an airport is divided almost evenly between public and private support. An exception to this occurred in North America. Trillium Terminal Three at the Lester B. Pearson International Airport in Toronto was built solely by a private concern. It was developed by a conglomerate of interests, each contributing to an aspect of the terminal's development. Although the development was not an entire airport undertaking but one terminal building on an airport facility, Trillium to this date has exceeded expectations.

In addition to heavy opposition by some in Washington, there are other hurdles to jump before implementing airport privatization. Ott (1992) highlights the fact that ownership can involve more than one political jurisdiction, hundreds of agreements, and a blend of public and private financing tools. These work against privatization agreements by their very nature and weight.

Others have cited the fact that present statutory regulation would have to be amended to allow easier access to the possibility of federal grants by private concerns. Cohan (1991), however, cites a major consideration that, in addition to all others, local opponents of privatization have pointed out that a private airport cannot use tax-exempt bonds, which could impede any expansion and renovation projects.

Still another major hurdle rests with the airline users themselves. Any privatization scenario poses the potential for increased costs to the private ownership and thus passes through increases to the ultimate airport user, the airlines. Even if privatization does act to improve efficiency and proficiency of operation, many airlines believe that the savings gained will be outweighed by the increased burdens imposed by private ownership.

Notwithstanding the fact that both publicly and privately owned airports can be profitable, the fury that envelops the privatization activity has been highly publicized and politicized and has polarized many to viable arguments from both sides. As a result, consensus does not exist among those concerned, the stakeholders.

The privatization of airport ownership is nothing new to the United States, since most of the 18,292 airports in the nation are privately owned. In fact, some of the

Figure 10-7. Range of Privatization of Airports

Full government ownership and operation	Government ownership with privatization of selected services	Government ownership and private management	Private ownership and management

major public-use airports in the nation today began as privately owned airports. One recent example of a conversion from private to public ownership in the United States was the purchase of the Hollywood-Burbank Airport from the Lockheed Corporation by the Hollywood-Burbank-Pasadena Airport Authority. Since this conversion in 1979, however, the trend has been in the other direction, with private ownership a goal and private contract operation of public airports a possible "way-station." According to Airport Privatization, developed in 1992 by the American Association of Airport Executives in association with the Airport Development Foundation Board, the range of possible options available to airport operations is depicted by figure 10-7.

Although it is not the concern of this discussion to optimize or evaluate the issues of privatization or total governmental controls of the airport system, it does seem likely that the future holds different financial horizons for the airlines and airports to navigate. How financing is to be achieved will be a major concern for the privatized airport of the future.

Conclusions

Airport finance has evolved substantially over the past twenty years. At airline airports, airline deregulation has gradually moved airport finance away from financing via the lease/use agreement to other vehicles of finance. Tax changes have forced airports to focus their fund-raising and building programs on tax-exempt projects related to the airfields or buildings rather than on nonaeronautical projects such as hotels.

Another big change was the advent of congressionally approved PFCs after a long period of being illegal. However, the reality is that PFCs and AIP together still are not enough to meet all of the airport finance needs. Therefore local, state, and private sources of funds will continue to be a crucial part of the funding mix. Airlines still have a strong voice in the conduct of large-scale airport expansion projects. For example, the "third airport" for Chicago near Peotone, Illinois, has received federal and state funds for planning studies but little or no airline support. The reason is the tremendous investment that the airlines have made and are still making in Chicago O'Hare and Midway Airports.

Another trend is privatization. While the impact in terms of new private ownership of airports has been small, the impact on contract operations of airports has been somewhat greater. Airport operating bodies wanting more efficiency than they are getting may opt for such management of their airports as a way to have more money to invest on the capital side.

Finally, airport finance is increasingly global, with the United States involved in international airports and international finance involved with U.S. airports. This global involvement has expanded the potential sources of money for airports. It has also changed the rules in terms of who actually controls the flow of such funds. Airport projects can now be multinational in character and finance.

In the end, airport finance is a multilayered partnership among several levels of government as well as between the public and private sectors. While there is no equity market for airports directly (you cannot buy stock in most airports), there is a market in bond issues for large capital projects for airports. In addition, you can purchase shares in the private companies that are now vying to run airports on contract: Lockheed Air Terminal, Johnson Controls, BAA, Aeroports de Paris, Commarco, and others.

The future needs and proliferation of airport facilities are an indication that the industry will change dramatically in the future. No industrial evolution has been accomplished without an associated capital investment. The aviation industry, more specifically airport, metamorphosis offers great promise if the means exist to bring that promise to fruition. There exists in the industry a willingness to end the "business as usual" mind-set. With the growing entrepreneurial spirit permeating the aviation industry, times are changing in airport finance.

Suggested Readings and References

Airport and Airway Improvement Act of 1982 Amendment, Pub. L. No. 100-223, sec. 534 (1987).

Airport and Airway Improvement Act of 1982 Amendment, Pub. L. No. 102-581, sec. 116 (1992).

Association of American Airport Executives, Airport Research and Development Board. (1992). *Special report, airport privatization.* Washington: Author.

Aviation Safety and Capacity Expansion Act of 1990, Pub. L. No. 105-508, sec. 9114 (1990).

Cohan, P. (1991, September). Airport privatization yet to be resolved. *American City & County 106,* 34.

Delgado, Victor. (1998). *The federal role in financing the national airport system.* Unpublished master's thesis, Southern Illinois University, Carbondale.

Federal Aviation Administration. *Federal aviation regulations.* 14 CFR 156. Washington: Author.

Federal Aviation Administration Reauthorization Act of 1996, Pub. L. No. 104-264, sec. 147 (1996).

Federal Aviation Administration, Office of Airport Planning and Programming. (1993). *Introduction to the airport improvement program.* Washington: Author.

Federal Aviation Administration. *Annual report of accomplishments under the airport improvement program.* (1982, 1983, 1993, 1994, 1995, 1996). Washington: Author.

Harrian, M., & Vasigh, B. (1994, Autumn). Airport privatization: Procedures and methods. *Transportation Quarterly 48,* 393–403.

Kirchoff, Andrew. (1997). *A review of the FAA state block grant program.* Unpublished master's thesis, Southern Illinois University, Carbondale.

Mecham, M. (1993, September 20). Firm financing will let Macao open in 1995. *Aviation Week & Space Technology 139,* 47–49.

Mecham, M. (1994, March 28). Kansai expansion wins key backing. *Aviation Week & Space Technology 140,* 51.

Mecham, M. (1995, June 5). China seeks formula for foreign funding. *Aviation Week & Space Technology 142,* 39–40.

Merlis, E. A. (1998, February). *Views of the air transport association concerning reauthorization of the airport improvement program.* Transcript of statement presented to the U.S. Senate Committee on Commerce, Science, and Transportation hearing on reauthorization of the Airport Improvement Program, Washington.

Moody's Investors Service. (1996, October). *Moody's bond record.* New York: Author.

Northwest Airlines, Inc., et al. v. County of Kent, Michigan, et al., 49 U.S.C. App. 1513[a] and [b].

Ott, J. (1992, May 11). Bush order opens door for airport privatization. *Aviation Week & Space Technology 136,* 24–25.

Standard & Poor's rating guide. (1995). New York: McGraw-Hill.

U.S. General Accounting Office. (1994). *Airport improvement program: Program funding by state relative to enplanements for selected years (GAO/RCED-94-7FS).* Washington: Author.

U.S. General Accounting Office. (1996). *Airport improvement program: State block grant program (GAO/T-RCED-96-86).* Washington: Author.

Wells, A. T. (1992). *Airport planning and management.* 2nd ed. Blue Ridge Summit, PA: Tab Books.

Whitlock, E. M. (1992, Winter). Financing airport facilities. *Transportation Quarterly 46,* 99–114.

Zorn, C. K. (1990, Spring). The airport and airway trust fund: A continuing controversy. *Public Budgeting and Finance 10,* 13–25.

11

PREPARATION OF A BUSINESS PLAN

Whether you are a start-up airline, a new fixed base operator, or an existing company seeking new funding, you must develop a business plan. There are no formal rules for writing a plan, nor is there any defined length. The purpose is to make every aspect of a business clear to prospective investors and lenders while defining your objectives. When meeting with a lender, you need a well-defined and thorough plan. Below is a generalized outline for writing a plan for your organization.

Starting and Running a Business

The Small Business Administration (SBA) has reported that almost 90 percent of business failures result from poor management. Poor management is defined in terms of unfamiliarity with the business itself, accounting practices, managerial techniques, inventory control, employee relations, record keeping, and a host of other idiosyncrasies. A major problem area cited is poor capitalization.

It is amazing how many people are eager to start a business but have only a vague notion of what they want to accomplish. Generally, they come up with an idea for an enterprise and then begin discussing it with others. It is in this preliminary stage that they need a plan. Most people fail to do this, but developing a business plan forces entrepreneurs to be specific about the products or services they intend to offer, the industry where the venture will take place, and the capital required to finance such a venture. According to military tactician Sun Tzu, "All battles are won before they are fought." If this is so, then management, like the art of war, is a tactician's venue, and the key to survival is thorough preparation. Unless an entrepreneur spends adequate time and effort preparing a business plan, it may end up, unread, in the banker's or venture capitalist's wastebasket.

According to Joseph Mancuso, director of the Center for Entrepreneurial Management in New York, a good business plan takes at least five months to write. Then the author has to convince readers (bankers, SBA, venture capitalists, friends, and other interested parties) within five minutes not to throw the plan away.

There is no such thing as the perfect business plan, but there are some ways to pique interest. No plan can guarantee acceptance, because every reader has different concerns and desires in his/her approach to financing. However, several students have used the following plan to their advantage. So successful was one that, without any collateral involvement on his part, he was able to secure financing in excess of $100,000, enough seed money to successfully start his business.

Define and Identify Objectives

Before writing a successful plan, you must know who the readers will be, what they already know about your organization, what they are apt to ask, what you are willing to divulge, and how the information will be used.

Outline the Plan

Your outline can be as general or as detailed as you desire. Your goal is to obtain capital, be it venture capital or borrowed funds/equity. So you should consider the following:

- The market analysis may be the only basis for your estimation of prospective sales and pricing estimates. Be sure to indicate the market need for the product and/or service and indicate how a need can be met and how you would make a profit at the defined needs level.
- In all areas pro forma financial data should be indicated for at least five years.
- Stress your management team's relevant skills, education, background, and anticipated contribution to the success of the organization.
- Investors want to know that the borrower understands their primary objective: to gain a return on their investment. Therefore, be flexible in developing investor opportunities.

Review the Outline

Identify areas that should be presented in detail or summary form in the final product. The plan should describe your organization at a fairly high level, and extremely detailed descriptions should be avoided except where absolutely necessary. In preparing and reviewing the outline, keep in mind that you must be prepared to provide detailed support for your statements and assumptions apart from the plan itself.

Write the Plan

The order that follows will vary depending on the age of your company, its stage of development, and a host of other variables. There are as many forms of business plans as there are writers. Below you'll find two approaches to covering the important elements of your plan. The first approach is less detailed than the second. Depending on the intent, either example will help you develop your outline.

Typical Business Plan Outline I

I. Cover letter, individualized to the specific reader

II. Cover Sheet

    A. Name of business

    B. Address and phone number of business

    C. Name of principals

    D. Date

III. Statement of purpose

IV. Table of contents (Give the page number of every topic and subtopic. This makes it easy for prospective lenders to refer to sections of interest.)

V. The business

    A. Description

    B. Market and target customers

    C. Competition

    D. Marketing strategy

    E. Business location

    F. Management, legal form of business

    G. Personnel

VI. Financial data

    A. Sources and applications of funding

    B. Capital equipment list

    C. Break-even analysis

    D. Pro forma income statements

        1. Detailed by month for first year

        2. Detailed by quarter for second and third years

    E. Pro forma cash flow

        1. Detailed by month for first year

        2. Detailed by quarter for second and third years

    F. Pro forma balance sheet

    G. Historical financial reports (for existing business only)

        1. Balance sheets for past three years

        2. Income statements for past three years

        3. Tax returns

VII. Supporting documents

    A. Resumes

    B. Personal financial statements (net worth/tax forms)

    C. Letters of reference

    D. Letters of intent

    E. Copies of leases, contracts, and other legal documents

    F. Other supporting information

Business Plan Outline II

Executive Summary

The executive summary should be more than a listing of the topics contained in the body of the plan. It should emphasize key issues. The executive summary is not only a prelude to the information contained therein. It also sets the tone for the reader's desire to continue further.

This very important area of information summarizes the business and explains briefly how it will be established and operated. This section should be kept brief, consisting of at least one page but no more than five pages. It should employ flat statements, not explanations. It should be made clear that these flat statements will be explored in depth later in the plan.

Remember: The summary should stimulate the lender's interest. He/She may never read the rest of the plan. Therefore, the executive summary must demonstrate that you have a realistic plan that will succeed so that you will be able to repay any loan and remain a viable business.

    A. Purpose of the plan

        1. Attract investors

        2. Document an operational plan for controlling the business

    B. Market analysis

        1. Characteristics of your target market (demographic, geographic, etc.)

        2. Size of your target market

    C. The company

        1. Needs the company will satisfy

        2. Products or services the company will offer to satisfy these needs

    D. Marketing and sales activities

        1. Marketing strategy

        2. Sales strategy

3. Keys to success in the competitive environment

E. Product or service research and development

    1. Major milestones

    2. Ongoing efforts

F. Organization and personnel

    1. Key managers and owners

    2. Key operations employees

G. Financial data

    1. Funds required and their use

    2. Historical financial summary

    3. Prospective financial summary

Market Analysis

This section should reflect knowledge of the industry and present highlights and analysis of market research. Detailed market research studies should augment specific concerns. These reports should be contained in the appendices. Included in this section should be the size of the market in terms of dollars and customers, a history of the market, and the type of customers the company will attempt to service.

A. Industry descriptions and outlook

    1. Description of the primary industry

    2. Size of the industry

        a. Historical

        b. Current

        c. Anticipated

            i. Five years

            ii. Ten years

    3. Industry characteristics and trends

        a. Historical

        b. Current

        c. Future

    4. Major customer groups

        a. Businesses

        b. Governments

        c. Consumers

B. Target markets

  1. Distinguishing characteristics of the primary target markets and market segments

    a. Critical needs

    b. Extent to which needs are currently being met

    c. Demographics

    d. Geographic location

    e. Purchase decision makers and influencers

    f. Seasonal trends

    g. Cyclical trends

  2. Primary target market size

    a. Number of prospective customers

    b. Annual purchases of products or services meeting the same or similar needs as those to be provided

    c. Geographic area

    d. Anticipated market growth

  3. Market penetration indicates the extent and demonstrates rationale that level of penetration is possible based on market research

    a. Market share

    b. Number of customers

    c. Geographic coverage

    d. Rationale for market penetration estimates

  4. Pricing/gross margin targets

    a. Price levels

    b. Gross margin levels

    c. Discount structure

  5. Methods of target market identification

    a. Directories

    b. Trade association publications

    d. Reservations systems

    e. Government records

  6. Media for communication with target market

    a. Publications

    b. Radio/television

    c. Advertising

d. Publicity

e. Sources of influences

7. Purchasing cycle of potential customers

   a. Identification of needs

   b. Research for solutions to needs

   c. Solution evaluation process

   d. Determining who has final solution selection responsibility and authority

8. Key trends and anticipated changes in primary target markets

9. Secondary target markets and key attributes

   a. Needs

   b. Demographics

   c. Significant future trends

C. Market test results

   1. Potential customers contacted

   2. Information/demonstrations given to potential customers

   3. Reaction of potential customers

   4. Importance of satisfaction of targeted needs

   5. Test group's willingness to purchase products/services at various price levels

D. Lead times (amount of time between customer order placement and product/service delivery)

   1. Initial orders

   2. Repeat orders

   3. Volume purchases

E. Competition

   1. Identification (by product line or service and market segment)

      a. Existing

      b. Market share

      c. Potential (How long will your window of opportunity be open before your initial success breeds new competition? Who are your new competitors likely to be?)

      d. Direct

      e. Indirect

2. Strengths (competitive advantages)

a. Ability to satisfy customer needs

b. Market penetration

c. Track record and reputation

d. Staying power (financial resources)

e. Key personnel

3. Weaknesses (competitive disadvantages)

a. Ability to satisfy customer needs

b. Market penetration

c. Track record and reputation

d. Staying power (financial resources)

e. Key personnel

4. Importance of your target market to your competition

5. Barriers to entry into the market

a. Cost (investment)

b. Time

c. Technology

d. Key personnel

e. Customer inertia (brand loyalty, existing relationships, etc.)

f. Existing patents and trademarks

F. Regulatory restrictions

1. Customer or governmental regulatory requirements

a. Methods for meeting the requirements

b. Timing involved

c. Cost

2. Anticipated changes in regulatory requirements

Company Description

The company description section must summarize how all elements of your company fit together, without going into detail.

A. Nature of the business

1. Marketplace needs to be satisfied

2. Methods of need satisfaction

3. Individuals or organizations with the needs

B. Your distinctive competencies (factors that will lead to your success)

1. Superior customer need satisfaction

2. Production/service delivery efficiencies

3. Personnel

4. Geographic location

5. Route structure

Marketing and Sales Activities

Both general and specific marketing and sales information must be included. The objective is to describe the activities that will allow the organization to meet the sales and margin levels indicated in your prospective financial statements. This section should contain all aspects of getting the product/service to the customer. These include advertising, promotions, pricing, selling, delivering, and servicing the business. Explanation should include how a workable strategy exists for marketing the product or service compared with the approach that the competition uses. Define the objectives of the marketing program.

A. Overall marketing strategy

1. Marketing penetration strategy

2. Growth strategy

   a. Internal

   b. Acquisition

   c. Franchise

   d. Horizontal (providing similar products to different users)

   e. Vertical (providing the products at different levels of the distribution chain)

3. Distribution channels (include discount), profitability levels (at each stage)

   a. Original equipment manufacturers

   b. Internal sales force

   c. Distributors

   d. Wholesalers

   e. Travel agents

   f. Military operations

   g. Retailers

4. Communication

   a. Promotion

   b. Advertising

   c. Public relations

   d. Personal selling

   e. Printed materials (catalogs, brochures, etc.)

  B. Sales strategies
    1. Sales force
        a. Internal
        b. Independent representatives
        b. Size
        c. Recruitment and training
        d. Compensation
    2. Sales activities
        a. Identifying prospects
        b. Prioritizing prospects
        c. Number of sales calls per period
        d. Average dollar size per sale
        e. Average dollar size per reorder

Products and Services

Special attention should be paid to the users of the business plan. Too much detail can have a negative impact on external users. Avoid turning this section into a policies and procedures manual.

  A. Detailed product/service description (user's perspective, not employees)
    1. Specific benefits of product/service
    2. Ability to meet needs
    3. Competitive advantages
    4. Present stage (idea, prototype, small production runs, etc.)
  B. Product life cycle
    1. Description of the products'/services' current position within life cycle
    2. Factors that might change the anticipated life cycle
        a. Lengthen the cycle
        b. Shorten the cycle
  C. Copyrights, patents, and trade secrets
    1. Existing or pending copyrights or patents
    2. Anticipated copyright and patent filings
    3. Key aspects of your products/services that cannot be patented or copyrighted
    4. Key aspects of your products/services that qualify as trade secrets
    5. Existing legal agreements with owners and employees
        a. Nondisclosure agreements
        b. Noncompete agreements

D. Research and development activities

   1. Activities in process

   2. Future activities

   3. Anticipated results of future research and development activities

      a. New products or services

      b. New generation of existing products or services

      c. Complementary products or services

      d. Replacement products or services

   4. Research and development activities of others in the industry

      a. Direct competitors

      b. Indirect competitors

      c. Customers

Operations

A. Production and service delivery procedures

   1. Internal

   2. External

B. Production and service delivery capability

   1. Internal

   2. External

   3. Anticipated increases in capacity

      a. Investment

      b. New cost factors

         i. Direct

         ii. Indirect

      c. Timing

C. Operating competitive advantages

   1. Techniques

   2. Experience

   3. Economies of scale

   4. Lower direct costs

D. Suppliers

   1. Identification of the suppliers of critical elements of production

      a. Primary

      b. Secondary

   2. Lead time requirements

3. Evaluation of the risks of critical element shortages

4. Description of the existing and anticipated contractual relationships with suppliers

Management and Ownership

The management team is truly a unique aspect of the company. This section must emphasize team members' talents and skills. List names, ages, current positions, educational attainments, and employment histories. In particular, describe their past business successes. This aspect is very important, particularly when the company needs to borrow money. Lenders are generally fond of managers with impressive records. Ensure that all outside related advisers, such as attorneys, consultants, and accountants, are also included.

A. Management staff structure

    1. Management staff organization chart

    2. Narrative description of the chart

B. Key managers (complete resumes should be presented in an appendix)

    1. Name

    2. Position

    3. Brief position description

    4. Primary duties

    5. Primary duties and responsibilities with previous employers (include levels of authority)

    6. Unique skills and experiences that add to enhancement of company

    7. Compensation basis and levels

C. Planned additions to the current management team

    1. Position

    2. Primary responsibilities and authority

    3. Requisite skills and experience

    4. Recruitment process

    5. Timing of employment

    6. Anticipated contribution to the company's success

    7. Compensation basis and levels

D. Legal structure of the business

    1. Corporation

        a. C corporation

        b. S corporation

2. Partnership
    a. General
    b. Limited
3. Proprietorship

E. Owners
  1. Names
  2. Percentage of ownership
  3. Extent of involvement with the company
  4. Form of ownership
    a. Common stock
    b. Preferred stock
    c. General partner
    d. Limited partner
  5. Outstanding equity equivalents
    a. Options
    b. Warrants
    c. Convertible debt
  6. Common stock
    a. Authorized
    b. Issued

F. Board of directors
  1. Names
  2. Position on the board
  3. Extent of involvement with the company
  4. Background
  5. Ownership in company, if any
  6. Contribution to the company's success
    a. Historically
    b. In the future

Funds Required and Their Uses

A. Current funding requirements
  1. Amount
  2. Timing

    3. Type

       a. Equity

       b. Debt

       c. Other

    4. Terms

B. Funding requirements over the next five years

    1. Amount

    2. Timing

    3. Type

       a. Equity

       b. Debt

       c. Other

    4. Terms

C. Use of funds

    1. Capital expenditures

    2. Working capital

    3. Debt retirement

    4. Acquisitions

    5. Other

D. Long-range financial strategies (liquidating investors' positions)

    1. Taking company public

    2. Leveraged buyout

    3. Acquisition by another company

    4. Debt service levels and timing

    5. Liquidation of the venture

Financial Data

This section contains the financial representation of all the information presented in the previous sections.

A. Historical financial data (past three to five years, if applicable)

    1. Annual statements

       a. Income

       b. Balance sheets

       c. Cash flows

2. Level of CPA involvement (name of firm)

    a. Audit

    b. Review

    c. Compilation

B. Prospective financial data (five-year pro forma)

    1. Next year (by month or quarter)

        a. Income

        b. Balance sheet

        c. Cash flows

        d. Capital expenditure budget

    2. Final four years (by quarter or year)

        a. Income

        b. Balance sheet

        c. Cash flows

        d. Capital expenditure budget

    3. Summary of significant assumptions

    4. Type of prospective financial data

        a. Forecast (management's best estimate)

        b. Projection ("what if?" scenarios)

    5. Level of CPA involvement

        a. Assembly

        b. Agreed-upon procedures

        c. Review

        d. Examination

C. Analysis

    1. Historical financial statements

        a. Ratio analysis

        b. Trend analysis with graphic presentation

    2. Prospective financial statements

        a. Ratio analysis

        b. Trend analysis with graphic presentation

Appendices or Exhibits

This section should contain any additional detailed or confidential information that could be useful to the readers but is not appropriate for distribution to everyone receiving the body of the plan. You should be able to expand or delete this section, depending on your purpose.

A. Resumes of key managers

B. Pictures of products or services provided

C. Professional references

D. Market studies

E. Pertinent published information

F. Patents

G. Significant contracts

    1. Leases

    2. Sales contracts

    3. Purchases contracts

    4. Partnership/ownership agreements

    5. Stock option agreements

    6. Employment/compensation agreements

    7. Labor union agreements

    8. Insurance

        a. Product liability

        b. Officers' and directors' liability

        c. General liability

Suggested Readings and References

Advances in applied business strategy. (1984). Greenwich, CT: JAI Press.

Bangs, D. H. (1989). *Business planning guide: Creating a plan for success in your own business.* Dover, NH: Upstart.

Buskirk, R. H., Davis, M. R., & Price, C. H. (1991). *Program for writing winning business plans.* Denver: Premier Entrepreneur Programs.

Crego, E. T. (1986). *How to implement a business plan.* New York: American Management Associations.

Crego, E. T., Deaton, B., & Schiffrin, P. D. (1986). *How to write a business plan.* New York: American Management Associations, Extension Institute.

Dean, J. W. (1981). *Business policy and strategy.* Durham, NC: Eno River Press.

DeThomas, A. R., & Reierson, V. (1992). *Financing your small business: Techniques for planning, acquiring, and managing debt.* Grants Pass, OR: Oasis Press.

Gillen, L. (1989). *Alternative approaches to financing business development.* Prepared for the

U.S. National Council for Urban Economic Development, Economic Development Administration. Washington: Government Printing Office.

Glassman, C. A. (1993). *The weakening role of banks in financing small business.* Washington: Banking Research Fund of the Association of Reserve City Bankers.

Hicks, T. G. (1987). *One hundred and one ways to get 100+% financing quickly for real estate and business.* Merrick, NY: International Wealth Success.

Lindberg, R. A. (1979). *Long-range planning.* New York: American Management Associations.

Mazzo, W. L. (1990). *A business plan and evaluation, simple as 1-2-3: Three easy steps for a simple do-it-yourself business plan.* N.p.: Business Plan.

Nersesian, R. L. (1989). *Computer simulation in business decision making: A guide for managers, planners, and MIS professionals.* New York: Quorum Books.

Poole, K. E. (1987). *Financing tools and techniques: A guide to planning for business development.* Prepared for the National Council for Urban Economic Development. Washington: Government Printing Office.

Rowe, R. H. (1993). *Financing a small business in the securities markets.* New York: Practicing Law Institute.

Sitarz, D. (1991). *The complete book of small business legal forms: All the legal forms and documents you will need to successfully operate your small business.* Carbondale, IL: Nova.

Strategic management journal. (1980). New York: Wiley.

Sutton, C. J. (1980). *Economics and corporate strategy.* New York: Cambridge University Press.

GLOSSARY

INDEX

GLOSSARY

accelerated depreciation. An accounting method that allows a company to write off an asset's cost at a faster rate than the traditional method.

accountant. A person who records and examines individuals' or businesses' finances.

accounting. The principles and techniques in establishing, maintaining, and analyzing the records of the transactions of a business, individual, or governmental operation.

accounting equation. Assets = Liabilities + Owner's Equity. Variations on the equation are based on this standard formula.

accounts payable. Money that a company owes for merchandise or services bought on credit.

accounts receivable. Money owed to a company for merchandise or services bought on credit.

accrual basis. Accounting method in which income and expenses are accounted for as they are earned or incurred, although they may not have been received or paid yet.

acid test ratio. This ratio is computed by deducting inventories from current assets and dividing the remainder by current liabilities.

agency problem. A potential conflict of interest between stockholders and management or between stockholders and creditors (debt holders).

air traffic liability. The amount of money collected by the airlines from ticket sales on flights that have not yet been taken.

American Stock Exchange. The third most active market in the United States, behind the New York Stock Exchange and the NASDAQ Stock Market. The exchange was founded in 1842 in New York City. Most stocks traded on it are those of small to midsized companies. Also called AMEX and the curb exchange.

AMEX market value index. A stock index that measures the performance of more than 800 companies representing all major industry groups on the American Stock Exchange.

amortization. The accounting procedure that companies use to write off intangible rights or assets, such as goodwill, patents, or copyrights. More commonly known as the gradual elimination of debt through periodic payments.

annual report. A report issued annually by a corporation to its stockholders. It contains basic financial data, as well as management's opinion of past operations and future prospects.

appreciate. An increase in an asset's value over time.

asked. The price that someone is willing to accept for a security or an asset. In the stock market, the ask portion of a stock quote is the lowest price anyone is willing to accept for a security or an asset at that time.

asset allocation. Dividing investment money into a variety of instruments and markets.

asset-backed securities. Securities backed by loans or accounts receivable. For example, an asset-backed bond is created when a securities firm bundles some type of debt, like car loans, and sells investors the right to receive the payments that consumers make on those loans.

asset management ratios. A set of ratios that measure how effectively a firm is managing and using its assets.

assets. Everything a company or individual owns or is owed. May be cash, receivables, inventory, land and buildings, patents, or goodwill.

audit. An independent review by a certified public accountant to determine whether a company's financial statements fairly represent the financial results and condition of the entity and conform to generally accepted accounting principles.

auditor's report. The independent accounting firm's opinion on whether the company's financial statements conform to generally accepted accounting principles.

available seat miles (ASM). The number of seats on an aircraft multiplied by the total number of route miles flown in a specified period.

average annual yield. A way to calculate the return on investments of more than one year. It is calculated by adding each year's return on investment and dividing that number by the number of years invested.

averages. In the stock market, averages are indicators that measure price changes in representative stock prices. The most popular indicator is the Dow Jones industrial average, which measures the performance of thirty industrial stocks.

balance sheet. Financial statement that lists a company's assets and liabilities as of a specified date.

bankruptcy. A legal process governed by the U.S. bankruptcy code for people or companies unable to meet financial obligations. The bankruptcy code is divided into chapters that provide different types of relief. Chapter 7 governs liquidation rather than reorganization. Chapter 9 provides for municipal debt adjustments. Chapter 11 provides for reorganization and repayment for individuals, partnerships, and corporations that are domiciled in the United States. Chapter 12 governs reorganization and repayment for farmers or closely held farming corporations having debt of no more than $1.5 million. Chapter 13 provides for individual debt adjustments and is an alternative to liquidation under Chapter 7.

bearer stock. Stock certificates that are not registered in any name. They are negotiable without endorsement by any person.

bear market. When security prices decline 15 percent or more.

bid. The price that someone is willing to pay for a security or an asset. In the stock market, the bid portion of a stock quote is the highest price anyone is willing to pay for a security at that time.

board of directors. The elected representatives of a corporation's or a sub-s corporation's stockholders.

bond. An interest bearing certificate of debt that pays a set amount of interest on a regular basis. The issuer promises to repay the debt on time and in full. Bonds are bought and sold on the market.

bond, bearer. A bond payable to the holder that does not have the owner's name registered on the books of the issuing company.

bond, callable. A bond that the debtor has declared to be due and payable on a certain date prior to maturity, in accordance with the provisions of an issue to be redeemed.

bond, collateral trust. An issue of bonds for which collateral has been pledged to guarantee repayment of the principal.

bond, convertible. A bond that provides its owner the privilege of exchanging it for other securities of the issuing company on a preferred basis at some future date or under certain conditions.

bond, government. An obligation of the U.S. government, regarded as the highest-grade issues in existence. Types of government bonds include treasury bills and treasury notes.

bond, income. A type of bond on which interest is paid when and only when earned by the issuing corporation.

bond, mortgage. A bond that has a mortgage placed on properties of the issuing corporation as repayment security.

bond, municipal. A bond issued by a state or political subdivision (county, city, etc.) or a state agency or authority. In general, interest paid on municipal bonds is exempt from federal income taxes and state and local taxes in the state of issue.

bond, refunding. A bond issued to retire a bond that is already outstanding. Refunding bonds may be sold for cash and outstanding bonds redeemed in cash, or they may be exchanged for outstanding bonds.

bond, revenue. A bond whose principal and interest are to be paid solely from earnings. Such bonds are usually issued by a municipally owned utility or other public service enterprise, such as an airport. The revenues generated by the use of items purchased by the bond money are pledged as repayment.

bond, sinking fund. A bond secured by the deposit of specified amounts of money. The issuing corporation makes deposits to secure the principal.

bond rating. Appraising and rating a company's ability to repay the bond upon maturity. Ratings are based on the reputation of the organization, its record of previous payments, profitability, etc. The major bond rating agencies are Standard & Poor's and Moody's.

book value. The difference between a company's assets and its liabilities usually expressed in per-share terms. It takes into account all money invested in the company since its founding, as well as retained earnings. It is calculated by subtracting liabilities from assets and dividing the result by the number of shares outstanding. Comparing book value to share price is one way to gauge if a company's stock is undervalued or overvalued.

bottom line. Accounting term for the net profit or loss.

breakeven. The point at which the income from the sales of a product, service, or business unit equals total expenses. Normally, this figure is arrived at by using a formula related to fixed and variable costs. Another way of determining breakeven in the airline business is through the use of direct operating costs and fully allocated costs.

breakup value. The dollars per share the company would be worth if it were completely sold off and converted to cash.

broker. A person who gives advice and handles orders to buy or sell stocks and bonds.

budget. A document establishing income and expenses for a clearly defined future period.

business productivity. The Labor Department's monthly measurement of output or production per hour of work.

call. The issuer's right to redeem a bond or preferred share before it matures.

call provision. A provision in a bond contract that allows the issuer to call in and pay off the bond under specified terms before the stated maturity date.

callable bond. A bond that can be redeemed by the issuer before it matures.

capital asset. An asset held for more than a year that is not bought or sold in the normal course of business. Capital assets generally include fixed assets, such as land, buildings, equipment, and furniture.

capital budgeting. The process of planning expenditures on assets whose cash flows are expected to extend beyond one year.

capital gain. The difference between the purchase price and the sale price of an asset when the sales price exceeds the purchase price.

capital goods. Items that are normally expected to last for a long time and are used by the business to produce goods or services.

capital lease. See financial lease.

capital loss. The difference between the purchase price and the sale price of an asset when the sales price was less than the purchase price.

capital markets. The financial markets for stocks and long-term debt (one year or longer).

cash flow. Net income after depreciation and other noncash charges are subtracted, usually measured by profits before deductions of noncash items such as depreciation. This figure shows the flow of cash through a company. It indicates the net cash generation and requirements each month.

cash flow cycle. The way in which actual net cash, as opposed to accounting net income, flows into or out of a firm during some specified period.

certified public accountant (CPA). Accountant who has met certain educational and experience requirements and has passed a licensing examination of the American Institute of Certified Public Accountants.

closely held. Companies in which stock and voting control are concentrated in the hands of a few investors, although the companies' shares may be traded to a limited extent.

closing price. The last trading price of a stock when the market closes.

collateral. Stock or other property that borrowers are obliged to turn over to lenders if they are unable to repay a loan. Property pledged by a borrower as security on a loan.

commercial bank. A bank owned by shareholders that accepts deposits, makes commercial and industrial loans, and provides other banking services for the public. Also called a full-service bank.

commercial paper. Unsecured short-term promissory notes of large firms usually issued in denominations of $100,000 or more and having interest rates slightly below prime rate.

commodities. Bulk goods such as grains, metals, livestock, oil, cotton, coffee, sugar, and cocoa. They can be sold either on the spot market for immediate delivery or on the commodity exchanges for later delivery. Trade on the exchanges is in the form of futures contracts.

common stock. Represents partial ownership of a company. Holders of common stock have voting rights but no guarantee of dividend payments.

common stock equity (net worth). The capital supplied by common stockholders—capital stock, paid-in capital, retained earnings, and reserves. Total equity is common equity plus preferred stock.

comparative ratio analysis. An analysis based on a comparison of a firm's ratios with those of other firms in the same economic sector.

consumer comfort index. A measure of consumers' feelings about their finances and the economy as a whole. The numbers are calculated through a weekly survey by *Money* magazine and ABC News.

consumer credit. Money loaned to individuals, usually on an unsecured basis, requiring monthly repayment. Bank loans, credit cards, and installment credit are examples of consumer credit.

consumer price index (CPI). A gauge of inflation that measures changes in the prices of consumer goods. The index is based on a list of specific goods and services purchased in urban areas. It is released monthly by the Labor Department.

convertible bond. A bond that investors may exchange for stock on some future date under certain conditions.

convertible security. A security, usually a bond or preferred stock, that can be converted into common stock at the option of the holder.

corporate bonds. Bonds issued by corporations.

corporation. A legal entity created by a state, separate and distinct from its owners and managers, having unlimited life, transferability of ownership, and limited liability.

correction. A reverse movement, usually downward, in the price of an individual stock, bond, commodity, index, or the stock market as a whole.

cost basis. In accounting, the valuation of an asset that includes the cost of the asset and factors in such items as depreciation, capital gains, and dividends.

cost of living. The level of prices of goods and services required for a reasonable standard of living.

cost-push inflation. A sustained rise in prices caused by businesses passing on increases in costs, especially labor costs, to purchasers.

coupon. The interest rate specified on a bond when it is originally issued.

coupon rate. The stated annual rate of interest on a bond.

credit ratings. Formal evaluations of a government body or company's credit history and ability to repay its debts.

currency. Money that circulates in an economy. Also refers to a country's official unit of exchange.

current account balance. One of the components of a country's balance of payments, the current account balance covers the imports and exports of goods and services.

current assets. Assets that will be readily and quickly realized in the regular course of business, usually within a period of one year or less.

current liabilities. Liabilities that are due or will become due in the next year or the next operation cycle, whichever is longer. ·

current ratio. This ratio is computed by dividing current assets by current liabilities. It indicates the extent to which the claims of short-term creditors are covered by assets expected to be converted into cash in the near future.

current yield. A measure of an investor's return on a bond. Calculated by dividing the coupon rate by the purchase price, then multiplying by $1,000.

debenture. A certificate issued by a corporation that states the amount of a loan, the interest to be paid, and the time for repayment. It is backed only by the corporation's reputation and good word, not by collateral.

debt. Securities such as bonds, notes, mortgages, and other forms of paper that indicate the intent to repay an amount owed.

debt-equity ratio. A comparison of a company's total debt to the total equity (or net worth).

debt management ratios. A set of ratios that indicate the level of debt used by a firm.

debt ratio. The ratio of total debt to total assets.

default. Failure to pay principal or interest on a financial obligation. It can also refer to a breach or nonperformance of the terms of a debt instrument.

defensive securities. Stocks with investment returns that do not tend to decline as much as the market in general in times when stock prices are falling. Those include companies with earnings that tend to grow despite the business cycle, such as food and drug firms, or companies that pay relatively high dividends, such as utilities.

deflation. A decline in the general price level of goods and services that results in increased purchasing power of money. The opposite of inflation.

depreciation. A decline in value. In accounting, a reduction of earnings to write off the cost of an asset over its estimated useful life.

depression. A severe downturn in an economy that is marked by falling prices, reduced purchasing power, and high unemployment.

derivative. A complex investment whose value is derived from or linked to some underlying financial asset, such as stocks, bonds, currencies, or mortgages. Derivatives may be listed on exchanges or traded privately over the counter. For example, derivatives may be futures, options, or mortgage-backed securities.

discount. In general, the amount by which one security price is less than another. In financing, it is the interest withheld when a note, draft, or bill is purchased.

discount bond. A bond that sells for less than its par value. This occurs when the coupon rate is lower than the going rate of interest.

discount rate. The interest rate charged by the Federal Reserve on loans to banks and other financial institutions. This rate influences the rates that these financial institutions then charge to their customers.

dividend. A portion of a company's income paid to shareholders as a return on their investment.

dividend policy decision. The board decision concerning how much of current earnings to pay out to stockholders as cash dividend and how much to keep and reinvest in the firm's growth.

double entry system. An accounting system requiring two entries, a debit and a credit, to be made for each transaction. Debits record increases in assets and expenses or decreases in liabilities. Credits record increases in liabilities, owner's equity, or income and record decreases in assets. Debits must always equal credits.

Dow Jones averages. There are four Dow Jones averages that track price changes in various sectors. The Dow Jones industrial average tracks the price changes of the stock of thirty industrial companies. The Dow Jones transportation average monitors the price changes of the stocks of twenty airlines, railroads, and trucking companies. The Dow Jones utility average measures the performance of the stock of fifteen gas, electric, and power companies. The Dow Jones 65 composite average monitors the stock of all sixty-five companies that make up the other three averages.

Dow Jones equity market index. Index that measures price changes in more than 100 U.S. industry groups. The stocks in the index represent about 80 percent of U.S. market capitalization and trade on the New York Stock Exchange, the American Stock Exchange, and the NASDAQ stock market. The equity-market index is market-capitalization weighted, which means that a stock's influence on the index is proportionate to its size in the market.

Dow Jones world stock index. An index that measures the performance of more than two thousand companies worldwide that represent more than 80 percent of the equity capital on twenty-five stock markets.

durable goods orders. Monthly survey of the backlog in orders for durable goods that is compiled by the Commerce Department. Durable goods are products expected to last more than three years.

earnings. Income after a company's taxes and all other expenses have been paid. Also called profit or net income.

earnings before interest and taxes (EBIT). Earnings net of direct operating expenses but before any interest and taxes due are deducted to determine net income. The figures are often used to gauge the financial performance of companies with high levels of debt and interest expenses. EBIT is also a measure of a firm's ability to generate positive cash flow.

earnings per share (EPS). A portion of the company's earnings allocated to each share outstanding. Calculated by dividing the number of outstanding shares into earnings.

economic indicators. Key statistics used to analyze business conditions and make forecasts.

emerging markets. Financial markets in nations that are developing market-based economies and have become popular with American investors, such as China and Peru.

entrepreneur. A person who organizes, manages, and assumes the risk of a business enterprise.

equity. In property, equity is the difference between the property's current market value and the claims against the property. In securities markets, equity is the part of a company's net worth that belongs to shareholders.

equity capital. The amount of the investment through cash or retained profits in a company. Sometimes called shareholders' equity, book value, or net worth of a company. Also, the difference between the assets and the liabilities of the company.

eurodollars. Dollar-denominated deposits in banks outside the United States.

European monetary system. An exchange-rate system adopted by European Union members in an effort to move toward a unified European currency.

European-style option. An option that may be exercised only on its expiration date.

European Union (EU). An intergovernmental organization of twelve Western European nations created under the Maastricht treaty of December 1991 with its own institutional structures and decision-making framework. Before the Maastricht treaty went into effect in November 1993, the organization was known as the European Community or the Common Market. Its members are Belgium, Denmark, France, Germany, Greece, Ireland, Italy, Luxembourg, The Netherlands, Portugal, Spain, and the United Kingdom. Its council of ministers and the European Commission are based in Brussels, Belgium, and its parliament is based in Strasbourg, France.

exchange. A centralized place for trading securities and commodities, usually involving an auction process.

expenses. The cost of doing business. A decrease in owner's equity by any transaction except a withdrawal or payment of a dividend. The cost of assets used up in producing revenue or carrying out other activities that are part of the business's operation.

expiration date. The date after which an option may no longer be exercised.

exports. Goods and services that one country produces and sells to others.

face value. The monetary value of a bond printed on its face. The exact amount for which a note is written. Face value and market value often differ.

federal debt. The total amount the federal government owes because of past deficits.

federal deficit. The amount of money the federal government owes because it spent more than it received in revenue for the past year.

Federal funds rate. The interest rate that banks charge on overnight loans to banks that need more cash to meet bank reserve requirements. The Federal Reserve sets the interest rate.

Federal Reserve Bank. The central bank of the United States. The Federal Reserve oversees money supply, interest rates, and credit with the goal of keeping the U.S. economy and currency stable. Governed by a seven-member board, the system includes twelve regional Federal Reserve banks, twenty-five branches, and all national and state banks that are part of the system. Also called the Fed.

Financial Accounting Standards Board. The primary rule-making body for accountants.

financial lease. A lease that does not provide for maintenance services, is not cancelable, and is fully amortized over its life. Also known as capital lease.

financial service corporations. Firms that offer a wide range of financial services including investment banking, brokerage, insurance, and commercial banking.

financial statement. Any report summarizing the financial condition of a company. Key reports are the balance sheet, income statement, and cash flow statement.

fiscal year. The twelve-month period that a corporation or government uses for bookkeeping purposes.

fixed assets. Machinery, aircraft, furniture, or fixtures used in the service or production of other assets or services. Their serviced life extends beyond the limits of a single accounting period.

fixed base operators. An operator of one or more aircraft who has a permanent fixed aviation service facility at an airport. FBOs usually engage in aviation activity such as flight instruction, fuel sales, repairs, aircraft rental and sales, and air charter.

float. In securities, the number of outstanding shares in a corporation available for trading by the public. Also, the time between the deposit of a check in a bank and the check's payment.

floating an issue. Offering stocks or bonds to the public for the first time. It can be an initial public offering or an offering of issues by companies that are already public.

force majeure. A condition that permits a company to depart from the strict terms of a contract because of an event or effect that cannot be reasonably anticipated or controlled.

foreign exchange. Money instruments used to make payments between countries.

foreign exchange market. Market in which foreign currencies are bought and sold and exchange rates between currencies are determined.

full-service brokers. Brokers who execute buy and sell orders, research investments, help investors develop and meet investment goals, and give advice to investors. They charge commissions for their work.

fundamental analysis. Analysis technique that looks at a company's financial condition, management, and place in its industry to predict a company's stock price movement.

futures. An agreement to purchase or sell a given quantity of a commodity, security, or currency at a specified date in the future. Also called a futures contract.

General Agreement on Tariffs and Trade (GATT). A trade pact ratified in 1994 that cut tariffs worldwide, reduced agricultural subsidies, standardized copyright and patent protection, and set up arbitration panels. GATT was also an institution that oversaw international trade issues. The institution changed its name to the World Trade Organization after the trade pact was ratified.

general ledger. A ledger that contains all accounts appearing in the trial balance.

general obligation bond. A government bond that is approved either by the voters or by their legislature. The government's promise to repay the principal and pay the interest is constitutionally guaranteed, based on its ability to tax the population. Also called a full-faith-and-credit bond.

general partner. A co-owner in a partnership who is fully liable for all partnership debts.

generally accepted accounting principles (GAAP). Guidelines that explain what should be done in specific accounting situations as determined by the Financial Accounting Standards Board.

goodwill. In accounting, goodwill is any advantage, such as a well-regarded brand name or symbol, that enables a business to earn better profits than its competitors. If such assets are sold for less than book value, the difference is negative goodwill.

government-sponsored enterprises. Government-sponsored agencies such as the Federal National Mortgage Association (Fannie Mae), the Federal Home Loan Mortgage Corporation (Freddie Mac), the Student Loan Marketing Corporation (Sallie Mae), and the Tennessee Valley Authority (TVA).

Great Depression. The worldwide economic hard times generally regarded as having begun with the stock market collapse of October 28–29, 1929. It continued throughout most of the 1930s.

greenmail. A firm offers to buy back its own stock from a raider at a premium over market price to avoid a takeover. The offer is not extended to all shareholders.

gross domestic product (GDP). The total value of goods and services produced by a nation. In the United States, it is calculated by the Commerce Department, and it is the main measure of U.S. economic output.

gross national product (GNP). The dollar value of all goods and services produced in a nation's economy. Unlike gross domestic product, it includes goods and services produced abroad.

hedging. Buying or selling a product or a security to offset a possible loss from price changes on a future corresponding purchase or sale.

holding company. A company whose principal assets are the securities it owns in companies that actually provide goods or services. A holding company enables one corporation and its directors to control several companies by holding a large stake in the companies.

hostile takeover. An acquisition of one company by another over the objections of the target company's board. Often an acquirer will take its transaction directly to the shareholders of the target company, offering to buy their shares through a tender offer, or seeking their approval to remove opposing members from the target company's board.

housing starts. The Commerce Department's monthly survey of the number of housing permits issued by local government authorities.

income statement. A summary of the revenues and expenses for a specified period of time. It can also be called a "profit and loss statement."

initial public offering (IPO). The first time a company issues stock to the public. This process often is called "going public."

interest. The cost of borrowing money. May also be referred to as the "cost of money."

intermediate-term bonds. Bonds that mature in five to ten years.

inventory turnover ratio. The ratio computed by dividing sales by inventories.

investment bank. A securities firm, financial company, or brokerage house that helps companies take new issues to market. Additionally, an investment bank handles the sales of large blocks of previously issued securities and private placements. Most investment banks also maintain brokerage operations and other financial services.

investment banking houses. Financial institutions that underwrite and distribute new securities issues and assist businesses in raising capital.

investment grade. An assessment of a debt issue by a credit-rating firm that indicates investors are expected to receive principal and interest payments in full and on time.

investment grade bonds. Bonds that are rated A or BBB; many institutions are prevented by law from investing in any bonds that are below this level of risk.

junk bonds. High-yield bonds that credit-rating agencies consider speculative. The bonds typically offer higher yields and carry higher risk than bonds with investment-grade ratings.

lagging economic indicators. A composite of seven economic measurements that tend to trail developments in the economy as a whole. Those indicators are duration of unemployment, ratio of inventories to sales, index of labor costs per unit of output, average prime rate, outstanding commercial and industrial loans, ratio of outstanding consumer installment credit to personal income, and consumer price index for services. Compiled by the Commerce Department.

leading economic indicators. A composite of eleven economic measurements developed to help forecast likely changes in the economy as a whole. It is compiled by the Conference Board. The components are average work week, unemployment claims, orders for consumer goods, slower deliveries, plant and equipment orders, building permits, durable order backlog, materials prices, stock prices, M2 money supply, and consumer expectations.

lease. A long-term rental agreement.

leasee. The party who uses and pays for leased property.

ledger. Summations of journal entries, by category, that show the effects of each transaction on the balance in each account.

lessor. The owner of leased property.

letter of credit. A bank's promise that a shipment of goods will be paid for on arrival. Used mostly in foreign trade, but also used domestically to guarantee payment of securities.

leverage. The use of borrowed assets by a business to enhance the return to the owner's equity. The expectation is that the interest rate charged will be lower than the earnings made on the money. In securities markets, leverage refers to money borrowed to cover part of the cost of a purchase.

leveraged buyout (LBO). A situation in which a group, often the firm's management aided by an LBO specialist, uses credit to purchase the outstanding shares of the company's stock.

liabilities. The claims against a corporation or other entity. They include accounts payable, wages and salaries, dividends, taxes, and obligations such as bonds, debentures, and bank loans.

LIBOR. The London Interbank offered rate. A floating interest rate that serves as a base for many lending agreements.

lift. The number of available seats (ASMs) in a specific city pair market.

limited partner. A member of a limited partnership whose losses are limited to the amount invested. Limited partners usually do not participate in management or investment decisions of the partnership.

line of credit. An agreement in which a bank or group of banks will lend funds up to a specified maximum amount during a designated period.

liquidation. The process of converting stock or other assets into cash. When a company is liquidated, the cash obtained is first used to pay debts and obligations to holders of bonds and preferred stock. Whatever cash remains is distributed on a per-share basis to the holders of common stock.

liquidity. The ease of converting an asset to cash.

liquidity ratios. A set of ratios that show the relationship of a firm's cash and other current assets to its current liabilities.

load factor. A measurement of business and efficiency for airlines. It is the percentage of available seats that are occupied.

long bond. Slang for a thirty-year bond issued by the U.S. Treasury. It is considered a key indicator, or benchmark, of trends in long-term interest rates.

long-term assets. Tangible assets of a relatively long life that are not intended for resale and that are used in the operation of a business.

long-term bonds. Bonds with maturities of more than ten years.

long-term debt. Borrowings due more than one year from the balance sheet date.

long-term liabilities. Financial obligations not due in the next operating period.

market capitalization. The total market value of a company or stock. Market capitalization is calculated by multiplying the number of shares by the current market price of the shares.

market share. A comparison of a company's sales to the industry total sales. In the airline industry, a comparison of an airline's RPMs to other airlines' RPMs in the same market.

maturity date. The date on which the par value of a bond must be paid to the bondholder; the redemption date.

maturity value. The total of principal added to accumulated interest.

merchant banking. A form of banking where the bank arranges credit financing but does not hold loans until maturity. A merchant bank invests its own capital in leveraged buyouts, corporate acquisitions, and other structured finance transactions. It is a fee-based business, in which the bank assumes market risk but no long-term credit risk.

merger. The formation of one company from two or more previously existing companies through pooling of common stock, cash payment, or a combination of both.

monetary aggregates (M1, M2, M3). Measures of a country's money supply. M1 consists of funds that are readily available for spending, including cash and checking accounts that pay interest and those that don't, and currency. M2 consists of M1 and all savings or short-term deposits. It also includes certain short-term assets such as the amounts held in money market mutual funds. M3 is the total of M1 and M2 as well as the assets and liabilities of banks. Also called money supply measures.

monetary base. The sum of reserve accounts of financial institutions at Federal Reserve banks and currency in circulation. It is the ultimate source of the nation's money supply and is controllable, to some degree, by Federal Reserve monetary policy. The adjusted monetary base data are compiled weekly by the Federal Reserve Board and the Federal Reserve Bank of St. Louis.

monetary policy. A government's efforts to control its money supply. The Federal Reserve influences the money supply through its control of bank reserves and lending rates between itself and other banks and the lending rate of bank to bank.

mortgage. A security interest in property given by a borrower (mortgagor) to a lender (mortgagee).

mortgage-backed securities. Debt issues backed by a pool of mortgages. Investors receive payments from the interest and principal payments made on the underlying mortgages.

mortgage bonds. Debt issues secured by a mortgage on the issuer's property, such as buildings or equipment.

multinational firm. An organization that operates in two or more countries.

municipal bonds. Bonds issued by local government authorities, including states, cities, and their agencies.

NASDAQ. An electronic stock market run by the National Association of Securities Dealers. Brokers get price quotes through a computer network and trade via telephone or computer network.

NASDAQ composite index. An index that covers the price movements of all stocks traded on the NASDAQ.

NASDAQ national market. A subdivision of the NASDAQ that contains the largest and most actively traded stocks. Companies must meet more stringent standards to be included in this section than they do to be included in the other major subdivision, the NASDAQ small-cap market.

net income. The amount left after a company's taxes and all other expenses have been paid. Also called earnings or profit.

net loss. The amount by which expenses exceed revenues. The excess of all expenses and losses for a period over all revenues and gains for that same period. Negative net income.

net worth. The amount by which assets exceed liabilities.

New York Stock Exchange. The largest U.S. stock market in terms of capitalization. The total market value of roughly 2,300 companies whose shares are listed there is about $5 trillion. It was founded in 1792.

Nikkei. There are several Nikkei indexes. Most often it refers to the daily average of 225 large-capitalization stocks on the Tokyo Stock Exchange.

normal profits. Those profits which are close to the averages for all firms in that category and are sufficient to attract capital.

note. A written promise by a government or corporation to repay a debt. The date for repayment is generally one to ten years later.

NYSE composite index. An index that covers the price movements of all stocks listed on the New York Stock Exchange.

offering price. The price at which initial public offerings are set.

operating cash flows. Those cash flows which arise from the normal conduct of business operations; the difference between sales revenue and cash expenses.

operating costs. Expenditures arising out of current business activities.

operating income. Net income excluding income derived from sources other than the company's regular activities and before income deductions. Also called net operating income or net operating loss.

operating lease. A lease under which the lessor maintains and finances the property.

operating leverage. The extent to which a firm's fixed costs are used in a firm's operations.

operating merger. A merger in which the operations of the two firms will be combined and integrated in the hope of achieving synergy and economies of scale.

options. An agreement allowing an investor to buy or sell something, such as shares of stock, during a specific time for a specific price. Options are traded on several exchanges, including the Chicago Board of Options Exchange, the American Stock Exchange, the Philadelphia Stock Exchange, the Pacific Stock Exchange, and the New York Stock Exchange.

over-the-counter market. A market in which securities transactions are conducted by dealers through a telephone and computer network connecting dealers in stocks and bonds. Also called OTC trading.

over-the-counter securities. Securities that are not listed and traded on an organized exchange. Also called OTC securities.

owner's equity. Assets minus liabilities. What would remain for a firm's owners if the company were liquidated, with all of its assets being sold off and all its debts paid.

par value. The nominal or face value of a stock or bond. It has no relationship to the market price.

partnership. An agreement between two or more people to share in the operation and profits of a commercial undertaking.

payment date. The date that a stock's dividend or a bond's interest payment is scheduled to be paid.

payout ratio. The percentage of earnings paid to shareholders as dividends.

performance shares. A type of incentive plan in which managers are awarded shares of stock based on the firm's earnings per share performance over a fixed interval of time.

pink sheets. The printed quotations of the bid and ask prices of over-the-counter stocks, published by National Quotation Bureaus Inc.

poison pill. An action taken by a firm's management to make the firm financially unattractive to potential buyers and thus avoid a hostile takeover.

portfolio. A collection of securities held by an investor.

portfolio insurance. A method of hedging, or protecting, the value of a stock portfolio by selling stock-index futures contracts when the stock market declines. The practice was a major contributor to the October 1987 stock market crash.

preferred stock. Ownership shares of a company that have no voting rights but that do have a set guaranteed dividend payment.

premium. In general, the amount by which one security price exceeds another security price.

premium bond. A bond that sells above its par value. This occurs when the coupon rate is above the going rate of interest.

present value. The current dollar equivalent of a future stream of income; the amount found by discounting the future stream by some selected interest rate.

price/earnings ratio. A ratio to evaluate a stock's worth. It is calculated by dividing the stock's price by an earnings-per-share figure. If calculated with the past year's earnings, it is called the trailing P/E. If calculated with an analyst's forecast for next year's earnings, it is called a forward P/E. Also called the P/E ratio or multiple.

pricing. The job of the underwriter to determine the price it will pay the company for a security. This is usually done the day before the sale of the security.

primary markets. Markets in which corporations raise capital by issuing new securities.

prime rate. The interest rate that banks charge their most credit-worthy commercial customers. Banks use the prime as a base to set rates for credit cards, home equity loans, and other loans, including loans to small and medium-sized businesses.

private placement. The sale of stocks or other investments directly to an investor. The securities in a private placement don't have to be registered with the Securities and Exchange Commission.

pro forma results. A projection of a financial statement that shows how the actual statement would look under certain conditions. For example, pro forma results are used to show the earnings that newly merged companies would have achieved had they been combined throughout the entire period.

producer price index (PPI). A group of statistics compiled by the Labor Department that are used to gauge inflation at the wholesale level. The index for finished goods—which tracks commodities that will not undergo further processing and are ready for sale to the ultimate user—is the most prominently reported of the statistics.

profit. The amount left after the company's taxes and all other expenses have been paid. Also called net income or earnings.

profit margin. A measure of a company's profitability, cost structure, and efficiency, calculated by dividing a measure of profits by sales. Gross margins are based on gross profits—sales minus the cost of producing the goods sold. Pretax profit margins are based on pretax profits—sales minus all operating expenses. After-tax profit margins are based on after-tax profits—sales minus operating expenses and taxes.

profit margin on sales. This ratio measures income per dollar of sales and is computed by dividing net income by sales.

profit maximization. The maximization of the firm's net income.

profit taking. Selling securities after a recent, often rapid price increase.

profitability ratios. A set of ratios that show the combined effects of liquidity, asset management, and debt management on operating results.

promissory note. A document specifying the terms and conditions of a loan, including interest rate, term, and amount.

proprietorship. The sole owner of a company.

prospectus. A formal written offer to sell securities that sets forth the plan for a proposed or existing business. The prospectus must be filed with the Securities and Exchange Commission and given to prospective buyers. A prospectus includes information on a company's finances, risks, products, services, and management.

proxy. A document giving one person the authority to act for another, typically, to vote shares of common stock.

proxy fight. An attempt to gain control of a firm by soliciting stockholders to vote for a change in management.

proxy statement. A document mailed with a proxy that gives information about the company or group seeking the proxy votes and matters scheduled for consideration at the shareholder meeting.

public company. A company that sells shares of its stock to the public. Public companies are regulated by the Securities and Exchange Commission. Also called a publicly held company.

put option. An agreement that gives an investor the right but not the obligation to sell a stock, bond, commodity, or other instrument at a specified price within a specific period.

qualitative analysis. A research technique that deals with factors that cannot be precisely measured such as employee morale and management expertise.

quantitative analysis. A research technique that deals with measurable assets such as the value of assets and the cost of capital.

quote. A bid to buy a security or an offer to sell a security in a given market at a given time.

ratio. The relationship between two items on a financial statement.

recession. A downturn in economic activity, broadly defined by many economists as at least two consecutive quarters of decline in a nation's gross domestic product.

recovery. In a business cycle, the period after a downturn or recession when economic activity picks up and the gross domestic product increases.

regional exchanges. Securities exchanges located outside New York City. They include the Boston, Philadelphia, Chicago, Cincinnati, and Pacific stock exchanges. Stocks listed on the New York Stock Exchange or the American Stock Exchange also may trade on regional exchanges.

repurchase agreement. An agreement between a bank and an investor for the bank to borrow money from the investor for a short time, usually less than ninety days. Repurchase agreements are widely used on the money market by governments' central banks. Also called a repo or buyback.

reserve borrowing capacity. The ability to borrow funds at reasonable rates as and when the need arises.

reserve requirement. The Federal Reserve's limit on the level of financial assets that banks must keep on reserve and not lend out or reinvest. These reserves help determine how much money the banks can lend.

residual value. The value of leased property at the end of the lease term.

retail sales. A monthly survey by the Commerce Department that measures the sales of durable and nondurable goods sold to consumers. A durable good is a product that is expected to last more than three years.

retained earnings. That portion of net income that has been saved by the firm rather than paid out to stockholders as dividends.

return on assets (ROA). The ratio of net income to total assets.

return on common equity (ROE). The ratio of net income to common equity. Measures the rate of return on common stockholders investment.

return on equity. A measure of how much the company earns on the investment of its shareholders. It is calculated by dividing a company's net income by its common shareholders' equity.

return on investment. A measure of how much the company earns on the money the company itself has invested. It is calculated by dividing the company's net income by its net assets.

revenue. Money that a company takes in, including interest earned and receipts from sales, services provided, rents, and royalties.

revenue bond. A bond backed only by revenue from the airport, roadway, or other facility that was built with the money it raised.

revenue passenger miles (RPM). The number of paying passengers carried by an air carrier multiplied by the number of miles those passengers flew in a specified period.

revolving credit. A line of credit that may be used repeatedly up to a specified total, with periodic full or partial repayment.

revolving credit facility. A line of credit extended to a business for a certain period without a fixed repayment schedule. The borrower may use the full amount at any time and repay it in full without penalty.

risk. In a financial context, the chance that a loan or note will not be paid back.

sales. Money that a company receives from the goods and services it sells. In some cases, the amount includes receipts from rents and royalties.

sales and leaseback. A process by which a firm sells assets such as aircraft, land, or buildings to another firm and leases the property back for a specific period. This procedure usually results in lower operating costs or increased cash flow.

S corporation. An arrangement whereby a corporation may be taxed as a partnership under the provisions of the Internal Revenue Code.

secondary markets. Markets in which securities and other financial assets are traded among investors after they have been issued by corporations.

secondary offering. The sale to the public of a large block of stock that is owned by an existing shareholder.

secured loans. Loans that require collateral for protection against nonpayment by the debtor.

Securities and Exchange Commission (SEC). The federal agency that enforces securities laws and sets standards for disclosure about publicly traded securities, including mutual funds. It was created in 1934 and consists of five commissioners appointed by the president and confirmed by the Senate to staggered terms.

security. A financial instrument that indicates the holder owns a share or shares of a company (stock) or has loaned money to a company or government organization (bond).

self-liquidating. An investment or loan for a purpose that is expected to yield a return sufficient to retire the loan and interest.

senior security. A security with claims on income and assets that rank higher than certain other securities. For example, mortgage bonds are senior to debentures.

service business. A business that provides people with labor services, such as airlines and fixed base operators, as opposed to those providing a tangible product, such as automobile manufacturing, restaurants, etc.

share. An investment that represents part ownership of a company or a mutual fund.

short selling. A trading strategy that anticipates a drop in a share's price. Stock or another financial instrument is borrowed from a broker and then sold, creating a short position. That position is reversed, or covered, when the stock is repurchased to repay the loan. The short seller profits if he or she is able to repurchase stock at a lower price than he or she received in creating the short position.

short-term gain or loss. For tax purposes, the profit or loss from selling capital assets or securities held six months or less. Short-term gains are taxed at the highest ordinary income-tax rate.

sinking fund. A required annual payment designed to amortize a bond or preferred stock issue.

small capitalization stocks. Shares of relatively small publicly traded corporations, typically with a total market value, or capitalization, of less than $600 million. Also called small cap stocks or small caps.

social responsibility. The concept that businesses should be actively concerned with the welfare of society at large.

sole proprietorship. A business owned by one individual.

specialist. A stock exchange member who is designated to maintain a fair and orderly market in a specific stock. They are required to buy and sell for their own account to counteract temporary imbalances in supply and demand.

spot market. A market for buying or selling commodities or foreign exchange for immediate delivery and for cash payment.

spread. In stocks, the difference between the bid and asked prices. In fixed-income securities, the difference between the yields on securities of the same quality but different maturity or the difference between the yields on securities of the same maturity but of different quality.

Standard & Poor's 500 stock index. A benchmark index of 500 large stocks, maintained by Standard & Poor's, a division of McGraw-Hill. Also called the S&P 500.

statement of cash flows. A statement reporting the impact of a firm's operating, investing, and financing activities on cash flows over an accounting period.

statement of retained earnings. A statement reporting how much of the firm's earnings were not paid out as dividends. The figure that appears is generally the sum of the annual retained earnings for each year of the firm's history.

stock. An investment that represents part ownership of a company. There are two different types of stock: common and preferred. Common stocks provide voting rights but no guarantee of dividend payments. Preferred stocks provide no voting rights but have a guaranteed dividend payment. Also called shares.

stock appreciation rights. An executive compensation plan, usually linked to stock options, that gives recipients the opportunity to benefit from an increase in the company's stock price without exercising the options. Stock-appreciation-rights payments can be in cash, an equivalent amount of stock, or some combination of the two.

stock dividend. Dividends paid in stock instead of cash.

stockholder wealth maximization. The appropriate goal for management decisions; considers the risk and timing associated with expected earnings per share in order to maximize the price of the firm's stock.

stock option. An agreement allowing an investor to buy or sell something, such as shares of stock, within a stipulated time and for a certain price. Also, a method of employee compensation that gives workers the right to buy the company's stock during a specified period at a stipulated exercise price.

stock repurchase. A transaction in which a firm buys back shares of its own stock, thereby decreasing the number of shares outstanding, increasing earnings per share, and often increasing share price.

stock split. A change in a company's number of shares outstanding that doesn't change a company's total market value, or each shareholder's percentage stake in the company. Additional shares are issued to existing shareholders at a rate expressed as a ratio. A 2-for-1 stock split, for instance, doubles the number of shares outstanding. Investors will own two shares after the split for each share they owned before the split.

stop order. An investor's order to a broker to buy or sell a security when its market price reaches a certain level.

strategic business plan. A long-term plan that outlines in broad terms the firm's basic strategy for the next five to ten years.

strike price. A specified price at which an investor can buy or sell an option's underlying security.

strip. The practice of splitting a bond's principal and coupon (the interest rate that the bond issuer promises to pay) and then selling them separately. The Treasury issues one variation, known as Strips, an acronym for Separate Trading of Registered Interest and Principal of Securities.

Student Loan Marketing Corp. A government-sponsored enterprise that purchases student loans on the secondary market, provides financing to state student loan agencies, and sells debt. Its shares trade on the New York Stock Exchange. Also called Sallie Mae.

subordinated debenture. A bond that has a claim on assets but only after all senior debt has been paid off.

swap. An agreement that exchanges one security's return for another's return.

tender offer (13D). An offer to buy the stock of a firm directly from its shareholders. Tender offers must be filed on Form 13D with the SEC.

times-interest-earned ratio (TIE). The ratio of earnings before interest and taxes (EBIT) to interest charges; measures the ability of the firm to meet its annual interest payments.

treasurys. Securities (bonds, notes, or bills) issued by the U.S. government. A treasury bill is a certificate representing a short-term loan to the federal government that matures in three, six, or twelve months. A treasury note matures in two to ten years. A treasury bond matures in more than ten years. Among bonds, the thirty-year issue is considered a key indicator of trends in long-term interest rates.

trend analysis. An analysis of a firm's financial ratios over time used to determine the improvement or deterioration of its financial situation.

trial balance. A list of all accounts that have balances in the ledger to verify the equality of the debit and credit sides of the ledger.

turnover. In accounting terms, the number of times an asset is replaced during a set period. In trading, the volume of shares traded on the exchange on a given day. In employment matters, turnover refers to the total number of employees divided by the number of employees replaced during a certain period. In the United Kingdom, the term refers to a company's annual sales volume.

underwriter. In the securities business, a company that for a fee brings an issue of stocks, bonds, or other securities to market. The underwriter buys all or most of the issue, then resells it to investors.

unemployment rate. The percentage of people in the workforce who aren't working and are looking for jobs. The numbers are compiled monthly by the Labor Department and are adjusted for seasonal variations. Two rates are distributed: one for the civilian workforce and one for the overall workforce.

unsecured loan. Loans that require no collateral, usually provided to those who have class A credit ratings.

Value Line composite index. A gauge that covers about 1,700 stocks that are tracked by the Value Line Investment Survey and traded on the New York Stock Exchange, the NASDAQ, and the American Stock Exchange.

variable costs. Those costs that vary directly with the level of business activity.

venture capital. Financing for new businesses. In return for venture capital, investors may have a say in the company's management, as well as some combination of profits, preferred shares, or royalties.

volatility. The characteristic of a security or market to fall or rise sharply in price in a short-term period.

volume. Number of shares traded in a company or an entire market during a given period.

warrant. A security that allows an investor to purchase stock at a specified price within a certain period.

working capital. A firm's investment in short-term assets such as cash, marketable securities, inventory, and receivables.

yield. The annual rate of return on an investment, as paid in dividends or interest. It is expressed as a percentage, generally obtained by dividing the current market price for a stock or bond into the annual dividend or interest payment.

yield (airline industry). The total number of revenue passenger miles divided by the total revenue received during a specified period.

yield to maturity. The rate of return earned on a bond that is held to stated maturity.

zero-coupon bond. A bond sold at a deep discount. It does not pay periodic interest payments to investors; instead, investors receive their return on investment at maturity. The return is equal to the difference between the bond's price at issuance and its face value.

INDEX

Robert W. Kaps earned a bachelor of science degree in business administration from Washington University, a master of arts in legal studies and a master of arts in human resource development from Webster University, and a doctorate in workforce development from Southern Illinois University. He is an associate professor of aviation management at Southern Illinois University Carbondale, where he teaches in the aviation management baccalaureate and the master of public administration programs. He spent over twenty-two years in various executive positions with major and national air carriers. His first book was *Air Transport Labor Relations*.

Southern Illinois University Press
Series in Aviation Management
    David A. NewMyer, Editor

Corporate Aviation Management
    Raoul Castro

Air Transport Labor Relations
    Robert W. Kaps

Aviation Maintenance Management
    Frank H. King

Aviation Industry Regulation
    Harry P. Wolfe and David A. NewMyer